(IN)SIGHTS

(IN)SIGHTS

Peacemaking in the Oslo Process
Thirty Years and Counting

Gidi Grinstein
with
Prof. Ari Afilalo

gefen
publishing house בית הוצאה לאור
JERUSALEM ♦ NEW YORK Est. 1981

Cover Design: Leah Ben Avraham
Typesetting: www.optumetech.com

ISBN: 9789657801482

Gefen Publishing House Ltd.
6 Hatzvi Street
Jerusalem 9438614,
Israel
972-2-538-0247
orders@gefenpublishing.com

Gefen Books
c/o Baker & Taylor Publisher Services
30 Amberwood Parkway
Ashland, Ohio 44805
516-593-1234
orders@gefenpublishing.com

www.gefenpublishing.com

Printed in Israel
Library of Congress Control Number: 2023943833

To the matriarchs of our families
and to our beloved children

Betty Grinstein   Brigitte Dayan Afilalo

Eliyahu Attias
Yosef, Tanya, Noam and Eden Attias
Michael, Noa, Netta, and Shaked Attias   Maya, Liora and Rami Afilalo
Noa and Yael Grinstein

This is our legacy and wish for you:

"Seek peace and pursue it" (Psalms, 34-14)

"בַּקֵּשׁ שָׁלוֹם וְרָדְפֵהוּ" (תהילים, לד-טו)

"Let us work together until the day comes
when they beat their swords into plowshares
and their spears into pruning gooks." (Isaiah 2.4)

President Anwar Sadat, March 26, 1979
signing of the Israel-Egypt Peace Treaty, The White House[1]

"I believe that this is the outline of a fair and lasting agreement.
This is the best that I can do…I have taken this as far as I can."

President Bill Clinton, December 23, 2000
Concluding remarks, The Clinton Ideas, The White House

---

1   As quoted from Henry Kissinger, *Leadership: Six Studies in World Strategy*,
Penguin Press Publishing 2022, p. 274.

Israeli Delegation to the Camp David Summit
At Dogwood Cabin, on the last day of summit (July 25, 2000):
Standing: Gilead Sher (L), **Grinstein** (with my peace doves novelty tie), Shlomo Yanai,
Danny Yatom, Dan Meridor. Seated: Yossi Ginossar Z"L (L), Shlomo Ben-Ami,
Amnon Lipkin-Shahak Z"L, Einat Glouska and Ehud Barak.

October 2000: Sharm Summit
Grinstein in a typical position,
on the keyboard.
Standing: Sher and Barak

December 2000: Clinton Ideas
Grinstein and Clinton. In the back:
Robert Malley, Mara Rudman, Sher (between
author and Clinton) and Sandy Berger.

Praises

"...expands our understanding of the Two-State Solution and highlights the critical importance of Israel's quest for peace for the long-term security and wellbeing of the Jewish People."

Ronald S. Lauder,
President of World Jewish Congress

"...a must-read for understanding Israel's approach to an agreement on Permanent Status. The contours of the FAPS that my government negotiated in 1999-2001 will shape any future agreement on Permanent Status."

Ehud Barak,
Prime Minister of Israel, 1999-2001 and
Minister of Defense 2007-2013

"...Gidi's acquaintance with all the different issues is quite extraordinary. Any future Israeli leader will have to read this book to be able to do what all of us until now did not achieve."

Ehud Olmert,
Prime Minister of Israel, 2006-2009

"Gidi Grinstein's book is the single best book on understanding the issues and the approaches of the different players, illuminating new and important dimensions, and its insights are essential for any future attempt to bring Israeli-Palestinian peace."

Amb. Dennis Ross,
Special Middle East Coordinator, 1993-2001
Distinguished Fellow at Washington Institute for Near East Affairs

"(In)Sights uniquely weaves the story of frontstage and backstage diplomacy, top-down policy and bottom-up work of civil society that shapes Israeli-Palestinian relations. It draws a clear line from the 1978 Camp David Accords, via the Oslo Process, through the Abraham Accords to the challenges of forging a normalization agreement with Saudi Arabia. Kudos to Grinstein-Afilalo."

Tom Nides,
Ambassador to Israel, 2021-2023

"While Gidi and I served different governments with different outlooks, and my views differ from Gidi's on many of the issues and politics generally, I was surprised to learn the extent to which our understanding, analysis and policies converged on multiple topics."

The Honorable Jason D. Greenblatt,
White House Envoy to the Middle East, 2017-19
and author of the widely acclaimed book "In the Path of Abraham"

"As a pro-Israeli and pro-Palestinian staunch Zionist, I believe Gidi's book is crucial in comprehending the complexities of the two-state solution. Gidi is one of the most esteemed thinkers in our field…".

Noa Tishby,
Former Special Envoy for Combating Antisemitism and
Delegitimization of Israel for the Government of Israel,
Producer and Author of "Israel: A Simple Guide
to the Most Misunderstood Country on Earth."

"… some resolution to the Israeli-Palestinian conflict is critical for both peoples. (In)Sights opens a fascinating window onto what actually transpired in the Camp David negotiations and makes the audacious claim that Oslo may well still bear the seeds of peace."

Daniel Gordis,
Shalem College, Jerusalem and Author of
"Impossible Takes Longer: 75 Years after its Creation,
Has Israel Fulfilled its Founders' Dreams?"

"Grinstein used his vast experience in peacemaking to produce a fair and lively piece of history. Eloquent and thoughtful."

Prof. Shlomo Ben-Ami,
Israeli foreign minister, 2000-01 author of "Prophets Without Honor:
The 2000 Camp David Summit and the End of the Two-State Solution"

"Clear, intelligent, and fact-based insights on a much-contested historic period. It is of no surprise to those who had the privilege of acquaintance with Grinstein's superb work within government and without."

Attorney Gilead Sher,
former senior Israeli peace negotiator and Chief of Staff to PM Ehud Barak.
Fellow in Middle East Peace and Security at Rice University's Baker Institute.

"Gidi, my then-counterpart during the Camp David negotiations, uniquely offers a factual account, a sharp analysis and a fair representation of the Palestinian perspective. (In)Sights is an essential read for anyone interested in Israeli-Palestinian peace."

Ghaith Al-Omari,
Advisor to the Palestinian Delegation to the Camp David negotiations, 1999-2005
Fellow at the Washington Institute for Near East Affairs

"(In)Sights provides readers a front row seat and inside look at Israel's negotiating strategy and tactics at the 2000 Camp David negotiations ... the
structure of the book based on the draft framework agreement is a boon for
experts and casual readers."

Amb. Daniel Kurtzer,
former U.S. Ambassador to
Israel and Egypt, Professor at Princeton University.

"(In)Sights is one of the most important works about the Israeli-Palestinian
conflict and its possible solution. Grinstein is an observer-participant in the
formal and the informal efforts for peace. A must read for those who haven't
given up on peace..."

Dr. Yossi Beilin,
Minister in the Government of Israel (1995-2001),
Architect of the Oslo Process (1993), co-creator of Beilin-Abu Mazen
Understandings (1994-95) and Geneva Accord (2001-03).

"Written with keen insight and irrepressible hope, Gidi Grinstein offers a
unique personal perspective on what went wrong with the Palestinian-Israeli
peace process, what could have gone right – and may yet work in the future.
This compelling account has much to teach even those of us who were critical of the Oslo process – perhaps especially those of us who were critical of
Oslo. At a time of growing despair among Israelis and Palestinians, we desperately need the visionary pragmatism of Gidi Grinstein."

Yossi Klein Halevi,
senior fellow, Shalom Hartman Institute, author,
"Letters to My Palestinian Neighbor"

"Gidi's book highlights the potential of track-two policy work to impact historical transformations and how political and personal constraints affect statecraft. His work offers important insights to politicians, diplomats and peace activists."

Prof. Yair Hirschfeld,
Creator of the Oslo backchannel (1993), Co-Founder and
Director General of ECF, Prof. of Middle Eastern
History at University of Haifa.

"...edifying and remarkably accessible narrative of Israeli-Palestinian peace-making ... provides veteran and aspiring change-makers with indispensable handbook of heuristic best-practices."

Jonathan S. Kessler,
former AIPAC leadership development director
and founder/CEO of Heart of a Nation

Table of Contents

SECTION II
FRAMEWORK AGREEMENT ON PERMANENT STATUS

SECTION IV
THE PATH FORWARD

My Friend Gidi Has Stories
Foreword by Professor Ari Afilalo

On September 13, 1993, I was glued to the television, which was broadcasting a momentous event from the South Lawn of the White House in Washington, D.C.: U.S. President Bill Clinton—standing between hitherto sworn enemies, PLO Chairman Yasser Arafat and Prime Minister Yitzhak Rabin—gently guided the two men to a historic handshake. They had just signed the Declaration of Principles (DOP), a framework agreement that was supposed to guide their two peoples toward peace, thereby ending decades of strife. The DOP was supplemented by an equally historic exchange of letters of mutual recognition between Rabin, representing Israel, and Arafat, representing the Palestinian People. That ceremony filled me with tremendous hope, which was shared by millions of Israelis, Palestinians, and other peace-seeking people around the world. At the same time, many friends and family members were filled with fear and grave concern.

The DOP turned out to be the first of a series of agreements between Israel and the PLO—the Oslo Accords—that were signed from 1993 to 1999. In the following years, literally thousands of Israelis and Palestinians worked to implement, substantiate, and effectuate those agreements. Many were civil servants, while others worked at nonprofit organizations. Their goal was to reach peace, or Permanent Status, as they called it. One of those dedicated people was my friend-like-brother, Gidi Grinstein.

Some two decades ago, from August 1999 until March 2001, Gidi worked in the Office of the Prime Minister of Israel, as part of the Israeli delegation tasked with negotiating with the PLO a Framework Agreement on Permanent Status, known as FAPS. The highlight of that dramatic period was the Camp David summit in July 2000 with the participation of President Clinton, Prime Minister Barak, and Chairman Arafat.

At Camp David, Gidi was the youngest delegate at just 30 years old. Serving as secretary of the Israeli delegation and assistant chief negotiator, he wore many hats for the Israeli team, including note-taker, writer of policy papers, co-drafter of agreements, junior negotiator, and sometimes just a "fly on the wall." He was a witness—in person or through the reports of his bosses and colleagues—to almost every development during that historic period.

Gidi did not get to Camp David by a stroke of luck. By that time, he had already worked for five years on multiple aspects of Israeli-Palestinian-Jordanian relations. In the years since Camp David, he has been involved in many other ventures related to peacemaking. Gidi has worked top-down in government in formal negotiations and through backchannels, as well as bottom-up in the nonprofit and academic worlds. As founder and president of the Reut Institute, he directed hundreds of policy and strategy papers on this issue, earning the respect of his peers. I believe that his perspective is unique and singularly comprehensive.

I come from a different world. I am an American-Israeli-French-Moroccan professor of law at Rutgers University who focuses on international trade. I am also the president of a Sephardic synagogue on the Upper West Side of Manhattan. In those positions, I meet a lot of people—Jews and non-Jews; supporters of Israel and its detractors—who are opinionated about Israel and Israelis, Palestine and Palestinians, and the relationship among them. I am repeatedly surprised by their strong views and preconceived notions, which are matched by lack of knowledge and disregard for the other's perspective.

These dynamics of polarization are particularly evident on college campuses in the United States and other Western countries, where Israel has become a "wedge issue." Politically minded students and professors are expected to have an opinion on Israel, and, unfortunately, too many blame it for the failure to achieve peace. This can lead some to travel the road from criticism of Israel to its demonization and delegitimization, which are inappropriate, counterproductive, and morally flawed. That dogma surrounding the Israeli-Palestinian conflict inspired me to co-author this book with Gidi about Israel's peacemaking efforts through his eyes.

Beyond the historical value of documenting Gidi's stories, we also share some forward-looking goals for our book. Gidi's approach is comprehensive and pragmatic, seeing the opportunities for peacemaking as well as the risks and challenges involved. We hope that it will help mitigate the polarization between those highly critical of Israel and those who place all the blame on the Palestinians. We also want to share with Palestinians and Arabs the experiences of an Israeli who dedicated years of his life to the cause of peacemaking.

Our book is also designed to support future negotiations. Many, particularly in Israel, have acted as if the Israeli-Palestinian conflict is stable and contained, so much so that its resolution was not even a significant issue in Israel's multiple recent elections from 2020 to 2022. We do not accept this view, observing that the Israeli-Palestinian conflict continues to fester with ongoing violence and occasional flareups around Gaza and in the West Bank. Meanwhile, its foundational realities remain unchanged: millions of Israelis and Palestinians do not want to live in the same country, much less create a shared society. Hence, we are confident that circumstances will arise to allow for the resumption of negotiations on an agreement, which will facilitate a political separation between the two peoples.

In 2020, President Trump's peace plan—known formally as "Peace to Prosperity: A Vision to Improve the Lives of the Palestinian and Israeli People"—failed to achieve Israeli-Palestinian peace. This made Trump the fourth consecutive U.S. president who has foundered in an attempt to conciliate between the two sides since the last Oslo Accord was signed in 1999, nearly a quarter of a century ago.

Our book is designed to support the women and men who will be tasked with reaching that agreement and will want to learn from past experience. Among the dozens of books about Israeli-Palestinian peacemaking, most take a chronological approach, describing and analyzing events as they unfolded. Alas, past circumstances will not reoccur, particularly as most of the main characters in the diplomatic drama of 1993–2001 have retired or passed away.

Therefore, we took a more thematic approach, which is based on the Israeli draft of the FAPS that was negotiated in 2000. Each chapter in Section II of our book tells the story of an article of the FAPS through Gidi's stories and analysis, with the goal of bringing together as many relevant insights as possible. And while ours is not a history book, we worked hard to ensure factual accuracy. We apologize for any shortcomings in that regard and hope that they are insignificant to the larger points we are making.

While many of the stories in this book are Gidi's personal accounts and took place in 1995–2001, they also illuminate systemic issues and highlight topics that recurred under multiple Israeli prime ministers and U.S. presidents in the past three decades. They are all included in this book because they are certain to reemerge. And when they do, we want our work to be the first resource for future negotiators.

Prof. Ari Afilalo
Rutgers University
July 2023

Who Are You? Where Have You Been? Foreword by Gidi Grinstein

On Monday, July 17, 2000, I was at the Dogwood Cabin in Camp David, Maryland, the country retreat of presidents of the United States. That cabin was assigned to Prime Minister Ehud Barak, but it effectively served as the operations center of the Israeli delegation at Camp David, which was charged with negotiating a historic peace agreement with the Palestinians. That cabin, on that night, was at the center of one of the most dramatic events taking place in the world.

Around 10:00 PM it was time for snacks. Earlier, we had had a team meeting, and Barak gave a few directives to the staff, which Gilead Sher, our chief negotiator and my boss, turned into assignments. Sher, General Shlomo Yanai (who led the security portion of the negotiations), and I were now huddled in the living room around my laptop, crystallizing Israel's positions on the issue of security. The remainder of our delegation was hanging out in the dining room across the hall, providing a cheerful background buzz. All were distinguished professionals, and some, particularly our legal advisors, Elyakim Rubinstein and Daniel Reisner, also had a great sense of humor.

Suddenly, we heard loud coughing from the next room and then the sound of someone receiving strong whacks on his back. A few seconds later, Einat Glouska, the delegation's administrative assistant, shouted: "Call the bodyguards! The prime minister is choking!" Sher, Yanai, and I hustled over in time to see Barak staggering in the opposite direction. I quickly scanned the room. Shlomo Ben-Ami, the minister of public security and co-chief negotiator, raised his hands to his shocked face. Attorney General Elyakim Rubinstein clutched his head in his hands. Someone asked: "Does anyone know what to do?"

As the youngest and most junior member of our delegation, I was probably the only one still referring to Barak as "Mr. Prime Minister." Israelis tend to be highly informal, and many of my colleagues had known him for years. In such a setting, they referred to him by his first name, Ehud. But I still stuck to formalities: "Mr. Prime Minister, should I Heimlich you?" In response, he put his hands to his neck in the international sign of "I'm choking."

I straightened him up, stabilized him against my hip, and clasped my hands together to form a double fist under his diaphragm. Two hearty thrusts forced a cashew out of his throat. A few seconds later his bodyguards came rushing in, followed closely by Clinton's medical team. Barak refused to be treated, nor would he let Rubinstein say *HaGomel*, the traditional Jewish prayer recited after a brush with danger. Five minutes later, everyone, including Barak, was back at work.

My Heimlich of Barak was memorable enough to be mentioned in Clinton's autobiography and other accounts of the summit. But it was merely an esoteric footnote in a dramatic set of events known to history as the Camp David negotiations. They began in July 1999—when Barak became prime minister following a landslide victory over Benjamin Netanyahu—and ended in January 2001, just before Barak lost to opposition leader Ariel Sharon. That period began with high hopes of ending the Israeli-Palestinian conflict and ended in a devastating war that claimed the lives of thousands and has effectively prevented any prospect of a peaceful resolution between Israel and the Palestinians since that time.

For the duration of the Camp David negotiations, I was "just" the secretary of the Israeli delegation, neither a principal nor a major decision-maker. My role, however, placed me at the hub of these events due to my unique experience working on Israeli-Palestinian relations and my specific knowledge of the issues being negotiated, which allowed me to contribute beyond my official role. I was empowered by my bosses, particularly Sher, who sought my input and trusted me with delicate assignments and significant responsibilities.

By the time of Barak's choking incident on July 17, the Israeli, Palestinian, and American delegations had already been secluded at Camp David for a week. We were supposed to be well on our way to hammering out a frame-work agreement on the Permanent Status of Israeli-Palestinian relations, which would outline not only the resolution of all outstanding issues between the parties, but also the establishment of a Palestinian state and its future relations with Israel. A FAPS was also expected to formally establish an End of Conflict and Finality of Claims between the parties and usher in a new period of peace.

As much as there was to gain at Camp David, there was also much to lose. The five-year Interim Period of the Oslo Process had ended 14 months earlier, in May 1999. Multiple agreements between Israel and the PLO, initiated in September 1993 by the Declaration of Principles, also known as Oslo A, provided for Israeli withdrawals from the Palestinian populated areas within the West Bank and Gaza, the establishment of a self-governing Palestinian Authority (PA), and the delineation of its relations with Israel in all civic areas, particularly security and economics. At the same time, the Interim Period was meant to end with an agreement on Permanent Status. At Camp David, we had already missed the deadline for a FAPS by nearly fifteen months, and the Palestinian side was on the edge.

In an act of defiance, Arafat first threatened to declare Palestinian statehood unilaterally ahead of May 1999. Israel responded by announc-ing that such a declaration would constitute an abandonment of the Oslo Accords, which could lead to war. Under international pressure, Arafat postponed his declaration to May 2000, and then again to September 2000. Hence the Camp David summit was seen as a last chance to prevent a violent clash.

And yet, that first week at Camp David was an exercise in futility. Little progress was made in direct negotiations, and the American side was at a loss to forge a breakthrough. We were clearly on track to fail. Clinton, who was scheduled to fly to Japan for the G8 Summit on July 19, was frustrated with both sides. He had put his own political capital on the line, succumbing to Barak's pressures to convene this all-or-nothing summit. His second term in office would end six months later, and peacemaking in the Middle East was the crown jewel of his foreign policy and diplomatic legacy. Some said he was eyeing the Nobel Prize. No wonder he was not pleased.

Barak, however, was in a bind among a myriad of political, domestic, security, and foreign- affairs interests. Israel's unilateral withdrawal from Lebanon was carried out in May 2000, in keeping with his electoral promise to the Israeli public. It followed a breakdown of the negotiations for peace with Syria two months earlier. For most of that period, from September 1999 to April 2000, Barak put the political process with the Palestinians on the back burner.

But as of May 2000, Barak had refocused on the Palestinians, applying tremendous pressure on Clinton to call for a summit and on Arafat to attend it. He did so despite stark warnings from Israel's military intelligence and several senior diplomats, all of whom warned him that Arafat was not ready to sign a FAPS, which would establish End of Conflict and Finality of Claims, as Barak desired. They also cautioned that Arafat was entertaining the possibility of another round of violence, with the goal of forcing Israeli concessions at the negotiating table. Against this backdrop, Barak was concerned that Israel might be blamed for the failure of the negotiations, and ultimately emerge isolated and vulnerable during that forewarned military conflict. He needed to prove to the world, and particularly to the Americans, that Israel negotiated in good faith. Such proof would require a generous overture.

At the same time, his political situation was dire. His wide coalition of center, left, right, and religious parties had disintegrated just before he departed for the summit, primarily due to his advances toward an agreement with the Palestinians. He no longer had a governing majority, and remained in office because the Knesset was out of session. Early elections were looming. Fourteen months earlier, Barak had defeated Netanyahu, declaring the "dawn of a new day" for Israel. Now, he was in danger of becoming the shortest-serving premier in Israel's history.

For the imminent elections, Barak needed something to run on; a legacy, like a FAPS with a trophy case of strategic achievements that offset the painful concessions Israel would have to make. For example, Barak demanded a historic Palestinian recognition of the centuries-old Jewish connection to Temple Mount and the Wailing Wall, in addition to Israeli sovereignty over the Old City of Jerusalem. That, in turn, would require Israel to recognize Palestinian affiliation with al-Harem al-Shariff, the Arab name for Temple

Mount, and to place the Palestinian population of Jerusalem under management and sovereignty of the Palestinian state. It was also clear that the Palestinians would only drop their demand for a "Right of Return" for all Palestinian refugees in Israel if Israel withdrew from the West Bank and Gaza, where a Palestinian state was established. Because of his acute political needs, many critics accused Barak of being "desperate" and of sacrificing Israel's national interests for his political whims.

Pressures on Barak were compounding from the Palestinian side as well. As he determined to reach a FAPS, they moved to exploit his vulnerabilities to squeeze out more concessions. They were also legitimately concerned that Barak would be unable to ratify the FAPS in the Knesset, thereby exposing their flexibilities without the rewards of statehood. Such a scenario could lead to a challenge to Arafat's leadership that resulted in political instability or even violence.

By that fateful Monday, July 17, the urgency of the moment was palpable within our delegation. With no meetings with the Palestinians scheduled for the day, we held internal discussions and assessments. In the early afternoon, Barak convened us on the porch of his cabin to discuss Jerusalem. Over the next three hours, each member of our delegation presented his view of Israel's interests and positions. Some gave historical overviews, while others provided political analysis. Some spoke with pathos, while others leaned on logic and facts. Barak was seeking ideas but also legitimacy, particularly from those with strong security standing or right-wing credentials. All of this was in preparation for a late-night meeting with the increasingly impatient Clinton. Barak was heading to his own moment of truth.

That night, Barak met Clinton and presented him with a dramatic proposal: Jerusalem would house two capitals of two states, and Israel would hand over sovereignty over most Palestinian neighborhoods to Palestine. And while Israel would remain the sovereign in the Old City and carry the overall responsibility for security, the Palestinians would manage al-Harem al-Sharif and hold civic responsibilities for the Muslim and Christian Quarters of the Old City, both with predominantly Arab populations. From a historical, diplomatic, and political standpoint, it was a far-reaching conciliatory offer. Even Clinton and his team were stunned, and one American delegate thought that Barak "went too far." Nonetheless, by the end of the summit, Arafat had effectively rejected this offer.

These events changed the history of Israeli-Palestinian relations. Yes, the summit continued for another week, and Permanent Status negotiations for six more months. But once the public understood that the future of Jerusalem was in the balance, tremendous political energy was unleashed, leading to the eruption of a bloody war in the fall.

On March 7, 2001, our team, led by Sher, arrived early to the Aquarium, Israel's West Wing, to prepare for the transfer of prime ministerial powers. At exactly 9:30 AM, Barak received Ariel Sharon in a small ceremony on the ground floor of the Office of the Prime Minister, and then the two men climbed the wide stairs to the Aquarium on the first floor, where Barak's staff was waiting. As he approached the top step and walked toward us alongside Barak, Sharon smiled and waved to the small contingency of journalists who were documenting the historic moment. A minute later, Barak and Sharon secluded themselves in the prime minister's office for a transition that lasted about an hour. Meanwhile, both teams huddled around Barak's chambers, which would soon be Sharon's. After having run a heated and even nasty campaign, Sharon's crew was now benevolent, and the atmosphere was friendly; many had prior acquaintances with our team. They would later offer that some of us stay on with them, and they turned out to be true mensches in the following months.

Words alone cannot capture the intensity of those moments. Theory teaches that power is a zero-sum game: if one party has it, the other party does not. On that morning, Barak walked into the Aquarium with a team of bodyguards and an army of assistants. An hour and a half later, he walked out with a small security detail, one secretary, and access to a small office in Tel Aviv. Meanwhile, Sharon took the opposite path. After 27 years in politics, the veteran politician and former war hero was now in charge of all affairs of state.

When Barak left the Aquarium, so did we, his team. Four of us drove to Tel Aviv. We had shared an extremely intense and formative time during which we had simultaneously sought peace and waged war. We had started out as colleagues and became friends. Our small group was disappointed with Barak's loss to Sharon, but also proud of our work. We were convinced that soon enough we would be called upon to assist in "finishing the job" of peacemaking, as Sharon's team realized the indispensability of our knowledge and experience.

I had a different mindset. I had been awarded a Wexner Israel Fellowship and was scheduled to attend Harvard's Kennedy School of Government in July. I also realized that my chances of ever returning to a central position on Israel's negotiating team were slim. I knew how much good fortune I'd had in serving in that role and then remaining a part of the Prime Minister's team for nearly eighteen months. I doubted that Sharon would pursue a political process with the Palestinians given the recent escalation of violence, particularly suicide bombings, and his campaign pledge of a strong military response. And if I were to return, my intention was to take a more senior position, such as chief negotiator, chief of staff, foreign policy advisor, or government secretary. Then and there, I decided to move on.

In the few years that followed the Camp David negotiations, many members of the American, Israeli, and Palestinian delegations wrote accounts of that time. All of us were invited to join a veritable traveling circus of conferences, speeches, and roundtables, as well as to publish articles that expounded upon "what went wrong." The academic and think-tank worlds were fascinated by the political and diplomatic drama that we had been part of, and by the sudden shift from amicable peacemaking to brutal warring. All of us became hot commodities and were invited to expound on the positions of the parties, the psychology of the negotiations, the character of the leaders, the impact of domestic politics, and the substantive gaps that remained on the various issues. Most famously, the *New York Review of Books* ran a multipart exchange among Israeli, Palestinian, and American negotiators. Even Barak contributed an extensive piece to set the record straight from his perspective.[2]

---

2   Malley Robert and Agha Hussein, *Camp David: The Tragedy of Errors* (*New York Review of Books*, https://www.nybooks.com/articles/2001/08/09/camp-david-the-tragedy-of-errors/, August 9, 2001)
     Ross Dennis and Grinstein Gidi, *Camp David: An Exchange* (*New York Review of Books*, https://www.nybooks.com/articles/2001/09/20/camp-david-an-exchange/, September 20, 2001)

The debate quickly became polarized and politicized. The Israeli left and its partners around the world—especially in Europe, the United States, and among American Jewry—would not accept Barak's conclusion that "Israel did not have a partner for peace at this time." That contention devastated them, because it undermined their pro-peace positions. They therefore sought to disprove Barak's conclusion by arguing that he did not go far enough in his concessions or treat Arafat with the respect necessary to achieve peace. Indeed, in 2003, Dr. Yossi Beilin and Yasser Abed Rabbo concluded the Geneva Accord as a mock-FAPS in track-two negotiations to demonstrate that an agreement was feasible.

Meanwhile, the right wing was thrilled to have Barak validate their view that Israel had no partner for peace. While they vilified him for his willingness to divide Jerusalem and to give up land, they celebrated the failure of his overtures as proof that the "Two-State Solution" and "peace" were illusory. In fact, some analysts claimed that the failed summit formed the cornerstone of the subsequent two-decade reign of right-wing governments in Israel. In short, the left accused Barak of not doing enough and the right accused him of doing too much.

There was a debate within our team of negotiators as well. Some thought we could have reached peace if we had only had more time, if Barak had been nicer to Arafat, if the American Peace Team had put forward its bridging proposal in July as opposed to December, or if the Israeli positions had been more generous earlier in the process. In fact, Sher's book was entitled *Within Reach*. The natural implication of that view was that we should try again to reach a FAPS based on the lessons we had learned. Other members of our team subscribed to Barak's conclusion that the Palestinians would not be ready to make peace with Israel, at that time or ever. Even those who participated in the negotiating had differing accounts of the facts and radically varying interpretations of the outcomes.

My conclusions strayed from those of many of my colleagues. On the one hand, I subscribed to Barak's view that the Camp David negotiations revealed that Israel and the PLO were not ready to reach a comprehensive agreement on Permanent Status *at that time*. I also believed that such an

---

Morris Benny and Barak Ehud, *Camp David and After—Continued* (*New York Review of Books*, https://www.nybooks.com/articles/2002/06/27/camp-david-and-aftercontinued/ June 27, 2002)

agreement was the only one that Barak could have negotiated in 1999–2000. That, of course, made Barak a bit of a tragic figure, attempting to negotiate an agreement that could not be achieved. On the other hand, I saw a real possibility for a long-term *interim* agreement *within* the West Bank and Gaza that would have formalized a Palestinian state within *provisional* borders. I thought this could serve the interests of Israel and the Palestinians even better than an agreement on Permanent Status because it would make the process of peacemaking gradual. That approach became even more relevant following Hamas' takeover of Gaza in 2007.

I also concluded that while Israel had a key strategic interest in signing an agreement with the Palestinians, especially on Permanent Status, it could not subject its long-term interests to Palestinian consent. Therefore, Israel's fundamental approach to shaping its relations with the Palestinians needed to be based on unilateral moves, and particularly on recognizing the PA as a state. I will explain these ideas in the chapters to come.

Nevertheless, in the years following Camp David, I was reluctant to write my account. Frankly, I thought it would be bad for my career. Principals do not generally appreciate seconds who document and analyze their actions. Also, my bosses were publishing their own books, and I didn't want to contradict or be contradicted by them.

So I moved on. At the Kennedy School, I focused on Israel's long-term economic development and embraced the sport of long-distance running. But I was repeatedly invited to share my experience at the Camp David negotiations in speeches and on panel—nearly 75 times in one year! After my return to Israel, I launched the Reut Institute as a cutting-edge think-tank. As part of Reut's work, we developed an extensive body of analysis and knowledge regarding the emergence of a Palestinian state within provisional borders and a possible unilateral approach to secure a reality of two states for two peoples. Between 2006 and 2009, I was also part of a backchannel that convened in Madrid 26 times.[3] In the years that followed, I was intermittently involved in

---

3   The convener of the backchannel in Spain was the Toledo Institute, led by Prof. Shlomo Ben-Ami, who was the minister of public security, minister of foreign affairs, and co-chief negotiator during the Barak government. The Israeli side included Major General (Ret.) Giora Eiland and former head of the national security council, as well

many other initiatives, but the general level of engagement with the Israeli-Palestinian political process subsided.

There was one exception: dinner table conversations. Hundreds of times over the years, I was asked to analyze and comment on recent developments between Israel and the Palestinians, which led to lively conversations and debates. There were a few underlying themes: You gave them everything. What else do they want? Israel withdrew from Gaza only to be fired upon. What else can Israel do? Why is it so important for Israel to disengage from the Palestinians? Are Israel's relations with the PA stable or not? Can there ever be peace?

Meanwhile, there were significant developments in the high echelons of diplomacy and politics: in 2002–2003, the "Quartet"—including the U.S., Russia, the UN, and the EU—published the Roadmap for Peace and the Sharon government built a massive security fence in the West Bank; in 2005, Sharon led the unilateral withdrawal from Gaza; in 2006, Hamas won the elections to PA's legislative council, which set the stage for a constitutional stalemate that ended when Hamas took over Gaza in 2007; in 2007–2009, the Annapolis Process took place and Abu Mazen and Ehud Olmert attempted to reach a peace agreement; in 2013–2014, President Barack Obama and Secretary of State John Kerry attempted to improve on Clinton's efforts and reach a FAPS-type accord between Netanyahu and Abu Mazen; in 2014, 2015, and 2016, Abu Mazen threatened to unilaterally declare Palestinian statehood at the General Assembly of the United Nations; in 2017–2019, President Donald Trump "changed the playing field" by recognizing Jerusalem as Israel's capital, the Golan Heights as Israel's territory, and the legitimacy of the settlements ahead of publishing the Trump Plan in January 2020. There were also multiple cycles of violence around Gaza and in the West Bank, some of which escalated into large-scale military operations by the Israeli Defense Forces (IDF) and widespread firing of rockets on Israel by Hamas. And in an incredible turn of events, the Trump administration mediated the historic Abraham Accords and the normalization agreements among Israel and the United Arab Emirates, the Kingdom of Bahrain, and

---

as Adv. Yoram Raved, who was part of Sharon's team. The Palestinian side included Dr. Hussein Agha and Dr. Ahmad Khalidi, senior advisors to Abu Mazen.

the Kingdom of Morocco. Each of these game-changing developments provided additional backdrop for repeated discussions about the condition and direction of Israel's relations with the Palestinians.

As far back as 2017, my wise wife, Betty, told me it was time to write a book. She pointed out that people seemed to like my stories and appreciate my analysis, and that the summer of 2020 will mark 20 years since the Camp David Summit. I dismissed her: "No one is interested in the Israeli-Palestinian conflict anymore … everything about Camp David has been written…there is no urgency because the political process is stalled…my notes are buried in the archive…I am so busy…the dog ate my homework." But she persisted.

Then, in October 2019, we were invited to Shabbat lunch by our friends Prof. Ari Afilalo and his wife, Brigitte Dayan. The conversation randomly turned to my experiences in the negotiations. One anecdote followed another before Ari said: "Gidi, you have to publish a book." Betty immediately jumped in: "I have been begging him to do that for two years. Maybe he will listen to you." Predictably, the conversation shifted to my stubbornness and refusal to heed my wife's good advice. After that back-and-forth, I realized that if my wife and best friend think I should write a book, I'd better do it. So I challenged Ari: "If you co-author the book with me, I'll do it." And so we have.

This book is published just before marking thirty years of the Oslo Process on September 13, 2023. It highlights the successes of Oslo in creating the PA as a self-governing body for the Palestinians in the West Bank, which released Israel from direct control and management of that population. It also underscores the longstanding security and economic cooperation between the PA and Israel, which was nurtured by successive Israeli governments led by both right- and left-wing premiers. At the same time, the thrust of the Oslo Process to reach an agreement on Permanent Status effectively dissipated in 2014 and has not been resumed since. While the U.S. pays lip service to the "Two-State Solution," it seems as if all parties have accepted that the structures of the Interim Period are stable and long-lasting and may even represent an unexpected form of Permanent Status.

Our book presents a different outlook. We assume that there will be another effort to cement political separation and peace between Israelis and Palestinians based on the principle of two states for two peoples. After all,

millions of Palestinians and Israelis do *not* want to share a society and be part
of the same nation, effectively rejecting the notion of the current situation in
the West Bank as permanent. Their collective energy will, at some point, be
transformative. And some shocks are expected sooner: Abu Mazen, now 87
and unhealthy, will inevitably step down or pass away. Violence is simmering
and can always spiral out of control. Since the beginning of 2023, there have
been hundreds of terror attacks on Israelis, claiming the lives of dozens, while
the IDF has carried out many military operations that resulted in nearly one
thousand casualties.

In the bigger picture, Israel expands settlements and challenges the status quo on Temple Mount and in Jerusalem. Meanwhile, the Palestinian
side increases the diplomatic pressure on Israel in international fora, seeking to frame Israel as an "apartheid state" because of its so-called "de-facto
annexation" of the West Bank without granting equal political rights to its
Palestinian residents. Success in their campaign would be a stepping stone
toward Israel's isolation and delegitimization.

What should Israel or the U.S. do? We resist the temptation to front-load
another set of ideas about how to negotiate and what an agreement could
look like, which will be shelved alongside dozens of others similar attempts.
When you make it to chapter 12, you can read our views, including our
acknowledgment that there are many possible outcomes and scenarios. We
focus on sharing and expanding wisdom regarding Israeli-Palestinian relations in Permanent Status, rather than proposing a specific solution and then
defending it.

Multiple Israeli prime ministers and U.S. presidents have put their best
feet forward on this matter. Their collective work provides solid stepping
stones for any future negotiations. When considering the architecture of
future diplomatic initiatives, statespersons could reference the Oslo Process,
which calls for a comprehensive agreement on Permanent Status *before* a
Palestinian state emerges within *permanent* borders, as well as the Roadmap,
in which a Palestinian state within *provisional* borders is established *before*
a Permanent Status agreement. We support the latter over the former. And
when considering the endgame of negotiations, the Clinton Ideas are a reference point, as are multiple draft-FAPSs. For a starting point, such statespersons could thank President Trump for the Trump Plan, which established

Israel's minimal demands from the Palestinians. In addition, the collective experience of the Oslo Process and the Camp David negotiations, as well as of the Unilateral Disengagement from Gaza, provides vast insights into the structural and substantive difficulties that stand in the way of any agreement.

The goal of this book is to bring together those insights within one volume. And while we focus primarily on one episode—during Barak's tenure from 1999 to 2001—our book discusses issues that are longstanding and dynamics that are recurring. Indeed, our effort was shaped by the desire to remain relevant in case negotiations resume. Nearly all books about Israeli-Palestinian negotiations are arranged in chronological order, describing a series of events, and analyzing their underlying causes with the goal of answering bigger questions such as "What went wrong?" Alas, as Ari wrote in his opening remarks, past efforts at negotiation are unlikely to be recreated or even approximated, if only because so many of the participants have retired or died.

Therefore, we took a different approach to organizing our book. Section One, entitled *A Personal Introduction to Oslo*, shares my stories from before I became secretary of the Israeli delegation and highlights key aspects of the Oslo Process. Section Two, entitled *A Framework Agreement on Permanent Status*, follows the structure of Israel's draft FAPS from the Camp David negotiations, with each chapter dedicated to an article of the FAPS. For example, Article Two of the draft FAPS dealt with the establishment of a Palestinian state and with its future relations with Israel. Correspondingly, chapter four of our book deals with Palestinian statehood, highlighting the strategic dilemmas that Israel faced, and how they turned into specific formulations in the FAPS. And so on: chapters five to eight of our book correspond with the FAPS' articles three (territory), four (Jerusalem and holy sites), five (security), six (refugees), seven (economics) and eight (water). And each chapter could also be read as a stand-alone essay.

Section Three, entitled *System Effects*, deals with the role of the U.S. and describes the eruption of the war between Israel and the Palestinians as of September 28, 2000, to demonstrate the vulnerability of peacemaking efforts to the law of unintended consequences. And Section Four, *The Path Forward*, suggests an approach to the design of a future political process and to negotiations. We close the book with my *Note to Aspiring History Makers* and with our acknowledgements. In addition, we will launch a website–https://www. peacemaking.info–to share more information and elicit your feedback and input to improve future editions of this book.

We aspire for our book to remain relevant for many years to come, effectively until Permanent Status is reached. Clearly, only a rare set of circumstances can provide for another historic agreement between Israel and the Palestinians. Should that window of opportunity emerge, every ounce of knowledge will be essential. At that point, we hope that our book will be a primary source of wisdom serving negotiators, policy planners, and leaders, as they strive to bring peace to our land.

Gidi Grinstein
July 2023

Maps[4]

11/1947: Partition Decision
Mandatory Palestine was supposed to be divided into a Jewish State (52%) and an Arab State (48%). The Jews accepted; the Arabs rejected.

7/1949 to 6/1967: Armistice Lines
The ceasefire lines of 7/1949 were amended ~20 times to form the June 4, 1967 Lines (in this map).

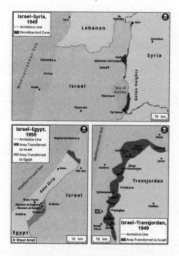

1949-1950s: Land Swaps
Note the swap in the Northern Triangle (bottom right), where Israel would suggest demographic swaps in 2000 and 2020.

June 10, 1967: After the 1967 War
Following the 1967 War, Israel gained control of Jerusalem, the West Bank, Gaza, Sinai, and the Golan Heights.

4   Credit: Shaul Arieli at https://www.shaularieli.com/en/category/maps/

9/1995: Interim Agreement

The Interim Agreement divided the West Bank and Gaza into Area A (full PL control); Area B (PL civilian control) and Area C (IL control).

Jerusalem for 1949 to 1967

W. Jerusalem (Yerushalayim) municipality covered 36 sq km. E. Jerusalem (Al-Quds) covered ~6 sq km including the Holy Basin.

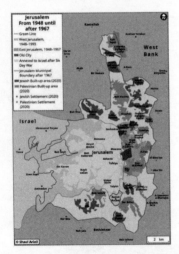

After the 1967 War: Expanded Jerusalem

Municipal borders of Jerusalem were expanded threefold to surrounding mountains and the Atarot Airport, which included 11 Arab villages.

Holy Basin and Old City

Note the size of the Muslim and Christian Quarters and of Temple Mount.

SECTION I

Personal Introduction to Oslo

CHAPTER 1

Birthday in Bethlehem

June 26, 1995 was my 25th birthday. On a leave from my active service in the Israeli Navy, I drove my mother's car from my parents' home in Holon, south of Tel Aviv, to Bethlehem, just south of Jerusalem. It took me a bit more than an hour to cover the distance and enter a different world. Crossing a checkpoint into the area of the Palestinian Authority, I turned left at the first major intersection, continued farther, and parked my car, with its Israeli license plate, on the street. That short journey was a surreal experience for me. When an Israeli military unit enters a Palestinian area, extensive preparations are required, which make the distance traveled feel much longer. Now, for the first time, I was meeting Palestinians as peers rather than in uniform or from the other side of a gun. When I entered the home of our hosts, the Hazboun family, as welcomed guest, I realized just how close we could be.

Going to Bethlehem was exciting and even felt adventurous. It was a period of dramatic political change taking place at breakneck speed: Oslo A was signed in September 1993, leading to the Gaza-Jericho Agreement, which was signed nine months later, in May 1994, in Cairo and launched an Interim Period of five years of Palestinian self-government. That agreement included the Paris Protocol, which regulated economic relations between the PA and Israel. Israel then withdrew from Gaza and Jericho to allow for Arafat to return triumphantly to Gaza in July 1994 so that the PA could be established and elections for its institutions could be held. After these initial steps of realizing the Oslo Accords, Israel and Jordan signed a peace treaty in October 1994. By June 1995, when I came to Bethlehem, intense negotiations were unfolding on yet another historic agreement that would be finalized in September and become known as the Interim Agreement or Oslo B, which regulated relations between Israel and the PA. While the overall sentiment was that history was unfolding before our eyes, this was also a time

of devastating mass-casualty terrorist attacks designed to derail the political
process. The first attack was carried out by an Israeli settler, and subsequent
ones by Hamas and Islamic Jihad.

The goal of my trip to Bethlehem was to join a meeting organized by
the Economic Cooperation Foundation (ECF), an Israeli nonprofit that spe-
cializes in relations with the Palestinians. Our Palestinian hosts, Dr. Samir
Hazboun and his brother, George, ran their own nonprofit, DATA Center for
Studies and Research. Also present were Dr. Rateb Amro, a retired Jordanian
general, and his son, Mohammed, who led the Horizon Center, a Jordanian
research institution in Amman. It was the ECF who brought together the
Jordanian and Palestinian sides, as well as the German Friedrich Naumann
Foundation, who underwrote the entire enterprise. Everyone's goal was to
establish the foundations for thriving Israeli-Jordanian-Palestinian economic
and trade relations. We assumed that an agreement on Permanent Status was
going to be signed by May 1999 and launch the Two-State Solution to the
Israeli-Palestinian conflict.

The ECF spent months working with DATA, Horizon, and the Naumann
Foundation to reach that moment, and my birthday was a good reason for
some real celebration. After a delicious lunch, during dessert—surprise!—a
Palestinian band appeared, followed by a multilayered chocolate birthday cake.
It was a surreal moment in a surreal day, which turned out to be the beginning
of an exciting chapter of my career dedicated to peacemaking. Two weeks later,
on July 11, 1995, I officially retired from the military and joined the ECF.

Constructive Ambiguity? Saving Oslo from Itself

The full story of the ECF's impact has yet to be told, and the following chapters capture the narrow perspective of my experiences working there. When
I joined the ECF in 1995, it had been in existence for five years. For the first
couple of years, its mailing address was a post-office box, but by 1992 it had
established its base of operations in a shabby apartment in Tel Aviv, with a
worn bluish carpet and cracks running down the walls. Most of the furniture
had been rescued from the garbage, and the tiny toilet was separated by a
thin wall from the kitchen, whose refrigerator was a definite health hazard.
But nobody cared about appearances in one of Israel's most important and
dynamic diplomatic hubs of that time.

Five men co-founded and led ECF: Dr. Yossi Beilin was president and the ECF's political leader, having served as a minister, member of Knesset, and government secretary, primarily on behalf of the Labor Party under the leadership of Prime Minister Shimon Peres; Dr. Yair Hirschfeld, a professor of Middle East history at Haifa University, served as director general and rainmaker of ideas and initiatives; Boaz Karni saw his mission as supporting Beilin's work while focusing on finances and operations; Dr. Nimrod Novik— an international businessman, former diplomat for Israel in Washington, and former foreign policy advisor to Peres—was chairman and the team's chief diplomat; and Dr. Ron Pundak—a historian, peace activist, and former journalist and agent of Mossad— led the execution of many of ECF's projects. All but Ron, a newcomer to the group, had longstanding ties that dated back to the Peres government and the Labor party of the mid-1980s.

In its essence, the ECF was a platform for diplomatic entrepreneurship in an era of dramatic change. Beilin, Novik, Hirschfeld, and Karni recognized that sea changes in international politics would profoundly affect Israel and create game-changing opportunities. The collapse of the Berlin Wall in 1989 had allowed for mass immigration of some one million Jews from the former Soviet Union to Israel. It also left the U.S., Israel's chief ally, as the world's only superpower, and dashed any Arab hope to destroy Israel by force. That initial insight was reinforced in 1991. The Gulf War brought together Arab countries, including Syria and Saudi Arabia, within a U.S.-led coalition, which then decimated Iraq's military. The outcome of the war allowed for the convening of the Madrid Conference for Peace, with the participation of Israel, a Jordanian-Palestinian delegation, Syria, Lebanon, and Egypt. Meanwhile, the European Union expanded to Central and Eastern Europe, and its Barcelona Declaration of 1992 pledged massive political attention and financial support to Mediterranean countries to enhance their economic, social, and political development. Finally, in 1992, Rabin was elected prime minister with a clear mandate to engage the Palestinians in peace negotiations.

Joining the ECF represented a profound personal and professional transition. I moved from the field of budgets and planning, which was the focus of my days in uniform, into the worlds of diplomacy and regional politics; from a system of hierarchy and discipline to an ecosystem of creative, intellectual, and diplomatic entrepreneurship; from a short commute to Israel's naval headquarters to regularly visiting European and Middle Eastern capitals; from uniforms to suits and ties; from Hebrew to English; and from a strictly non-partisan military service to deep involvement in international politics.

Hirschfeld brought me to the ECF. We had met in the spring of 1995, at a dinner arranged by a close friend who knew of my interests and passions. She thought that I should meet Hirschfeld because he had co-made history by initiating and participating in the backchannel negotiations in Oslo, which led to the signing of Oslo A. In November 1992 in London, Hirschfeld met the veteran PLO senior Ahmed Qurei, also known as Abu Alaa, who was a supporter of the Two-State Solution. Hirschfeld's unique experience in track-two diplomacy since the 1980s allowed him to spot the opportunity to structure a transformative negotiation process that would run in parallel to the official negotiations, which were currently deadlocked in Washington. That opportunity was seized shortly thereafter, in Oslo in January 1993, when Hirschfeld and Pundak met with Abu Alaa and his team.

Hirschfeld and Pundak were guided and supported by Beilin, Novik, and Karni. Theirs was a team of singular experience and capabilities, whose clout came from Beilin, then serving as Deputy Minister of Foreign Affairs. Beilin was very close with Peres, who was Minister of Foreign Affairs under Rabin. Hence, the axis of Beilin-Peres-Rabin made possible the elevation of the discussions in Oslo from an academic exercise into a transformative political intervention. Meanwhile, the clout of the Palestinian team came from Abu Alaa's stature, which afforded him direct access to Arafat and the PLO leadership in Tunis. While both teams operated in Oslo with full deniability by their leaderships, their access ensured that the ideas they raised were acceptable to their leaders.

This was an extremely intricate exercise. As discussions progressed, in March, Beilin updated Peres, and in May, Peres brought Rabin into the picture. Or at least so everyone thought; alas, at that point, Rabin had already learned about the talks in Oslo from intelligence briefings he'd received. Against the backdrop of stalemate in the negotiations in Washington, where the Israeli delegation was led by Elyakim Rubinstein, Rabin understood the potential of the deliberations in Oslo and allowed them to unfold without mentioning them to Peres or Beilin. But when Rabin and Peres agreed to embrace the Oso track as their primary channel of negotiations with the

PLO, they ordered a switch in the leadership of the Israeli side, appointing Joel Singer (for Rabin) and Uri Savir (for Peres) to lead them. At the time, Singer was Israel's chief specialist in international law and Savir was Peres' top diplomat. While Hirschfeld and Pundak had to take a back seat, the Oslo track they launched now became a full-fledged backchannel, operating in absolute compartmentalization from the official delegation, which was still futilely negotiating in Washington.

On August 20, 1993, a historic agreement was reached and signed in Oslo. The news of it would stun Israelis, Palestinians, and the entire world. But before the official signatures, Israel and the PLO—hitherto sworn enemies—needed to exchange letters of recognition, which are as historic as the agreement itself. At that point, President Clinton could call for a signing ceremony on the South Lawn of the White House, which included an iconic handshake between Rabin and Arafat.

The signing of the agreement in Washington did not go down without a nasty fight over the credit for the historic breakthrough in Oslo. Peres and his team sought to dwarf and marginalize the contribution of Beilin's team, so much so that Israel's Foreign Ministry would not provide two tickets for Hirschfeld and Pundak to participate in the ceremony at the White House. Fearing unnecessary embarrassment and potential injustice, the Government of Norway stepped in and invited the two Israelis to the ceremony as its guests. From Hirschfeld's perspective as an academic, this was a very rare case, perhaps singular: a meeting in London had turned into track-two informal discussions in Oslo, which matured into formal backchannel negotiations sanctioned by national leaders, which led to a historic official agreement—all within ten months!

So when I was seated across from Hirschfeld at the dinner table, I expected him to be proud, even boastful, of his work. We quickly struck up a conversation that cut through the rest of the table chatter. He had a lot to say, and I wanted to hear it all. I was surprised that he mostly expressed concern. Eighteen months into the Oslo Process, multiple agreements were signed and implemented in parallel to a frightening rise in terrorism and growing distrust among the parties. Powerful forces were pushing to expand the peace process, while equally powerful counterforces were mobilizing to prevent it.

Hirschfeld and Pundak were the biggest proponents of the Oslo Accords, but also the most intimately acquainted with their flaws. That night, I learned mostly about the shortcomings of the Oslo Process and the risk of its collapse.

But Hirschfeld also had a plan. He said that sustaining the peace process was like riding a bicycle: unless there was constant movement forward, the process could collapse. He spoke about an urgent need to connect Israeli and Palestinian civil societies and business communities and to create a "safety net" of relationships in case political negotiations failed. Such work, he claimed, could only be carried out by non-governmental organizations. Before our meal was over, he basically offered me the job of leading that effort.

My official title at the ECF was "project coordinator," a role that came with the responsibility of supporting all the Israeli experts of the eleven working groups sponsored by the Nauman Foundation. Horizon and DATA each had its own project coordinator with parallel responsibilities to coordinate their eleven teams. But I was a first among equals because the Israeli side had much stronger professional and administrative capacities, and because the ECF brought everyone together and was directly accountable to our funders.

Each of the eleven working groups was going to deal with an issue that was crucial for the emerging economic, business, and trade relations among the three nations, and all working groups were trilateral, with experts from the three sides. Their goal was to come up with joint recommendations that would be presented to our governments and to the international community. If this format sounds complicated and an administrative nightmare, well, it was.

In Israel, there was no shortage of talent for our effort. Many of Israel's most senior professionals were eager to contribute, so I worked with top government officials, world-class academics, leading businesspeople, and a few of Israel's most prominent lawyers. Our project allowed them to do their bit for peace. Israeli tax and customs experts worked with their Palestinian counterparts to envision arrangements that supported mutual economic development and bilateral trade. Bankers from the Bank of Israel and private banks did the same for connecting the three banking systems. The equitability of the undertaking made it possible for our Palestinian and Jordanian partners to receive Israeli input without suspicion or rancor. Indeed, copious amounts of knowledge were transferred, and many strong personal bonds were forged.

Mine was the best entry-level job into the peace process that anyone could have hoped for.

The five-year Interim Period that began in May 1994 was the keystone of the Oslo Process. In this period, the Palestinians would be self-governed by a Palestinian Authority, aka "the PA," which was created by the agreements between Israel and the PLO. The idea was that the PA would build its institutions and capacities during this period ahead of future Palestinian statehood and sovereignty. Additionally, the PA and Israel were meant to build trust.

The concept of an Interim Period was not invented in Oslo, but rather emanated from the Egypt-Israel Framework for Peace in the Middle East signed in Camp David in 1978, also known as the 1978 Camp David Accords, and from the Egypt-Israel Peace Treaty of 1979. Both agreements were signed by Prime Minister Menachem Begin, the legendary leader of the right-wing Likud party, and by President Anwar Sadat. But there were major differences between the Interim Period envisioned in the 1978 treaty and that which was provided for the Oslo Accords of 1993. Primarily, the Oslo Accords, and the accompanying letters exchanged between Rabin and Arafat, represented real historical concessions by both parties, which included mutual recognition, the establishment of the PA, an Israeli withdrawal, and suspension of all military action by the PLO. Furthermore, the Oslo Accords provided a framework for reaching the Permanent Status of Israeli-Palestinian relations by the end of the Interim Period in May 1999.

The underlying vision of the Oslo Accords was implicit yet clear: in Permanent Status there would be two states for two peoples, Israel and Palestine, within the so-called "Two-State Solution." Nonetheless, the words "Palestine," "Palestinian state," and "peace" were not mentioned in the Oslo Accords. All related matters—such as how a Palestinian state would be created, its territory and relations with Israel, as well as the resolution of the refugee problem—were to be hashed out during the Interim Period.

Rabin and Peres hoped that leaning on the 1978 Camp David Accords with Egypt, signed by Begin, would protect the Oslo Accords against right-wing attacks. That did not happen. They also hoped that the Interim Period would allow Israelis and Palestinians to accept the compromises that would be necessary for an agreement on Permanent Status. For example, many Palestinians refused to revoke their demand for the right of Palestinian refugees to return to Israel, and many Israelis would not accept a Palestinian state. Although polls on both sides indicated support for a comprehensive peace agreement, objections to key elements remained strong. Hence, the Oslo negotiators understood that "the devil is in the details" and that it was impossible to iron out the particulars of Permanent Status in 1993. That approach to Permanent Status became known as "constructive ambiguity."

The ECF team, however, was painfully aware of the pitfalls of their brainchild. The Interim Period was designed to foster mutual trust, but it also provided plenty of opportunity for posturing and maneuvering that would only engender *distrust*. Furthermore, five years seemed too short a time for the PA to stabilize its institutions and its relations with Israel, but it was plenty of time for opponents of the peace process to derail it through legitimate political means or by violence and terrorism.

In fact, by the spring of 1995, when I met Hirschfeld and the ECF team, those dynamics were already in motion. The Rabin government was implementing the Gaza-Jericho Agreement, which required Israeli withdrawals and transfer of powers to the PA, while negotiating the Interim Agreement (Oslo B). Meanwhile, opposition within Israel was mounting. Some criticized Rabin for making historic concessions, like recognizing the PLO and allowing the PA to emerge, without having first secured Israel's long-term interests. Others, farther to the right, opposed any compromise or even any engagement with the Palestinians as a matter of principle. Those farthest to the right saw Rabin's concessions as heresy and even treason. These zealots believed that the establishment of Israel in 1948 and the liberation of the Old City of Jerusalem and ancestral Judea and Samaria in 1967 were not just historic but redemptive in that they point toward imminent realization of a messianic vision of reestablishing Jewish ownership of the holy land and Jerusalem, rebuilding the Jewish Temple on Temple Mount in place of the mosques, and a coming of the messiah. For them, any Israeli withdrawal must be opposed by any means necessary.

On February 25, 1994, Dr. Baruch Goldstein, a settler from the Hebron area, walked into the mosque in the Tomb of the Patriarchs and opened fire, killing 29 Palestinians and injuring 125 more. It was the first major act of terrorism of the Oslo Process. Shortly thereafter, a wave of Palestinian suicide bombings shook Israel and produced an unprecedented number of casualties. Meanwhile, as negotiations continued and additional agreements were signed, Arafat's ambiguous approach to curbing terrorism was put under the spotlight, increasing criticism of the Oslo Process and incitement against Rabin, Peres, Beilin, and even Hirschfeld and Pundak. Against this backdrop, the ECF's budding effort to build bridges among Israelis, Palestinians, and Jordanians was quite bold.

The Beilin–Abu Mazen Understandings

Bolder still and stunningly ambitious was another track-two effort that the ECF committed to, in Stockholm. It was initiated in 1994 by London-based Dr. Hussein Agha and Dr. Ahmad Khalidi. Agha and Khalidi are senior advisors to Mahmoud Abbas, also known as Abu Mazen, then second in the PLO hierarchy and the head of its Negotiation Department. While the official delegations were hammering out the Interim Agreement, the goal of the track-two effort in Sweden was to design Permanent Status by formulating a mock framework agreement that addressed all the outstanding issues.

Every few weeks, Hirschfeld and Pundak would make their way to Stockholm via various European transit hubs, often adding "legitimate activities" like a conference in Paris or a meeting in London to veil their true destination. Between their joint sessions, they worked tirelessly in Israel, consulting with Beilin, Novik, and Karni, and initiating brainstorming meetings and research projects on various "theoretical scenarios," which were, in fact, feeding the Stockholm negotiations. Working in the same office, I had no clue about that dimension of their work.

The Stockholm Track produced the Beilin–Abu Mazen Understandings, which are a set of principles about Permanent Status that were designed to be embraced by Rabin and Arafat. Their context was the Gaza-Jericho Agreement, also known as the Cairo Agreement, which was signed in May 1994 to govern the Interim Period. It established that the official negotiations toward an agreement on Permanent Status would begin two years later, on May 4, 1996. The ECF team anticipated that such negotiations would immediately hit a wall, so they planned to finalize a draft agreement on Permanent Status in Stockholm before that date. The next step would be to convince Arafat and Rabin to endorse and sign it on May 4, 1996. Consequently, for the remainder of the Interim Period, from May 1996 to

May 1999, the parties would be negotiating the detailed reality of the Two-State Solution, as opposed to arguing its overarching principles. This would have been a game-changing political maneuver.

Hence, the Beilin–Abu Mazen Understandings were negotiated to be consistent with the public statements of Rabin and Arafat. They creatively introduced ideas that continue to impact all attempts to reach Permanent Status, up to and including the Trump Plan, such as demilitarizing the Palestinian state; land swaps based on the 1967 Lines and Israeli annexation of settlement blocs in exchange for land in the Negev; allowing for the return of Palestinian refugees to Palestine, except for a symbolic number that would return to Israel; and establishing two capitals of two states in the Area of Jerusalem, where the Jewish neighborhoods would be Israel's and the Arabs ones would be parts of Palestine, while sovereign and administrative powers in the Old City would be shared.

Abu Mazen and Beilin did not finalize and sign the final draft of their understandings, dated October 31, 1995. Allegedly, Abu Mazen then presented the Understandings to Arafat, who did not reject them. Now, it was Beilin's turn to brief Rabin, and a meeting was scheduled. Alas, tragically, Rabin was assassinated on November 4, 1995, as he walked out of a peace rally in Tel Aviv. Israel immediately descended into a state of mourning, shock, and soul-searching.

Rabin's funeral turned into an unprecedented demonstration of international support for the peace process. A caravan of world leaders arrived in Jerusalem. Clinton's speech touched the hearts of millions of Israelis when he concluded with the words "*Shalom, chaver*" ("Goodbye, friend"). But from the perspective of the peace process, Arafat's visit to Rabin's home to comfort his wife, Leah, was the most moving moment of that week, and demonstrated the bond that had been created between the two leaders.

Like all Israelis, the ECF team was shocked, but immediately regrouped. They believed that the tragic event might create an opportunity for a breakthrough with the Palestinians, using Peres' legitimacy as the new premier. Beilin presented Peres his understandings with Abu Mazen, but Peres decided to call for early elections. With a 30-point lead, he was confident of a decisive victory over Netanyahu that would grant him a clear mandate to reach an agreement with the Palestinians. And, of course, some of Peres' people were confident that they could negotiate a better deal than Beilin.

A bitter election campaign followed. A string of savage terror attacks and suicide bombings put Peres on his back foot, under pressure to respond with a heavy hand. He then approved the killing of Yahya Ayyash, head of Hamas's military wing in Gaza, which then led to more brutality on Israel's streets. Scenes of carnage dominated the news, as hundreds of Israelis were left dead or wounded. And when Peres decided to flex his military muscle in Lebanon, Operation Grapes of Wrath failed because the IDF mistakenly killed 106 civilians in Qana. Slowly but surely, Netanyahu closed in on Peres and eventually pulled off an extremely tight and stunning victory. Israel's left wing sunk into despair.

At the ECF, the shock lasted only a few days. On the following weekend, I penned a policy paper for my bosses. My argument: If Netanyahu pursued the path of the Oslo Accords, he would enjoy broad public and international support, including from political rivals on the left. But should he refuse to do so, and if he failed to be reelected, his successor would have a 16-month window to conclude a historic agreement with the Palestinians.

Why 16 months? Well, it was clear that by 1999 or 2000, pressure would mount on Israel to resume negotiations on Permanent Status. As a rule, the traditional instability of Israeli governments granted each coalition a window of two years to drive its primary agenda. I assumed that a new prime minister would seek to ratify an agreement in the Knesset within that amount of time.

I also realized that the civil service is not capable of preparing for and conducting such comprehensive negotiations, which touch upon the core issues of Israel's ethos. This presented a dramatic opportunity for the ECF. It was, in fact, our responsibility, as the non-governmental organization most closely associated with the Oslo Process, to fill this gap. Thus, in May 1996, I recommended undertaking a comprehensive research, strategy, and policy-planning exercise ahead of negotiations on Permanent Status that could begin three or four years later. In retrospect, that memo is one of the most important I've ever written, determining my professional and personal paths to the Bureau of the Prime Minister, the Camp David negotiations, and the Reut Institute. A direct line connects that memo and this book.

The Great Peace-Planning Exercise

In May 1996, however, my ideas were a bit premature, even for the ECF leadership, which was invested in promoting the Beilin–Abu Mazen Understandings. Despite the dramatic setbacks represented by Rabin's assassination and Peres' loss, Beilin and Co. still hoped that when negotiations resumed, it would be with an endorsement of his understandings with Abu Mazen.

Meanwhile, I believed that the ECF needed to lead a complementary effort. Even in the unlikely case that Netanyahu embraced the Oslo Accords, I saw no chance that he would confirm an agreement that was co-created by Beilin. Also, to legitimize any agreement, the bureaucratic process would have to unfold with the participation of "credible experts," including former generals, professors, ambassadors, and senior civil servants. After all, the Beilin–Abu Mazen Understandings represented only one possible outcome regarding Permanent Status, and any new negotiations could arrive at different conclusions. I believed that we needed to prepare the groundwork for those future negotiations by collecting relevant data, identifying experts, articulating Israel's interests, and gaining a better understanding of Palestinian positions. There was also much work to be done regarding how each issue affected all other issues. Such work needed to happen for every individual topic and for the entire agreement, as a whole is always more complex than the sum of its various parts.

It took me nearly six months to convince Hirschfeld to approve this initiative. The decisive moment came in Cairo, while he and I were participating in the Middle East North Africa Conference. In the evenings we took power walks, analyzing the events of the day and discussing next steps. Cairo comes alive at night when the temperature cools, and I loved walking along the Nile and across its bridges. It was during one of those walks that Hirschfeld gave me the green light.

For the following two and a half years, my primary task would be to establish and support working groups who researched and deliberated every topic of the future negotiations on Permanent Status. Dozens of top experts, often espousing a range of political and professional views, made up our working groups on Palestinian statehood, refugees, security, borders and territories, economics, water, and Jerusalem.

The most fascinating part of the work was engaging with Palestinians, Jordanians, and international experts on various aspects of Permanent Status. We would meet at different international conferences or bilateral brainstorming workshops, where we gained a deeper understanding of their perspectives, as well as of what would be feasible in future negotiations. No less important, these sessions also prepared our potential Palestinian interlocutors for future negotiations.

By 1999, we had a folder on every topic, including essential facts, figures, laws, and international agreements. We also had an articulation of Israel's interests and our best understanding of Palestinian interests. In some areas, we even had draft agreements, some formulated by our experts and others completed after extensive discussions with the Palestinians. In the area of economic and trade relations, we even had a fully fleshed-out mock-agreement that was "negotiated" between an Israeli team led by David Brodet, then-former director general of the Ministry of Finance, and a Palestinian team led by PLO-senior Dr. Maher Al-Kurd, a veteran of the negotiations in Oslo.

This was a period of intense intellectual, personal, and professional growth. We needed to create knowledge on hitherto-unexplored issues. Nobody had thought about the detailed implications of Permanent Status on a topic-by-topic basis, or as a systemic whole. Because the Beilin–Abu Mazen Understandings were kept confidential, we couldn't study them, beyond what Hirschfeld and Pundak shared. Their discretion turned out to be a blessing in disguise because it forced us to methodically work through every issue.

To support the different working groups, I had to become conversant in every subject area. That required quickly digesting huge amounts of material. For example, to support our working group on water, I needed to understand the existing and projected needs of Israel, Jordan, and the Palestinians; relevant international law regarding shared bodies of water, aquifers, and rivers; and even the basics of sewage treatment. I had to seek out precedents, meet experts, and seek international benchmarks. Of course, the same needed to be done for security, borders, Jerusalem, refugees, and the establishment of a Palestinian state. I often returned from travels toting tens of kilograms of books and publications rarely read by anyone not already an expert in the field, and I gradually became a "generalist" on Israeli-Palestinian Permanent Status.

All in all, it was a remarkable opportunity to work with some of Israel's most accomplished professionals. Indeed, many would advance to top positions in the private and public sectors: Prof. Avi Ben-Bassat, a member of our economic working group, became director general of the Ministry of Finance; Adv. Meir Linzen, our chief legal advisor and a board member of the ECF, became the managing partner of Israel's leading law firm; and Adv. Gilead Sher, the lawyer of our security working group, became Barak's chief of staff, his chief negotiator, and my boss.

The Peace Industry

Netanyahu's electoral victory in 1996 had the unanticipated effect of launching the so-called "peace industry." The ECF was now imbued with a sense of urgency to save the Oslo Process from collapse due to Netanyahu's hardline policies, Hamas' terrorism, and the fragility of the PA. Steadfast in our belief that a disengagement from the Palestinians was crucial for Israel's future, the ECF doubled down on its efforts.

At that point, European funding for our work became readily available. The Israeli-Palestinian and Israeli-Arab peace processes were cornerstones of the EU's Euro-Mediterranean Partnership, which was declared in 1995 in Barcelona and seen as vital for the future of Europe itself. The EU was now concerned that its vision and massive financial investments would be lost if the Oslo Process collapsed, so the European Commission and individual European countries pledged millions of euros to foster collaboration among Israeli and Palestinian civil-society organizations to keep the peace process afloat.

Henceforth, an entire ecosystem of organizations emerged with dozens of groups and hundreds of social entrepreneurs, academics, former diplomats and civil servants, activists, and even some charlatans. The "peace industry" rapidly expanded and now operated through conferences, research projects, track-two diplomacy, confidence-building efforts, and many people-to-people activities.

The ECF, together with the Peres Center, was at the epicenter of that ecosystem. Our team uniquely combined capacities for top-down political and policy work with bottom-up people-to-people operations. Namely, the ECF's mastery of the "big picture" guided its projects, which would all come together to support broader strategies. Ambassadors and diplomats frequented our offices, and we visited their embassies in Tel Aviv and their foreign ministries overseas. I got to tag along with Hirschfeld and Pundak on many of these meetings, where political and diplomatic assessments were shared and projects were discussed. As someone who loves history and appreciates diplomacy, I felt like a kid in a candy store.

Alas, oddly enough, despite the abundance of resources in the field, the ECF experience was one of scarcity. Hirschfeld, Pundak, and Karni would take on more commitments than they could serve and hired staff before securing funding. Salaries were modest—I was making much less than I did in the military—and every few months we were warned that our paychecks might be delayed. To Karni's credit, this never happened, at least not to junior employees. That said, there were many non-monetary benefits to working at the ECF. We got to travel to the most interesting places, meet fascinating people, and work on the most exciting initiatives. I had the opportunity to participate in track-two diplomacy and be a guest of ministers and ambassadors around the world. I visited Norway, Sweden, Denmark, Canada, the U.S., the UK, Spain, Belgium, the Netherlands, Switzerland, France, Germany, Austria, Greece, Italy, Turkey, Egypt, and Jordan. Of course, there were also many visits to Palestinian cities, and to places in East Jerusalem that few Israelis ever explore. It was an eye-opening and mind-expanding personal and professional period.

The Oslo-ization of Netanyahu

In November 1996, when Bill Clinton was reelected, the political landscape was set for a minimum of three years. Clinton supported the Oslo Process and the Two-State Solution, which he also saw as Rabin's legacy. The ECF had close ties with key people in his administration, which created a silver lining. Hirschfeld's approach was that peacemaking should be a national project led from the center, and not a pet project of Israel's left wing. The idea was that Netanyahu could be persuaded to embrace and even own the political process and relations with the Palestinians. Pundak supported this approach and emphasized that the Palestinians must be able to work with any Israeli government, not just the ones they liked. We expected that Netanyahu would seek to appease the Americans by publicly pledging his commitment to the already-signed agreements, while highlighting the process' flaws and making new demands that the Palestinians would reject—all with the goal of legitimately blocking the Oslo Process. Indeed, that is exactly what happened.

Given Netanyahu's policy, the ECF embarked on a counter-move: the Oslo-ization of Netanyahu. It entailed convincing the Palestinians to agree to his demands, thereby calling his bluff. Novik took the lead on that one. With superb diplomatic skills, he orchestrated a global diplomatic campaign involving Americans, Egyptians, Europeans, and Jordanians to soften Netanyahu's stance on the one hand and persuade Arafat to accommodate Netanyahu on the other. He diligently pieced together a system of unwritten understandings that served all stakeholders in Washington, Ramallah, Cairo, Amman, Brussels, London, and Paris, as well as in Jerusalem and Tel Aviv. And because he did it all from the comfort of his office in Herzliya, I often got to sit across from his desk and observe a master at work.

The policy goals were for Netanyahu to formally endorse the Oslo Process, recognize the PLO and the PA, and perhaps even sign additional Oslo Accords that would ratify all past agreements and provide for their implementation. The ECF's political goals were equally ambitious: If Netanyahu embraced Oslo, he'd lose the right-wing factions of his coalition, and if he blocked the political process and clashed with the U.S., he'd lose the support of his coalition's moderates. Either way, his chances in the next election would be compromised. Surprisingly, the ECF found allies for this approach within Likud and Netanyahu's government. Some wanted to moderate his hardline positions while others just hoped to accelerate his downfall.

As anticipated, shortly after his election, it became clear that Netanyahu had no intention of discussing Permanent Status with the Palestinians. He never resumed negotiations on Permanent Status, which were launched by the Peres government on May 5, 1996, two weeks before the election. Instead, he demanded to renegotiate the *implementation* of the Interim Agreement, particularly the withdrawal from Hebron, which was part of the First Further Redeployment (FRD1) of Israel's forces in the West Bank. At that point, Israel had already withdrawn from five Palestinian cities in the West Bank, and he claimed that the Palestinian side was not complying with its commitments. Of course, subsequent Second Further Redeployment (FRD2) and Third Further Redeployment (FRD3)—which required further military withdrawals and transfer of powers to the PA—would be deferred as well.

Initially, the Palestinians refused to renegotiate with Netanyahu's *outstanding* commitments of an *existing* agreement, which they had signed with Rabin. They demanded that Israel implement all its outstanding obligations *before* discussing the implementation of future commitments. But under persistent pressure from Washington, Cairo, and Brussels, orchestrated by Novik from Herzliya, they eventually agreed to "concede" to Netanyahu's demands. The outcomes were the Hebron Agreement, which was signed in January 1997, and the Wye River Memorandum, signed by Netanyahu, Arafat, and Clinton in October 1998. In this process, the Netanyahu government formally engaged with the Palestinians and the PLO and came to appreciate the PA's role in curtailing terrorism. Most important, they endorsed the Oslo Accords and pledged to implement them. In sum, the ECF effort unfolded to perfection: Netanyahu signed two Oslo accords with Arafat; shortly thereafter his government was brought down by his far-right coalition partners; and in May 1999 he lost to Barak.

CHAPTER 2

In the Aquarium

The Smartest Person in the Room

In July 1999, Ehud Barak finally became prime minister. He took his time forming his government after his stunning electoral victory in May, and now he immediately travelled to meet President of Egypt Hosni Mubarak, Arafat, and Clinton with the goal of resetting the diplomatic agenda. In Washington he made his first significant speech on the Palestinian issue, pledging that "in fifteen months we will know" whether an agreement on Permanent Status will be reached. Watching him on television, I was blown away. Four years earlier, in 1996, I anticipated that the prime minister who would follow Netanyahu would have 16 months to reach an agreement. Now Barak was speaking about 15 months.

At that point, I knew that a huge diplomatic drama was going to unfold, and that I was uniquely qualified to contribute to Israel's success. That speech confirmed for me that this was my moment to transition into government, if possible as secretary of the delegation for the negotiations with the PLO. As one of a handful of Israelis who worked on every issue of Permanent Status, I had the knowledge and the relationships. I was seasoned enough to support the prime minister, but young enough not to threaten other senior staffers. Hirschfeld had been encouraging me to make this move for months, and Sher had already asked for my help in advising Barak as prime minister–elect. The stars seemed to be aligning.

The process for joining the government as a professional appointee is challenging. There are only a few spots and much competition. For a few weeks, it wasn't at all clear that I would be offered the position. Then, on an early-August Friday, Sher called. He had just been appointed chief negotiator and needed an assistant. Basically, he said to me, "Our first meeting is tomorrow night in Jerusalem. If you show up, the position of secretary of the delegation is yours." I hung up and called Hirschfeld, Pundak, and Karni, who immediately encouraged me to take the plunge. The next evening, I joined Sher's meeting to take the first step in one of the most incredible journeys of my life.

Barak was elected as the rising star of Israeli politics. Four years prior, he had retired from the IDF as its lieutenant general and chief of staff. His exemplary career spanned 35 years in Israel's Delta Force, *Sayeret Matkal*, in the armored corps, and at headquarters. Not only was he the IDF's most decorated soldier, but he was also a confident officer who repeatedly took strong positions on the most critical politico-military issues of the 1980s.

Like many top generals, Barak had charisma, courage, and luck. What set him apart were his intellect, analytical skills, and remarkable memory. Over the years, he gained undergraduate degrees in mathematics and physics and a post-graduate degree—with distinction—in system analysis from Stanford University. He is well read in history, philosophy, and politics and admires Churchill, de Gaulle, and Ben-Gurion. He can also speak with confidence, knowledge, and sophistication about classical music, watches, wine, and cigars and plays the piano, favoring Rachmaninoff. Almost always, Barak is the smartest person in the room.

Barak is also exceptionally ambitious. The daring operations he led behind enemy lines required personal approval by ministers of defense and prime ministers, so he had been interacting with senior brass and Israel's top politicians since he was a junior officer. His ability to understand and explain the big strategic picture and its nuanced complexities led to his rapid rise. Every position was a stepping stone for promotion, including his tenure as the IDF's chief of staff, which served as an entryway into national politics. Indeed, four months after retiring from active service, he became minister of the interior in Rabin's government, positioned to inherit the role of chair of the party.

Barak's burning desire was to be "in the room where it happens," confident in his abilities to influence the course of history. Toward that end, as a politician, he built and disbanded coalitions, and made and broke promises. Many saw him as a Machiavellian instrumentalist who cold-bloodedly manipulates his closest allies. To him, though, such machinations were justified by "the bigger picture." After all, joining the Netanyahu government in 2010 to help curtail the Iranian nuclear project was more important than preserving the unity of the Labor Party in parliamentary opposition.

During his service in *Sayeret Matkal*, Barak not only designed and led hundreds of mind-boggling operations, but also crystallized many of its methods. One of them became known as "the matrix." It requires breaking down the most complicated operations into their basic elements and then synchronizing logistics, transportation, equipment, and the skills of the team, based on impeccable intelligence, into a perfectly timed sequence of actions. Success was a result of countless rehearsals, as well as optimal timing, disciplined execution, and the ability to improvise if anything went wrong. The final point of harmony, which allows for a go-ahead, materializes when "the matrix comes together" and yet another stealth operation behind enemy lines can unfold without anyone else even knowing it happened.

Barak brought that mindset to the military's top positions. As IDF chief of staff in 1991–1995, he argued for making the IDF "small and smart" in a unique "window of strategic opportunity" when Israel did not have a direct military threat for the first time in its existence. The collapse of the Soviet Union in 1989, which ended the Cold War with an American victory; the subsiding of the Palestinian Uprising, which began in December 1987; the decimation of the Iraqi military in the First Gulf War in 1991; and the exhaustion of Iran following the brutal Iran-Iraq war—all gave Israel the chance to modernize its military. Tanks, airplanes, and ships from the 1970s and 1980s were quickly replaced with precision weaponry that could win wars at greater distances with fewer casualties. Three decades later, Israel is still reaping the fruits of that revolution.

Wars are foggy and complex, just like forging peace or leading a political transformation. They are subject to the law of unintended consequences, with ripple effects and backlashes. Some general principles offer guidance, and some best practices are useful, but there is no manual to inform the endeavor. While strategizing and planning are essential, results also hinge upon unpredictable interaction among multiple elements. Sometimes, thoughtful well-intended efforts can end in disaster. Sadly, Israeli-Palestinian peacemaking in 2000 turned into a bloody war. In other times, symbolic gestures can have profound effects, as when Sadat came to Jerusalem in 1977.

Hence, whereas there is a lot that we can learn from history, outcomes cannot be predicted.

But complex is different from complicated. For example, building an airplane is complicated, requiring the assembly of millions of screws, metal plates, wheels, and wires. It is a "science" of great engineers and designers that create and follow detailed manuals. When working for Barak, I always felt that he aspired to turn the complex into the complicated. He would engineer moves involving diplomacy and politics, while aspiring for systemic effects. He would analyze a wide range of possible outcomes from his actions, connecting activities, outputs, outcomes, and strategic impact. Consequently, while some of his senior appointments could not even get his attention, in other cases he would drill down into basic elements, make tactical decisions, or dictate exact wording, which frustrated his team. For him, things were rarely simple and straightforward.

Barak also assumed that everyone was rational, like he was. He believed that political allies and rivals, advisers and staffers, Israelis and Palestinians could contain their emotions and arrive logically where he did, and that therefore pieces would eventually fall into place. His political maneuverings were rarely "personal," only "business"—the business of power and policy. On election night, standing on the balcony of Tel Aviv's Rabin Square, in front of tens of thousands of cheering supporters, he promised "a dawn of a new day," counting on the matrix to rein in the messiness of whatever came next.

Israel's Double Crisis

Upon his electoral victory in May 1999, Barak quickly faced a couple of compounding challenges: under a new electoral system—which was introduced in 1996 to consolidate power—he gained a broad personal mandate to effectuate his agenda. Alas, the Knesset was now fragmented, with both Barak's Labor Party and Netanyahu's Likud losing power to smaller factions. That made building and leading a ruling coalition excruciatingly difficult.

Meanwhile, Barak needed to face three urgent and interrelated foreign policy crises: first, in Lebanon, Israel and the South Lebanon Army (SLA) were fighting a war of attrition against Hezbollah, which Barak pledged to end within a year of taking office. Next, in Syria, President Hafez al-Assad was gravely ill, and Barak needed to act fast if he wanted a peace treaty, which would also allow him an honorable exit from Lebanon. And third, Israel faced the possibility of a Palestinian declaration of independent statehood following the end of the Interim Period in May 1999. In that context, it was rumored that Barak, as candidate, endorsed a promise to Arafat to accommodate Palestinian statehood in May 2000, if Arafat avoided a violent clash with Israel during the election, which was anticipated to serve Netanyahu.

Looming over these challenges was the end of Clinton's presidency. Clinton had become a beloved friend of Israel who also had clout and credibility with the Arab and Palestinian side. There was no guarantee that his successor would be equally committed to Israel's well-being. In other words, Barak had sixteen months, or less, to accomplish three big goals.

At that point, Barak was looking at two tried-and-tested approaches to establishing his coalition. He could have created a large national unity government with Likud, but such a coalition would tie his hands when it came to Syria, Lebanon, and the Palestinians. Another alternative was to build a center-left coalition, which would rely on the support of Arab-Israeli parties. But that coalition would lack the legitimacy to sign historic agreements with Syria and the PLO. In the aftermath of the Rabin assassination, Barak needed broad political and public support for the matrix to be realized.

Therefore, he came up with an original approach, piecing together the broadest coalition in Israel's history. It was made up of small parties ranging from the far-left secular-liberal Meretz party to the far-right religious MAFDAL party and included the ultra-orthodox party of Shas. This coalition was made possible by each party's desire to join the governing coalition and would be kept together by adhering to two principles: a preservation of the status quo on religious affairs and committing to a general referendum on any agreement that would require withdrawal of Israeli forces. Barak also pledged to a series of no's in his negotiations with the Palestinians: Israel would *not* return to the 1967 Lines, would *not* compromise its security needs, and would *not* allow the return of Palestinian refugees to Israel. Hence, Barak's coalition gave him the broadest possible mandate to *negotiate* comprehensive agreements with Syria and the PLO but not to *conclude* them. Barak hoped that a "yea" vote in the referendum would compel the Knesset to follow suit. In any case, that was a problem for a later date.

Syria First, Lebanon Second

Barak's first major policy decision was whether to pursue agreements with the PLO and Syria simultaneously or to prioritize one over the other. He quickly decided to focus first on Syria and then on an honorable exit from Lebanon. He hoped that negotiations with Syria would be "simpler" because Assad was a more "rational" adversary and the conflict with Syria was about tangibles like land, water, and security, while the conflict with the Palestinians involved religious issues and a clash between two national narratives. It might be needless to mention that having mutually agreed-on international borders with Syria, effective security arrangements, and normalized diplomatic relations would be a huge accomplishment for Zionism, which would "justify" eighteen years of sacrifice in Lebanon and fifty years of hostility with Syria. Further weakening of the Palestinians, who would be left alone in their struggle against Israel, was seen as a collateral bonus. Barak's decisions were backed by extensive polling that indicated wide public support for a Syria-first approach and for an agreement that allowed for peaceful withdrawal from Lebanon, if such an agreement is reached.

Barak's timeline was ambitious: He sought an agreement with Syria by early 2000, which would allow for a withdrawal from Lebanon in the spring. If he could not reach an agreement with Syria, there was a Plan B: to withdraw from Lebanon unilaterally. This idea was introduced to the Israeli public by Beilin after extensive consultations with military experts at the ECF. In a book published in 1998, Beilin argued that Syria was holding Israel captive in Lebanon,[5] and that herefore Israel should break the linkage between an agreement with Syria and its pullout to the internationally recognized border with Lebanon. The outcome of such a move would be erosion of support for Hezbollah, which could no longer claim to be fighting to liberate Lebanese territory, and a weakening of Syria's hand in future negotiations.

While most of the IDF's senior brass opposed unilateral withdrawal, some key generals endorsed Beilin's approach, and Barak paid close attention. I was in a unique position to see both sides of this process. At the non-governmental setting of the ECF in 1998 and 1999, I witnessed Beilin's ideas incubate,

---

5   Yossi Beilin, *A Guide to an Israeli Withdrawal from Lebanon* (Tel Aviv: Hakibbutz Hameuchad Publishing House, 1998) (in Hebrew)

crystallize, be published, and garner public support. Later, in the Office of the Prime Minister, I saw how the unilateral withdrawal unfolded. As early as January 2000, while negotiating with Syria, Barak ordered the IDF to prepare detailed plans for a pullout in case negotiations with Syria failed. And around May 22, 2000, when the line of defense in Lebanon collapsed, these plans were implemented without a single loss of life.

Going for a Meltdown Moment

Barak designed his coalition and the diplomatic processes that he led during his tenure around "meltdown moments" when a "truth is revealed," and the political systems are transformed. He anticipated that any agreement with Syria or the PLO would trigger one such moment. Up to that point, Barak would have a coalition and a government without a draft agreement. After that point, he would have a draft of a historic agreement, but no longer a coalition to support his government.

Barak's political strategy determined that Permanent Status negotiations had to be stalled during the negotiations with Syria, perhaps until the spring of 2000. At that point—and if his government survived a failed negotiation with Syria or an agreement, a referendum, ratification, and withdrawal from Lebanon—he could turn his attention to the PLO. And if Barak failed to reach an agreement with the PLO, there was a Plan B for that as well: to disengage from Palestinian areas and shape Permanent Status unilaterally. And all of that complexity was supposed to be compressed into fifteen months...

But Arafat would not simply take a back seat to the Syria negotiations after postponing the declaration of statehood from 1999 to 2000. He had promises from world leaders that he would be able to act unilaterally if Israel avoided negotiating with him. Therefore, Barak needed to establish a formal delegation to "negotiate" with the Palestinians but without making any progress that could destabilize the coalition and disrupt the talks with Syria. Furthermore, the Wye River Memorandum of 1998 promised the Palestinians further Israeli withdrawals within the West Bank. Each such withdrawal was a threat to Barak's coalition, so he needed to postpone even those measures. That entire strategy required walking on a diplomatic tightrope and could have collapsed at any moment into a full-blown conflict.

But Barak had limited tools for appeasing Arafat. The right-wing parties of his government had effective veto power to prevent even small gestures of goodwill. Paradoxically, while Israel could negotiate extensive territorial withdrawals, Palestinian statehood, and releasing thousands of prisoners in a Permanent Status deal, Barak could barely release a few dozen veteran prisoners as an act of goodwill. Though we were negotiating the dismantling of dozens of settlements, Barak had a hard time temporarily freezing construction in settlements. Those limitations compromised our ability to demand confidence-building measures from the Palestinians, such as tighter policing of terror suspects or curtailing the toxic anti-Semitic incitement in mosques, at universities, and in schools, which provided ample ammunition to Oslo's critics.

Sharm Memorandum: A Restructured Process

Sharm Memorandum
Article 1: Permanent Status negotiations:

a.   … the two Sides will resume the Permanent Status negotiations in an accelerated manner … to achieve their <u>mutual goal of a Permanent Status Agreement</u> …;

b.   … the <u>negotiations</u> on the Permanent Status will <u>lead to the implementation of Security Council Resolutions 242 and 338</u>;

c.   … a determined effort to conclude <u>a Framework Agreement on all Permanent Status</u> issues <u>in five months</u> from the resumption of the Permanent Status negotiations [i.e. FAPS no later than February 13, 2000 —GG];

d.   … will conclude a <u>comprehensive agreement on all Permanent Status</u> issues within <u>one year</u> of the resumption of the Permanent Status negotiations [i.e. CAPS no later than September 13, 2000 —GG];

e.   Permanent Status negotiations will <u>resume</u> … <u>not later than September 13, 1999</u>.

Article 4: Committees

a.   The <u>Third Further Redeployment Committee</u> shall commence its activities <u>not later than September 13, 1999</u> [parallel to the negotiations on the FAPS —GG]

Of course, Barak could not disclose his strategy of delaying negotiations with the Palestinians. He couldn't tell his negotiators because he needed us to be serious in our endeavors, nor could he reveal his strategy to fellow politicians who would leak it instantly. And Barak needed the Americans and Egyptians to believe that he was committed to Permanent Status negotiations so they would pressure Arafat to accept his proposals, although that meant that Arafat would be sidelined to allow for negotiations with Syria. Hence, Barak needed a new agreement regarding the *process* of negotiations and the *sequence* of implementing Israel's outstanding commitments, including from Netanyahu's Wye River Memorandum. Indeed, the timeline of the political process with the Palestinians had to be extended deep into 2000 to create a window of time for the Syria negotiations and the Lebanon withdrawal. The matrix was still missing a keystone.

The Sharm El-Sheikh Memorandum of September 1999 was designed to bring the matrix together in one agreement by recalibrating expectations among all stakeholders. Arafat was initially reluctant to negotiate, for the third time, Israel's withdrawal from the West Bank and Gaza, which had been originally laid out in the Oslo B Agreement of 1995. The Palestinian side felt that they had been patient with Israel from 1997 to 1998, when they contributed to the effort of calling Netanyahu's bluff, and then, in 1999, when they agreed to postpone their declaration of statehood. From their perspective, they had delivered on all their promises. After three challenging years since 1996, it was time for Barak to reciprocate their goodwill by treating Arafat with respect and fulfilling Israel's commitments.

Barak, though, had clout with the Americans, Europeans, and Egyptians. He convinced them that while he was absolutely committed to implementing the existing agreements and to pursuing a peace treaty, he also needed a new framework. Sher led the negotiations throughout August. Our arguments were logical and coherent, emphasizing the need to accommodate and nurture the historic opportunity created by Barak's election. And eventually, under tremendous international pressure, the Palestinians caved and all parties gathered on September 4, 1999 in Sharm El-Sheikh, which is in Sinai, Egypt, for a signing ceremony of the "Sharm Memorandum."

Negotiating the Sharm Memorandum was my first experience in international diplomacy, seeing "how the sausage was made." The Israeli side had the advantage of clear goals. We then formulated a draft that captured all that we wanted to achieve, which all parties used. Work was intense around the clock, and I had little time even to mourn my grandmother, who passed away that month. Then came the flight to Sharm El-Sheikh, my first international trip with the prime minister, which gave me a glance at the power politics of his bureau and at the complicated logistics, administration, and security that surrounds such travel. I saw the arm-twisting— and sometimes the begging—that determine who gets to travel or to sit close to the PM, as well as the dynamics between him and the traveling press cohort on the plane.

In the signing ceremony, Barak sat next to Arafat and Sher presented the Sharm Memorandum for his signature. This was a momentous occasion for me, worth wearing my novelty tie with small peace doves, which I kept for such special occasions. We now had a new framework for effectuating the Oslo Accords, setting February 13, 2000, as the target date for reaching a Framework Agreement on Permanent Status (FAPS) and September 13, 2000, as the target date for a Comprehensive Agreement on Permanent Status (CAPS). The Sharm Memorandum also rearranged the implementation of the Wye River Memorandum, which was the third postponement of the FRD2, notwithstanding Palestinians frustrations.

Furthermore, Israel's Third Further Redeployment, which was originally supposed to happen by January 1996, was now open-endedly attached to the negotiations on the FAPS and effectively deferred indefinitely. We realized that it would be impossible to reach an agreement with the Palestinians on FRD3 independent of the agreements on Permanent Status. And yet again, there was no mention of Palestinian statehood or a date for its establishment. On paper, the Palestinians now had a signed commitment by Barak for an ambitious framework for negotiating Permanent Status. In practice, the Sharm Memorandum allowed Barak to deprioritize them.

The signing of the Sharm Memorandum had immediate personal implications for me. Sher, my boss and patron, now understood Barak's plans to place the Palestinians on the back burner. He stepped down and went back to his law firm, knowing that Barak might call on him again when serious negotiations resumed. For the following weeks, there was no chief negotiator, and thus no negotiations. The Jewish holidays provided a useful cover for inaction, but the Palestinians were irritated. Their suspicions of Barak were being confirmed.

At long last, in late September, Ambassador Dr. Oded Eran was appointed chief negotiator, charged with leading a delegation that had no mandate to make any progress. He was a senior and respected diplomat, with a successful career that included postings in Europe, Washington, and Amman. He was smart, experienced, knowledgeable, hardworking, and genuinely interested in the task at hand. He also collected books about Jerusalem, which earned him the respect of our Palestinian interlocutors. The delegation he led was comprised of representatives of different ministries and security agencies that were relevant to the negotiations.

As part of his portfolio, Eran also became the founding director of Israel's Peace Administration, which was managed by Colonel (Res.) Shaul Arieli and by my friend Moty Cristal. Together, Arieli, Cristal, and I staffed the tremendous policy-planning work of readying Israel for a comprehensive multi-track, multi-issue negotiation. We tapped dozens of government agencies, building on Arieli's experience as a veteran of the Strategic Planning Branch of the IDF and of the Oslo B talks. Cristal was, and still is, an expert in orchestrating complex negotiations, and he was thrilled to co-lead such a high-stakes affair. Their vision for the Peace Administration was perfectly aligned with what I had foreseen in 1996 and was along the lines of ECF's efforts between 1997 and 1999. Naturally, I was excited to work with them in the immediate second circle to history- making.

Eran's initial task was to prepare for Permanent Status negotiations by crystallizing Israel's interests and determining, subject to Barak's approval, Israel's opening positions on all issues. While in some areas there was a government agency in charge and a legacy from Oslo B, in other areas, including statehood, Jerusalem, or refugees, there was no prior experience or any agency with clear responsibility. Hence, Eran and Arieli presided over long meetings with many participants, where representatives of each agency presented their suggested starting positions and demands of the Palestinians. There was little discussion of what Israel would be giving in return or any attempt to prioritize our expectations. Naturally, in the absence of a political directive to do otherwise, these positions were maximalist, and effectively impossible for the Palestinians to accept. Nonetheless, this was a very important exercise because dozens of senior civil servants had to seriously engage with the prospect of Permanent Status.

Eran envisioned leading historic negotiations with the Palestinians as a professional highlight of his career. But Barak wanted him to stall the negotiations without annoying the Palestinians, destabilizing the coalition, or distracting from the Syria negotiations. This made Eran a pawn in Barak's master plan, consumed by logistics and administration instead of diplomacy and statecraft.

Most frustrating for Eran were the hawkish and impossible positions that naturally emerged from the bottom-up bureaucratic process that he was tasked with leading. Only Barak, not Eran, could overrule government agencies, but Barak had no interest in doing so. Furthermore, Eran was repeatedly blindsided by direct discussions among Barak, Clinton, Arafat, Mubarak, and the Europeans, as well as by various backchannels that happened without him. He had a shiny title but no power or mandate to lead, and everyone knew it.

Meanwhile, the negotiations with Syria advanced toward their anticipated moment of truth. In December 1999, as originally planned by Barak, Clinton hosted a summit with Israel and Syria in Shepherdstown, West Virginia. While Assad sent his foreign minister, Farouq Al-Sharaa, Barak represented Israel, and their engagement clarified the contours of the deal: Assad demanded full Israeli withdrawal from the Golan Heights and insisted on "wetting his feet in the Sea of Galilee." And while this might sound like a perk that could be accommodated through an act of goodwill, it was actually a demand with dramatic implications for sovereign water rights in a system that includes the Jordan River, the Sea of Galilee, and the Dead Sea. Our side was adamantly opposed, and Assad's demand became a deal-breaker for Barak.

When no agreement came out of Shepherdstown, negotiations ensued while Assad's health continued to deteriorate. His final answer came in late March from Geneva: he would not compromise on Syria's access to the Sea of Galilee, so no agreement would be reached under his watch. He passed away shortly thereafter, his power bequeathed to his son, Bashar.

At that point, Barak had to implement the second phase of his scheme: unilateral withdrawal from Lebanon to the "Blue Line," the internationally

recognized border between the two countries, which dates from a 1923 agreement between France and Britain. A contingency plan to that effect had been
prepared by the IDF since January, with a target date in July 2000, per Barak's
pledge to get Israel out of Lebanon within one year of taking office. By that
point, Barak had embraced Beilin's view that full Israeli withdrawal would
erode the legitimacy of Hezbollah within Lebanon, as well as legitimize a
harsh Israeli military response to any aggression from Lebanon. He anticipated that those effects would calm the border area and create better security
for Israel and its northern communities. Barak even intended to invite the
United Nations to confirm that Israel had fully withdrawn from Lebanon.

But not everyone was a fan of Barak's plan. Top generals argued that
unilateral withdrawal broadcasted weakness. At the very least, they called
for keeping control of a few high points that overlooked Lebanon and protected Israeli communities from direct gunfire. Barak overruled them, arguing that any Israeli-controlled Lebanese hilltop would become a focal point
of fighting and a rallying cry for Hezbollah. Renewed confrontation would
lead to additional withdrawals and diplomatic humiliations. Furthermore,
if the IDF maintained its presence in Lebanon, all international support for
Israel's redeployment would be lost. It was a classic clash between national
security and political thinking on the one hand and a military approach on
the other.

In late April, following the collapse of the negotiations with Syria, the
pace of events accelerated. The South Lebanon Army (SLA), Israel's ally in
its war with Hezbollah, began to collapse once its soldiers—who were armed,
trained, and paid by Israel—understood that Israel would soon withdraw.
What began as a trickle turned into a flood around May 20. Outposts were
abandoned, as some soldiers fled north, even with the looming specter of
imprisonment by Hezbollah, and others decided to seek asylum in Israel with
their families.

The drama surrounding the collapse of Israel's line of defense in Lebanon
cannot be overstated. Barak faced an immediate and excruciating decision: to
double down in Lebanon by sending in large IDF forces to fill the gaps created by the implosion of the SLA, or to withdraw the IDF from its remaining
positions in Lebanon in short order. Against the advice of the IDF top brass,
Barak ordered an immediate withdrawal. On May 24, 2000, just 36 hours

later, the last Israeli soldier, Colonel Benny Gantz, crossed the border into Israel.

The Art of Stalling

The delay in the timeline of the Syria negotiations and the dramatic events in Lebanon affected the Palestinian negotiations. Clearly, Barak had no bandwidth to even try to reach a FAPS by February 13, the target date set in the Sharm Memorandum, and Eran had to lead the stalling through April and into May. Every few weeks, we met with the Palestinian delegation for a round of "negotiations" that lasted two or three days in a secluded location, often a hotel in Eilat.

Each round began with Eran and Yasser Abed-Rabbo, who headed the Palestinian delegation, ceremonially shaking hands across a long table, which was beautifully arranged with flowers. Both delegations, all formally dressed, were sitting on their respective sides. A photo was then immediately released to the media, as both sides wanted to show their publics that a serious diplomatic process was unfolding. Then, behind closed doors, we would begin to "negotiate."

Barak and Arafat agreed that the issue of security, which was considered "important for Israel," and territory, considered "important for the Palestinians," would be negotiated first. Naturally this was a simplification, since security was also important for the Palestinians and territorial issues were crucial for us. Israel took the lead of presenting its starting positions, which were clearly non-starters for the Palestinians: under the guise of security, Israel demanded permanent annexation to Israel of nearly 50 percent of the West Bank and a third of Gaza, and security arrangements that were an overreach even in the eyes of some of our own delegation. Of course, we did not mention Jerusalem, and when referring to the areas from which Israel would withdraw, we did not use the words "Palestinian state." Predictably, the Palestinians stuck to their guns and rejected our positions out of hand. We were talking past each other, and every so often we got into a futile historical argument, which sometimes escalated into a shouting match. After each round we broke for a few weeks, until the Americans would nudge us to meet again.

Israel's positions were approved by Barak himself, who wanted to make sure that they would not threaten the stability of his government. We knew that these positions were unacceptable to the Palestinians, and sometimes even humiliating when they denied the Palestinians the right to self-determination. As Dr. Saeb Erekat, the deputy head of the PLO Negotiation Department under Abu Mazen, angrily yelled at us at one point: "You are trying to perpetuate occupation in new ways." Six years after the Oslo Process began and after three years of a Netanyahu government, they expected much more of us. Even the Trump Plan, which was endorsed by Netanyahu, was significantly more generous to the Palestinians than Barak's initial offers.

The Palestinians were fundamentally suspicious of Barak not only for designing some of the most devastating commando operations against their leaders in Beirut, Tunis, and elsewhere, but also for emphasizing that legacy in his election campaigns. They found his iconic photo standing on the wing of a hijacked Sabena airplane with a gun in his right hand and his left foot on the head of a dead Palestinian terrorist to be humiliating. In short, they felt Barak had not transformed himself from a military general to a statesman who is capable of forging a "peace of the brave," as had Rabin, whom Arafat referred to as "my brother." The initial phases of the negotiations confirmed these Palestinian suspicions.

That said, there was also a more humane side to the negotiations. During meals, evening walks, and other off-hour opportunities, we struck up personal connections and even friendships. Eran spent a lot of private time with Abed-Rabbo, and they seemed to build a close relationship. Through these personal interactions, we also got the inside scoop on their internal politics and a better understanding of their flexibilities. While none of the Palestinians spoke fluent Hebrew, members of our delegation were fluent in Arabic. Sometimes we felt that through these informal conversations they were advising us how to better handle their own side.

Then, in April 2000, following the collapse of the Syria negotiations and the withdrawal from Lebanon, the path was cleared for real negotiations with the Palestinians. At that point, without informing Eran, Barak reached out to Sher to lead backchannel discussions. This was an institutional decision, without any animus toward Eran, who was part of the ministry of foreign affairs, which was notorious for leaks to the press and was led by David Levy, a politician who challenged Barak's leadership. And while Eran could not lead secret negotiations, Barak needed Eran to lead the formal track until it was clear whether the backchannel, led by Sher, could bear fruit.

Backchannel in Sweden

These developments transformed my position again. Since the signing of the Sharm Memorandum and Sher's departure, I was twice removed from the heart of the diplomatic action. Physically, our team was housed in the old old ministry of foreign affairs compound, while policy and diplomacy were led from the bureau of the prime minister. Hierarchically, I was reporting to Arieli, who reported to Eran, who was not part of Barak's inner circle.

When Sher took it upon himself to lead the backchannel negotiations, he asked me to support him. Barak agreed, but also instructed me to report only to Sher. Thus, I began to live a "double life": during the days, I worked at the peace administration and reported to Arieli and Eran, who were lead-ing the stalled negotiations. At night, I worked for Sher, who wasn't even a government employee. Many administrative regulations were compromised by this odd arrangement.

In late April, Par Nuder, a special envoy of the prime minister of Sweden, visited Israel. He invited Barak and Arafat to dispatch their rep-resentatives to hold direct and secret backchannel negotiations in Sweden. In 1994–1995, Sweden hosted the non-governmental Stockholm Track with Hirschfeld, Pundak, Agha, and Khalidi, which led to the Beilin–Abu Mazen Understandings. Allegedly, with Agha's advice, the Swedish government was now emboldened to step up their involvement. If Oslo, Norway had created the Interim Agreement, they wanted Stockholm, Sweden to provide for an agreement on Permanent Status.

Barak accepted the Swedish invitation on the condition that Arafat personally appointed his delegates to ensure that the Israeli delegation was negotiating with Palestinians who Arafat empowered. He then appointed Ben-Ami and Sher to be his representatives in Sweden, while he continued to operate the backchannel involving Amnon Lipkin-Shahak, Yossi Ginossar (Barak's special envoy), Mohammed Dahlan, Head of Preventive Security in Gaza, and Mohammed Rashid, Arafat's financial advisor. We expected Arafat to ask Abu Mazen to form the delegation as his deputy, as he was also the head of the PLO Negotiation Department and had a working relationship with the Swedes. Instead, Arafat dispatched Abu Alaa and Hasan Asfour, who were rivals of Abu Mazen. As soon as we got word of this, we knew that Arafat was setting up the Stockholm channel for failure by humiliating Abu Mazen and pitting his top deputies against one another.

Rumors about a secret channel began to circulate almost as soon as it was launched in late April. While Arieli and Crystal thought that a backchannel was necessary, they speculated about who was leading the talks and staffing them, eager to contribute as well. I had to keep my mouth shut and look the other way to avoid eye contact with my colleagues and friends. This uncomfortable situation was becoming unbearable. I feared that if Eran found out about my involvement, he'd justifiably fire me on the spot.

On May 19, at 16:00, the Israeli and Palestinian teams were scheduled to fly to Sweden on the Swedish prime minister's official airplane for a second round of negotiations. When Sher told me to join the delegation, I requested that Barak inform Eran that I was doing so at his directive. This was during the unfolding crisis in Lebanon, and understandably Barak had bigger things on his mind. At Sher's instructions, I waited at the airport, anxious to join the team. With only a few minutes left before departure, Barak finally spoke with Eran and I was cleared to go.

The conversation with Barak must have been difficult for Eran. He immediately told me that I was no longer welcome at the peace administration or as part of his team. He never spoke to me again, but it was an unpleasantness worth enduring for being part of a historic event. The backchannel and the negotiations on Permanent Status were going to happen with or without me, and I knew I could contribute to their success.

Eventually, Sher took care of me. After we returned from Sweden, Barak made him his de-facto chief negotiator, and Sher retained me as his assistant. In October, after a war broke out between Israel and the Palestinians, Barak asked Sher to become his chief of staff, and Sher invited me to join the bureau of the prime minister with the title of secretary of the delegation and assistant bureau chief. That's how I entered the so-called "Aquarium."

The trip to Sweden was a bittersweet experience of negotiations and generated its own set of anecdotes. The Swedish government hosted us at Harpsund, the official country retreat of Sweden's prime ministers. The estate has an imposing main building and a couple of guest houses on gorgeous grounds with a lake. It is beautifully minimalistic, almost spartan considering its use. Beyond Ben-Ami, Sher, and me, our delegation included a representative of the Shin Bet, Israel's security service responsible for relations with the PA. Our security detail was Michael Ben-Simon, who, like me, brought his camera to document history being made. The Palestinian side included Abu Alaa and Asfour, as well as Hiba Husseini, the niece of Faisal Husseini and a talented lawyer, as well as Abu Alaa's son, Alaa, who baffled the airhostess by his insistence to smoke a cigar midflight.

During our work sessions, Abu Alaa lived up to his reputation as a pragmatic and creative negotiator. While chain-smoking cigars and with the support of Husseini and Asfour, we reviewed the draft FAPS that Sher presented and made significant progress in identifying areas of agreement and points of discord ahead of a possible summit. In between sessions we ate together and had many personal conversations. Alas, Abu Alaa did not have the necessary political support to succeed. Abu Mazen, excluded from the process, resented the Swedish track, and three days later the backchannel was exposed in the media, which brought the entire exercise to a halt.

In the Aquarium

The offices of the prime minister of Israel are walled off by a bulletproof floor-to-ceiling glass wall with a glass door, which is manned by his security detail. Hence the name "the Aquarium." Wide stairs connect the Aquarium to the ground level, where the motorcade is parked, and to the second floor, where the secretariat of the government and the cabinet meeting room are located. The Aquarium is a small and tight space of roughly 3,000 square feet. The prime minister works in its far-right corner in a surprisingly cramped office paneled in mahogany with two doors leading to his secretariat and to the cabinet room. The interior design is quite basic: a large executive desk and a sitting corner that includes a folding single bed for rest. An Israeli flag, a library of books, a few paintings by Israeli artists, and the usual array of family photos completes the setting.

The Aquarium, which is the epicenter of political power in Israel, is bisected by a hall that leads to the cabinet room on its far end. Simple sofas accommodate visitors and advisors who wait for their meetings with the prime minister. When the prime minister is not punctual (and Barak was not), important dignitaries spend significant time hanging out there. The prime minister's secretariat and the office of the bureau chief are on the right side of that corridor, and the military attaché and the senior political advisors are on the left. Additional advisors have offices along a long corridor outside the Aquarium. When the prime minister is there, the Aquarium bustles, and when he or she is away, the place is nearly deserted. The juxtaposition is startling.

Having an office in the Aquarium represents the ultimate access to and influence on the prime minister. When Sher became chief of staff after the Camp David summit, he took over the designated office in the Aquarium, and I got a shoebox at the farthest end of the corridor. But my days—from early morning until late at night—were spent working closely with Sher in the Aquarium. I quickly found myself using the opposite side of his desk.

Our days in the Aquarium were a sprint-marathon of non-stop action. Often, Sher and I would only get to clear our mailboxes after midnight. The wives and children of our delegation were jokingly referred to as "widows and orphans." We often worked eighteen-hour days, running on fumes, exhausted but adrenalized. Weekends were spent catching up on sleep.

The Shaping Power of Polling

The inner circle around the prime minister was made up of a few groups: a policy cohort in charge of his security and foreign-policy agenda, which included Sher and Danny Yatom, former head of Mossad and the head of Barak's politico-military unit; his military secretariat, responsible for his relations with the IDF and other security services, headed by Brigadier General Gadi Eizenkot, who later became a lieutenant general and the IDF's chief of staff; the Government Secretariat, headed by Isaac Herzog, now president of Israel, responsible for coordinating the work of the government; a media and public relations team; the CEO of the office of the prime minister, Yossi Kutzik, responsible for coordinating Barak's domestic policy; and political advisors who managed his interactions with the Knesset and his coalition partners.

Above this fray and outside the Aquarium was another group of strategic advisors, who were responsible for monitoring Barak's approval ratings and managing his ongoing campaign for getting reelected. Toward this end,

Barak relied on extensive polling, which was paid for by wealthy donors, to assess public support for his government and for the agreements being nego- tiated with Syria and the Palestinians. Some polls tested specific scenarios, while others simply monitored the general mood.

The polling effort was a top-secret operation, which Barak led in per- son, formulating many of the questions and poring over the results. Even Sher was not privy to these polls, which helped Barak shape the negotiations with the Palestinians. I guess that he did not want to expose the interplay between his national security strategy and his political considerations. In any case, these polls consistently indicated that the Israeli public would support a comprehensive agreement with a Palestinian state in most of the West Bank and Gaza, whose capital is "Arab East Jerusalem." The conditions: "Jewish Jerusalem" is Israel's eternal capital; "appropriate security arrangements"; the large settlement blocs remain part of Israel; and End of Conflict is declared, leading to a "real peace." At the same time, there was adamant opposition to any return of Palestinian refugees to Israel based on the so-called Right of Return, although there was acceptance of their repatriation to Palestine. Symbolic humanitarian gestures by which some refugees could live in Israel would only be accepted as part of a comprehensive package that put the entire refugee issue to rest.

The polls also indicated that the Israeli public did not want another interim agreement that deferred the resolution of the outstanding issues yet again. The general sentiment was that Arafat and the Palestinians were not committed to peace but seeking to claim Israel step by step. In the early 1970s, the PLO embraced the Phased Plan, which called for gradually elim- inating Israel through continuous military struggle. By 2000, many Israelis saw the Oslo Process as a diplomatic manifestation of that slice-by-slice "salami approach." These findings reinforced Barak's determination to forge an agreement with End of Conflict and Finality of Claims—legal terms that became absolute political necessities.

The Chaos of His Bureau

The Aquarium is a place of inevitable surprises. You can never know how and when your day will end and what will unfold. A political crisis or a terror attack can take over the agenda, scrapping plans that were weeks in the making at a moment's notice. After all, the prime minister is a finite asset in terms of how many meetings, briefings, calls, or field visits she or he can attend. If one topic or group receives more attention, there is less to go around for others. Hence, a certain level of disorder is inevitable.

But the tenure of Barak was especially chaotic. The loosely held coalition generated countless crises, and the pace at which major events unfolded was breathtaking. This chaos was exacerbated by Barak's personality and mode of operation. Holding the matrix in his head, he compartmentalized his team, managing advisors directly and often in separation from one another through direct interactions and bypassing the chain of command. We rarely sat together as a team. Only Barak had the full picture at any given time, while Sher, Ben-Ami, and others worked in silos, and on a need-to-know basis. Every position had a backchannel, which often had another backchannel. Eran was chief negotiator and Sher led the backchannel in Sweden. And when Sher was chief negotiator, Ginossar—former deputy director of the Shin Bet and Barak's friend and neighbor—had his own relationship with Arafat and communicated directly with the prime minister. All were tools in Barak's master plan to shape Israel's history.

One day, as I walked into the secretariat, Barak suddenly emerged from his office. He put his hand on my shoulder and said, "Gidi, I need you to call the bureau chief of the *New York Times* and brief him on the negotiations." He then proceeded to give me very specific talking points, before telling me to keep confidential this completely random encounter. I was confounded: Should I update my boss or not? Should I update Barak's spokesperson or not? These kinds of requests broke organizational and hierarchical lines and repeatedly rattled the entire team, upending trust among the different factions of Barak's bureau. Luckily, Sher shielded me from many of these organizational machinations, which happened "above my pay grade."

There were also hundreds of big and small policy decisions. Since Barak would not share the matrix with anyone, his decisions were sometimes experienced as abrupt, hurried and haphazard. But I had a unique perspective on the evolution of his positions regarding Permanent Status, since I had already thoroughly studied many of the issues during my time at the ECF. Primarily, Pundak and I created and explored the key concepts of End of Conflict and Finality of Claims, which gave me understanding of the "zone of possible agreement" for a FAPS. I knew, for example, that a "generous proposal" equivalent to 85 percent of the West Bank would not cut it for an end-of-conflict agreement. So I was not surprised when "serious negotiations" about a FAPS eventually revolved around withdrawal from nearly 100 percent of the West Bank and all of Gaza. Also, as I sat in on some of Beilin's deliberations regarding the unilateral withdrawal from Lebanon and the interplay between negotiations with Syria and with the Palestinians, I could also appreciate the rationale of Barak's decisions during the pullout from Lebanon, or criticize them. Given my junior position, I was in a unique position to understand the dynamics of Barak's diplomacy and to contribute to it, through working for Sher, without being embroiled in the street fighting of his bureau.

Savage War for Peace

In April 1962, France's then-president, Charles de Gaulle, won an astonishing 91 percent majority in a referendum to approve the Evian Accords, ending 130 years of French control of Algeria. The Accords, signed with Algeria's government-in-exile, capped two years of secret negotiations held over multiple rounds in the Swiss Alps, and eight years of a bitter war between the Algerian National Liberation Front (FLN) and the French army and its local allies. The story of this dramatic period was captured in a phenomenal book by Alistair Horn entitled *A Savage War for Peace*.[6]

The Evian Accords contained 93 pages of detailed understandings.[7] In them, France recognized the Algerian right to self-determination, independence, and sovereignty, and committed to withdrawing its forces. The Accords also provided for prisoner release and for the protection and non-discrimination of all Algerian citizens, including the one-million- strong European-French community in Algeria, known as *Pieds Noir*. The agreement also established special economic relations between the two countries, including freedom of movement and work. In our terms, it was the equivalent of a CAPS.

6 Alistair Horne, *A Savage War of Peace: Algeria 1954–1962*, (*New York Review Books*, 2006).

7 *France-Algeria independence agreements (Evian Accords)*, (International Legal Materials, Vol. 1, No. 2, pp. 214–230, October 1962, https://www.jstor.org/stable/20689578).

The Evian Accords were negotiated by Ambassador Louis Joxe, a prominent French diplomat and minister.[8] Forty years later, Sher and I were at the
epicenter of a similarly dramatic political process. Sher was my boss and 15
years my senior, but we were a fully integrated team, trying to make sense of
the unprecedented challenge we faced and specifically of Sher's role as Barak's
chief negotiator. As we searched for context, a mutual friend suggested learning from the relationship between de Gaulle and Joxe.

De Gaulle was not a natural first choice of inspiration for Israelis. Before
the 1967 war, when Israel was under siege by Egypt, Jordan, and Syria, he
placed a weapons embargo on all parties to the conflict—at a time when
Israel's air force was dependent on French planes. He was also the creator of a
longstanding French diplomatic approach in favor of the Arab world, known
as *politique Arabe*. Many Israelis deeply resented him.

That said, de Gaulle was undoubtedly a great leader, and Barak admired
him. During World War II, he was the commander of the Free French Army,
which fought Nazi Germany and the Vichy government. After the war, he
led France, but then abruptly retired from politics, only to return in 1958.
By that time, the war in Algeria had been raging for four years, and his electoral pledge was to "keep Algeria French." Beyond signing the Evian Accords
and ending the war in Algeria, additional highlights of his 11-year tenure
included a constitutional reform that launched the Fifth Republic, and part-
nering with Germany to create the Luxembourg Accords that would eventually seed the European Community.

There are, of course, differences between the France-Algeria and Israel-
Palestine situations. The French affiliation to Algeria was colonial; Israel's
affiliation is ancestral. France and Algeria are separated by the Mediterranean
Sea, while Israel and the Palestinian areas are geographically entwined. And
the Algerian resistance neither claimed France as its own nor denied France's
right to exist.

Still, the similarities are undeniable. First, the future of France and its
society were at stake because of its control of Algeria, a colonial venture that
risked draining French resources and transforming the demographic and
societal makeup of France itself. The debate over Algeria created a fault line

---

8   Based on Wikipedia, *Louis Joxe* at https://en.wikipedia.org/wiki/Louis_Joxe.

in French politics and society, where the left favored Algerian independence, and the right, with strong support within the military, saw France and Algeria as inseparable. The far right even challenged the fundamental constitutional legitimacy of the French government to decide on disassociating France from Algeria.

Furthermore, about one million Pieds Noir settled in Algeria in major cities and in large farms in the countryside, while many Algerians presented as French, working for France's government and serving in its military against the FLN. The entire world had been watching the struggle over Algeria, and in 1957, Albert Camus, the French writer and philosopher, won the Nobel Prize in Literature for his book, *The Stranger*, about his childhood in Algeria.

The challenge for de Gaulle and Joxe was to envision a future for two independent countries—one a centuries-old Christian nation, the other a new Muslim country—that were fundamentally different yet deeply connected. Realizing this vision required ending the war and setting the stage for future security collaboration; ensuring the personal rights and legal status of the Pieds Noir, as well as of the Algerians who were associated with France; providing for future economic and trade relations; and ensuring French access to Algerian oil.

The Algeria talks were a classic case of complex negotiations in which all the issues were interrelated. None of them could be negotiated separately in silo, and all needed to be discussed together within an overarching idea that came from de Gaulle himself. Furthermore, there were many possible packages of understandings that could conclude an agreement with different trade-offs. Even the religious rights and status of the Sephardic Jews of Algeria, who were Algerians with deep ties to the French administration, were negotiated.

But what was de Gaulle's framework? Well, we learned that his understanding of French interests and of the Algerian side evolved during the conflict and the negotiations. Clearly, he understood that ending the war required agreeing to an Algerian state and ending hostilities. But initially his big idea had been to "keep Algeria French" by limiting the sovereign powers of Algeria and providing for French political and economic domination by subordinating the Algerian parliament to the French parliament and maintaining an extensive French military presence in Algerian territory, including control of nuclear test sites and naval bases. But as negotiations progressed, de Gaulle's mindset changed when he realized that his real goal should be to save France from Algerian influence. With that reframing, the goal suddenly changed to minimizing the connection between the two countries.

Sher and I, though, were interested in another dimension of the story. We wanted to understand how the negotiations were structured, how they unfolded, how France's interests were defined, and how those interests evolved right up to the closing of the deal. We were particularly fascinated by the interaction between de Gaulle and Joxe. We learned that although they were close, de Gaulle could not fully confide in Joxe. He did not disclose his final positions to Joxe because he needed him to fight hard to extract gains, some of which were renegotiated later.

The lesson for Sher and me was that we couldn't expect clarity from Barak regarding red lines and final positions until the very end of the talks, both because he would not disclose them and because he was crystallizing them himself as negotiations progressed. Consequently, while we followed his directives, we also had to assess his future flexibilities and explore them with caution beyond our formal mandate.

We also learned that many critical ideas and provisions of the Evian Accords were never implemented. Indeed, it seems that de Gaulle knew they were unlikely to ever be realized but needed them to ensure public support. For instance, while the Evian Accords provided for the legal and political rights of the Pieds Noir in Algeria, it was unrealistic to expect that after such a bitter war, they could remain safely in place without retribution. In fact, the exit of the French administration and military forces from Algeria led to an exodus of these settlers, many of whom became refugees in their motherland. This episode also highlighted de Gaulle's ruthlessness in pursuing that which he believed to be in the best interests of his country.

The most interesting aspect was de Gaulle's political U-turn. As mentioned, famously, de Gaulle was elected on a promise to keep Algeria French, but in the end, he nearly severed formal ties between the two countries with the support of 91 percent of his citizenry. Namely, within two years he completely reversed public opinion.

Managing that political U-turn took outstanding political skill. In *Savage War for Peace*, Horn details de Gaulle's public statements as a two-steps-forward, one-step-back dance that slowly seduced his constituents. He repeatedly challenged the notion of a French Algeria and began to legitimize the idea of France and Algeria becoming two independent political entities. The process was accelerated by escalating violence in Algeria and even by rebellion within the French military, which convinced many others to support the agreement. De Gaulle masterfully prepared the French public for future compromises before knowing that an agreement could be reached.

In the process, he gradually replaced his cabinet and found new political allies who favored his strategy. As he disassociated himself from his alliances on the right, he created new ones on the left among groups that had previously opposed him. It was an extremely precarious political maneuver that few leaders could have navigated successfully. In fact, most leaders who embark on a U-turn in politics are cast aside, and some are murdered by the camp that they have betrayed: President Sadat was assassinated by Islamist radicals after making peace with Israel; Mikhail Gorbachev was ousted after withdrawing Soviet forces from Eastern Europe; and George H. Bush lost his bid for reelection after breaking his "no new taxes" pledge. Indeed, there were reportedly more than 20 attempts on de Gaulle's life, primarily by right-wing activists. A fun fact is that the Mossad helped avert one of them.

The relevance of the French-Algerian model was evident to us. We knew that if Barak reached a historic deal with the Palestinians, he would also have to walk back some of his election pledges. While Barak was careful in how he framed his election promises, some of them, primarily regarding the territory of a future Palestinian state and its status in Jerusalem, would have to be compromised.

Barak would have wanted to follow in the footsteps of de Gaulle and reorient Israel toward separating from the Palestinians, but in 2005, it was Prime Minister Ariel Sharon who embarked on a dramatic political U-turn clearly inspired by the legendary French leader. Two years earlier, in 2003, he had opposed withdrawal from Gaza and claimed that Netzarim, a small settlement at the heart of the Gaza Strip, was as vital to Israel as Tel Aviv. In 2005, he led the disengagement from Gaza, dismantling and uprooting all settler communities there, including Netzarim, famously saying, "What you see from here [i.e., as prime minister] you don't see from there [i.e., as leader of the opposition]."

To accomplish his goal, Sharon, too, had to reconfigure his base. Entering the premiership, he was the political patron of the settler movement. Once he decided to withdraw from Gaza, he lost his right-wing supporters and came to be hated by those who had adored him. Eventually, he left his party, Likud, to create a new one, Kadima, as he gained political traction in the center and on the left.

The most dramatic moment before the Gaza Disengagement was a face-off between the government, in the form of thousands of police and military personnel, and tens of thousands of anti-disengagement protestors attempting a march to Gaza to prevent the withdrawal. For a few hours, it seemed as if the foundations of Israel's democracy were shaking. But although Israel stood at the abyss, Sharon did not budge. He was willing to be ruthless in serving Israel's interests, a move straight out of de Gaulle's playbook.

SECTION II

Framework Agreement on Permanent Status

CHAPTER 3

FAPS Article 1:
End of Conflict and Finality
of Claims

FAPS + CAPS = PSA

Sharm Memorandum, Article 1: Permanent Status negotiations [Provisions a–d]:

a. … the two Sides will resume the Permanent Status negotiations … to achieve … <u>a Permanent Status Agreement</u> …;

b. … <u>negotiations</u> on the Permanent Status will <u>lead to the implementation of Security Council Resolutions 242 and 338;</u>

c. a determined effort to conclude <u>a Framework Agreement on all Permanent Status</u> issues <u>in five months</u> …;

d. … a <u>comprehensive agreement on all Permanent Status</u> issues within <u>one year</u> …;

FAPS, Preamble

–   [P: Reaffirming that the Palestinian people have the <u>right to self-determination</u> under international law]

–   Reiterating their commitment to <u>United Nations Security Council Resolutions 242 and 338</u> and confirming their understanding that the FAPS is based on [I: provides the basis for] [P: and will lead to] the <u>implementation of these resolutions</u> and for the <u>settlement of the Israeli-Palestinian conflict.</u>

FAPS, Articles 1: Purpose of the FAPS [Provision 2, 5–7]

2. The FAPS establishes <u>firmly</u> the basic principles that will determine the [P: core] content of the Comprehensive Agreement on Permanent Status (hereinafter "CAPS") that will be concluded so as to complete the process towards peace and final and effective reconciliation.

5. The FAPS sets forth the <u>principles, mechanisms and schedules for resolving each of the issues</u> [I: outstanding] [P: reserved for Permanent Status negotiations] between the Parties and contains the <u>modalities of the negotiation towards the CAPS</u> and the transition to Permanent Status …

6. The CAPS will embody the detailed arrangements relating to the matters <u>agreed upon in the FAPS</u> and will provide for the modalities of their resolution …

7. <u>The FAPS and the CAPS</u> shall be read together as constituting the <u>Permanent Status Agreement</u> … creating a permanent condition of peace and reconciliation between the Parties…"

FAPS Article 6: Refugees [Provisions 92–95]

92. The wishes and claims of the Palestinian refugees shall be taken into account to the extent and manner agreed between the Parties in the FAPS and CAPS.

94. Israel shall have <u>no further commitment or obligation</u> emanating from the Refugee issue beyond those specified in this Agreement [i.e FAPS establishes Finality of Claims —GG].

95 The implementation of this Article and the completion of the Commission's work as described in paragraph [X] shall resolve the Palestinian refugee problem in a permanent way thus amounting to the <u>implementation of all relevant international resolutions</u> [i.e. implementing the FAPS means implementing UNGAR 194 and UNSCRs 242 and 338 —GG].

FAPS, Annex 1: Protocol on Negotiating the CAPS [Provision 1–3]

1. The <u>Parties to the CAPS</u> shall be the Government of Israel (GOI), on the one side, and the Palestine Liberation Organization (<u>PLO</u>) and the State of <u>Palestine</u> for the Palestinian side, on the other.
2. The <u>Palestinian Authority</u> shall nominate the Palestinian delegations for the negotiation on all issues pertaining to the future <u>bilateral relations</u> between Israel and Palestine, excluding those issues and elements specifically reserved for the PLO.
3. Negotiation on the CAPS shall commence immediately pursuant to the initialing of the FAPS. All such negotiations prior to the approval and subsequent signature of the FAPS shall be *ad referendum*. The negotiations on the CAPS shall address all the issues referred for CAPS in this Agreement.

Clinton Ideas: The End of Conflict

… <u>the agreement</u> [i.e. FAPS —GG] clearly marks the <u>end of the conflict</u> and <u>its implementation</u> puts an <u>end to all claims</u> [i.e. Finality of Claims when CAPS implemented]. This could be implemented through <u>a UN Security Council Resolution that notes that Resolutions 242 and 338 have been implemented</u> and through the <u>release of Palestinian prisoners</u> [i.e. Clinton was not clear when Palestinian prisoners will be released —GG].

By 1998, all the working groups on Permanent Status, which were initiated by the ECF, were in full swing. We held regular meetings with Israel's top experts and traveled to meet our Palestinian partners in the West Bank, Amman, and overseas. But as the work advanced, it grew increasingly clear that we needed a framework to streamline our efforts and help everyone make sense of their various tracks. For instance, future economic relations would be heavily influenced by whether the security group would provide for free movement between the two countries.

Our dominant assumption was that we were preparing for negotiations on an agreement on Permanent Status that would resolve all the outstanding issues. This goal of reaching a "Final Status agreement" was stipulated in Oslo A,[9] building on a long history that dated back to United Nations General Assembly Resolution 194 from December 1948[10] and to the Camp David Accords of 1978.[11]

That said, what kind of an agreement on Permanent Status should we aspire to: A document of principles like Oslo A, or a detailed agreement like Oslo B? The answer was unclear. While the Beilin–Abu Mazen Understandings resembled Oslo A, our working groups were forging detailed arrangements more like Oslo B. Furthermore, while the Oslo Accords referred to a "Final Status agreement" as a singular event, it made sense to reach Permanent Status in steps: first a FAPS and then a CAPS. We had to decide which path to take.

A FAPS, while a less detailed document, was not easier to reach than a CAPS. It had to establish all the trade-offs that would create a historic compromise to end the conflict and eventually usher in peace, as well as to outline future relations between Palestine and Israel in all key areas. Coherence in the FAPS would be essential to successfully negotiating the CAPS. For example, if the FAPS called for free movement of goods and services, the CAPS would have to detail appropriate arrangements of customs, standards, security, and policing. And if the FAPS established that Palestine could use Israel's international airport for its commercial and civil flights in exchange for forfeiting its own airport, the CAPS would have to establish how goods from Palestine would be transported through Ben-Gurion Airport. If the FAPS was going to be a "constitutional" agreement, the CAPS had to detail the "rules and regulations."

The principles delineated in the FAPS also had to provide the checks and balances—and incentives—to ensure compliance, as well as to sequence the key milestones of implementation. When would the agreement be ratified and formally signed? When would the Palestinian state be formally established?

---

9   Declaration of Principles on Interim Self-Government Arrangements (DOP / Oslo A), signed on September 13, 1993. See Article I.

10 Article 5 of UNGAR 194 refers to a "final settlement of all the questions outstanding between them." See also UNSCR 242 (November 1967), Article 1, and UNSCR 338 (October 1973), Article 2.

11 Egypt-Israel Framework for Peace in the Middle East (hereinafter 1978 Camp David Accord) (September 1978). See Preamble and Article 3, Section 7.

When would Israeli forces redeploy? Would redeployment happen in phases or at once? Furthermore, when would negotiations on the CAPS commence: before or after Palestine was established? And, most important, when would the parties declare "peace": upon signing the FAPS, once Palestine was declared independent, upon concluding the CAPS, or later still when the CAPS was implemented?

So, yes, the FAPS was going to be a monumental undertaking, requiring both sides to make painful decisions that were politically explosive. Take, for example, the issue of Jerusalem. Sharing sovereignty in the city would be a highly charged political decision for Israel that would require delineating a border through a densely populated urban area. If the FAPS called for a physical barrier that cut through the city, additional barriers would also need to be built along the border in the West Bank, around Gaza, and along both sides of the safe passage between them. On the other hand, if Jerusalem were to be "open," allowing for free movement between its Palestinian and Israeli parts, the entire Israeli-Palestinian economic space could allow for similar freedom of movement. One way or another, the agreed-upon border arrangement in Jerusalem would have systemic effects on economic relations, security, and policing. And that was just one of dozens of issues in which one piece of the FAPS would inevitably and intimately affect the others.

We now know that the Camp David negotiations failed to reach peace and collapsed into war and violence. In 2020, even Netanyahu failed to ratify and implement the Trump Plan, which he endorsed, and all other attempts to conclude a FAPS failed as well. Is achieving peace between Israel and the Palestinians simply impossible? In retrospect, I am surprised that this possibility was rarely discussed at the ECF or within Israel's center-left circles.

To be sure, the leadership of the ECF was uniquely qualified to appreciate the immense complexity and potential explosiveness of the path to an agreement on Permanent Status. They experienced how difficult it was to launch and sustain the Oslo Process; were well acquainted with the weaknesses of Arafat and the Palestinian leadership; knew best the substantive gaps between the parties; and personally suffered from threats and intimidation by the protestors against Oslo. Nonetheless, of this group I only remember Hirschfeld ever raising concerns about the capacity of the two sides to reach and implement an ambitious agreement like a FAPS. As a historian, he brought a deeper perspective and repeatedly warned that striving for a FAPS could lead to an implosion of the Palestinian leadership and an explosion of violence. However, though Hirschfeld was the director of the ECF, his concerns never developed into a wider questioning of prevailing assumptions. And we never explored an alternative course of action, such as establishing a Palestinian state before seeking a comprehensive peace treaty.

Indeed, we were working at full speed toward an agreement on Permanent Status. In 1998, Pundak and I began to formulate a document, which we named "FAPS," and worked through its chapters. He obviously had the Beilin–Abu Mazen Understandings in mind, but our comprehension of Permanent Status evolved, fueled by the working groups and by changes in the political reality.

When Barak was elected, the politics of his government and the legacy of the Oslo Process prevented him from even questioning the architecture of the Oslo Process. Seeking a FAPS was the only legitimate way to go. To be clear, at the time, I, too, supported this all-or-nothing approach. When I began to work for Sher, our first assignment was to negotiate the Sharm El-Sheikh Memorandum, which stipulated that "the Permanent Status agreement would include two components: A FAPS … and a CAPS..." Indeed, the idea of first seeking a FAPS turned out to be the framework of all future negotiations, except for the 2003 Roadmap for Peace of Bush and the Quartet. The 2000 Camp David summit, the Clinton Ideas, the 2003 Geneva Initiative, the 2007–2009 Olmert–Abu Mazen negotiations, and the 2020 Trump Plan— all are different versions of a FAPS.

On a personal level, the Sharm Memorandum was a special milestone. It was my introduction to international negotiations, when I saw an idea, which began in the ECF, turning into an official government policy. Even the acronyms that Pundak and I created stuck: FAPS and CAPS. That was a first for me.

What Do They Want?

Since the beginning of the Oslo Process and during the Camp David negotiations, the Israeli public debated over the Palestinians' intentions. Our delegation too had doubts about the motives of Arafat and the Palestinian leadership, except that we had extensive firsthand knowledge of the Palestinian narrative, interests, and positions. Even IDF intelligence officers, who had spent years studying the Palestinian side, argued about Arafat's real goals.

We were fully aware, and constantly updated about, the range of views on the Palestinian side. In simple terms, we divided them into two camps. One supported a "historic compromise" with Israel based on the principle of two states for two peoples, aka the Two-State Solution. It was led by the Fatah movement, a fundamentally secular party that was founded and led by Arafat as the largest Palestinian political organization and has led the PLO since its inception. We referred to members of this group as "two-staters." In general, they were willing to recognize Israel's right to exist and to peacefully coexist alongside it in exchange for Israel's accepting the Palestinian "core demands" based on "international law" and "international legitimacy." Those overarching principles meant that the borders of the Palestinian state in the West Bank and Gaza would be based on the 1967 Lines, with Al-Quds as its capital, and that the Right of Return of the refugees would be recognized, even if implemented primarily in Palestine. Most important, these Palestinians understood Oslo A of 1993 to embody their "historical compromise," in which they effectively recognized Israel based on the 1967 Lines, namely in approximately 76 percent of Mandatory Palestine. Hence, since the area of the British Mandate covered 25,590 square kilometers, in Permanent Status, the area of Israel would be roughly 19,500 square kilometers and Palestine would have about 6,100 square kilometers in Gaza and the West Bank. They were generally willing to have Jerusalem house two capitals with special arrangements regarding holy sites; to address Israel's security concerns, if they did not lead to unacceptable infringements on Palestinian sovereignty; and to allow the large settlement blocs to be incorporated into Israel in exchange for adequate territorial compensation in other areas.

Most Palestinian two-staters held the 1947 Partition Decision by the UN to be fundamentally unjust, which is why it was rejected. But they also recognized that the 1948 War turned Israel into an undeniable reality and Jews into co-inhabitants of Mandatory Palestine. Hence, Oslo A irreversibly cemented their 1948 defeat, and the FAPS was tasked with implementing a division of land that gave them 6,100 square kilometers, with borders roughly following the 1967 Lines.

Within this camp, there was a big debate about what strategy to embrace. Some, like Abu Mazen, rejected the armed struggle altogether and believed in peaceful resistance and diplomacy. Others, like Marwan Barghouti, the leader of Tanzim, Fatah's military wing, believed that the armed struggle remained a relevant and legitimate option in case the peace process collapsed. Along that line, in 2006, Barghouti's militia participated in the war against Israel, and he was subsequently jailed for life. Some two-staters even distinguished between soldiers or settlers within the West Bank and Gaza, who remained "legitimate targets," and Israeli civilians within Israel, who were no longer targeted. While there were countless nuances among them—after all, this camp included terrorists and peaceniks—we referred to all of them as "two-staters" for whom diplomacy or military action were means to the end of establishing a Palestinian state within the 1967 Lines alongside Israel.

The other camp believed in struggle with Israel and rejected the Zionist ideology that it represented. We called them "the resistance camp," and its primary political organization has been Hamas, which emerged in the 1980s as a social movement associated with the Egyptian faction of the Islamic Brotherhood. Hamas then developed into a political party with a military wing that took over Gaza en route to leading the PLO and the Palestinian national movement. They too had a range of views. Some believed in the armed struggle; their symbol was an AK-47 rifle. In principle, they rejected Israel's fundamental legitimacy, and therefore opposed the peace process or any normalization with Israel. "Moderates" among them were willing to acknowledge the *reality* of Israel's existence without confirming Israel's legitimacy. Their "Two-State Solution" was not a Permanent Status but a formalized *Hudnah*, a transitional long-term ceasefire, at the end of which, when the balance of power tilted in the direction of Palestine, Israel's existence would be challenged anew. Naturally, they rejected the notion of End of Conflict, and they certainly could not accept any Finality of Claims, which would sign off on the Palestinians' historical claims on Israeli territory.

Arafat's outlook was confounding. Some on the Israeli side believed that he was a two-stater, gradually leading his people toward peace after crossing the Rubicon of recognizing Israel in 1993. He seemed to have struck a partnership with Rabin that allowed him to swallow painful historical concessions at grave personal risk. Holding Arafat to be a peace-seeking two-stater gave him the benefit of the doubt when he fell short of curbing Palestinian terrorism or when he insinuated that the struggle continued. The Palestinian side claimed that Arafat didn't have internal legitimacy to act decisively because Israel had not implemented its obligations, and that he could only deliver "real security" for Israel after "real peace" was achieved.

Others saw Arafat as a wolf in sheep's clothing who was resistant to Israel's very existence and seeking its elimination. They argued that he embraced diplomacy only because the armed struggle failed; would only sign an agreement that was effectively a Hudnah; and would never agree to End of Conflict or to Finality of Claims, let alone declare peace. Though this camp acquitted the government of Israel when it caved to right-wing pressure—for example, when it expanded the settlements—they couldn't stomach Arafat caving to his own right wing on matters of security or refugees. They showed no sympathy to the challenges he faced, and nothing he did was ever enough.

These opposing views were similar in that they both attributed to Arafat a masterminded plan and a nuanced outlook that guided his statements and actions. It was also believed that the Palestinians acted coherently as a unified group in the service of their "national interests." But the reality I saw was much messier: the Palestinians were discombobulated, fragilely structured, and riven by infighting. Their negotiators—Abu Mazen, Saeb Erekat, Yasser Abed-Rabbo, Mohammed Dahlan, Abu Alaa, Hassan Asfour, and others—all clearly seemed to be two-staters, notwithstanding their differing perspectives and priorities. They too were often at a loss when trying to discern Arafat's intentions.

Unlike us, the Palestinians had neither a forum nor a process to discuss strategy and policy. We were legalistic; they were not. We had top-notch professional backing; they had barely any. Our lawyers were seasoned; most of theirs were inexperienced. To the best of our knowledge, the Palestinians did not have a single thorough discussion regarding their priorities for the FAPS and did not know what they were willing to compromise. They never presented a comprehensive approach to the resolution of any of the outstanding issues. In fact, it often seemed that their understanding of their own interest evolved in response to our positions.

These gaps were exacerbated by the differences in personality between Barak and Arafat. Barak was logical, thrived on complexity, and acted from within a strategic framework. Arafat was a man of simple, even simplistic, notions and symbolic gestures, who often acted on intuition and instinct. Barak read texts, remembered their details, and diligently analyzed them. A senior Palestinian negotiator told Sher and me that Arafat likely had not even read the Oslo Accords or fully understood what they included. Barak was authoritative, giving clear guidelines and taking full responsibility. Arafat let his negotiators explore options at their own peril and always assigned the blame to them. The differences between the two leaders could not have been starker.

Indeed, as late as the Camp David summit, the Palestinians had not accepted the framework of End of Conflict and Finality of Claims, or, perhaps, did not fully understand the importance of these ideas to our side. This became clear on the seventh day of the summit, when a working group was tasked with discussing the structure of the FAPS. Gaith al-Omari, the secretary of the Palestinian delegation, was a Jordanian who wore a stylish pointed beard and ponytail and smoked unfiltered French Gitane cigarettes that he would patiently roll himself. He was warm and professional, and we became—and remain—friends. As we discussed the chapters of the FAPS, al-Omari asked to add a chapter entitled "Israeli Compensation for the Occupation." This demand had been a traditional PLO position, one that we rejected and refused to even discuss for a variety of reasons. Regardless, in the months before the summit, the Palestinians had not repeated it with Ben-Ami or Sher, so we conveniently assumed that they had dropped it. Now, re-raising such an explosive and complicated issue at Camp David was seen as an attempt to sabotage the summit and prevent reaching a FAPS.

Naturally, we were angry, and Ben-Ami was furious with what he called "Palestinian pathologies." Poor al-Omari found himself at the receiving end of Ben-Ami's rage. As the Palestinians' lawyer, he was probably instructed to raise the issue, likely by Abu Mazen, without forewarning about its history to that date. Unintentionally, al-Omari provided the Israeli side with further proof that the Palestinians had no intention of reaching an agreement at Camp David.

Ending the Conflict

FAPS, Articles 1: Purpose of the FAPS [Provisions 1, 3 and 4]

1. [I: The FAPS marks the end of the conflict between the Parties] [P: The End of Conflict between the Parties will occur with the full implementation of the CAPS].

3. [I: The FAPS identifies] [P: The FAPS and the CAPS identify] all the claims of the Parties emanating from the conflict and arising from events occurring prior to its signature. No further claims may be raised by either Party. Save as agreed, the settlement of these claims will be achieved by the conclusion of the CAPS. Any further issues claims arising from the past relations of the Palestinian People and Israel will be raised only in as much as they are recognized within the FAPS [P: and / or the CAPS.

4. [I: The Parties shall conclude arrangements to ensure that claims, emanating from the conflict and arising from events occurring prior to the signature of the FAPS, shall not be raised by individuals or either Party against the other Party]

FAPS, Articles 17: General Provisions FAPS [Provision 141]

141. ... The FAPS will be submitted to the United Nations, calling for both General Assembly and Security Council confirmation that the FAPS constitutes the sole agreed basis and mechanism for the fulfillment and implementation of all relevant United Nations Resolutions.

FAPS, Side Letter: Declaring Palestinian Statehood [Provisions 1–6]

1. On January 1, 2001, the independent sovereign State of Palestine shall be established based on and realizing the legitimate right of the entire Palestinian people for self-determination.

2. The Government of Palestine shall be the sole representative of the Palestinian state in its international affairs ... to sue and be sued in the name of Palestine and Palestinians ... to conclude contracts etc.

3. Upon the <u>establishment of Palestine</u>, [the <u>Palestinian Authority</u>] [Palestinian Provisional Government] <u>shall cease to exist</u> and <u>Palestine shall assume all its remaining undertakings</u> and obligations, as well as all those concluded for its benefits by the PLO.

4. The Palestinian Side undertakes that its legislation, and executive and judicial decisions shall be consistent with this Agreement.

5. This FAPS is a historic compromise … <u>an irrevocable renunciation of any claims</u> for [territories] that are under the sovereignty of the other side.

6. The <u>PLO shall modify its title, charter, structure, objectives and modes of operation</u> … [and] <u>shall not represent Palestine</u> in all of its international affairs.

Clinton Ideas: The End of Conflict

… <u>the agreement</u> [i.e. FAPS —GG] clearly marks the <u>end of the conflict</u> and its <u>implementation</u> [i.e. not clear when —GG] puts an <u>end to all claims</u>. This could be implemented through a <u>UN Security Council Resolution</u> that notes that <u>Resolutions 242 and 338 have been implemented</u> and through the <u>release of Palestinian prisoners</u>.

As Pundak and I deliberated the FAPS, we realized that Israeli-Palestinian relations remained officially in a state of "conflict." Though multiple agreements had been signed as part of the Oslo Process, this fundamental legal fact remained in force. One way or another, the FAPS had to change this reality to have a chance of being ratified by the Knesset. But how should we describe the new state of relations? What big political statement did we want to make by signing a FAPS-type agreement? And when would peace be declared between Israel and the Palestinians? With Egypt, peace was declared upon the signing of the peace treaty in March 1979, six months following the framework agreements, which were signed at Camp David. With Jordan, peace was declared when the two countries signed the first agreement in October 1994. Meanwhile, Oslo A named the end state of Israeli-Palestinian negotiations only as "final status," purposely avoiding the word "peace." That language seemed to indicate that sometime *after* an agreement on Permanent Status, "peace" would be declared.

Pundak and I believed that it was in Israel's interest to declare "peace" as early in the process as possible. From Begin to Netanyahu, every prime minister wanted to achieve "peace" because it represents acceptance of Israel by the Arab world and a historic milestone in Zionism's century-long quest for legitimacy. So Pundak began to test different timelines with his Palestinian counterparts, most of whom had not even thought about the issue. These theoretical conversations did not go very far. The Palestinian we spoke to suspected that once Palestine was established and "peace" officially declared, Israel would lose the incentive to fully implement the agreements. Reluctant to hand Israel the prize of a peace agreement, their instinct was to defer its declaration as far into the future as possible. Pundak and I quickly realized that emphasizing the issue would only complicate the negotiations and give the Palestinians more leverage over a matter that was primarily declaratory. Indeed, in 2016, Netanyahu would demand that Abu Mazen recognize Israel as the "nation state of the Jewish People" before renewing negotiations. Not surprisingly, Abu Mazen rejected Netanyahu's demand, which became an effective way to avoid negotiations altogether.

This is the origin story of the demand for "End of Conflict." We concluded that the signing of the FAPS must mark an official end to the conflict between Israel and the Palestinians. The era that would follow the FAPS can be creatively characterized as "peace," "permanent status," "transition to peace," or "transition to permanent status." But End of Conflict was the minimal demand that Israel had to put forward, which the PLO could not reject.

Pundak and I also came to understand that a FAPS should establish a path toward resolving the longstanding claims of the Palestinians that had fueled the conflict. We were concerned with a scenario in which, while the FAPS is presented to the Knesset for ratification, additional claims surface from the Palestinian side. Therefore, we began to systematically map Palestinian grievances. Later, in 1999, Col. Daniel Reisner, the brilliant commander of the International Law Department of the IDF, broke down the concept of Finality of Claims into a three-step process: both parties would present all their claims; all claims would be negotiated into the FAPS to their full resolution or to an agreed-to process for such resolution; and after signing the FAPS, the only mutual demand would be its implementation. No additional claim from a past conflict could ever be raised again.

Achieving Finality of Claims required copious negotiations, primarily because all claims needed to be brought forth and clarified. Oslo A had listed "outstanding issues" that the parties needed to resolve: Jerusalem, refugees, settlements, security, water, borders, and other issues of common interest.[12] Now, each outstanding issue had to be unbundled and resolved before finality could be reached. That was the primary reason why it was essential for Israel that the PLO remained the "sole legitimate representative of the Palestinian People" until the FAPS was signed, so that it could declare Finality of Claims on behalf of all Palestinians and the future Palestinian state.

Clearly, one of the trickiest issues was refugees, about which the Palestinian side had a host of demands. They initially wanted Israel to recognize that Palestinians had a right to return to their former homes in Israel and to acknowledge its "responsibility" for the creation, preservation, and resolution of the refugee problem. They also demanded financial compensation for both lost property and "distress." Furthermore, reaching Finality of Claims required addressing the personal status of refugees, which included ensuring that they became permanent citizens in their final places of residence; losing their formal status as "refugees"; dissolving the United Nations Relief and Works Agency (UNRWA), which had been created to serve Palestinian refugees; and transforming "refugee camps" in Syria, Jordan, Lebanon, the West Bank, and Gaza into permanent "neighborhoods" of nearby cities. Certainly, there could be no "refugees" or "refugee camps" when Palestine existed in Permanent Status.

An additional batch of Palestinian claims were not even referenced in Oslo A. Most important among them was their demand for "self-determination" in their state. That demand had profound constitutional implications for Jordan and Israel because a significant number of Palestinians lived in both countries. The PLO also demanded compensation for the "occupation" or for Israel's use of "Palestinian water." There was also the major issue of prisoner release, and minor issues such as the status of holy sites and graveyards.

---

12   DOP, *Ibid*, Article 5.

Finally, the Palestinian side clung to a vision allowing individual Palestinians to present their private claims against Israel in international fora. Of course, we wanted none of that.

Finality of Claims was a legal concept that carried significant political and historical consequences. For Israel, it meant forgoing the quest for sovereignty over ancestral lands of the Jewish People in Judea and Samaria. It also meant preventing Israelis from suing the Palestinian state for damages related to terrorism, at least in Israeli courts. For Palestinians, it meant foregoing their claims within Israel and abandoning the decades-old strategy known as the Phased Plan, which inspired their perpetual struggle against Israel. In simple terms, Finality of Claims meant that the Palestinians would formally and irrevocably give up on their quest to destroy Israel.

As anticipated, the concepts of End of Conflict and Finality of Claims had a formative impact on the Camp David negotiations. The Palestinian side tried to defer End of Conflict as much as they could and effectively rejected the notion of Finality of Claims in the FAPS. At the Camp David summit, Arafat said that End of Conflict would be reached after the *implementation* of the CAPS, namely in years to come. His position meant that Israel's concessions and territorial withdrawal, as well as the emergence of Palestine, would occur while the state of "conflict" formally persisted. The Palestinian side may have had some legitimate concerns about the timeline of future political steps, but from the Israeli perspective, they confirmed suspicions that the Phased Plan was alive and kicking in Arafat's mind. Indeed, 20 years later, in the Trump Plan, the ideas of End of Conflict and Finality of Claims endured, with a declared goal to "…end the conflict between Israelis and Palestinians and clear all claims made by both parties to the conflict."[13]

Managing the Text

As soon as Sher invited me to support the backchannel in Sweden, we began to develop a draft agreement to guide our work. Initially, we patched together texts from different sources, primarily those that I worked on at the ECF. Then we spent long sessions editing the draft FAPS to fit Barak's directives

---

13   *Peace to Prosperity: A Vision to Improve the Lives of the Palestinian and Israeli People,* January 2020 (hereinafter The Trump Plan), p. 38.

and to ensure coherence and consistency. Naturally, some areas needed mild touch-ups, others needed massive rewrites, and a few topics were missing altogether. Over time, we formulated a full draft FAPS. Though we never shared it with the Palestinians or the Americans, it was a "live document" that guided our work.

Negotiating the FAPS was a complex effort because each topic was complicated and all topics were interconnected. Someone had to be looking at the big picture, making sure that each team was working within its mandate and that all mandates were synched and aligned with Barak's directives. This was Sher's responsibility, and I was his right hand in that effort by "managing" the draft FAPS. We updated it as we received input from our teams and through our engagements with the Palestinians in formal negotiations or even during side conversations. Areas where we anticipated agreement were formulated as a shared legal text, and in areas where we expected disagreements, we bracketed our position with an "I" and the Palestinian position with a "P" to have an ongoing accurate assessment of the state of the negotiations.

Hence, Sher and I knew every provision and every trade-off made among all topics and across all the tracks, and how they all came together. This made me one of a handful of people with full knowledge and a comprehensive view of the Camp David negotiations. That fact is likely one of the reasons I was invited to join our delegations to the backchannel in Sweden, the Camp David summit, and the negotiations of the Clinton Ideas. In short, I became essential to the success of my bosses.

Flashing Red Lights

In May 1999, after Barak was elected and before he formed his government, Hirschfeld and I were in Cairo for a conference. We used the opportunity to pay a visit to the U.S. ambassador to Egypt, Dr. Dan Kurtzer. He and his wife Sheila warmly welcomed us on a Sabbath, and I was struck by how they balanced observant Jewish life with the responsibilities of an ambassadorship in a Muslim country. Kurtzer was a seasoned diplomat, having served in multiple postings related to the Middle East including in Tel Aviv, Cairo, and Washington. The ECF team saw him as one of the wisest American diplomats on the Israeli-Arab issue and specifically on Israeli-Palestinian relations.

He was very friendly to Hirschfeld and particularly close to Novik after their postings in Tel Aviv (Kurtzer) and Washington (Novik).

After some niceties, Hirschfeld detailed how we envisaged Permanent Status negotiations, which were about to unfold; the huge amount of preparatory work we had done; and the hope that these efforts would lead to "peace." Kurtzer listened carefully and then responded. In a calm voice and with chilling clarity, he anticipated the collapse of the Palestinian leadership under the pressure to conclude an agreement on Permanent Status, and the likely eruption of unprecedented violence that could spill into Israel and engulf Arab Israelis. He even predicted that violence would erupt in Jerusalem around the Al-Aqsa Mosque. In short, he was deeply pessimistic about the prospects of peacemaking, and saw the attempt to reach a historic agreement as a precursor to a historic war.

It was a masterful act of policy analysis, done on the fly by a brilliant diplomat. It also proved to be prophetic. I spent the evening in the hotel with a shaken Hirschfeld, preparing a detailed report for our team. Given how hopeful we were, it was difficult to hear such a pessimistic forecast from a close friend, and even more difficult to countenance a change in plans. Indeed, we continued to pursue our approach, despite Kurtzer's warning.

A few months later, on the weekend of September 3, 1999, the ECF held a retreat in the gorgeous Dan Caesarea Hotel. On the following Sunday morning, I was supposed to fly to Egypt, as part of Barak's delegation and in my capacity as secretary of the Israeli delegation. The goal of the trip was to conclude the Sharm El-Sheikh Memorandum, which was going to restructure the Oslo Process so that we could pursue a FAPS and then a CAPS to achieve End of Conflict and Finality of Claims. For the ECF, this was going to represent another dramatic success: Barak would embrace their framework for the political process.

I hesitated to join that workshop. Though the ECF was highly respected, and Barak repeatedly tapped it for input, it was also subject to deep suspicion because of its legacy of successful track-two negotiations that had blindsided Rabin and Peres. Now, many expected the ECF to engage in another track-two exercise to impose on Barak their ideas about Permanent Status, which were embodied in the Beilin–Abu Mazen Understandings. Barak had already been briefed by Beilin about the content of his discussions with Abu Mazen and thought that Beilin had gone too far. Against this backdrop, I was under a cloud of suspicion as being the "ECF guy" within the premier's team. Still, with Sher's blessing, I joined their retreat. They were, after all, my former bosses and my friends, and I knew that their political wisdom was second to none.

The special guest at the ECF retreat was a remarkable strategist from South Africa by the name of Andre Zaimaan. I met Andre in 1997, when he facilitated a process of envisioning Israel 30 years in the future. He impressed us with strategic thinking. In facilitating the meeting, Zaimaan used the methodology of scenario planning, in which participants identify two "critical uncertainties" before forming four alternative scenarios, which are then assessed for their implications. After two intense days, the ECF team concluded that the most likely outcome of an attempt to reach an agreement with End of Conflict and Finality of Claims was a collapse of negotiations and an eruption of violence that would expand to Israel's Arab population. These conclusions were remarkably similar to Kurtzer's.

Zaimaan was further concerned about the long-term implications of such a full-on conflict. With artistic talent, he drew on the flipchart the flywheel effect of multiple cycles of violence that gradually, over years, would delegitimize the Oslo Process and the PA, compromise the Israeli and Palestinian "peace camps," and discredit the Two-State Solution altogether. These dynamics would culminate in an implosion of the PA that would then suck Israel back into the West Bank and Gaza, this time irreversibly. After everybody left the room, I tore off from the flipchart the pages with Zaimaan's prophetic analysis. Two days later, on September 5, 1999, Israel and the PLO signed the Sharm El-Sheikh Memorandum. No additional agreement has been signed since.

But in the hopeful, even exuberant initial period of Barak's tenure, we could not stomach the doomsayers' conclusions that an all-out war was the most likely outcome of the upcoming peace initiative. I don't even remember having a conversation with Sher about Zaimaan's prediction. In retrospect, we were particularly susceptible to the collective denial born from a sense of omnipotence that emanates from working in the Aquarium.

Indeed, within months, Israel's intelligence agencies were warning that there was no ZOPA—Zone of Possible Agreement—between Barak and Arafat because Barak's maximum concessions did not meet Arafat's minimum demands, which were based on the "core positions" of the PLO. They fore-warned that Arafat might create a crisis by declaring a Palestinian state and even allow for a "contained conflict" to pressure Israel into making further concessions that met Palestinian demands. The Camp David summit vali-dated that prediction, demonstrating that the Palestinian leadership had no will or capacity to sign a FAPS that included End of Conflict and Finality of Claims.

Still, Barak and our team were "heating up the system" by pushing for a comprehensive deal. Barak believed that Arafat would only compromise under pressure, so he raised the temperature by "taking Arafat to the mat" in Camp David. Against that backdrop, two months later, a small event—Sharon's visit to Temple Mount on September 28, 2000, which was fully coordinated with the Palestinians—led to a blowup and then to an all-out war.

Twenty years later, the architecture of a FAPS and then a CAPS remains the dominant paradigm of a peace agreement. The five best-known models for an agreement on Permanent Status—the Beilin–Abu Mazen Understandings of 1995; the draft FAPS created under Barak in 2000; the Geneva Accord signed in 2003; the draft agreement between Olmert and Abu Mazen from the 2007–2009 negotiations; and the 2020 Trump Plan—are all FAPS's.

But I and others have since thought better of that approach. We came to realize that the sequence forged in Oslo—in which a monumental com-prehensive agreement brings into being a Palestinian state as a stepping stone toward Permanent Status—locks both sides into an all-or-nothing process that is more likely to end in nothing, or worse. As Zaimaan predicted in 1999, Israel's repeated failures to secure an outcome of two states for two peoples may lead to a disastrous "one-state reality," namely one polity for the two peoples.

In hindsight, if I had to choose one model for the Israeli-Palestinian political process, it would be the 2003 Quartet Roadmap for Peace, which President Bush led and Sharon accepted. It is simply more realistic for Israel to welcome a Palestinian state in *provisional* borders, thereby eliminating the threat of a one-state reality, while postponing End of Conflict, Finality of Claims, and peace to a later phase. Once established, Palestine can work with Israel on shaping Permanent Status. This approach has its own funda-mental shortcomings, but it stands a much better chance of nudging Israeli-Palestinian relations toward Permanent Status.

CHAPTER 4

FAPS Article 2:
Palestinian Statehood

Clinton Ideas: On Refugees

The solution will have to be <u>consistent with the two-state approach</u> that both sides have accepted as a way to end the Palestinian-Israeli conflict: the <u>state of Palestine as the homeland of the Palestinian people</u> and the <u>state of Israel as the homeland of the Jewish people</u>.

Arab Peace Initiative

… calling for <u>full Israeli withdrawal from all the Arab territories occupied since June 1967</u>, in <u>implementation of UNSCRs 242 and 338</u> and [for] … Israel's acceptance of <u>an independent Palestinian state</u> with <u>East Jerusalem as its capital</u> … in return for the establishment of normal relations in the context of a comprehensive peace with Israel…

What's National about National Security?

In 2015, IDF Major General (Res.) Gershon HaCohen published an important book entitled *What's National about National Security?*[14] in which he argued that the purpose of a national security doctrine is to protect the physical existence of a country and its ethos. Hence, in the case of Israel, a national security doctrine should also account for demographic makeup and

---

14 Gershon HaCohen, *What's National about National Security?*, (Tel Aviv, Israel: Universitah Meshuderet [online university]), 2014.

immigration, the state's relationship with world Jewry, strategic alliances, and even Israel's international standing and legitimacy.

The distinction HaCohen makes between "national security" and "security" is profound because some threats to the ethos of a country are not military. For example, Russian intervention in the 2020 U.S. presidential elections was an assault on American national security conducted without spilling a drop of blood. Similarly, the campaign to deny the right of the Jewish People to self-determination and of the State of Israel to exist is a non-violent assault on Israel's national security.

In this respect, the establishment of a Palestinian state following an agreement with Israel was going to be a formative moment for Israel's national security and for Zionism. On the one hand, Israel would then recognize the existence of another people who are indigenous to the land. On the other hand, such an agreement would imprint the right of the Jewish People to its own state through an irrevocable confirmation by its most bitter enemy. A similar drama would unfold for the Palestinians: they would celebrate statehood and self-determination after a century-long struggle in exchange for recognizing the legitimacy of their bitter enemy, Israel. This is why, of all the issues of the FAPS, Palestinian statehood was the most significant to Israel's long-term identity and national security.

Alas, the two sides were at odds regarding the *process* of establishing a Palestinian state. For the Palestinians, statehood would represent the realization of their inalienable right to self-determination. Establishing their state was a matter of "how," not "if," and they came to negotiate the details of implementing that right. From their point of view, Israel could not negate Palestinian statehood or set conditions on its realization, and only once Palestine was established would they negotiate its relations with Israel and possibly agree to compromises regarding its sovereign powers and responsibilities. This approach shaped the early phases of the Oslo Process, when the Palestinians insisted on first establishing the PA in Gaza and Jericho in May 1994, and only then negotiating the Interim Agreement, which was signed in September 1995.

We had a different view. Israel did not dispute that the statehood of Palestine would represent the realization of the Palestinians' right to self-determination, but Palestine also needed to satisfy additional conditions, primarily relating to Israel's security. Namely, Palestine could only emerge with Israeli consent. And the FAPS was supposed to combine both approaches, providing for a Palestinian state whose powers did not compromise Israel's security.

Twenty years later, the Trump Plan—led by Trump's son-in-law and chief negotiator Jared Kushner, Ambassador David Friedman, and Special Envoy Jason Greenblatt—embraced and sharpened Israel's demands. Whereas the cornerstone of the Trump Plan is the Two-State Solution and it recognizes the Palestinian right to self-determination, it also conditions Palestinian statehood on meeting the expectations set forth in the plan, such as demilitarizing Gaza and stopping all incitement against Israel to the full satisfaction of Israel and the U.S. These demands were probably unacceptable to the Palestinians, but they rejected the Trump Plan before it was even unveiled after Trump's decision to move the U.S. Embassy to Jerusalem in December 2017.

Why Not Just Recognize?

FAPS, Article 2: Declaring Palestinian Statehood [Provisions 9, 11]

9. The right of the Palestinian people … to establish [I: its] [P: their] independent State shall be exercised by the Palestinian Party…
11. The State of Israel shall recognize the State of Palestine … upon its establishment. The State of Palestine shall immediately recognize the State of Israel …

FAPS, Side Letter: Declaring Palestinian Statehood [Provision 1]

1. On January 1, 2001, the independent sovereign State of Palestine shall be established …

The words "State of Palestine" and "Palestine" do not appear in the Oslo Accords. This was at the insistence of Rabin to negotiate down any symbol and attribute of Palestinian statehood. Arafat's title, for instance, was

"chairman," not "president," and the PA was not empowered to sign international agreements, establish a foreign ministry, issue a currency, or dispatch
diplomatic missions. The final status of the PA, namely its statehood and sovereign powers, was not even explicitly mentioned as an "outstanding issue" to
be discussed during the Permanent Status negotiations. Back in 1993, when
Oslo A was signed, deferring statehood was agreed on by Israel's left and right
and coincided with the interests of the PLO, which was based in Tunis and
wanted to first establish its hold on the PA.

When I became involved with the Israeli-Palestinian political process in
the late 1990s, I thought that establishing a Palestinian state was the sim-
plest issue on the agenda. The Two-State Solution provided a clear framework whereby two states would coexist side by side; all that remained was
to recognize the PA as a state. Furthermore, by the time of the Camp David
negotiations in 2000, the PA had already been the Palestinians' self-governing
entity since 1994, with elected executive and legislative branches and many
other attributes of statehood. It controlled nearly 93 percent of all prospec-
tive citizens of Palestine, who lived in Area A of the West Bank, which then
already covered 18 percent of the West Bank and two-thirds of Gaza.

The PA also had significant international recognition in its aspiration
for statehood. In 1988, the PLO declared Palestinian independence from
Algiers. That proclamation was recognized by nearly 140 countries, and PLO
diplomatic missions around the world were often treated with the protocols accorded to state representatives. That international legitimacy was then
carried over to the PA when some 30 countries dispatched diplomatic missions to Ramallah. In fact, one could argue that by 2000, the Palestinian
national movement had already gained "collective conditional recognition"
of its future statehood.

The international stature of the PA has been further upgraded since
2000. In 2003, the Sharon government signed an agreement with the PA
as its partner, and following the Gaza Disengagement in 2005, Palestinians
have full control of all of Gaza, while Israel has withdrawn any claim to sovereignty there. Since the 1970s, Arafat and then Abu Mazen were given the
stage at the UN General Assembly along with other heads of state, and in
2012, the status of the PA in the UN was upgraded from an "observer entity"
to a "non-member observer state."

Nonetheless, Palestinian statehood—at the time and since— is yet to be formally realized and recognized. What is missing? Why couldn't we assume, as a starting point for negotiations on Permanent Status, that a Palestinian state exists, and that its government is the interlocutor of the government of Israel? Well, beyond the clear statement of the Oslo Accords that the PA is *not* a state, and that the PLO is Israel's interlocutor, two important attributes are lacking. For one, the PA does not have full control of its population or territory, which includes its external borders, airspace, water, customs, and external security. All of those are determined by Israel, which also controls Area C covering roughly 61 percent of the West Bank.

Yet, a lack of control of territory in and of itself need not prevent statehood. In fact, many territories and populations have received international recognition of their independent statehood even while under the control of a foreign power. Indeed, the second missing factor has been that Israel and the U.S. do not recognize the PA as a state. Without their recognition, key attributes of sovereignty are denied to the Palestinians. In legal terms, the PA lacks a "critical mass of recognition" as a state.

At the ECF, it was assumed that Palestine would come into being by way of a peace treaty with Israel, the result of which would be flourishing state-to-state relations. But for Israeli government officials, recognizing Palestinian statehood was perceived as a valuable "asset" that should only be given away during the final phase of the negotiations, when Israel's interests and demands had been met, and in exchange for significant Palestinian concessions. The U.S. and other countries endorsed this approach.

Israel's logic was practical: life in the West Bank and Gaza was regulated by a mix of legal systems that emanated from the status of these areas as "disputed territories" that were taken from Jordan and Egypt in 1967 but never officially annexed by Israel. Some 80 square kilometers of the West Bank were incorporated into the Jerusalem municipality in 1967 and are treated like any other part of Israel. Eighteen percent of the West Bank have the status of Area A and are controlled by the PA, while all Israeli settlements and settlers in Area C are governed by Israeli law. Meanwhile, the overarching formal sovereign body in the West Bank is the IDF, through its central command and civil administration, and not the Government of Israel. If it sounds complicated, well, it is.

Against this backdrop, Israel worried that recognizing the statehood of the PA without agreeing on its provisional or permanent borders would confer powers upon Palestine that conflict with the responsibilities of the IDF, particularly in Areas B and C. This conflict of powers could create many complications, including exposure of Israeli authorities to prosecution in international fora.

Hence, Barak posited that Palestine would come into existence as an *outcome* of an agreement that would articulate its various powers and responsibilities. In other words, the establishment of a Palestinian state was *not* a foregone conclusion, and Palestine would emerge in the "permanent status" of its development. For Israel, when it came to Palestinian statehood, nothing was agreed until everything was agreed. Notwithstanding Barak's *official* position, a Palestinian state was the cornerstone of the Camp David negotiations. In fact, we could not discuss any of the outstanding issues without assuming Palestinian statehood. And although Barak did not publicly acknowledge the imminent emergence of a sovereign Palestine, the draft FAPS that Sher and I prepared included a chapter to this effect. Olmert and Netanyahu would later embrace a similar approach.

Alas, there was an even more fundamental question regarding Palestinian statehood, which was never discussed at the ECF or in government. Namely, is postponing Palestinian statehood in Israel's interest? Perhaps the establishment of Palestine is an idea that Israel should advance because of its own interests. As I've mentioned, the traditional Israeli position has been that accepting Palestinian statehood represents a huge giveaway to be saved as leverage for the last stage of the negotiations.

By 2000, however, some members of our delegation began to doubt this longstanding approach. The new view held that Israel's control of the Palestinian population was a "burden" that threatened Israel's long-term ethos as the nation-state of the Jewish People. Hence, the sooner we brought a Palestinian state into being, the better it would be for Israel. We feared a scenario in which no agreement on Permanent Status would be concluded, a reality of two-states-for-two-peoples would not materialize, and a solution of one-state-for-two-peoples would become the inescapable result. To avoid that catastrophic scenario, Israel needed to be proactive about Palestinian statehood.

To that end, we entertained the notion of reversing the sequence of the political process: to first establish a Palestinian state and only then to design Permanent Status. Back then, these ideas were not only embryonic, but also radical. On the left, decoupling Palestinian statehood from the Permanent Status agreement and from "peace" was unfathomable. On the right, Palestinian statehood was a big "no," let alone in the absence of historical concessions by the Palestinian side.

Toward May 2000, a historic opportunity presented itself. The five-year Interim Period of Oslo, which was scheduled to last from May 1994 to May 1999, had now been overextended by one year. In May 1999, when the Interim Period officially ended, Arafat threatened to unilaterally declare Palestinian independence. He agreed to postpone that declaration in exchange for a promise that the international community would recognize Palestinian independence in May 2000, even if declared unilaterally.

The territorial scope of his would-be-declared independent Palestinian state was not clear. It may have included Area A and Area B while demanding sovereignty over Area C until the 1967 Lines. Another possibility was that Arafat would declare independent the entire "occupied territories," namely all of the West Bank, Gaza, and the areas of the West Bank, which were annexed to Jerusalem. Arafat could also declare a state without any specified borders, which could have invoked concerns in Israel that he espoused a vision of Palestine that superseded Israel. Nor was it clear which additional powers Arafat would claim once statehood was declared, or if there would be any practical change on the ground. Israel was going to fully withdraw from Lebanon to the international border without an agreement, so Arafat was under pressure to make his own move. His critics observed that he had negotiated peace with Israel but gotten nothing in return, while Hezbollah fought Israel to full withdrawal.

At that point, without any serious contemplation, the Israeli side readied itself for battle to deter such a Palestinian declaration of statehood. The Peace Administration took part in extensive meetings and discussions, led by the IDF, that were entitled "Circumventing a Palestinian Unilateral Declaration of Independence." The deliberation of Israel's strategic interests was skipped,

and the possibility that such a declaration by Arafat would actually be beneficial for Israel was not even explored. We immediately dove into an operational
conversation about sinking Palestinian intentions. Indeed, eventually, under
tremendous international pressure, Arafat agreed to postpone the declaration
of statehood again, this time until September 13, 2000, which was the target
date for the CAPS according to the Sharm El-Sheikh Memorandum.

By May, I had already formed a dissenting view that it was in Israel's
interest to have a Palestinian state *prior* to finalizing a FAPS, and then to
shape Permanent Status gradually via state-to-state negotiations. I became
convinced that this was a better approach than seeking a comprehensive
agreement between Israel and the PLO. According to this approach, Arafat
was offering Israel a golden opportunity by threatening to declare statehood
unilaterally. Therefore, my recommendation was to let Arafat go ahead with
his threats. Our immediate response would then be protests and halfhearted
sanctions, but then we could restructure the diplomatic process to better suit
our interests in a graduality rather than an all-or-nothing FAPS.

But, being the youngest and most junior member on the team, I was not
in a position to challenge the foundational premise of the IDF. To drive home
that point, in one of our meetings, a colleague and mentor scribbled on a
yellow Post-it note: "If you want to be invited to such forums in the future,
keep your 'smart' ideas to yourself." To be clear: he agreed with me, but he
would not stand up to the power of the IDF.

In retrospect, I believe that in April–May 2000, Israel did not have the
bandwidth to consider the radical shift of strategy that I proposed. In the
spring of 2000, negotiations with Syria had just collapsed; the SLA was
imploding; and internal pressure in Israel to withdraw from Lebanon was
mounting and would lead to the unilateral withdrawal on May 24. Politically,
Barak's coalition was shaky and could not stomach such pivots. Perhaps, in the
bigger picture, it made more sense to postpone Palestinian statehood after all.

Thus, when negotiations on Permanent Status got serious, roughly in
April 2000, their sequence and architecture were set. The FAPS would establish End of Conflict and a Finality of Claims, create a Palestinian state, and
determine that state's future relations with Israel. It was diplomatic all-or-
nothing at the highest level. Eight months later, the Clinton Ideas would
follow a similar logic. For years to come, this framework continued to shape

Israeli-Palestinian negotiations, with the goal of concluding an agreement on Permanent Status as a prelude to a Palestinian state. This was true under prime ministers Olmert and Netanyahu and during the Obama and Trump administrations.

The one exception to this approach was the Quartet's 2003 Roadmap for Peace, published in coordination between Bush and Sharon.[15] The Roadmap was the only American-European plan to reverse the order of events, calling for the establishment of a Palestinian state within *provisional* borders first, and then reaching an agreement on Permanent Status. It was never implemented, and its parameters have not been seen since. Unfortunately.

Finally, in 2015–2017, Abu Mazen repeatedly threatened to unilaterally declare Palestinian statehood during the United Nations General Assembly. Three times the Netanyahu government opposed this move and successfully thwarted it. I thought Israel should have done the exact opposite: let Abu Mazen declare statehood and then offer to negotiate its terms. My logic has been simple throughout the years: only a reality of two-states-for-two-peoples can eliminate the serious threat of a one-state solution.

Palestinian Representation and Arab-Israelis

FAPS, Article 2: Declaring Palestinian Statehood [Provisions 9–10, 18, 20]

9. The right of <u>the Palestinian people</u>, by virtue of [I: <u>its</u>] [P: their] <u>right to Self-Determination</u>, to establish [I: <u>its</u>] [P: their] independent State shall be exercised … <u>within the international borders</u> agreed in [Article III of the FAPS] [This agreement].

10. … upon the coming into existence of Palestine, all the functions at present performed by the entities constituting the Palestinian Party will pass to Palestine. Palestine shall replace the Palestinian Council and the <u>Palestinian Authority</u>, which <u>shall hereupon stand dissolved</u>.

---

15 *President Discusses Roadmap for Peace in the Middle East: Remarks by the President on the Middle East The Rose Garden*, National Archives and Records Administration. National Archives and Records Administration, March 14, 2003. https://georgewbush-whitehouse.archives.gov/news/releases/2003/03/20030314-4.html.

All the undertakings and obligations by the PLO and the PA will be succeeded by Palestine.]

18. The parties are committed <u>not to intervene in each other's internal affairs</u> or to take any action that may undermine the security or economic and social integrity of the other party. Neither party shall <u>provide or attempt to offer to provide diplomatic representation</u> in any way, shape, or form <u>to citizens of the other party</u> … [I: Accordingly, except as specifically agreed, <u>no individual may hold dual Israeli-Palestinian citizenship</u>].

20. [I: In view of the beginning of the new era of peace, <u>the PLO undertakes upon the declaration of Palestine, to cease its former existence,</u> [and] to <u>change its title, charter</u> and <u>stated objectives</u> to reflect the requirements of the new era of peace and the coming into being of Palestine.]

FAPS, Side Letter: Declaring Palestinian Statehood [Provisions 1-6]

1. On January 1, 2001, the independent sovereign <u>State of Palestine</u> shall be established based on and realizing the legitimate right of the <u>entire Palestinian people</u> for self-determination.

2. The <u>Government of Palestine</u> shall be the <u>sole representative</u> of the <u>Palestinian state</u> in its international affairs … to sue and be sued in the name of Palestine and Palestinians … to conclude contracts etc.

3. Upon the establishment of Palestine [the <u>Palestinian Authority</u>] … shall <u>cease to exist</u> and <u>Palestine shall assume all its remaining undertakings and obligations</u>, as well as all those concluded for its benefits by the PLO.

4. The Palestinian side undertakes that its legislation, and <u>executive and judicial decisions shall be consistent</u> with this Agreement.

5. This FAPS is a historic compromise … an <u>irrevocable renunciation of any claims</u> for territories that are under the sovereignty of the other side.

6. The <u>PLO shall modify its title, charter, structure, objectives and modes of operation</u> … [and] shall <u>not represent Palestine</u> in all of its international affairs.

Initially, creating a Palestinian state seemed relatively simple. All that was required was an act of recognition by Israel, immediately followed by the U.S. and other nations. Indeed, in all draft agreements regarding Permanent Status, such as the Beilin–Abu Mazen Understandings and the Geneva Accord, the section regarding the establishment of Palestine and its diplomatic relations with Israel is relatively straightforward. Even the Trump Plan simplistically creates symmetry between Israel and Palestine as "nation states"[16] of the Jewish people and the Palestinian people respectively.

But the emergence of a Palestinian state turned out to have many implications and complications. I began to think about these issues only when I joined Sher for the backchannel in Sweden, when we formulated the draft-FAPS. At the ECF, we tended to assume good faith on both sides, and that Palestine would act and operate in the spirit of peacemaking. We also assumed that agreeing on state-to-state relations in all spheres, such as security or economics, was like co-designing Palestinian statehood alongside Israel. We never considered the constitutional implications for Israel or Jordan.

But the outlook in government tends to be risk-averse and inclined to assume bad faith. That's why Sher and I entertained scenarios of potential friction and even conflict that could result from Palestinian statehood. But we had no one to talk to in Israel about these issues. Barak did not trust the discretion of his Foreign Ministry, which was headed by a political rival, or of the IDF, so we could not tap their teams of talented international lawyers. The political stakes were also high: how could we—Barak's negotiation team—engage government officials on the implications of Palestinian statehood when Barak had not yet acknowledged that there would be a Palestinian state? To our advantage, Sher was an accomplished lawyer and an expert in the art of negotiations. For my part, I had extensive experience with the ECF. In the end, Sher had to trust himself, and me, to work through these issues.

This is how Sher and I came to visit with Prof. Sir Eli Lauterpacht, a friend of Israel and a British giant of international law. The Lauterpacht family had a longstanding relationship with Israel. Eli Lauterpacht represented Israel in international mediations and in secret negotiations on highly sensitive matters. He had taken over for his father, Sir Hersch Lauterpacht QC,

---

16   *Trump Plan*, ibid, p 7.

who was a prosecutor of the Nazis in the Nuremberg Trials and advised Ben-Gurion on formulating Israel's Declaration of Independence.

My first meeting with Lauterpacht had occurred two years earlier with Hirschfeld in Lauterpacht's Cambridge home. We travelled there to discuss issues related to Palestinian refugees, taking the train from London and a British cab to a very English cottage. Lauterpacht's home office was the size of a living room, with thousands of books organized in a floor-to-ceiling library. There were cozy sofas and big windows on both sides of the room, which overlooked lush green manicured lawns. The house and its surroundings—the opulence, the beauty, the tweeting of birds in the background—were exactly as you would expect from a member of the British intellectual elite in Cambridge, projecting wealth without extravagance. And, of course, we were served tea and biscuits.

Professor Lauterpacht must have been in his seventies, but he was still as sharp as could be. He listened intently to every dilemma presented by Hirschfeld, and then asked further questions to better understand the issue at stake. His answers were diligently thought through and expressed eloquently; it was a legal masterpiece packed into a few minutes of speech. He referred to multiple sources and gave us many new ideas. I felt that I was in the presence of a very special man. That afternoon, Hirschfeld and I strolled along the beautiful narrow streets of historic Cambridge and spent hours in local bookstores.

When the Swedish Track was launched in May 2000 in absolute secrecy, I suggested to Sher that we seek Lauterpacht's guidance. Sher was already familiar with him, and a meeting was arranged at a famous resort on the northern shore of the Netherlands. We met on a windy day that coincided with an annual kite festival. The view was breathtaking, with dozens of colorful kites filling the sky. This second meeting with Lauterpacht was as fascinating for me as the first. We discussed various aspects of Palestinian statehood and the legal implications of our demand for End of Conflict and Finality of Claims. In many ways, our entire approach to the emergence of a Palestinian state and its succession of the PLO and the PA was shaped by Lauterpacht.

How did "Palestinian representation" become so important to Israel? First, there was the practical matter of the PLO's legitimacy. After the Declaration of Principles was secretly signed on August 20, 1993, in Oslo,

Rabin understood that he needed the PLO to represent all Palestinians. At that moment, Israel's interests switched from diminishing the stature of the PLO to bolstering it. Six years later, we were facing a similar challenge. Up until the signing of the FAPS and perhaps also the CAPS, we wanted maximum legitimacy for the PLO as the sole representative of all Palestinians because of the historic concessions that the Palestinian side was expected to make. But after the Palestinian state was established, we wanted Palestine to become the sole legitimate representative of all its *residents and citizens*, but not of other Palestinians around the world, particularly in Jordan and Israel. Our meeting with Lauterpacht helped us understand how delicate and important this transition would be.

The second big issue concerned Arab-Israelis. We were adamant that the PLO did not represent them, and that the Palestinian state could not represent them after its founding, because Israel is the sole legal representative of all its citizens. This meant that while the PLO, during the struggle against Israel, may have claimed to represent Arab-Israelis, now, during the Permanent Status negotiations and in Permanent Status, neither the PLO nor Palestine could speak on their behalf. That had to be clear and official. And a similar challenge was going to face Jordan because some 60 percent of Jordanians have a Palestinian origin.[17] Since Jordan's stability greatly affects Israel's security, we had to think through the implications of Palestinian statehood for Jordan as well.

The relationship between Arab-Israelis and the Palestinian state became an even more sensitive matter because Arab members of the Israeli Knesset were advising Arafat on how to handle Israel during the negotiations. Even if those discussions were entirely focused on peace-building, this consultation did not go over well with the Israeli public. The right wing saw the discussions as a form of treason, and this view amplified fears of irredentism once a Palestinian state was established.

The potential impact of Palestinian statehood on Arab-Israelis represented the most sensitive challenge for us. The Arab population in Israel amounts to nearly 20 percent of all Israelis, about 1 million people in 2000,

---

17   Luisa Gandolfo, *Palestinians in Jordan: The Politics of Identity* (London, United Kingdom: I.B. Tauris, 2012).

not including 200,000 Arab residents of East Jerusalem. They hold full Israeli citizenship, carry Israeli passports, vote in Israel's elections, and enjoy equal civil and political rights. While there are many grievances about unfair allocation of budgets and other government resources, it is undisputed that since 1948 this constituency has experienced a remarkable leap in "human development" measured in terms of life expectancy, education, and per-capita income.

The term "Arab-Israeli"—with "Israeli" as the noun and "Arab" as an adjective—was controversial. It was a legal and constitutional designation that embodied an aspiration of Israeli society. Of course, when we used the term, we were immediately accused of patronizing. Others used "Israeli-Arabs," implying that the identity of Israel's Arab citizens was primarily shaped by their association with Arab culture, language, and legacy. Another view posited that Arab-Israelis were "Palestinians," who were either "Israeli-Palestinians" or "Palestinian-Israelis." As I described earlier, the notion of a Palestinian people with a distinct cultural, sociological, and political identity emerged in the 1920s and 1930s and was effectively rejected by Israel and most Israelis until at least the 1980s. Hence, using the term "Arab-Israelis" was mainstream, and "Israeli-Arabs" was also acceptable. But "Palestinian-Israelis" or "Israeli-Palestinians," which implies recognizing the existence of a Palestinian People, was too radical then, and may still be unacceptable today. In any case, I believed then and still believe now that Israeli society must strive for its Arab citizens to be as Israeli as its Jewish citizens. So I go with "Arab-Israelis."

This may sound like a theoretical debate among academics, sociologists, and lawyers. But based on our polling, the answers from Arab-Israelis were also muddled. Most view themselves as Palestinians in their origin, which predates 1948, and many have relatives in the PA and Jordan, both refugees and non-refugees. But their state affiliation is much more complicated. In fact, while supporting the establishment of a Palestinian state, an overwhelming majority of Arab-Israelis—as many as 68 percent in 2020[18]—view themselves primarily as Israelis. They speak Hebrew, hold degrees from Israeli

---

18   Abu Toameh, Khaled, *The Israeli Arabs Don't Want to Live in a Palestinian State, and for Good Reason,* (Mida, February 4, 2020 – in Hebrew).

universities, and are integrated into Israel's labor market. Even among those who associate themselves primarily with the Palestinian people, few would consider relocating to Palestine if it is established.

This debate had fundamental implications for Permanent Status. Anticipating extensive movement of goods and services between Israel and Palestine, the Arab-Israeli community was going to be a living bridge between the two states, with expanding business, cultural, and even family ties. In such a reality, consistent with the goals of End of Conflict and Finality of Claims, we did not want Palestine to have any claim to represent Arab-Israeli individuals or the entire community. We wanted as few gray areas as possible: to us, the right to self-determination of the entire Palestinian People would be realized only within Palestine. And we expected Jordan to support us on that point, because a vision of a Greater Palestine would come primarily at its expense.

Our quest for Finality of Claims highlighted another fundamental question regarding the "singularity" of the Palestinian People. Israel's approach was based on the idea that all Palestinians are represented by the PLO as their sole legitimate representative. Hence, the PLO is entitled to make political concessions on their behalf, as a nation and as individuals. Being Israeli Jews, we had an intimate understanding of that dilemma since Israel sees itself as the nation state of the Jewish People, although many Jews reject the notion that Israel represents them. Other nations, too, are concerned with their collective identity. In the past, standard parlance was "The United States *are…*", implying a collective of individual states, but today we say "The United States *is…*". In the same vein, should we say: "The United Nations *are…*" or the "United Nations *is…*"? Well, it was important for us to say: "The Palestinian People *is…*".

Our Palestinian interlocutors were initially oblivious to the entire issue, but then began to insist on keeping the "p" small when referring to the "Palestinian people." They brought up English grammar rules to support their point and accused us of being overly legalistic and of making an issue out of a non-issue. Even among our team there was doubt about our concerns.

But a group of us, led by Sher, felt that wavering on this point could open the door to unnecessary problems in the future. We were concerned that the Palestinian side wanted to keep the door open for individual

Palestinians to field claims against Israel in Permanent Status. Erekat confirmed our suspicions when he argued that the PLO could only negotiate collective issues like territory or control of Temple Mount, and could not settle individual claims that might result from a long-ago loss of property or personal injuries suffered at the hands of Israeli authorities. Those claims, he said, should be settled directly between Israel and individual claimants, and could not be resolved in the meantime. His position only galvanized our demand to capitalize the word "People" and to emphasize the singularity of the Palestinian People to strengthen the power of the PLO to make historical concessions.

In hindsight, I came to understand that the Palestinian position made more sense for Israel. Our quest to emphasize the singularity of the Palestinian People across the FAPS would have complicated matters for the PLO when it presented the FAPS for ratification. Meanwhile, our concerns were theoretical and long-term. But we were locked into our own narrative and made this issue into a matter of principle. My big take-away from that episode is simple: Listen carefully to the other side. Sometimes their position is better for you than your own.

As I mentioned earlier, our challenge in negotiating Permanent Status was to imagine Israeli-Palestinian relations with End of Conflict and Finality of Claims, and to do so in detail for every article of the FAPS. For issues like borders and territory or refugees we could envision a finite outcome. But for Palestinian statehood it was more difficult to do so because relations between states are dynamic. Clearly, Israel and Palestine would establish diplomatic relations and have embassies in Yerushalayim and Al-Quds – the Israeli and Palestinian areas of Jerusalem. But we had to go further and imagine the different scenarios that might unfold after Palestine was established.

We realized that the structure of the succession from the PLO and the PA to Palestine was crucial for peace. The PLO had been the "sole legitimate representative of the Palestinian People" and was now negotiating with Israel the establishment of a Palestinian state. In other words, the PLO and Israel were the co-creators of Palestine. So who would represent the Palestinian people *after* Palestine was established? Surprisingly, the Palestinian side had not thought about these issues, were surprised by our concerns and demands, and were suspicious of our intentions, as we were of theirs.

The cornerstone of our approach was that Palestine would fully realize the right to self-determination of *all Palestinians* but would only be the representative *of its citizens and residents*, none of whom would remain refugees. All Palestinians who chose to live in other places would be represented by the governments of their places of residence, whether in Jordan, Lebanon, Syria, or any other country. This meant that in Permanent Status the PLO could no longer claim to represent Palestine, and Palestine would not represent diaspora Palestinians. Neither could claim to be the "sole representative of the Palestinian People." For us, this principle seemed to be straightforward, obvious, and fair.[19]

We also wanted to prevent a scenario in which the PLO remained a platform for continuing the Palestinian struggle against Israel by Palestinians who oppose Israel and reject the FAPS. We wanted the PLO to commit to change its name, charter, founding documents, and stated goals. For starters, after Palestine was established, the PLO could no longer claim to be the Palestine *Liberation* Organization because the Palestinian territorial struggle would have ended. Henceforth, we wanted to deal directly with the government of Palestine regarding all matters related to its territory and people. In other words, post-FAPS, we wanted the PLO to disappear from the international scene altogether, or, at most, to morph into a nonprofit organization that helped settle refugees and encouraged economic development, similar to the model of the Jewish Agency for Israel.

Sadly, we never had an in-depth discussion of these matters with the Palestinians or the Jordanians, or on the Israeli side. But the issue of Palestinian representation is central to shaping Permanent Status and could have prevented an agreement, even if all other issues were resolved. Unfortunately, two years later, the Geneva Accord proposed that Palestine would succeed the PLO with all its rights and obligations.[20] This implies that Palestine may seek to represent all Palestinians, including those living in Jordan, Syria, and Lebanon, and maybe even in Israel. This is a bad idea for Israel and for peace.

In the years that passed, the issue of Palestinian representation continued to bubble: Arafat, and then Abu Mazen, remained chair of the PLO and chair

---

19   Sher, Gilead, *The Israeli-Palestinian Peace Negotiations 1999–2001 – Within Reach* (Tel Aviv, Mishkal, 2001, p. 421, section 2.9) (in Hebrew)

20   See the Geneva Accord, article 2.2, on Relations between the Parties.

of the PA, alternating between these titles as they saw fit; the Palestinian Basic Law, which was passed in 2002, preserves the special status of the PLO as the representative of all Palestinians even after Palestine is established;[21] and the draft constitution of the Palestinian state, formulated in 2003, implies that Arab-Israelis would have legal status in Palestine.[22] These are not semantics but profound constitutional and strategic matters, some of which are non-starters for Israel.

Meanwhile, the balance of power within the Palestinian political system has shifted since 2000. The stature of the PA rose, and it became the recognized address for all international affairs relating to the PA-controlled West Bank and to Hamas-controlled Gaza, with a foreign minister and ambassadors dispatched to foreign capitals. At the same time, the stature of the PLO declined, as it became a political shell without operational capabilities or substance in its myriad fora. Nonetheless, the PLO continues to hold the mantle of representation of the Palestinian People and retains the power to sign agreements on its behalf. Hence the goal of Hamas to gain control of the PLO.

Moment of Inversion

Sometime between the publication of the Quartet Roadmap for Peace in April 2003 and the Disengagement from Gaza in August 2005, a dramatic shift occurred in the Palestinian strategy toward Israel. To that point, the Palestinians sought a state as soon as possible, even in *provisional* borders with the hope of later expanding its territory and legitimizing its standing. This was the essence of the Phased Plan. In fact, in 1988, they even declared independence without any territorial foothold in the West Bank or Gaza. Likewise, during the Oslo negotiations, they fought for whatever attribute of statehood they could acquire.

Things began to change around the time of the Camp David summit. Until 1999, Israel refused to discuss Palestinian statehood, sought to defer it, and diminished any attribute of statehood by the PA. And from 1999, as the

---

21   The Palestinian Basic Law, *2003 Amended Palestinian Basic Law* (February 15, 2012, https://www.palestinianbasiclaw.org/basic-law/2003-amended-basic-law).

22   The PA drafted (but did not pass) a citizenship law that made Arab-Israelis eligible for Palestinian citizenship.

Interim Period neared its end, Israel fought to prevent Arafat from declaring statehood, which was seen as the ultimate trophy for the Palestinians in a Permanent Status agreement.

But following the failure of the Camp David negotiations and in the aftermath of the ensuing war, Israel began to entertain the notion of a Palestinian state in *provisional* borders with limited powers. This idea became the centerpiece of the Quartet Roadmap in 2003, and by the late 2010's it gained acceptance among Israel's right wing. Prime minister Naftali Bennett spoke about a PA with "augmented powers," while Netanyahu endorsed the Trump Plan, which referred to a state with "limited sovereignty."

Meanwhile, the Palestinians gravitated in the opposite direction. They pointed to the expansion of settlements during the Interim Period and to the absence of a "political horizon" for a fully independent state with contiguous territory. They noted the experience of the PA, which Israel had used to dominate them without carrying the full military, administrative, financial, and diplomatic burden of "occupation." They feared that an ill-planned non-contiguous Palestinian state with limited powers and sovereignty would remain permanently subjected to similar Israeli domination in Permanent Status. Hence, they would not "accept statehood" until their "core demands" were met.

The early signs of these dynamics could already have been spotted during the Camp David negotiations. Palestinian negotiators were not eager to discuss their own statehood, an issue that was brought up by the Israeli side. They understood that "occupation" was a burden on Israel that they would alleviate only when Palestinian demands were addressed. Meanwhile, their passivity revealed Israel's double game: Negotiating as if Palestinian statehood was a trophy, while seeing the establishment of Palestine as an essential interest to thwart the One-State Solution.

Eventually, these glacial movements led to the inversion of positions sometime around 2004, when the PLO reversed course on statehood. While the official position of the PLO and the PA remained support of the Two-State Solution,[23] a growing number of Palestinians now called for disman-

---

23   At a press conference on June 9, 2020, Mohammed Shtayyeh, the Palestinian prime minister, said "We submitted a counter-proposal to the Quartet [vis-à-vis the Trump

tling the PA and challenging Israel to assume responsibility for the entire Palestinian population in the West Bank. In 2005, they even objected to the Gaza Disengagement, which would have been celebrated as a massive victory just a few years earlier. In more recent years, PA leadership has begun to threaten dismantling the PA and its own self-exile to lay the burden of "full occupation" on Israel. Together, this set of events represented an astonishing inversion of Israeli and Palestinian interests, which had been long in the making.

Hamas' takeover of Gaza in June 2007 complicated matters further. Hamas contests Fatah's leadership of the PLO and seeks to lead the Palestinian national movement with its Islamic-nationalist ideology that rejects the Oslo Accords and Israel.[24] Therefore, Hamas refused to recognize the PA, which emanated from the Oslo Accords. Nonetheless, Hamas participated in and won the 2006 elections for the Palestine Legislative Council, allowing it to form the next government of the PA. Its victory sent the Palestinian political system into a deadlock, as Israel and the U.S. demanded that the PA's Hamas-led government endorse the Oslo Accords, but Hamas refused. In June 2007, Hamas took Gaza by force; it has controlled it ever since.

All attempts to achieve Palestinian reconciliation between Hamas and Fatah have failed, and Gaza and the West Bank have grown to represent two distinct political realities. The PA in the West Bank is an internationally recognized entity bound by the Oslo Accords and financed by Israel and by Western countries, and it also officially represents Gaza. Meanwhile, Hamas-controlled Gaza rejects the agreements with Israel in perpetual defiance, which occasionally erupts into violent conflict. And while the West Bank remains "disputed territory," Gaza is now an independent Palestinian territory to which Israel has no claim.

Plan —GG] ... which proposed the creation of a 'sovereign Palestinian state, independent and demilitarized' with 'minor modifications of borders where necessary'..."

24 Mahmoud Zahar stated that Hamas "want[s] to join the PLO—but on the basis of a new program, not of the Oslo program and the agreements ... right now the PLO is a dead body ... we will revive this organization by means of new programs and methods." (See MEMRI, 11/14/05). On the struggle between Arafat and Hamas throughout the Oslo Process, see Barry Rubin, *The Transformation of Palestinian Politics* (Cambridge: Harvard Press, 1999, p. 13).

At the same time, the two entities clash over their competing claims to represent both the West Bank and Gaza: the PA by the power given to it by the PLO and the Oslo Accords, and Hamas based on its electoral victory. These realities undermine the premise of all existing agreements and peace initiatives, including the Trump Plan, that propose that Gaza and the West Bank remain a single territorial unit and that a Palestinian state will be demilitarized. Thus the "bilateral" Israeli-Palestinian conflict has morphed into a "trilateral" conflict among three distinct and competing political entities: Israel, the West-Bank PA, and Hamas in Gaza.

Arafat, Please Be Ben-Gurion...

Many of Israel's expectations from Arafat regarding imminent Palestinian statehood emanated from the experience of the Jewish national movement in the leadup to the creation of the State of Israel. As of 1936, under the leadership of Ben-Gurion and during the British Mandate, the Jewish national movement pragmatically accepted partition of the land with the Arabs and engaged in a remarkable effort of state-building, called "state in the making" (*HaMedinah SheBaDerech*). Until 1948, every key function of the future state was created and developed, including healthcare, welfare, education systems, a seaport, and utilities companies. Ben-Gurion also acted with a heavy hand to discipline all armed factions and to control the use of force against the British Mandatory government. Shortly after the 1948 War, Israel would establish diplomatic relations with Britain and pursue a path of immigration absorption and remarkable economic development.

During the Interim Period and the Camp David negotiations, Israel wanted Arafat and the PA to walk a similar path. They were urged to use their security forces to rein in the radical military factions; to build the capacities of the would-be Palestinian state; to drive toward remarkable economic development such that "Gaza becomes the Singapore of the Middle East"; to negotiate a comprehensive peace on behalf of the entire Palestinian people; to lead a historical reconciliation with Israel and to accept a Palestinian state in only 22 percent of the territory of Mandatory Palestine; and to end the conflict with Israel based on Finality of Claims. We were disappointed on all counts.

Indeed, the legacy of Ben-Gurion was even raised in our side conversations with the Palestinians. Some of them, like Gibril Rajoub, spent their time in Israeli jails learning Hebrew and educating themselves about the history of Zionism and Israel. They too respected the heavy-handedness of Ben-Gurion during Israel's nation-building, even if they blamed him for their *naqba*. Alas, in these conversations, one fact was conveniently ignored: Ben-Gurion did not want to finalize Israel's borders, because he hoped that one day they would be expanded. So, in fact, we wanted Arafat to take a step beyond Ben-Gurion: to establish finality of all claims for all time.

CHAPTER 5

FAPS Article 3:
Borders, Settlements & Territorial Arrangements

June 1967 Lines: Disputed or Occupied Territories?

FAPS, Article 3: Borders, Settlement & Territorial Arrangements [Provisions 22, 27]

22. This article and Map no. 1. attached hereto provide the <u>permanent borders</u> and the <u>related territorial arrangements</u> between Israel and Palestine.

27. The Parties shall view the delimitation of their <u>permanent international borders</u> and the creation of the agreed <u>permanent Special Arrangements</u> as the <u>implementation of UNSCRs 242 and 338</u> and shall recognize them as <u>final, permanent, irrevocable, and inviolable</u>. The Parties may maintain territorial claims solely with regards to those areas specified in Map no. 1 as territories whose permanent sovereign status or permanent arrangements are reserved in the FAPS for future negotiations.

Clinton Ideas: Territory

"...the solution should be in the mid-90%'s, <u>between 94%–96% of the West Bank territory</u> of the Palestinian State. The land annexed by Israel should be compensated by a <u>land swap of 1%–3%</u>, in addition

> to <u>territorial arrangements</u> such as a <u>permanent safe passage</u> ... the swap
> of leased land to meet their respective needs ... develop a map consistent
> with the following criteria: 80% of settlers in blocs; contiguity; minimize
> annexed areas; minimize the number of Palestinian affected."

"Barak was willing to give Arafat 95 percent—or 99 percent—of the land. How could Arafat walk away from such an extremely generous offer?!" This is the most common question and comment I hear about the Camp David negotiations. It is indeed perplexing, but only if you subscribe to the Israeli position that the West Bank and Gaza were "disputed territories" that needed to be bargained for and divided between the two parties. Meanwhile, if you accept the Palestinian position that these territories are "occupied," Arafat's position is easier to understand. To be clear, for us, like for most Israelis, these territories are disputed. Chapter 2A of this book, which is available online, provides the historical background for this contention.

The foundation of the Israeli argument is historical. It holds Judea and Samaria—the southern and northern parts of the West Bank respectively, with Jerusalem at its center—to be ancestral lands of the Jewish People. Jews have had an uninterrupted lineage and presence in these areas for thousands of years. This claim is documented in the Bible and other historical documents and validated by countless archeological findings.

There is also a legal argument: in 1917, the Balfour Declaration recognized the right of the Jewish People to a "national home" in its historical homeland, which came under the control of Britain following World War I. In 1920, the San Remo Conference gave Britain the mandate to prepare the Jewish and Arab populations living in that territory for political independence, but in 1921, Britain recognized the area *east* of the Jordan River as a separate political entity, to be called Trans-Jordan and later become the Hashemite Kingdom of Jordan. Henceforth the struggle between Arabs and Jews focused on Mandatory Palestine, which stretched from Lebanon in the north to Egypt and Jordan in the south, and from the Jordan River to the Mediterranean. In 1937, the Zionist movement accepted the findings of Britain's Peel Commission and acknowledged that Arabs also have valid indigenous claims to sovereignty in Mandatory Palestine. It thereby accepted the principle of two-states-for-two-peoples and the framework of the Two-State Solution for the resolution of its territorial dispute with the Arabs.

The recommendations of the Peel Commission shaped UN General Assembly Resolution 181, also known as the Partition Decision, which provided for an "Arab state" in 48 percent of that territory and a "Jewish state" in the remaining portion. While the Zionist Movement accepted UNGAR 181, the Palestinian leadership and Arab side rejected it and lost the ensuing war, which also resulted in the mass displacement of Palestinians that created Palestinian refugeeism. In 1967, Israel's existence was challenged again by Arab countries, and their defeat in the war led to Israel's seizing the West Bank, Gaza, Sinai, and the Golan Heights. Taken as a whole, these events cemented the Israeli perspective that areas that Israel held prior to 1967 are undisputedly Israeli, whereas the sovereign status of the West Bank and Gaza remains to be determined.

The perspective of Palestinian two-staters is radically different. Until 1948, there was a clear Arab majority in Mandatory Palestine—92 percent in 1918, 72 percent in 1936, and 68 percent in 1947[25]—so the entire area should have been an Arab state. This means that the Peel Commission of 1936 and the Partition Decision of 1948 were justifiably rejected. At the end of the 1948 War, Israel controlled 76 percent of Mandatory Palestine, and then in 1967 it took over the remaining areas. These events—called by Palestinians *naqba* (the catastrophe of 1948) and *naqsa* (the defeat of 1967)—inspired the PLO to fight for Israel's elimination and for establishing a Palestinian state in its stead.

In 1993, by signing Oslo A and in his letter to Rabin, Arafat broke with that tradition, recognized Israel, and effectively withdrew Palestinian claim for any territory that Israel had held before 1967. Hence, with the Oslo Accords, the PLO tacitly cemented the political and military defeats of the Palestinians in 1936–1948. That Palestinian concession could be seen as a grand success for the Zionist Movement, allowing it to consolidate the achievements of its journey of repatriation and territorial acquisition, which began in the 1880s. But the PLO's historic compromise came with the expectation that a Palestinian state would be established in the West Bank and Gaza on the remaining 24 percent of Mandatory Palestine, which covered roughly 6,100 square kilometers. Namely, Zionism's historic achievement is

---

25   Jewish Virtual Library, *Jewish and Non-Jewish Population of Israel / Palestine (1517 to Present)* (ND, https://www.jewishvirtuallibrary.org/jewish-and-non-jewish-population-of-israel-palestine-1517-present, updated April 2023).

conditioned upon Israel's accepting that some Jewish ancestral lands will be part of Palestine.

Hence, from the Israeli perspective, the task of the Camp David negotiations was to divide the West Bank and Gaza—that same 6,100 square kilometers—between Israel and Palestine, while accommodating the Jewish neighborhoods of Jerusalem, Israeli settlements, security needs, and water rights. In that vein, Barak's agreement that the area of Palestine would cover around 95 percent of West Bank and Gaza was extremely generous, and Arafat's rejection of that offer was mind-boggling.

But for the Palestinians, the purpose of any agreement on Permanent Status was to effectuate the division of Mandatory Palestine that was *already agreed upon* in 1993, which was based on the 1967 Lines and which granted them 6,100 square kilometers. The Palestinians did not budge from this principle, not even under tremendous American pressure at Camp David from Clinton himself. They insisted on adequate territorial compensation for any part of the West Bank that would be annexed to Israel. So while Israel wanted a territorial settlement *within* the West Bank and Gaza, the Palestinians wanted Israel to withdraw *from* those areas completely. In crude terms: regarding territory, while Israel came to Camp David to "bargain," the Palestinians came to Camp David to "collect."

The Palestinians Historic Compromise   Trump's Plan

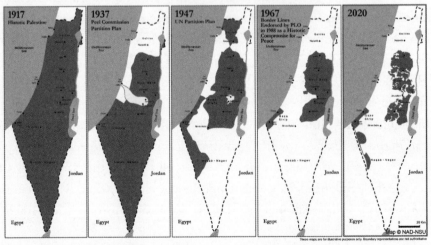

Palestinian Perspective on Territorial Negotiations

This document was used by Abu Mazen to present the diminishing Palestinian territory.
(Credit: Palestinian Negotiations Support Unit)

Here is a deeper dive into the numerical aspect of the Israeli-Palestinian territorial dispute: as mentioned earlier, Mandatory Palestine covered 25,585 square kilometers, and according to the position of the PLO, Oslo A established that Israel would have 19,500 sq km in that territory. The debate in the Permanent Status negotiations was: Who would have the remaining 6,100 sq km, which represents "100 percent of the West Bank and Gaza"? But before we delve into that debate, it is important to mention that Israel challenged this Palestinian "benchmark" of 6,100 sq km representing 100 percent of the West Bank and Gaza. We claimed that an area of about 309 sq km—including the no-man's land close to Latrun (~46 sq km), the areas annexed to Jerusalem (~73 sq km) and the Dead Sea (190 sq km)—is part of Israel, and not to be negotiated. So Israel's "100 percent of the West Bank and Gaza" was closer to 5,800 sq km. And given that Gaza's territory amounts to 363 sq km, Israel held the "disputed area" of the West Bank to be 5,428 sq km.

For those of you still with us, here is the bottom line: the PLO claimed that the West Bank covered 5,737 sq km so every 1 percent amounted to approximately 57 sq km, while Israel claimed that the disputed territory of the West Bank amounted to 5,428 sq km, which meant that every 1 percent equals 54 sq km. These discrepancies are not simple gaps that could be bridged through bargaining. For instance, ahead of Camp David, when Israel wanted to annex 14 percent of the West Bank for settlement blocs and its security needs, we were targeting an area of about 800 sq km *in addition* to 309 sq km in Jerusalem, the Dead Sea, and Latrun. Therefore, Israel's territory in Permanent Status was going to be 20,609 sq km, leaving 4,976 sq km for Palestine. Meanwhile, when the Palestinians said that they were willing to swap 4.5 percent of West Bank territory for settlement blocs and Jerusalem, they meant that Israel's area would be 19,500 sq km and Palestine would be 6,100 sq km. Namely, the disputed area between the Israeli position ahead of Camp David in July 2000 and the Palestinian position in Taba in January 2001 was 1,124 sq km, or a full 20 percent of the territorial aspirations of the PLO. No minor matter! And you should keep these gaps in mind when you read my account about the territorial offerings Israel and the PLO made throughout the negotiations.

Oslo's ambiguity left the status of the territories—whether "occupied" or "disputed"— unresolved, so both sides entrenched their positions during the Interim Period and ahead of the Permanent Status negotiations. Israel expanded the settlements, and the Palestinians built in Area B and Area C. Israel celebrated the *English* version of UNSCR 242, which could be understood to call for *partial* Israeli withdrawal "from territories" captured in 1967, while the Palestinians clung to the *French* version of UNSCR 242, which is understood to call for *full* Israeli withdrawal from "*the* territories" that were captured in 1967. This was largely a zero-sum game: more for us meant less for them and vice versa.

That is why Arafat and Barak were talking past each other during the Camp David summit and negotiations. For Barak, as a matter of principle, Israel could not withdraw from 100 percent of the West Bank and Gaza, thereby endorsing the Palestinian position regarding the West Bank and the 1967 Lines as a basis for future borders. Barak knew all too well that there was no political expediency to any such agreement. Consistent with this approach, Israel initially demanded annexing 40 percent of the West Bank, leaving 60 percent to Palestine; gradually decreased its demand to 14 percent on the eve of the summit, withdrawing its claim from Gaza; and by December offered 92 percent of the West Bank, claiming the remaining 8 percent for settlement blocs and security needs. Meanwhile, in December, the Clinton Ideas, which Israel conditionally accepted, offered Arafat some 95 to 99 percent of the land. Throughout that time, Arafat insisted on future borders being "based on the 1967 Lines" and incorporating a land mass of roughly 5,629 square kilometers. He was willing to accommodate including the settlement blocs in Israel, but only in exchange for territorial swaps equal in size and quality. So the principled gap remained wide: Israel never agreed to give the Palestinians 100 percent of the land, and the Palestinians would not accept anything less.

Thus, the status of the 1967 Lines—also known as "June 4th Lines" or the "Green Line"— is at the crux of the territorial dispute between Israel and the Palestinians. The term "1967 Lines" refers to the de-facto border between Israel and the West Bank and Gaza that existed on the eve of the 1967 Six-Day War and was shaped by agreed amendments to the 1949 ceasefire lines. Multiple United Nations resolutions—primarily UNSCRs 242 and 338— made the 1967 Lines a reference point for all future territorial arrangements between Israel and the Palestinians. Maps of the 1949 Armistice Line, land swaps, and the 1967 Lines appear at the beginning of this book.

The term "1967 Lines" gives the impression of a visible line in the sand that can be walked along. But the Armistice Line of 1949—which was the basis for the 1967 Lines—did not necessarily follow clear topographies such as a middle of a valley or a watershed line. And while each country erected fences on their respective sides, the exact line often remained unmarked. After the 1967 War, it was further blurred.

In 1996 and 1997, I joined Pundak on excursions to try to determine the exact location of the 1967 Lines. We drove along old patrol roads, which now serve agricultural vehicles, and climbed barren, sun-baked hills. We were looking for remnants of old fences and bunkers, comparing our findings to official maps. In some places, especially where Israel had built new communities on the West Bank side of the border, there was no trace of the 1967 Lines whatsoever. In Jerusalem's Abu Tor neighborhood, we stood on a street corner where a house on one side had been Jordanian prior to 1967 and the house on the other side was Israeli. Now both houses were part of an expanded Jerusalem. We also visited the so-called Northern Triangle, the densest area of Arab-Israeli population, where the 1967 Line runs through populated areas, for example separating Baqa al-Gharbiyye on the Israeli side from its sister West Bank community of Baka ash-Sharqiyya.

In early 2000s, traces of the 1967 Lines were further eliminated when the Sharon government built a security fence to block suicide bombings. The fence was built within the West Bank, and its construction erased the old border markings. In Jerusalem, the fence largely follows the municipal boundary of expanded Jerusalem and incorporates most of the Palestinian West Bank areas that were annexed to Jerusalem, often separating Palestinian neighbors and families. Also, crossing points between Israel and the West Bank, which used to be made up of simple mobile structures that were placed on the armistice line, were relocated eastward into the West Bank and built up into massive permanent concrete structures on the path of the fence.

The construction of the security fence may sound like a land-grab by Israel, and it was strongly opposed by the Palestinians. But at the time, it was also seen as an important signal by Sharon, who personally oversaw its delineation. The fence roughly follows the future borders of Palestine as suggested by the Barak government and does not prevent the contiguity and viability of the Palestinian state. In addition, the fence leaves the Palestinian neighborhood of Qalandia, which is officially part of municipal Jerusalem, and its population of 30,000 people, *outside* of the fence on the Palestinian side. In 2005, Sharon withdrew from Gaza and from three settlements in Samaria in the northern West Bank. In so doing, he was understood to be *gradually* designing the permanent borders of Israel, working off de Gaulle's playbook.

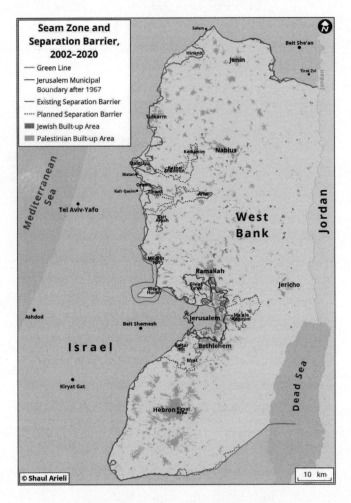

6/2002: Security Fence and Seam Zone
Following the 2001-02 suicide bombings, the Sharon government built a security fence roughly along the 1967 Lines incorporating the settlement blocs and municipal Jerusalem. The fence was seen as an indication of Sharon's plans for Permanent Status.
(Credit: Shaul Arieli)

These changes did not diminish the political significance of the 1967 Lines. Their stature was preserved by Palestinian insistence, UN resolutions, European diplomacy, and the position of Arab countries, as well as by Israeli actions. In 1982, Israel withdrew to the 1967 Lines of its border with Egypt, except in Gaza; in 1994, Israel and Jordan established their permanent border along the 1949 Armistice Lines; in 2000, the Barak government pulled Israel out of Lebanon to the international border; in 2005, the Sharon government withdrew to the pre-1967 border of Gaza; and in 2020, the Trump Plan was implicitly based on the 1967 Lines, enshrining their status as a reference point for any territorial arrangement between the Palestinians and Israel in the West Bank.

As we know, Israel is largely alone in its view that the West Bank is a "disputed territory." Meanwhile, every peace proposal from the international community held the West Bank to be "occupied," and thus belonging to the Palestinians. The one exception is the Trump Plan, which granted Israel the equivalent of 14 percent of the West Bank in Permanent Status, while offering the Palestinians a non-contiguous territory equivalent to 86 percent of the West Bank, including land swaps in the Negev. Trump's proposals would not even be read by the Palestinians.

In this context, the Clinton Ideas represent a virtuous attempt to bridge these positions. Clinton offered the Palestinians a state in 94 to 96 percent of the West bank, along with an additional 1 to 3 percent in land swaps in exchange for annexing the settlement blocs to Israel. Namely, Palestine would cover between 95 and 99 percent of the West Bank, the entirety of Gaza, and a land corridor that connected the two territories. Read one way, the Clinton Ideas view the West Bank and Gaza as "disputed territories" to be divided between the parties, with 95 to 99 percent of it going to Palestine. Read another way, the Palestinians get the equivalent of 100 percent of the land, but that includes "special arrangements" such as a safe passage between Gaza and the West Bank, a platform in Ashdod seaport, and a terminal in Ben-Gurion Airport. Clinton concludes his suggestions by saying that such arrangements would be considered implementation of UNSCRs 242 and 338.

Third Further Redeployment

9/1993: Declaration of Principles, Article 13 and 14: Redeployment of Israeli Forces

13. After the entry into force of this Declaration of Principles … <u>a redeployment of Israeli military forces</u> in the West Bank and the Gaza Strip will take place...

14. Israel will withdraw from the Gaza Strip and Jericho area...

9/1995: Interim Agreement, Articles 10–11: Redeployment and Land

10-1. The <u>first phase</u> of the Israeli military forces' <u>redeployment</u> will cover <u>populated areas</u> in the West Bank—cities, towns, villages, refugee camps and hamlets—… and will be completed <u>prior to the Palestinian elections</u>…

10-2. <u>Further redeployments</u> of Israeli military forces to <u>specified military locations</u> will … be gradually implemented … to be completed within 18 months…

11-2. ….. <u>West Bank and Gaza Strip territory</u>, <u>except for issues</u> that will be <u>negotiated in the Permanent Status</u> negotiations, will come <u>under the jurisdiction of the Palestinian Council</u> in a phased manner, to be completed <u>within 18 months</u>…

(a) <u>Land in populated areas</u> (Areas A and B) … will come under the jurisdiction of the Council during the <u>first phase of redeployment</u>

(d) The further redeployments … to specified military locations will be gradually implemented … <u>in three phases</u>, … to be completed within 18 months …

(e) … <u>powers and responsibilities</u> … will be <u>transferred gradually to Palestinian jurisdiction</u> … <u>except for the issues that will be negotiated in the Permanent Status</u> negotiations

(f) The specified military locations … will be determined in the further redeployment phases … will be negotiated in the Permanent Status negotiations

---

9/1999: Sharm Memorandum, Permanent Status negotiations and Further Redeployments [Provisions 1e and 2]

1e. <u>Permanent Status negotiations</u> will resume <u>after the implementation of</u> ... <u>second stage of the First and Second Further Redeployments</u> ...

2. The Israeli Side undertakes the following with regard to <u>Phase One and Phase Two</u> of the <u>Further Redeployments</u>: On September 5, 1999, to transfer 7% from Area C to Area B; On November 15, 1999, to transfer 2% from Area B to Area A and 3% from Area C to Area B; On January 20, 2000, to transfer 1% from Area C to Area A, and 5.1% from Area B to Area A.

In August 1999, when Barak appointed Sher to negotiate the structure of the political process, the highest hurdle we faced was the "further redeployments." The implementation of the DOP of September 1993 began with Israel's exit from Gaza City and Jericho to allow the PA to be established. The Interim Agreement of September 1995 committed Israel to further withdrawals *within* the West Bank and Gaza in three phases within eighteen months—hence the term "further redeployments" or "FRDs." At the end of FRD3, Israel pledged to remain in military installations, settlements, and other areas that would be discussed in the Permanent Status negotiations.

Accordingly, in FRD1 Israel committed to withdrawing from six Palestinian cities. But after pulling out from Jenin, Nablus, Ramallah, Bethlehem and Jericho, and during the wave of terrorism of early 1996, Peres postponed the withdrawal from Hebron. He then lost the May 1996 election to Netanyahu, who renegotiated the pullout from Hebron until January 1997. Thereafter, Netanyahu negotiated the Wye River Memorandum with Arafat for 18 months, until the PLO agreed to break down FRD2 into three "phases." After carrying out one phase, Netanyahu's government fell.

Enter Barak. While restructuring the Permanent Status negotiations, he also needed to implement Israel's outstanding commitments from the Wye River Memorandum without destabilizing his coalition. So the Palestinians were asked to renegotiate the second and third phases of FRD2. Barak wanted

to improve on Netanyahu's agreement, so he demanded to break down the
outstanding two "phases" of FRD2 into three "stages." At the same time,
the open-ended definition of "miliary installations" and "settlements" diminished the prospects of an agreement on FRD3, because any area that Israel
withdrew from would no longer be discussed in the Permanent Status negotiations. Grudgingly, the Palestinians understood their conundrum: seeking an
agreement on FRD3 meant postponing an agreement on Permanent Status.
To save face, they agreed to establish a "committee" to discuss FRD3 *in parallel* to negotiating the FAPS, in effect conceding that FRD3 would never
happen.

Settlements and Israeli-Palestinians?

FAPS, Article 5: Security Relations [Provision 65]

67. The Parties agree to establish procedures and arrangements for
    ensuring the security of the Israeli settlements in Palestine [i.e. iso-
    lated settlements —GG], and for free, secure the unimpeded access
    thereto.

Clinton Ideas

The Parties should develop a map consistent with the following criteria:
80% of settlers in blocs; Contiguity; Minimize annexed areas; Minimize
the number of Palestinians affected.

The terms "settlement" and "settler" have come to represent the Israeli communities and their residents who live in areas captured in 1967. Most settlements are indistinguishable from any other Israeli community. The bigger
ones have mayors and municipal governments, and the smaller communities are parts of regional councils. All have roads, houses, low-rise buildings,
schools, and sports facilities. Some settlers choose to live in the West Bank for
ideological reasons, while others are just looking for affordable housing and
more tightly knit communities.

But one aspect of settlers' lives differs drastically from that of other Israelis: as soon as they cross the checkpoints into Judea or Samaria in the West Bank, they transition into a different legal setting that governs their families, property, and communities, and that separates them from all things Palestinian. When my son sits on his balcony overlooking a Palestinian village, he sees a community with separate utilities and educational and legal systems. On the Israeli side, the police protect the residents and enforce the laws of their elected government. On the other side, Israel's security forces are viewed as occupiers and aggressors, empowered by military law to treat the local population with hostility and distrust.

By 2000, there were nearly 200,000 settlers in nearly 102 communities in Judea and Samaria, including illegal outposts.[26] Some 80 percent of them lived in major settlement blocs close or adjacent to the 1967 Lines. The Greater Jerusalem Block includes Ma'ale Edomim to the east of Jerusalem, the Gush Etzion block to the south of Jerusalem, and Givat Ze'ev to its north; the Modi'in Ilit block expands the "Jerusalem corridor" and the block of Ariel and nearby Karnei Shomron. Ariel is the largest Jewish city in the West Bank, deep in Samaria, and its location interrupts Palestinian contiguity. There are also a dozen or so communities adjacent to the 1967 Lines, some 20 communities in the Jordan Valley and the Jewish community of Hebron. These numbers don't include the   approximately 130,000 Jewish residents in the Jewish neighborhoods of Jerusalem, which were built in areas annexed after the 1967 war. Israelis view them as Jerusalemites, while the Palestinians hold them to be settlers.

Israel's generations-long effort to settle the West Bank was motivated by ideology and security needs. Ideologically, Judea and Samaria are the ancestral cradle of Jewish civilization, where the right to settle is inalienable. In places like Gush Etzion, Hebron, and the Jewish Quarter of the Old City of Jerusalem, Jewish communities existed long before the 1948 War. After Jordan's army destroyed those communities, their resettlement amounted to a legal right. And to the extent that the West Bank is in fact "disputed territory," Israel acted to create facts on the ground to affect the outcome of any

---

26   Peace Now, *Number of Settlers by Year* (https://peacenow.org.il/en/settlements-watch/settlements-data/population, May 7, 2019).

future political process. Furthermore, most Israeli communities were built on government land or land purchased from Palestinian owners. In this respect, they are also legal.

The presence of settlements is also a matter related to security. Those on the western slopes of the Samarian hills are on high ground that was once used by the Jordanian army to threaten the residents of Israel's coastal plain. They now overlook the urban sprawl of Tel Aviv, with its two million residents, and Ben-Gurion Airport, Israel's international gateway. Slightly to Tel Aviv's north is Israel's "narrow waist"—a corridor of land that was 10 miles wide before 1967 and connects Israel's north and its south. To a lesser degree, the settlements in Gaza were seen in a similar light. There too, a tiny Jewish community existed prior to 1948; settlements were built on government land; and compelling security arguments supported settling 7,000 Jews among nearly 2 million Palestinians.

For the Palestinians, settlements represent a continued act of state aggression. Multiple government agencies are involved in their systematic "expropriation," including Israel's Land Authority identifying Palestinian properties that could be seized; the Ministry of Justice defending shady land acquisitions in heavily biased courts; and the Civil Administration evicting Palestinian squatters who live on lands that were sold by their non-resident owners to Jews. Additional expropriations of private land then ensue to provide for roads or infrastructure needs, and strict security measures are put in place to protect the unwanted new neighbors. Separate Israeli government agencies provide for water, electricity, roads, security, and transportation, and the Supreme Court provides little protection against state overreach, as it limits its interventions to instances of blatant illegality.

Therefore, from the Palestinian perspective, all settlement construction in the West Bank is illegal. Worse, it is "colonial" and discriminatory in that Israeli policy distinguishes between Jewish Israelis and Palestinian natives. They hate the regime that Israel created to ensure the safety and wellbeing of settlers, including roadblocks, checkpoints, and sometimes entirely separate transportation and road systems. Furthermore, they see settlement expansion as creating irreversible facts on the ground that threaten their goal of a contiguous state. Indeed, it is estimated that by 2020, some 30 percent of the West Bank was subjected to Israeli security, infrastructure, and settlement needs.

Palestinian dislike of the settlements runs so deep that some who reject terrorism against Israeli civilians in Israel proper nonetheless legitimize targeting "civilian colonizers." Others who support coexistence with Israel reject coexistence with settlers, likening the relationship to one "between a horse and its rider." Therefore, the PA made selling land to Jews illegal with a potential penalty of death. Some sellers were murdered, sometimes in extremely brutal ways, or were forced to flee.

And yet the settlements were not, as many expected, the most contentious issue in the negotiations. The reason was simple: we agreed that, in Permanent Status, there would not be settlements whose status is disputed. Every community would either be "Israeli" or "Palestinian," and the entire issue was incorporated into the negotiations over territory. The Palestinians had also accepted that the major settlement blocs, along with some smaller communities that were adjacent to the 1967 Lines, would be included in Israel. At the time, polls showed that this arrangement was a clear expectation among the Israeli public regarding Permanent Status.

But the negotiations began in a different place. Barak's initial goal was to have as many settlements as possible on the Israeli side of the permanent border, while allowing most other settlements and settlers, on the Palestinian side of the border, to stay in place enjoying a "special status." His opening position did not envision any significant relocation of communities or individuals, consistent with the Beilin–Abu Mazen Understandings and with the Trump Plan.

But then our negotiating team and the Peace Administration, led by Arieli, began to explore the implications of leaving isolated Israeli communities within Palestinian territory. We quickly realized that such an arrangement would create impossible complications. For example, who would protect these communities and their members? Which police would enforce the law? Who would collect taxes? How would electricity and water be provided? There were dozens of practical challenges like these, and every solution seemed to introduce more problems.

And there were strategic implications as well. As explained earlier, we held Arab-Israelis to be primarily Israelis of Arab and Palestinian descent. We tried to prevent the PLO and Palestine from seeking to represent them as Israeli-Palestinians, namely as Palestinians who were living in Israel. We were now concerned that demanding special status for Israelis in Palestine would conflict with blocking special status for Arabs in Israel.

Hence, a technical question became strategic and ethical: Could we envision a community of Israelis with *special status* existing within Palestinian territory in Permanent Status? And if a special status could *not* be secured, could there be a community of Israeli-Palestinians? Should we even give Israelis the *option* of staying in their homes in Palestine in Permanent Status after the final redeployment of Israeli forces? Or should all Israelis be repatriated, even against their will? The recommendation of our team was eventually crystallized: no settlements or settlers should be allowed to stay within Palestine in Permanent Status. An estimated 50,000 people should be relocated into Israel. Of course, we had yet to experience the tremendous upheaval caused by the relocation of some 7,000 settlers from Gaza during the Disengagement of 2005.

Barak's coalition included right-wing factions that represented these settler communities, so he could not simply switch his position on isolated settlements without achieving some other significant gains, such as securing the future of the settlement blocs. Furthermore, some settler leaders expressed a preference for staying in their homes in Judea and Samaria under Palestinian sovereignty, rather than repatriating to Israel. A minority among them had built good relations with their Palestinian neighbors and believed in coexistence. Others were nationalist zealots and provocateurs who were willing to challenge and disobey the government in the hopes of scuttling the FAPS. None of us could understand why a Jewish national would choose to remain in Palestine over life in Isarel.

The Palestinian side was also conflicted. Some Palestinian representatives would not have any Israelis living in Palestine in Permanent Status. They justifiably feared that if their security is threatened, the IDF would be called to intervene within Palestine. Others had no objection to Jews or Israelis living in Palestine as citizens or residents with similar rights as all Palestinians. For sure, everyone opposed to any *special status* to Israeli communities or individuals in Palestine in Permanent Status, and we quickly realized that there was no chance that the Palestinians would agree to such demands. And even if they would, it would not serve our interest because such arrangement would result in endless friction and conflict, straying us from the goal of End of Conflict.

In sum, this issue combined a myriad of ethical, political, strategic, and practical considerations. It became clear that leaving settlements in place made sense politically but was impossible practically. Therefore, we recommended holding on to the issue as a chip to be traded later in the negotiations. Astonishingly, despite its dramatic implications, our side never had a serious discussion of this matter.

Safe Passage

FAPS, Article 3: Borders and Territorial Arrangements [Provisions 23–26]

23. A number of matters or specific areas, as shown in Map no. 1, will be covered by temporary or permanent Special Arrangements ... will include ... divisions of jurisdiction, and responsibilities, ... and long-term special regime ... or lease arrangements ... details shall be agreed upon in the CAPS.

24. Special Arrangements through, and within Israeli and Palestinian territories respectively shall include: (a) routes for joint usage ... (b) areas populated by Israeli and Palestinian citizens within the territory of the other party [i.e. isolated settlements —GG].

25. Special Arrangement through, over, or within Israeli territories shall include: (a) the Safe Passage between the West Bank and the Gaza Strip aiming to provide for efficient and unimpeded movement of Palestinian persons, vehicles, and goods, under Israel sovereignty; (b) Civil flight arrangements between the West Bank and Gaza; (c) Palestinian economic needs [i.e. platform in Ashdod Port, terminal at Ben-Gurion airport or desalination sites in Israel —GG]

26. Special Arrangement through, over, or within Palestinian territories shall include: (a) passageways to provide for the movement of Israeli citizens and security forces; (b) usage and control of the airspace and electromagnetic spheres; (c) Israeli strategic defense and security needs within specified locations, zones or areas as detailed hereinafter.

FAPS, Article 5: Security [Provisions 63–64]

63. Israel and Palestine recognize <u>Palestinian sovereignty over its air-space</u>. Both Parties further acknowledge that, for security and safety reasons, the Israeli <u>and Palestinian airspace is practically indivisible</u>. In light of the above, and in recognition of the vital importance of the airspace to Israel's security interests, the Parties have agreed that <u>the airspace shall remain under unified Israeli control and adminis-tration</u>, in accordance with arrangements detailed in Annex...

64. Israel and Palestine recognize Palestinian sovereignty over its <u>electro-magnetic spectrum</u>. Both Parties further acknowledge the fact that, due to geographical and topographical realties, it is practically impos-sible to administer this electromagnetic spectrum in separation from Israel's' electromagnetic spectrum. In light of the above, and in rec-ognition of the vital importance of the electromagnetic spectrum to Israel's security interests, the Parties have agreed that <u>the electromag-netic spectrum shall remain under undivided Israel control and man-agement</u>, in accordance with the arrangements detailed in Annex...

The most valuable card that Israel held in the territorial negotiations resulted from the Palestinian need to create a Safe Passage between the West Bank and Gaza through Israel. The Safe Passage was a concept developed in Oslo B in 1995. It made concrete a pledge, made in the 1978 Camp David Accords and reaffirmed in Oslo A, that Gaza and the West Bank would be under a "single authority" and remain a "single territorial unit."[27] Oslo B provided for four routes that connected Gaza to the West Bank, which Palestinians could use subject to special security arrangements.[28] Following the wave of terrorism in 1995–1997, most Palestinian traffic along the Safe Passage was halted, and Gaza and the West Bank were effectively separated. In 1999, upon resuming Permanent Status nego-tiations, reinstating the connection between the two parts of the PA was a top pri-ority for the Palestinians, which Barak and Ben-Ami accommodated by October 1999 with an agreement on the reactivation of the safe passage.

---

27   DOP / Oslo A, *ibid*, Article IV

28   Interim Agreement, / Oslo B, *ibid*, Annex II and Annex III

But toward Permanent Status, we had to re-envision the safe passage, which was a formative issue for Permanent Status. It affected border arrangements between Israel and Palestine; entry and exit points to Palestine through airports, seaports, and border crossings with Jordan and Egypt; and the future of Jerusalem. For example, would someone entering Gaza from Egypt be able to travel freely through the Safe Passage to the West Bank, then enter Jerusalem, and travel to Tel Aviv? If so, the entry point at the Gaza-Egypt border would effectively become an entry point into Israel. Obviously, we could not agree to that.

Israel's leverage on this matter derived from the fact that the Safe Passage was a novelty of the Oslo Accords. UNGAR 181 of 1947 envisioned a contiguous Arab state, but the 1948 War left Gaza and the West Bank separated. Now the Palestinians were demanding that Israel withdraw to the 1967 Lines, which did not include a safe passage. This demand gave us our negotiation card.

Unfortunately, we never used it. Israel's position that the West Bank and Gaza were *disputed* territories effectively meant that the Safe Passage was negotiated as part of the territorial package. The natural inclination was to assess the area of the Safe Passage as part of the territorial trade-off, but that area would not amount to much. For example, if the Safe Passage was 50 kilometers long and 200 meters wide, it would cover ten square kilometers, or an insignificant 0.15 percent of the West Bank. Nonetheless, this was Israel's position until the last stretch of the negotiations. The Clinton Ideas offered the Palestinians 95 to 99 percent of the West Bank and Gaza *in addition* to a Safe Passage, which rounded up the territorial package to an equivalent of 100 percent.

I thought that our handling of the Safe Passage was a mistake. As Barak edged toward agreeing to withdraw from most of the West Bank and all of Gaza, it would have made more sense to give the Palestinians the equivalent of 100 percent of that territory and create a new set of trade-offs around the Safe Passage. At that time, we were already discussing with the Palestinians a platform in the Ashdod seaport and a possible terminal in Ben-Gurion airport. In 2008–2009, Olmert would offer them desalination sites on the Israeli coast to ensure abundant water supply. Together with a the Safe Passage , these represented Palestinian "intrusions" into Israel's sovereign space, which were crucial for the future of Palestine. In return, we could have asked for some Israeli "intrusions" into Palestine's sovereign space in the form of control of its airspace, the sliver of sovereignty in the Jordan Valley, entry and exit points, water rights, or access to holy sites.

But as crucial as the issue of the Safe Passage was, it was never discussed in detail within our delegation or with Barak. Nor was it ever extensively negotiated with the Palestinians, who were even more clueless about its implications than we were.

Leases, Land Swaps, and Demographic Swaps

Land swaps have occurred many times between Israel and Arab countries, particularly Jordan, since 1948. In 1950, a significant land swap between Israel and Egypt shaped the borders of the Gaza Strip, giving Israel fertile land in Gaza's north in exchange for a much larger lot in its South. And in 1951, Israel gave Jordan fertile lands in the Beit Shean Valley in exchange for an area in Wadi Arah that was essential for travel between Tel Aviv and northeast Israel and included some 20 Arab communities, from Taibe and Tirah in the south to Jat in the north, with Kafr Qasim, Qalansawe, and Umm al-Fahm at the center. Today, Wadi Arah is a contiguous urban area known as the "Northern Triangle" and houses nearly 300,000 Arab-Israelis,[29] and in 2000, Umm al-Fahm became the first Arab-Israeli community to be recognized as a city.

Nonetheless, when the notion of land swaps was reintroduced by the Beilin–Abu Mazen Understandings in 1995, it was framed as a radical novelty. For the first time, a senior Israeli politician was accepting the principle that the entirety of the West Bank and Gaza, or the equivalent thereof, was Palestinian. Hence, if Israel demanded annexation of the settlement blocs or the Jerusalem neighborhoods, which covered roughly 5–7 percent of the West Bank, it would have to give the Palestinians territory of equal size and quality elsewhere. This has been the Palestinian position since the Oslo Accords. In fact, as late as 2020, Mohammed Shtayyeh, the Palestinian prime minister since 2019, reiterated a commitment to the principle of "minor modifications of borders [i.e. the 1967 Lines —GG] where necessary … as well as exchanges of land *equal in size and volume and in value—one to one*."[30]

---

29   *Israel Central Bureau of Statistics, Regional Statistics, (https://www.cbs.gov.il/en/settlements/Pages/default.aspx?mode=Yeshuv)*

30   Boxerman, Aaron, *PA Submits Counter-Proposal to US Plan, Providing for Demilitarized Palestine* (*The Times of Israel*, June 9, 2020, https://www.timesofisrael.com/pa-prime-minister-says-palestinian-state-will-be-declared-if-israel-annexes-land/)

The question is, where? Beilin pointed to Halutza, in the western Negev, close to the Egyptian border and adjacent to Gaza, which was less important to Israel and very important to the Palestinians. But Abu Mazen insisted on also swapping territories in the West Bank, so both parts of the Palestinian state benefit from a Permanent Status agreement. Hence, the Beilin–Abu Mazen Understandings also suggested a land swap in Mount Hebron, north of Arad. At the time, the idea of land swap was dismissed as a dangerous left-wing fantasy, but it has since become a permanent feature of all territorial arrangements, including the Trump Plan.

Barak, who was loyal to the notion of the West Bank as *disputed territories*, was not initially willing to discuss land swaps. His rationale was in part political, as such negotiations could have destabilized his coalition. However, to our negotiation team, it was clear that territorial exchanges would have to be negotiated for a FAPS to be concluded. To that end, Arieli secretly prepared a set of maps that depicted different swaps in the Negev adjacent to Gaza, in the Hebron mountains, and in the Beit Shean and Jordan Valleys. Of course, the fact that the peace administration was entertaining ideas so far beyond Barak's stated positions could have been a political bombshell if it had been revealed. Barak, however, never instructed us not to consider such swaps, so Sher planned for future contingencies.

On September 28, 2000, Sharon's visit to Temple Mount led to the eruption of violent riots in the West Bank that spilled into Israel and culminated in the killing of eleven Arab-Israeli citizens by police. One of centers of violence was Wadi Arah, where protestors blocked the main highway and entrapped thousands of people in their vehicles amid a raging crowd. These televised events traumatized the Israeli public. Though the deaths of eleven Arab-Israelis was unfathomable, violent protests in support of the Palestinian "enemy" and against the Israeli government were equally unacceptable. After decades of efforts to integrate Arabs into Israeli society, a deep rift had been exposed.

For Barak, this was a particularly unfortunate turn of events. One of the pledges of his election campaign had been for "equality and integration" of the Arab population in Israel. Early in his term, he appointed a task force to create an unprecedented master plan for planning, zoning and development of infrastructure in Arab communities with an investment of $1.2 billion.

The plan was scheduled to be announced during the week of the protests and was of course delayed for a few years before becoming government policy. And Barak's relationship with the Arab community never fully rebounded.

These events had a profound effect on our negotiation team. In September 2000, before the outbreak of violence, we had already been discussing a Palestinian state in nearly all of Gaza and some 90 percent of the West Bank, including most of the Jordan Valley, but without discussing land swaps. Once the violence broke out, many of Barak's advisors urged him to break off the negotiations or to sanction the Palestinians. But Barak was determined to continue the diplomatic process and even raised the stakes. Like Rabin, he felt that changing the trajectory of the Israeli-Palestinian conflict was bound to face harsh protests and even violence, so he saw the September 2000 outbreak as inevitable "growing pains." While he was running out of time because his government was disintegrating, he became more determined to present to the public a finalized draft-FAPS worthy of all the sacrifice. So while Israel was flexing its military muscle against the rioters, it also unleashed its diplomats, namely us, and ramped up the negotiations.

With elections in the U.S. just a few weeks away, Barak was now inclined to make even more concessions. For the first time, he was open to accepting the principle of land swaps. That evolution in his position did not surprise our delegation. We realized, perhaps before Barak did, that Israel would have to accept the 1967 Lines as the basis for its permanent borders with Palestine if it wanted to reach a FAPS with End of Conflict and Finality of Claims. At that point, we needed to optimize the size of the areas we demanded to annex in the settlement blocs or the Jordan Valley, as well as the swapped areas.

The shocking and violent clashes with Arab-Israelis in early October turned our attention to the Northern Triangle and sent Pini Meidan-Shani, the representative of Mossad in our delegation, and me to pen a policy paper entitled "Demographic Swaps." Our suggestion was for Israel to offer that the southern side of the Northern Triangle, south of highway 70, would be part of the swap in exchange for the settlement blocs. The population in the two areas was roughly the same and the size of the swapped area was significant. We recommended holding local referendums offering each community the choice between remaining in Israel in Permanent Status or becoming part of Palestine. If they voted to join Palestine, the Israel-Palestine border would run west of their communities, whose land would then count as part of the land swap. If they voted to remain in Israel, the land swap would take place in other regions, as originally planned. We believed that the PLO could not refuse such an offer.

Demographic swaps, as we suggested, offered Israel a win-win. If the Arab residents of the Northern Triangle voted to remain part of Israel, it would be a historic vote of confidence by Arab-Israelis who preferred Israel over Palestine. If they chose to join Palestine, we would be spared the need to allocate additional land in Mount Hebron, Halutzah, or the Beit Shean Valley. We were excited about our idea and proud of our work.

Unfortunately, Barak did not have the bandwidth to focus on a new and radical strategy, which had not been raised with the Americans or the Palestinians. He read the memo but did not respond with a clear directive. We got the impression that he liked it but was too distracted to order a reorientation of the negotiations toward swapping populated areas, which was much more complicated than trading empty spaces. In the end, it was too complex an issue to introduce in the final stretch of negotiations, and it never took off.

In 2014, Yisrael Hasson, a member of our delegation, joined the party of Avigdor Lieberman, and shared the idea of demographic swaps with him. Lieberman, a right-wing politician, immediately saw its political potential and made demographic swaps a highlight of his campaign. He ignored the sections that called for a referendum and added a new slogan: "No citizenship without loyalty." Most of his followers, though, failed to realize that "demographic swaps" meant accepting the 1967 Lines as the baseline for the territorial agreement...

Territorial Bargaining and the Thinning of the Jordan Valley

Israel's starting position in the territorial negotiations was unacceptable to the Palestinians. We demanded annexing 40 percent of the West Bank to Israel in Permanent Status, without swaps, which meant giving the Palestinians 10 percent more territory than they already had in the Interim Period. But it was a suitable starting point for bargaining with the Americans. As allies, they could challenge our security demands in a way that the Palestinians could not, and as "honest brokers," their goal was to nudge our positions to a point at which the Palestinians would be willing to engage. But they had no leverage on Israel while Barak negotiated with Syria. So until March 2000, Israel's position on the future borders with Palestine barely moved. Our offers to accommodate Palestinian frustrations with a few additional percentage points of territory were rejected out of hand.

The initial focus of the negotiations was on the Jordan Valley, a 71-kilome-ter-long section of the Syrian-African Rift, a geological fault line that stretches from Ethiopia to Lebanon and creates a valley that separates Jordan and Syria on its east side from Israel and the Palestinian areas on its west side. The Jordan River flows southward in the middle of the rift from its source in the border area of Israel, Syria, and Lebanon, through the Sea of Galilee, and onward to the Dead Sea. There are towering mountains on both of its sides and ancient transportation routes that run east to west connecting Mediterranean seaports with the Arabian Peninsula and the Arabian Sea. One of these routes connects the ancient seaport of Jaffa with Jerusalem, on a mountaintop of the West Bank, via Jericho in the Jordan Valley to Amman, Jordan's capital, on the mountains of the East Bank—altogether, a three-hour drive with no traffic.

Israel's starting position in the Permanent Status negotiations emanated from decades of unwavering pledge by Israeli politicians from all parties to keep the Jordan Valley under Israeli sovereignty. It was then home to some 20 communities and 12,000 Israelis. Many of these settlers were associated with the Labor Party, which distinguished them from other settlement com-munities that tended to be more right-wing. Except for Beilin, who included a phased withdrawal from the Jordan Valley in the Beilin–Abu Mazen Understandings, the consensus was that the Jordan Valley must remain Israeli.

Alas, that consensus was based on outdated scenarios and partial informa-tion. Long-range precision weaponry obviated the need for the IDF to station large forces in that area, as did the peace treaty with Jordan and the decimation of the Iraqi army in 1991. In addition, many of the settlers in the Jordan Valley preferred relocating to Israel with a generous compensation package over living in a stretch of Israeli territory, bound by Jordan and Palestine on both sides. The founding generation braved hardships and clung to the barren land with idealism and determination, but many of their children migrated elsewhere. For those who remained, a FAPS was seen as a good opportunity to repatriate to Israel.

The Jordan Valley is also populated by some 60,000 Palestinians, who live in small towns and dozens of tiny, impoverished communities. Some

Bedouin tribes live nomadically in tents and tin sheds, and their communities were not even recognized by the Jordanians. Many camp on government land and are then pushed around by Israeli authorities; they are often left with no stable access to infrastructure and water. Visiting these communities often requires driving off-road in four-wheelers up the slopes of the Judean mountains, where there is barely any greenery. I went on such an expedition myself, and when we got out of our air-conditioned jeeps, the heat was stifling. I could hardly believe that such poverty and vulnerability could exist in Israeli-controlled areas. Furthermore, some 20,000 Palestinians lived in Jericho, which was recognized in Oslo B as one of six Palestinian cities under full control of the PA and happened to be the hometown of the Erekat clan and Saeb's family. If Israel annexed the Jordan Valley, Jericho would be enclaved in Permanent Status.

At roughly 1,670 square kilometers, the Jordan Valley is four to five times larger than all the settlement blocs combined. If it were to be annexed, it would be nearly impossible to find enough vacant territory in Israel for land swaps, even in the western Negev. Furthermore, some 60,000 Palestinians who live in the Jordan Valley would then become Israeli citizens, whose communal rights to land and water would have to be regulated under Israeli law. Additionally, Israel and Palestine would be thrown into complicated negotiations over water rights, because whoever is the sovereign of the Jordan Valley has rights in the water system of the Jordan River and the Dead Sea.

The IDF had its own concerns about annexing the Jordan Valley because it would have created nearly 1,000 kilometers of *additional* borders in difficult terrain along the eastern and western sides of the annexed area, on both sides of the envisioned land corridors from west to east, around settlement blocs and isolated settlements, and in the urban area of Jerusalem. The IDF cautioned that even multi-billion-dollar investment in state-of-the-art border fences and technologies and thousands of soldiers dedicated to border protection would not suffice for sealing the border to terrorists, criminals, and illegal trafficking of weapons, drugs, goods, and labor.

In May, following the collapse of the negotiations with Syria and ahead of the unilateral withdrawal from Lebanon, Barak turned his attention to the Palestinians. By that time, it was clear that in Permanent Status Israel would have to withdraw from most of the West Bank and Gaza if not from their entirety.

Because this meant that Barak could not get a FAPS while remaining in the Jordan Valley and other territories, Israel's demand for sovereignty over the Jordan Valley began to wither. The pressure to compromise came from the goal of achieving End of Conflict, but also from growing internal doubt among senior officers, civil servants, and politicians about the practicality of our own demands.

Indeed, over time, Israel's interests crystallized. Barak insisted on a "sliver of sovereignty" between Palestine and Jordan that would prevent the integration of the two territories into one hostile entity. Furthermore, we realized that the IDF did not have to be physically present in the Jordan Valley or along that border to prevent a military attack from Jordan, and that an American peacekeeping force could do the job just as well. We focused our demands on having areas for military deployment in times of emergency, access roads for deployment of those forces, and early-warning stations on a few mountaintops. This made strategic sense to everyone. Eventually, by the final phases of the negotiations leading up to the Clinton Ideas, we agreed to nearly full military and civilian withdrawal from the Jordan Valley except for the guarantee of that sliver of sovereignty and that our security concerns would be addressed through "special arrangements."

In numerical terms, by April, ahead of the backchannel in Sweden, Palestinian territory on the Israeli maps grew to 77 percent of the West Bank.[31] That offer was sufficient for the Americans to view Israel as forthcoming, yet mild enough not to destabilize Barak's coalition. By June, ahead of the Camp David summit, Israel raised its offer to a withdrawal from 86 percent of the West Bank. According to this map, while Palestine would incorporate nearly 97 percent of all Palestinians, 80 percent of all settlers, as well as all Israeli Jerusalemites, would be part of Israel in Permanent Status. Following Camp David, the bargaining continued; by September, Israel was willing to withdraw from nearly 90 percent of the West Bank and began to discuss some land swaps, and by January, Israel presented to the Palestinians a map that gave them 92 percent of the West Bank and all of Gaza, while conditionally accepting the Clinton Ideas, which suggested a withdrawal from 95 to 99 percent of the West Bank and Gaza with land swaps and a Safe Passage.

---

31   Sher, *Within Reach*, *Ibid*, p. 25.

For some in our delegation, Barak's willingness to withdraw from 86 percent of the West Bank was astonishing, let alone withdrawing from 92 percent while offering land swaps. But for a few of us, primarily Arieli, Ephraim Lavie, the intelligence officer of oru delegation, and me, it was clear that even these "generous positions" were not enough for an End-of-Conflict FAPS. We thought that instead of fighting tooth and nail for every square kilometer within a framework that was fundamentally unacceptable to the Palestinians, Israel should have presented a package that was equivalent to 100 percent of the West Bank and Gaza, while securing its interests in the settlement blocs and in military needs, airspace, and access to holy sites. In short, instead of bargaining about the extent of our withdrawal, we should have negotiated a package of territorial arrangements that would have accommodated everyone's interests. Unfortunately, even when Israeli territorial concessions reached 92 to 99 percent of the West Bank, this reframing of Israel's positions never materialized.

As Israel gradually agreed to withdraw from the Jordan Valley, we held on to six demands: control of the external perimeter of Palestine and monitoring of those who entered it; securing areas for military deployment and access to them; early-warning stations on two mountaintops; a sliver of sovereignty along the Jordan River; control and usage of the airspace and electromagnetic sphere; and distinguishing water rights from land ownership. (You can read more about these topics in coming chapters.) The Palestinians rejected our demands, framing them as attempts to dominate Palestine in Permanent Status, but were willing to work with us on them because they were "legitimate security concerns." That, at least, kept the prospects of reaching a FAPS alive. Nonetheless, in negotiating borders, their framework remained land-for-land based on the 1967 Lines.

As negotiations continued, we came up with creative ideas that distinguished sovereignty and ownership from control and use. For example, we offered that Israel would acknowledge the Jordan Valley as Palestinian land if Palestine leased key areas to Israel for extended periods. Such ideas followed in the footsteps of the peace treaty with Jordan and the Beilin–Abu Mazen Understandings. Of course, when discussing leases, the Palestinian side wanted shorter periods—seven to twelve years—and we spoke about 25 years or more—which as of this writing would have been up soon, in 2025.

Spring 2000: Barak's Initial Offer

Barak's initial offer included wide land corridors and continued control of the Jordan Valley. *(Credit: Shaul Arieli)*

1/2001: Barak's Closing Offer in Taba

In the Taba talks, Israel offered the Palestinians ~92% of the West Bank and all of Gaza. No land swaps are indicated on the map. *(Credit: Shaul Arieli)*

2008: Annapolis

By 2007-09, Olmert offered nearly 94% of the West Bank and all of Gaza with equal size land swaps and other territorial arrangements e.g. in seaports, airports and desalination sites (not on the map). *(Credit: Shaul Arieli)*

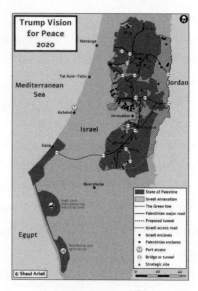

1/2020: Trump Plan

Trump offered Palestine equivalent to 86 percent of the West Bank and all of Gaza. Swaps were supposed to happen in the Negev and in the Northern Triangle (demographic swaps). *(Credit: Shaul Arieli)*

Who's Drawing the Maps?

I first dealt with the delineation of borders in the ECF, where we created a set of maps and accompanying aerial photos. This was before Google Maps made military-level accuracy and imagery available to anyone. We shopped for standard aerial photos and 1:50:000 maps at specialized stores, which served us well enough.

When I moved to government, though, even map-gathering had to go through the proper channels of procurement. There was a political challenge as well: the strategic planning branch of the IDF, which was responsible for the territorial arrangements, and the intelligence branch, which controlled the military mapping unit, wanted to monopolize the territorial negotiations and control map-making. Of course, we needed the IDF's input to finalize territorial arrangements, but not to explore new ideas.

The relationship grew even more strained in later phases of the negotiations over Jerusalem and the settlements. Some top IDF officials were more hawkish than Barak, and there were constant leaks to the media about the ideas we were discussing. We suspected that the leaks were deliberate attempts to sabotage the negotiations. In short, I saw significant distrust between Barak's bureau and senior military personnel. So Arieli used his skills and pulled his connections to create a set of maps for us. My takeaway for future negotiations? It's essential for chief negotiators to control map-making.

Anecdotally, throughout the Camp David negotiations, the Palestinians never saw any of our maps because Barak insisted on establishing the principles of territorial arrangements before sharing maps. He was concerned that such maps would determine Palestinian expectations and the starting point of future negotiations. He only relented in the final round of negotiations, in Taba, Egypt, in January 2001. There and then, for the first time, the Palestinians saw their state on Israeli maps. But it was too late.

Pictorial History of the Oslo Process (1978-2020)

9/1978: Camp David Accords

Begin, Carter and Sadat ahead of the summit that yielded the Framework Agreement for Middle East Peace. Annex III is the blueprint for the Oslo Process. The CD Accords are the cornerstone of Israeli-Arab peace including with Jordan and the Abraham Accords *(Wikipedia, Carter Presidential Library, unknown)*

8/1993: Secret Signing of DOP / Oslo A"

Oslo A was signed after nine months of negotiations. Seated: Savir (R); Norway MOFA; Abu Alaa. Standing: Pundak (R), Hirschfeld, Singer, Larsen and Juul, Peres, Asfour (second from left). *(Ron Pundak)*

2/1994: Massacre in Hebron

Baruch Goldstein, a settler from Kiryat Arba, killed 29 Moslem worshipers in the mosque before being killed. This massacre triggered Hamas suicide bombings, that eventually derailed the Oslo Process. *(Credit: Hemis / Alamy Stock Photo)*

5/1994: Gaza-Jericho Agreement in Cairo

First agreement to implement the DOP / Oslo A. After six months of negotiations, Arafat refused to sign the maps on stage until agreeing. Iconic picture captures Peres (Left, fingering Arafat), Rabin, Mubarak, Arafat, Christopher. *(Credit: Tsvika Israeli)*

4/1994 to 3/1995: Suicide Bombings in Israel

Following the Hebron massacre and in order to derail the Oslo Process, Hamas and Islamic Jihad carried out 13 bombings killing 149. A picture from Jerusalem (8/95). *(Avi Ohayon)*

7/1994: Arafat Returns to Gaza

Thousands of Gazans cheer Arafat upon his return to begin the implementation of Oslo A and the Gaza-Jericho Agreement and to launch the PA. *(Credit: Ahmed Jadallah / Reuters)*

10/1994: Israel-Jordan Peace Treaty
The treaty was signed following the 1978 Camp David accord, Oslo A, Gaza-Jericho Agreement and launch of PA. On stage: leaders of the US, Israel, Jordan . Standing: Commanders of both militaries. *(Israel Government Press Office)*

12/1994: Nobel Peace Prize
Rabin, Peres and Arafat shared the Nobel Peace Prize for the leadership of the Oslo Process. This was their peak moment. *(Credit: Sa'ar Ya'akov)*

9/1995: Interim Agreement / Oslo B

The maps were signed in the White House East Room to avoid a repeat of the scene in Cairo (5/94). From left: Singer, Rabin, Mubarak, Clinton, Hussein, Arafat and Erakat.

(Avi Ohayon)

10/1995: Beilin-Abu-Mazen Understandings

Abu Mazen and Beilin in Ramallah, date unknown. Their understandings attempted to outline the FAPS ahead of the Permanent Status negotiations.

(Credit: The Israel Internet Association, Author unknown)

11/4/1995: Assassination of PM Rabin
After Rabin's assassination Peres became PM (11/95-5/96), suicide bombings continued and Netanyahu won the elections (5/96). In picture: a page with the song of peace, stained with Rabin's blood *(IPPA, Dan HaDani Collection)*

10/1998: Wye River Memorandum
Arafat and Netanyahu signed the Hebron Agreement (1/97) and the Wy River Memorandum (10/98) to implement the Oslo Accords and particularly FRD2. Netanyahu's government then fell and Barak became PM (5/99). *(Credit: Sa'ar Ya'akov)*

9/1999: Sharm El-Sheikh Memorandum

Barah and Arafat sign an agreement to restructure the Oslo Process with the goals of FAPS and CAPS. Barak then turned his attention to Syria. Seated: Barak and Arafat. Standing: Sher (L), Mubarak, Albright, Erekat. *(Credit: Moshe Milner)*

10/1999-3/2000: Israel-Syria Negotiations

Clinton walks Barak and foreign minister of Syria, Farouk A-Shara at Sheperdtown for the peace summit between Israel and Syria. *(Credit: Avi Ohayon)*

5/24/2000: Israeli Withdrawal from Lebanon
In May 2000, after the collapse of the negotiations with Syria, Israel unilaterally withdrew its forces from Lebanon to the international border line. *(Credit: Milner Moshe)*

4-5/2000: Backchannel in Sweden
Following the collapse of the negotiations with Syria and after the withdrawal from Lebanon, Permanent Status negotiations were accelerated via a backchannel in Sweden. From Left: Ben-Ami, Grinstein, Sher, Abu Alaa in Harpsund, Sweden. *(Credit: Grinstein)*

July 11-25, 2000: Camp David Summit

The summit was convened following the collapse of all earlier negotiations. Barak designed a "moment of truth" around July 18 on Jerusalem. Pictured: Barak, Clinton, Arafat and Helal during a Shabbat dinner. *(White House)*

7/2000: US Peace Team at Camp David

Led by Amb Dennis Ross, the PT played a central roll in the Oslo Process since Madrid, 1991. Clinton (back to camera). From Left: Miller, Berger, Ross (behind Berger) Bruce Reidel, Mara Rodman, Helal, Malley, John Podesta, Albright. *(White House)*

9/28/2000: Sharon Visit to Temple Mount

Sharon's visit to Temple Mount, following significant advancement in negotiations, sparked a war that would last till 2004 with thousands of casualties. Pictured: Sharon surrounded by bodyguards and police. *(Source: AP Photo/Eyal Warshavsky)*

10/2000: Outbreak of Israeli-Palestinian War

Sharon's visit triggered mass-riots in Jerusalem, West Bank and Gaza with many casualties. Attempts to stop violence failed, and violence escalated. In picture: riots in Israel's Northern Triangle. *(Credit: AP Photo, Elizabeth Dalziel)*

12/2000-1/2001 - Clinton Ideas

On 12/23/2000, Clinton presented principles for a FAPS. Israel accepted them as "a basis for negotiations." Arafat was seen as not. In picture, Clinton meets both delegations on 12/17/00. Opposite Berger, Clinton and Albright: Helal (L), Dahlan, Erakat, Abed Rabbo, Ben-Ami, Sher, Meidan-Shani. In the back row: Malley and Miller *(Credit: White House)*

March 7, 2001: Transition between Barak and Sharon

Sharon became prime minister and shifted focus to fighting terrorism. He resumed diplomatic initiatives in 2003 and later withdrew from Gaza *(Credit: Avi Ohayon)*

Pictorial History of the Oslo Process (1978-2020)

10/2000 to 12/2004: War of Terror and Suicide Bombings
~130 suicide attacks claimed ~550 lives, eventually leading to Operation Defensive Shield and to building the security fence. In picture: aftermath of attack on Sbarro restaurant (8/01) killing 15. *(Credit: Avi Ohayon)*

3/02 and 03/07: Saudi Peace Initiative
The SPI, initially introduced to Tom Friedman, offered a path to Arab recognition of Israel following peace with the Palestinians. It was twice endorsed by the Arab League (3/02 and 3/07) Pictured: King Fahed of Saudi Arabia at the Arab League Conference in Beirut. *(Credit: AP Photo/Santiago Lyon).*

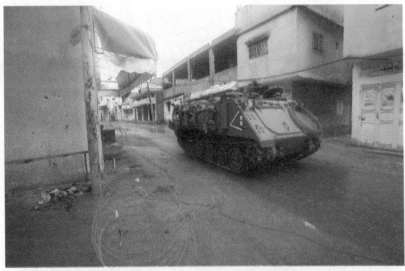

3/2002: Retake of West Bank / Defensive Shield
Following suicide bombings, IDF re-took Palestinian cities in Area A to eliminate terror
network. In picture: IDF armored vehicle in Palestinian Tul Karem
(Ra'anan Cohen, IDF Spokesperson)

6/2002: Security Fence
To stop suicide bombings, Sharon
government built a security fence that
roughly followed the outline of the
Settlement Blocks. Its path was seen
as an indication of Sharon's vision for
Permanent Status .
(Credit: Moshe Milner)

Pictorial History of the Oslo Process (1978-2020)

6/2003: Quartet Roadmap for Peace

The Roadmap offered an alternative structure to the Oslo Process with Palestinian state in provisional borders ahead of Permanent Status. Israel accepted but the Palestinian did not.
(Credit: Laam)

8/2005: Gaza Disengagement. West Bank Realignment

In 2005, the Sharon government withdrew all Israeli presence in Gaza to the 1967 Lines, and from an area in Samaria (with 3 settlements) as part of the Realignment Plan. In picture: police evicting settlers in Gaza *(Credit: Moshe Milner)*

11/2007-1/2009: Second Attempt at Permanent Status
In 11/07, following Hamas takeover of Gaza (6/07), Olmert, Abu Mazen and Bush
launched another attempt to reach Permanent Status based on the Roadmap.
(Credit: Wikipedia. U.S. Navy photo by Gin Kai)

2008-2014: Obama-Kerry
A third attempt to reach a FAPS. Netanyahu made far-reaching to Abu Mazen but no deal
was reached. This was Netanyahu's last attempt to reach an agreement with Abu Mazen.
(Credit: LAAM, Author unknown)

Pictorial History of the Oslo Process (1978-2020)

1/2017-1/2020: The Trump Administration
In 5/2018 President Trump moved the US Embassy to Jerusalem and in 1/2000
he publihsed the Trump Plan, which incorporated key aspects of the Camp David
negotiations e.g. equivalent of 86% of West Bank to Palestine.
Pictured: Mr. and Mrs. Netanyahu, Ivanka and Jared Kushner. *(Credit: Avi Ohayon)*

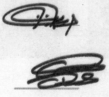

9/2020: Abraham Accords
The UAE, Morocco and Bahrain
signed normalization agreements
with Israel following Israel's withdrawal from its plans of annexing
the West Bank. *(Credit: The White
House from Washington)*

CHAPTER 6

FAPS Article 5:
Security

A Power Play by the IDF

FAPS Article 2: Palestinian State [Provisions 16–17]

16. [I: Israel and Palestine <u>shall not enter any ... union or confederation with third parties</u> whose objectives are directed against the interest of the other Party...]

17. [I: Neither Party shall be a party to <u>an agreement or alliance</u> with third parties, which has political military, economic or social intentions or objectives directed against the other parties or which is <u>inconsistent with their agreements</u>]

FAPS Article 5: Security [Provisions 56–59, 61–62]

56. The <u>demilitarized Palestine state</u> shall maintain <u>a non-military Palestinian Police and Security Force</u> (PPSF), comprised of ground and maritime elements for the purpose of ensuring internal security, law enforcement and public order and the fight against terrorism.

57. The size, armament deployment, activities, structure, facilities, infrastructure, capabilities, and equipment of the PPSF shall be approved and required for the fulfillment of its <u>responsibilities for internal security, law enforcement and public order</u> as shall be detailed in Annex. ... <u>No armed forces shall be established and operated by Palestine</u>. Accordingly, Palestine shall ensure the <u>dismantling of all other armed elements within its territory</u>.

---

58. Palestine shall not allow the entry into, deployment, stationing or operation in or passage through its land, air or sea of any military or security forces, personnel, armament, equipment, or material of any third party unless otherwise agreed by both states.

59. The <u>Palestinian Party shall not maintain any military forces,</u> capacities or infrastructure in any location, <u>nor shall it become party to any alliance</u>, agreement or cooperative activity that is of a military, paramilitary or security character.

61. <u>Israel ... shall maintain a land force presence and early warning facilities in specific zones, locations and areas</u> ... as delineated in Map no. 1. <u>Special arrangements concerning the ... movement of Israeli security personnel and equipment</u> to and from the zones, locations and areas, the jurisdiction and division of responsibilities therein and the status of Israel security personal are detailed in annex...

62. In case of an <u>imminent threat</u> of an armed attack, <u>Israel may</u>, by notice to Palestine, <u>temporarily reinforce</u> its military forces in the zones, locations or areas for the duration of that threat.

In November 1999—after two months of stalling that included the Jewish High Holidays—we headed to Eilat for the first session of Permanent Status negotiations. Barak and Arafat agreed that we would focus initially on the issues of security, which was framed as "important for Israel," and on the issue of territory and borders, which was considered "important for the Palestinians." These were conveniently simplistic definitions because the Palestinians had security concerns and we had territorial issues. In fact, security and territory were deeply entwined, and the IDF Planning Branch, headed by Major General Shlomo Yanai and Brigadier General Mike Herzog, were to lead both working groups on behalf of Israel. From a historical perspective, this was a momentous occasion: for the first time, Israel negotiated Permanent Status issues with the PLO while tacitly assuming the establishment of a Palestinian state. But the historicity of the moment was quickly lost on all participants.

After a brief ceremony that included a photographed handshake between Eran and Abed- Rabbo across a beautifully set table, we began the work session behind closed doors. Yanai shared a detailed presentation of Israel's security concerns and requirements. Anecdotally, his deck was still dubbed as "secret and confidential" although it was presented to a Palestinian delegation. For the following 45 minutes, Yanai described Israel's outlook and interests, while throwing at the Palestinians a host of strategic and military terms. He then focused on the threat of the "eastern front"—referring to a scenario in which Arab armies invade Israel from Jordan through its eastern border—which was the concern that shaped Israel's approach to the FAPS. As Yanai progressed through his slides, which were rich with aerial photos, maps, and arrows, the Palestinians grew impatient. They were annoyed with being a captive audience in a crash course on Israeli national security, which diligently laid the grounds for unacceptable territorial claims. They also understood that the real audience of Yanai's presentation were the Americans and Europeans who were not in the room. When he finally presented a sketch of the map of Palestine in Permanent Status, trifurcated among areas that would remain under Israeli control, the Palestinian delegation was outraged.

Their anger was expected. Barak, favoring the Syrian track, had no intention of allowing any progress with the Palestinians. His opening premise was that Israel would retain sovereignty and control of expanded municipal Jerusalem, settlements blocs and all isolated settlements, key holy sites, and all areas deemed by Israel essential for its security and water needs. This approach left the Palestinians with some two-thirds of Gaza and 60 percent of a non-contiguous West Bank that is segmented by wide east-to-west corridors that divided Palestine into three enclaves in the West Bank addition to Gaza.

The Palestinians felt betrayed. Abu Mazen and other Palestinian leaders had long pledged to accommodate Israeli security concerns. But they did not expect their goodwill to legitimize Israeli demands to encircle and divide their state. Erekat said bluntly: "You want to continue the occupation in a new way." Furthermore, during the Netanyahu government of 1996–1999, their left-wing Israeli friends—including my former bosses at the ECF—had pleaded with them to have strategic patience. They had gone along with the logic of acquiescing to Netanyahu's demands and "call his bluff" and signed the Hebron Agreement in 1997 and the Wye River Memorandum in 1998. In May 1999, they agreed to postpone their declaration of independence in anticipation of Barak's premiership, hoping for a Permanent Status agreement based on the 1967 Lines. Now, with Israel's opening positions on security, they realized how long and difficult their path to statehood would be. They told us that Barak's positions didn't even fall within the realm of the Israeli peace camp, which only confirmed their earlier suspicions of him.

The American Peace Team was also left with mouths agape. The Clinton Administration, which had invested political capital in Barak, were now hearing of security needs that were oceans away from any zone of possible agreement. Indeed, the first round was a fiasco for anyone who expected rapid progress in these negotiations. For Barak, though, it was what he had planned: a launch into a standstill. And he knew that no one would pressure him on his hard line as long as he was committed to peacemaking with Syria.

General Shlomo Yanai, our top person on security, was an outstanding tank man. He had joined the armored corps, became a tank commander and an officer, and was severely burned in the 1973 War, receiving a citation for outstanding bravery in battle. He then returned to service and rose to senior military leadership. His journey of service required courage, management skills, superior technical proficiency, discipline, and tight teamwork. It was in the armored corps that Yanai met Sher, who was also a brigade commander in the reserves. They understood and respected each other.

As mentioned, Yanai was head of the strategic planning branch of the IDF that handles all aspects of capacity building of Israel's military. A key division under his command was responsible for all "politico-military affairs," which includes the interface with Israel's diplomacy, such as the negotiations with the Palestinians and relations with foreign militaries. That unit was led by a deputy of Yanai, Mike Herzog, who currently serves as ambassador to Washington. Because of the importance and sensitivity of our negotiations, both men reported directly to chief of staff, Lieutenant General Shaul Mofaz.

In shaping Israel's positions on security and borders, Yanai and Herzog focused on the "eastern front" as the primary threat to Israel. In 1948, Arab armies invaded Israel from the east and nearly emerged victorious. In 1967, a similar threat was made by Jordan, Syria, and Iraq, and in 1973, Iraqi forces joined Syria in the fierce fighting against Israel. Later still, in 1991, Saddam Hussein fired Iraqi missiles into Israel from the east. These experiences, the size of the Iraqi and Syrian armies, and Saddam's violent rhetoric underscored

Israel's nightmare military scenario of a coalition of armies moving through Jordan across the river into the West Bank to take over Judea and Samaria, seize Jerusalem, and conquer Israel. In response, Israel viewed the Jordan River as the *last* line of defense and prepared to intercept any foreign military entering Jordan far from the border. Therefore, Israel entrenched in the east-facing slopes of the mountains overlooking Jordan, built a string of settlements and a system of roads in the Jordan valley, and developed offensive capabilities to operate deep in the Jordanian territory if such a need ever arose.

Now, ahead of the Permanent Status negotiations, Mofaz, Yanai, and Herzog established a few principles. Most important, Israel should be the sovereign in the Jordan Valley to prevent Arab territorial contiguity from Iraq and Jordan to the Palestinian state. They also wanted Israel to hold on to the mountaintops of the West Bank to monitor Jordanian airspace and prevent aerial attacks from Iraq or Iran. The IDF also demanded wide east-west territorial corridors that would allow forces to be transferred from Israel through the Palestinian state to the Jordan Valley. They also required the ability to move forces "across the front," north-south along the Jordan-facing eastern slopes of the Samarian and Judean mountains (the orange area of the map).

This approach may have been relevant for three decades, since 1967, but by 2000 it was less so. The IDF had developed and deployed long-range precision weapons in addition to building remarkable capabilities in its air force, particularly during Barak's tenure as IDF chief of staff in 1991–1995. So now Israel had the capability to dismember any hostile military coalition formed in Jordan. And while these systems were still top-secret, all members of our team knew that there was no longer any real military need to annex large portions of the Jordan Valley or to deploy significant forces in it. In addition, Jordan had maintained a tacit miliary alliance and security collaboration with Israel since the early 1970s (before the peace treaty of 1994), when Israel declared that any entry of military forces from Iraq or Syria into Jordan would be considered a declaration of of war. Indeed, in September 1970, it was Israel who deterred Syria from encroaching on Jordanian territory.

Furthermore, we intended that after we had concluded the FAPS with the Palestinians, we would negotiate an Israeli agreement *with Jordan* that would ensure the bilateral interests of our countries. (You can read more about this in Chapter 9.) That Israel-Jordan agreement was going to include a chapter on security, with arrangements for monitoring military deployments and even demilitarizing some border areas on the *Jordanian side*—all with the goal of ensuring long-term stability. None of these additional layers of security were detailed in the IDF threat assessments or influenced its suggested response. Instead, the full onus of Israel's security against an eastern front was placed on the Palestinians.

For Sher, Ben-Ami, and our negotiating team, the positions presented by the IDF were frustrating because of the politics that the IDF was playing with Barak. The IDF did not articulate "concerns" or "interests," as they should have, and instead put forward rigid positions. The military interest of circumventing an eastern front could have been served with Israeli sovereignty in the Jordan Valley, but also by American forces stationed between Palestine and Jordan. By presenting only one option, they tied the negotiators' hands. And there was no way for Sher to overrule Yanai or Mofaz.

Why would Barak—a former minister of defense and lieutenant general—allow the IDF to present Israel's security positions in a way that compromised his flexibility to negotiate? Polls revealed that the Israeli public wanted any Permanent Status agreement to include effective security arrangements. Therefore, Barak needed Mofaz and his senior officers—primarily Yanai, the chief of the Central Command overseeing the West Bank, the commander of the Air Force, and the head of intelligence—as well as influential veterans of the IDF and other security services to endorse the FAPS. In other words, Barak's dependence on his senior officers gave them power over him.

In truth, these positions served Barak's political interests at least until March 2000 during the Syria negotiations. But when the backchannel in Sweden began, Barak needed to direct the IDF to focus on Israel's actual security concerns. The power play between Barak and the IDF continued to unfold throughout his tenure. The military leadership knew that its positions would circumvent a FAPS because their own intelligence officers told them so. But it was more convenient for Mofaz and Yanai to have Barak be the "bad guy" who rolled back the IDF's demands. Hence, as much as Barak wanted his generals to assume responsibility for the security arrangements of the FAPS, the IDF generals wanted Barak to assume that responsibility himself. Eventually, they got their way. The onus was placed on Barak.

Counterterrorism: Israeli Safety, Palestinian Security

> **FAPS Article 2: Relations Between Palestine and Israel [Provisions 13–14]**
>
> 13. ...the two states shall endeavor to ensure the <u>freedom of movement of persons, vehicles, goods and services</u>...
> 14. Without prejudice to the freedom of expression and other human rights ... Israel and Palestine shall <u>create the appropriate atmosphere for a long-term peace</u> and reconciliation by promulgating laws to put an <u>end to incitement</u> for terror and violence by vigorously enforcing them through the appropriate <u>programs in the respective education systems</u>.

"It's all bullshit. One big bullshit." I heard that sentence—in Hebrew, as in *"Ze ha'kol bullshit. Bullshit echad gadol"*—dozens of times during the Camp David negotiations. The speaker was Yisrael Hasson, the representative of the Shin Bet in our delegation, who was trying to synthesize for me what was really going on in the talks. He was cross-referencing what we heard from our interlocutors—when they spoke with pathos in front of their colleagues, or in side-conversations with us—and the ample intelligence he was receiving every day, which gave him insights into what they were saying in private and what was really happening on their side.

Hasson had already served as deputy director of the Shin Bet and head of its Jerusalem District, with prior postings in Gaza and Lebanon. As far as Shin Bet agents go, he'd seen it all, and was now contending for the top position in the organization. His family of 10 siblings—including a famous professor, a leading businessperson, and other high achievers—came from Haleb in Syria. He was "an Arabist," fluent in Arabic and in Arab and Palestinian customs, specializing in human intelligence, namely operating agents. Later, he would become a member of Knesset on behalf of Lieberman's right-wing party, and then the head of Israel's Antiquity Authority.

With his background, Hasson played a crucial role in the negotiations. He held countless informal conversations in Arabic with the Palestinian delegates, often during cigarette breaks and especially when we were traveling.

Like all intelligence officers, he focused on the underlying motivations and politicking on the Palestinian side, but sometimes he was very cynical about our side as well. It was up to him, together with Meidan-Shani, to "read the room" by deciphering the body language and gestures of the Palestinian side, to make sure that we really understood them, and to ensure that they correctly understood us, so that nothing was lost in translation.

Hasson probably saw me as a young talent that needed to be groomed to understand "real life." He was always patient with me, sharing his insights and analysis that focused on human dynamics. When he said: "Gidi, it's all bullshit..." he meant that it was all a show. And there was also a sociological undertone to his remarks. In our internal discourse, Sher and I, as well as Arieli, Crystal, Herzog, Reisner, and Yanai, were *"Ashkenazim,"* which meant western, European, English-speaking, or fair-skinned. It also meant, however, that we were overly logical, analytical, legalistic, sophisticated, prepared, or organized, and therefore often incapable of deeply understanding and effectively communicating and connecting with the Palestinian side. The term *Ashkenazim* could be used derogatively, lovingly, amicably, critically, seriously, or jokingly, depending on the circumstance, and sometimes it would insinuate all the above at once. Being an *"Ashkenazi"* reflected attitude more than origin: Ben-Ami, Morocco-born and an Oxford and Tel Aviv University professor of history, who spoke in English with a perfect British accent; Arieli; and Ephraim Lavie, our intelligence officer, were included among the *"Ashkenazim,"* despite their Middle Eastern origin, while Meidan-Shani—a former Mossad agent and an Arabist—was excluded from that identity tag, although his family came from Europe.

Mohammed Dahlan—also known as Abu Fadi, named after his eldest son, Fadi—led the security negotiations for the Palestinian side. He had grown up in a refugee camp in Gaza, joined the Fatah Hawks during the first uprising, and spent time in Israeli jails before joining the PLO leadership in Tunis. With loads of street smarts and charisma, he rose to become head of the PA's Preventive Security in Gaza, which was responsible for monitoring internal insurgencies and for Arafat's personal safety. In that capacity, he developed close collaboration with the security services of Israel, Egypt, and the U.S., because all of them had an interest in the stability of the PA and in Arafat's longevity.

By 2000, Dahlan had become a rich and powerful man. He struck a close business partnership with Arafat's economic advisor, Mohammed Rashid, and former Shin Bet agent Yossi Ginossar. Together, the trio were rumored to split commissions for facilitating movement of goods between Israel and the PA. During the negotiations, Dahlan maintained the charismatic manner- isms of a street leader, except he was now wearing tailored suits and expen- sive watches and ascending from position as a military and security leader to being a national political figure who positioned himself to contend for PLO leadership. After Arafat's death, he became the leader of Fatah in Gaza and a bitter rival of Hamas, until the Hamas coup in 2007, when his people were brutalized, and he had to flee to Ramallah. A few years later he also chal- lenged Abu Mazen, and he eventually wound up living a comfortable life in Abu Dhabi.

Dahlan's co-delegates accepted his natural leadership, and he would often act as the leader of the delegation, although Abed-Rabbo or Erakat were for- mally its heads. We used to refer to Dahlan and Rashid as the "Young Turks"— inferring the legendary political group of Kemal Ataturk, which modernized Turkey in the 1920s—since they were challenging the old guard of the PLO to be pragmatic and modernize. We appreciated his directness and pragma- tism, and particularly liked the nonchalant way Dahlan would dismiss some of the legalistic ideas that came from the Palestinian Negotiation Support Unit (NSU), which tended to be purist, impractical, and often simply radical.

In June 2000, at Bolling Air Force Base, Dahlan and I struck up a conver- sation. He mistook me for being tech-savvy and said, "I want to buy Fadi a laptop computer." Back in 2000, they were an expensive toy. I suggested that it would be better to buy a brand that could be serviced in Gaza, to which he replied: "Don't worry. If it breaks, we'll get a new one." Years later I read that Fadi was a businessperson in Abu Dhabi, specializing, among other things, in Bitcoin.

If the IDF held the file of military security, the Shin Bet, Israel's general secu- rity service (also known as the SHABAK), led the file on personal security and anti-terrorism. The initial days of the Oslo Process and the establishment of the PA in 1994 required a radical shift within the Shin Bet from seeing the Palestinians as adversaries to working with them as partners. Palestinian prisoners, who were convicted for terrorism and other military and political activities, were released from Israeli jails to become commanders and leaders of the PA's newly established security forces. At once, former enemies needed to work side by side against a common enemy, radical Islamists.

That partnership was tested in the spring of 1994, when Hamas and Islamic Jihad orchestrated a wave of suicide bombings that killed nearly 140 Israelis and wounded many more. Israel demanded decisive preventive action against the terrorists, but Arafat refused to unleash his forces against other Palestinians. While he cited fears of a civil war, he also hoped to create some leverage over Israel through his measured response to the violence, favoring a softer approach such as by "recruiting" militants to the Palestinian police to co-opt them. In its frustration, Israel began to take more aggressive action within Palestinian areas, including arrests and even killing of militants and terrorists.

That gap in approach irreversibly changed the course of the Oslo Process, since Israel no longer saw the Palestinian side as "friends" and allies but rather as "frenemies," a portmanteau word combining "friends" and "enemies." Unfortunately, the "frenemy-ness" of the Palestinian forces was often on full display. For most of the three decades of the Oslo Process, significant security collaboration led to countless operational successes in preventing terrorism. But in a few cases—such as in October 1996, May 2000, or during the early part of the war as of October 2000—Palestinian police used their guns against Israelis.

Israel's approach to Permanent Status was shaped by the experiences of the Interim Period. Our trauma was the campaign of terror that came from the Palestinian side in 1994–1996, and our primary goal was to prevent a recurrence of that experience. So the challenge facing the Shin Bet, together with the IDF, was monumental. It included the design and operation of the future border apparatus between Israel and Palestine along a convoluted line of hundreds of kilometers, as well as the Safe Passage and Palestine's external perimeter—all with their fences, barriers, crossing points, and monitoring and verification tools. It also included significant collaboration with Palestinian law-enforcement agencies and the regulation of "hot pursuits" of terrorists escaping from Israel into Palestinian areas and preventive security operations within Palestine.

These arrangements have profound political implications. For instance, for the Palestinians, a Safe Passage with unchecked movement would demonstrate the "integrity" of Palestine, while overburdening security arrangements would be seen as "continued occupation" and delegitimize the agreement. For the Israeli side, a physical barrier within Jerusalem would depart from the pledge to keep Jerusalem unified and open, while adequate monitoring arrangements at the entry and exit points to Palestine were essential for ratifying the FAPS. These issues were formative for the openness of the Israeli-Palestinian space to movement of people and goods. And while security negotiations created many clashes over sovereign rights, they also highlighted shared interests. Most important, it was in Palestine's long-term security interest to address Israel's short-term security needs, because if Israelis would not be safe, Palestine would not be secured.

When tackling these dilemmas, we had the Interim Agreement of 1995 and the experience of implementing it as an important reference point. For example, the Shin Bet was physically present, behind blackened glass, in the Palestinian crossing points to Jordan and Egypt (before Hamas' takeover), with access to lists of passengers and goods. That arrangement seemed to be working well. In addition, hundreds of "hot pursuits" were carried out in collaboration with Palestinian intelligence and security forces, and without destabilizing the PA.

Both sides also got much better at facilitating movement of goods, services, labor, and businesspeople. Although there is always room for improvement, by 2000, cross-border arrangements had become reliable, sophisticated, and technologically advanced to a level at which flowers from Gaza would be sold in Europe within 48 hours. In the mid-1990s, sniffing dogs would check for explosives, and when they needed to rest their noses, the crossing point would be shut down. Fast-forward to 2023, and container-size screening machines and robust security protocols allow for uninterrupted shipping of goods from Europe via Israel to the PA, Jordan, and the Arab world.

Israel's approach to security in Permanent Status was practical: if it isn't broken, don't fix it. Namely, the procedures that were already working well during the Interim Period could stay in place, perhaps with some necessary adjustments such as in the Jerusalem area. But the Palestinians' national pride mandated pushing Israel out of monitoring the Safe Passage or the perimeter.

That approach would have required wholesale changes to existing security arrangements, forcing a separation between the economies and a division of Jerusalem. It also highlighted the paradox that the Palestinians faced: given the imbalance of power and the absolute economic dependency of Palestine on Israel, Israel's safety was essential for Palestinian security and prosperity.

Not much ended up happening among Yanai, Hasson, Dahlan, and Rajoub on the security front. With no directive from Barak or Arafat on the type of border in Jerusalem, the nature of the Safe Passage, or Israel's ability to monitor the Palestinian perimeter, there was no framework for negotiations on security in Permanent Status. Nonetheless, the longest-lasting collaboration created by the Oslo Process has been in the area of security.

Palestinian Prisoners

Sharm Memorandum, Article 3: Release of Prisoners

3b.   ...Israel shall release Palestinian and other prisoners who committed their offences prior to September 13, 1993, and were arrested prior to May 4, 1994.

3c.   The first stage ... on September 5, 1999 ... 200 prisoners. The second stage ... on October 8, 1999 ... 150 prisoners;

3d-e The joint committee shall recommend further lists of names to be released ... The Israeli side will aim to release Palestinian prisoners before next Ramadan.

Clinton Ideas: The End of Conflict

... the agreement clearly marks the end of the conflict and its implementation put an end to all claims. This could be implemented through ... the release of Palestinian prisoners.

Throughout the Permanent Status negotiations, we were upset with the Palestinians for refusing to accept the framework of End of Conflict and Finality of Claims or committing to its implications. But on one issue that was central to the Palestinians—release of more than 10,000 prisoners detained in Israeli prisons—the same was true of Israel: we refused to commit to their release.

For Palestinians, their prisoners are living symbols of their national struggle and a testament to the heavy-handedness and injustices of Israel's "occupation." Erekat once told us that every extended Palestinian family had at least one member in an Israeli jail at any given moment. While we could not confirm his claim, it largely made sense: one of every 500 Palestinians was in our prison system for offenses ranging from membership in illegal associations, stone throwing, demonstrations, incitement, attacks on military targets, support of terrorist activities, or even planning and carrying out brutal murders and mass-casualty terrorist activities. Regardless of their party affiliation, freeing prisoners was a national cause highlighted by powerful pressure groups as a test for the ability of Fatah, led by Arafat, to serve all Palestinians.

During the Netanyahu government, no prisoners were released before the end of their terms, so the issue of prisoner release was a top priority for Arafat coming into the negotiations on the Sharm Memorandum. The Palestinian side initially wanted Israel to release nearly 2,000 prisoners, but Barak negotiated them down to 350 veteran ones, less than 5 percent of all prisoners. A key argument Israel made was that Permanent Status negotiations were soon coming, and release of all prisoners could be discussed then; this was a rehashing of a similar argument that was made in 1995 ahead of the Interim Agreement. But after signing the Sharm Memorandum, Barak turned his attention to Syria and stalled Permanent Status negotiations for nearly 10 months. Meanwhile, the frustrated Palestinian side repeatedly asked that Israel release more prisoners as an act of goodwill to help calm the anger bubbling on the Palestinian streets. But Barak did not want to risk the stability of his coalition and rejected these requests.

Come May, the Palestinian side entered Permanent Status negotiations with a chip on their shoulder, feeling that they were tricked by Israel into keeping most prisoners in jail during the Oslo Process and for far longer than they were led to agree to. Now they presented an unyielding demand that all prisoners must be released upon the signing of a *FAPS* for its ratification to go through their parliament. That position was notwithstanding Arafat's position that End of Conflict would be declared only upon the full implementation of the *CAPS*. On that point, Clinton chose a middle ground, promising full release of prisoners but remaining vague regarding the timing:

Would it be upon the signing of the FAPS, or upon declaring Finality of Claims?

While refusing small gestures, Israel informally acknowledged that many, perhaps most, prisoners would be released upon the signing of the FAPS and the declaration of End of Conflict, perhaps as early as September 13, 2000. Clearly, all those imprisoned for minor offenses would be let go, and many others as well. But we would not discuss exact numbers, rejected ever releasing murderous terrorists, and refused to even negotiate with the PLO the release of Arab-Israelis.

We clung to these positions, although we knew their weaknesses all too well and that they would have to be compromised for a FAPS to be finalized. First and foremost, there were multiple precedents of Israel releasing many prisoners, including terrorists and Arab-Israelis, in exchange for hostages or kidnapped soldiers. The record in this respect was set by the Netanyahu Government in 2011, when it released to Hamas some 1,027 prisoners for one Israeli soldier, Gilad Shalit. But all Israeli governments had refused to do the same for the PA and the PLO, with whom we were collaborating on security and negotiating peace. Indeed, the Palestinian side used to cynically joke with us that "Israel only understands power," which is what we used to say of them...

Palestinian National Security and Finality of Claims

In hindsight, the strangest aspect of the security talks was that Palestinian concerns were neither presented nor discussed, except in response to our demands. Oslo A mentioned that security would be negotiated toward a Permanent Status agreement, and everyone seemed to assume that Israel's concerns would shape that discussion. But Palestinians had their concerns, and they are entitled to their own vision of the national security of Palestine.

The gap in professional capabilities was again striking. Israel had an entire apparatus—including the national security council, the strategic planning branch of the IDF, the politico-military department in the ministry of defense, and the planning unit of the ministry of foreign affairs, as well as multiple think tanks and academics—that relied on thousands of professionals. Meanwhile the Palestinian side was led by former resistance fighters and current counterterrorist security men. We identified only one scholar, Prof.

Yezid Sayigh, as well as the work of Khalidi and Agha, as thought leaders on this topic for the Palestinians. My guess is that the Palestinian side had never articulated their own framework for their national security, and, as in other areas, they evolved their positions in response to ours. Certainly, there was no trace of any comprehensive approach in the intelligence we received.

For the Palestinian side, the overwhelming military strength of the IDF was a reality that could not be challenged. Therefore, the foundation of their national security was going to be the agreement with Israel, which would establish permanent borders for Palestine and be enshrined in international law. In this vein, assurances from leading nations for the implementation of the Permanent Status agreements would be critical. That is why it was "easy" for the PLO to agree to the demilitarization of their future state and to a "non-military Palestinian Police and Security Force."

Nonetheless, their approach to the national security of Palestine was full of paradoxes. First, they held "occupation" to be the biggest impediment to the security of Palestinians, compromising their well-being, infringing on their self-government, and preventing any progress on the refugee issue. Hence, they wanted to end occupation as soon as possible, but the continuation of occupation was their biggest leverage on Israel. So they were torn between these conflicting logics. Furthermore, Palestine and Israel will always be interconnected in key areas such as security, environment, economics, water, holy sites, and Jerusalem. Hence, for the Palestinians, the opposite of "occupation" is not full "independence" from Israel, but rather a healthy interdependence with Israel.

They also believed that the biggest threat to Palestine would come from Israel. Therefore, acknowledging and addressing Israel's security concerns was essential for Palestine. In that respect, the interests of both states were aligned. But at what price? How should the PLO balance accommodating Israeli demands and maintaining Palestinian dignity and the legitimacy of their government? Take, for example, monitoring the perimeter of Palestine: while it may seem to violate Palestinian sovereignty, it is also essential for Palestinian security and prosperity that Israel's far superior capabilities be used to prevent terrorism, thereby alleviating some responsibility on Palestine's part.

The challenge for the Palestinians was Israel's excessive security demands that breached Palestinian sovereignty beyond the essentials: land corridors, safe passages through Palestine, military sites on mountaintops, sovereignty in the Jordan Valley, control of the perimeter, use of airspace, management of the electromagnetic sphere, and right for "hot pursuits." For Palestinian negotiators and politicians, these demands amounted to an unacceptable package of concessions. In matters of security, then, the Palestinians too needed some finality of claims. In other words, Israel could be the biggest threat to Palestinian security, but also its guarantor, allowing Palestine to be like Costa Rica, whose military was disbanded in 1948: without the need for an army, the country is free to focus on its economic and social development.

The Palestinian dilemma has only grown worse since 2000. Arafat combined diplomacy with violence beginning in the late 1980s. He authorized a diplomatic process toward a Palestinian state alongside Israel while allowing for so-called armed resistance and even terrorist activities. We summarized the idea in a pithy statement: Arafat kept the dog of terrorism on a leash, extended or shortened as he saw fit. By the late 1990s, during the tenures of Netanyahu (1996–1999) and Barak (1999–2001), Israel grew weary of Arafat's behavior, particularly after the wave of terrorism in 1994–1996. Israel insisted on determined security measures against terror groups as a precondition for further political progress. But Arafat avoided doing so, flipping the equation and insisting that political progress toward Palestinian statehood was a precondition for such resolute action in the service of Israel's security. These conflicting conditions put Israel and Arafat on a collision course.

Meanwhile, Clinton and CIA director George Tenet, as well as the EU, tried to balance the conflicting demands. They repeatedly asked Arafat "to do more in fighting terrorism," and he promised to do so. But when Arafat broke his pledge, our allies would sympathize with his "political constraints" and ask Israel to minimize its response. Meanwhile, we knew from our intelligence that Arafat would not hesitate to make false promises and even lie to his Israeli, American, European, and Egyptian interlocutors about his intentions and actions. This give-and-take imploded on September 28, 2000, when the Israeli-Palestinian war, commonly referred to as the Second Palestinian Uprising, broke out. Still, the U.S. and the EU continued to try to restore some semblance of calm, and they convinced Barak to hold back the IDF and to give political negotiations a chance to resolve the conflict. As late as January 2001, amidst ongoing violence, Clinton still hoped to hammer out the Clinton Ideas as a framework for future negotiations on Permanent Status.

This policy changed when Sharon became prime minister in March 2001 and President Bush refused to play Arafat's double game. In April 2001, the IDF intercepted a large weapons shipment from Iran that was headed to the PA. With that, Bush was done with Arafat. In March 2002, following a string of horrific suicide bombings in Israel, Sharon ordered the IDF to invade the PA and weed out terrorists. As of September, Sharon laid siege to Arafat's headquarters in the Mukataa in Ramallah, and the siege continued until Arafat departed the PA for the last time in October 2004. A month later, he died in exile in Paris.

When Abu Mazen succeeded Arafat in November 2004, he quickly transformed the concept of Palestinian national security by ceasing the armed struggle in favor of diplomacy and nonviolent resistance. Abu Mazen had supported a historic compromise with Israel and opposed the armed struggle for nearly 20 years, and the Israeli side knew that he was deeply frustrated by Arafat's approach. He believed that international legitimacy—support from the global community for Palestinian demands—would propel the Palestinian national struggle toward statehood within the 1967 borders. Now, in power and dealing with the trauma of the IDF's re-conquest of Palestinian cities in 2002, Abu Mazen convinced his security services that terrorism was a bigger threat to Palestinians than to Israel. For most of the following years, PA security services would fight terrorism, often in collaboration with Israel and even when political negotiations were blocked during the Netanyahu and Trump administrations.

Alas, Abu Mazen's big bet on diplomacy and nonviolence seems to have failed the Palestinian struggle. At this writing in 2023, Abu Mazen is 87, and a Permanent Status agreement seems to be unlikely, as is Palestinian independence; Hamas controls Gaza; Israeli presence in the West Bank and Jerusalem has expanded; contiguity of Palestinian territory is increasingly compromised; and Jewish presence on al-Harem al-Sharif has increased. Therefore, while the PA in the West Bank has enjoyed relative peace and economic prosperity for nearly 20 years, it has also experienced significant setbacks to its national goals of statehood, territorial integrity, sovereignty, and the designation of Al-Quds as its capital.

Meanwhile, Hamas has been promulgating an alternative model for Palestinian national security by defying and rejecting Israel. Around Gaza, a new equilibrium has emerged that is in essence an informal Hudna. Israel now acknowledges the reality of a Hamas government and no longer seeks to topple it, allowing it to be funded in cash by Qatar and facilitating movement of goods, labor, and businesspeople across the border. As of the spring of 2023, thousands of Gazans cross to Israel daily. In return, Hamas helps to keep the border quiet, while Israel has built defenses above and below ground. Hamas seems to be inching toward a similar path of coexistence with Israel, like the one that Fatah took in the 1980s: de-facto recognition of Israel's *existence* without abandoning the commitment to the struggle with Israel and to the PLO's Phased Plan.

As I've discussed earlier, Gaza and the West Bank remain fundamentally different in one crucial sense. Around Gaza, Israel is deployed along the 1967 Lines, defines Gaza as "foreign territory," and has no claim to any of it. This means that an independent Palestinian polity has emerged in Gaza—namely in a portion of "historic Palestine"—with tacit Israeli recognition. That, of course, is a very significant move toward a reality of two-states-for-two-people.

No End of Conflict

Barak's directive to seek End of Conflict and Finality of Claims in declaratory and practical terms could be achieved with regard to borders, but not to security. Friction between Israel and Palestine was likely to continue in Permanent Status because of their different interests and since many Palestinians, backed by Iran, were still pledged to the struggle against Israel.

Hence, in the absence of a feasible End of Conflict, Israel wanted to use the conclusion of the FAPS as an opportunity to enhance its long-term security guarantees. The Clinton administration all but pledged to renew and upgrade America's commitment to Israel's security with an annual multi-billion-dollar package of support that would preserve Israel's technological superiority. Clinton also indicated his willingness to grant an additional special package of aid—which we estimated at $60 billion over 20 years—to underwrite the relocating of the IDF and settlers out of the West Bank, bolster Israel's intelligence and defense systems, and build modern fences and state-of-the-art crossing points. Furthermore, an American force deployed along the Jordan River and acting as a "tripwire" against an attack from the east would have been a tremendous asset for long-term peace.

On a diplomatic level, it was assumed that peace with the Palestinians would boost Israel's legitimacy and further diminish Israel's detractors. We expected a warming of peace with Egypt and Jordan and new treaties with Saudi Arabia, Morocco, Gulf states, and other Muslim nations such as Malaysia and Indonesia, which would dramatically increase Israel's diplomatic stature and open vast markets for its exports and investments. In fact, all of this happened when Israel signed the Abraham Accords with Morocco, the UAE, and Bahrain in 2020.

Still, the primary benefits were supposed to accrue on the level of Israel's national security. At the cost of withdrawal from ancestral lands, the threat of a so-called One-State Solution would finally and irreversibly be quashed. Furthermore, Zionism, as the national movement of the Jewish People, would get the ultimate stamp of approval from its primary adversary, the Palestinian national movement. Delineating permanent borders with Palestine would leave only those with Syria undetermined. A journey of nearly 20 centuries of exile would be over, and the 120-year struggle of the Jewish national movement would come to an epic close with the Jewish People in possession of a defined, undisputed space to call their own.

Sadly, today these goals seem to be a dream. An agreement on Permanent Status iI unlikely; Hamas-controlled Gaza is armed to the teeth, making the demilitarization of Palestine unrealistic, and the firing of rockets from Gaza seems to make a withdrawal from the West Bank impractical. In other words, the conundrum of Israeli and Palestinian security has only grown more complex. True, the Abraham Accords— although signed without the Palestinians—represent a significant achievement. Still, they too may be upended by the ongoing instability between Israel and the Palestinians.

Barak, a Lefty?

Barak came out of his two-year tenure in office a beaten politician. With a handful of exceptions, most accounts of his leadership were scathing. The left accused him of not going far enough in his overtures and then falsely concluding that Israel didn't have a partner for peace at this time. Meanwhile, the right despised Barak for his willingness to give up too much, or anything at all. And everyone blamed him for the war that erupted in 2000.

From my perspective, Barak's approach of seeking a FAPS with End of Conflict and Finality of Claims was the only viable path available to him in the complicated circumstances of 1999–2001, with one caveat: he should have allowed Arafat to declare statehood in May 2000.

Many outsiders believe that Israelis are divided by their political views regarding the settlements. They assume that right-wing Israelis support them and object to any territorial compromise, while left-wing Israelis support withdrawals. The reality is more nuanced: many leftists view Judea and Samaria as ancestral lands, would never willingly give away the City of David, and would fight to include the settlement blocs within Israel. Meanwhile, even among the moderate right wing, there is an understanding that settlements which compromise Palestinian contiguity are contrary to Israel's interests. Barak embraced these dichotomies, attempting to inspire a new centrist political bloc that would rechart the course of Israel's history. Clearly, that did not happen.

CHAPTER 7

FAPS Articles 4 and 4A: Jerusalem and the Holy Sites

Explosion at Bolling Air Force Base

In mid-December of 2000, the Israeli and Palestinian delegations convened at Bolling Air Force Base (BAFB) near Washington, D.C. to get the political process back on track. With Barak's tenure clearly sunsetting and Clinton's term scheduled to end in two months, Dennis Ross, Special Middle East Coordinator under President Clinton and the leader of the American Peace Team, framed the situation to both sides: "There is one last bullet in the barrel."

Three months earlier, in September, we had a most promising week of deliberations, which began with a great meeting between Barak and Arafat and continued with fruitful discussions in Washington. But then, on September 28, Sharon's visit to Temple Mount triggered a chain of events that led to an all-out war, which unfolded in parallel to ongoing diplomatic efforts to end violence and resume the peace process. The story of these dramatic events is detailed in chapter 11, *The Butterfly Effects that Changed the Middle East*.

Now, at last, we thought that there might be "ripeness" to finalize a draft FAPS that could be ratified in a referendum or in a general election. Barak was seeking to cement his historical legacy and needed a platform for the imminent elections. Arafat wanted to consolidate his astonishing diplomatic achievements of the past few months. He was within reach of a state based on the 1967 Lines with Al-Quds as its capital and an economic package of $20 billion dollars to kick it off. Clinton sincerely wanted Israel and the PLO

143

to reach peace, but he was also eyeing a crowning diplomatic achievement worthy of a Nobel Prize. He pledged to spend his remaining days in office in pursuit of this goal. The scene was set for an American-led final act of supreme diplomacy. Again, as in August-September, we were looking toward a possible second summit.

It was clear that we needed to resume the discussion of Jerusalem if we wanted to prepare a summit and achieve a FAPS. In July, at Camp David, and since then, Israel's offer regarding Jerusalem had crystallized. We suggested that the area of Jerusalem would include the capitals of Israel and Palestine; Arab neighborhoods would be Palestinian and Jewish neighborhoods will be Israeli; there would be a special regime in the Holy Basin, which includes the Old City and Temple Mount, whereby the Palestinian areas would be associated with Palestine, but Israel would have overall security control. But that was not enough for a deal. The Palestinians wanted sovereignty over Temple Mount and had a few other demands.[32] We were at a standoff. Another clinch was needed.

The overture was made by Ben-Ami. He began one of the working sessions at BAFB by framing the conversation as a "noncommittal exchange of theoretical ideas about possible arrangements in the Old City and on Temple Mount." He stressed that he was presenting "his ideas," which ventured beyond the mandate given to him by Barak. This gave the prime minister plausible deniability. Ben-Ami then observed that both sides needed a "safe space" to honestly discuss their "needs" and explore the zone of possible agreement.

Ben-Ami acknowledged that both parties were deeply attached to the Holy Basin, the Old City, and Temple Mount, so peace required a surgical division of sovereignty, powers, and responsibilities. Focusing on Temple Mount, he suggested some upstairs-downstairs ideas. Upstairs, above the massive stone platform that upholds the mosques, Palestine would be the sovereign, but it would designate a space for Jewish prayer—a very large open-air synagogue of sorts. This would be significant for Israel because, at the time, there were no Jewish prayers on Temple Mount at all. He also suggested that Israel would "own" the space beneath the platform, where the holy of holies

---

32   Sher, *Within Reach*, Ibid, p. 82.

of the Jewish Temple was buried, emphasizing that the Palestinians could never "excavate" there. This was a stunning proposal, and it surprised even the Israelis in the room.

Ben-Ami expected the Palestinian side to appreciate his openness and engage in a good- faith exchange of ideas around his incredible offer. But his overture was rejected by Abed- Rabbo and Asfour, who refused to limit Palestinian sovereignty on al-Harem al-Sharif and to accept Israel's claim to the space beneath the mosques. They reiterated Arafat's agreement that the Jewish People, aka Israel, would own the Kotel and the Jewish Quarter, and that this should be enough. They went on to accuse Israel of exaggerating the Jewish affiliation to Temple Mount to deny their own claims to the place. Simply put, their narrative largely excluded ours.

Incredibly, this was the second time that we had encountered such an arrogant or ignorant Palestinian position. At Camp David, they similarly rejected the authenticity of our connection to Temple Mount. Then too, Ben-Ami could not believe what he was hearing, and the meeting deteriorated into a heated exchange. In a moment of calm, Ben-Ami—an Oxford historian by training—noticed an Oxford Dictionary of Religions on the bookshelf and opened it to the term "Jerusalem." The entry referred to the Jewish People dozens of times, to Islam a few times, and to the Palestinians once.

The discussion of Jerusalem at BAFB quickly deteriorated into a multi-party vein-popping screaming match, the worst that I witnessed during the Camp David negotiations. Ben-Ami was furious and spoke harshly to the Palestinians. As a historian, he was intellectually offended, unable to fathom a Palestinian position that was so disrespectful of Jewish history. As an aspiring politician, Ben-Ami was now badly exposed, having gone out on a limb only to be left hanging. He respected and liked Barak, but he could also easily imagine being thrown under the bus if the news of his proposals became public. For starters, Ben-Ami was certain that Peres—his intra-party nemesis, who was now maneuvering to seize the leadership of the peace negotiations and the Labor Party ahead of the coming election—would eagerly tarnish him. Things quickly got personal to a point where Abed-Rabbo stormed out of the room threatening to leave BAFB altogether.

These events threw our delegation into a major internal crisis. Hasson, backed by Meidan-Shani, was as upset with Ben-Ami as he was with the Palestinians. He believed that Ben-Ami had breached Barak's mandate and accused him of compromising national interests for party politics. Chain-smoking and fuming, Hasson also criticized Ben-Ami for positing his ideas with the wrong Palestinian interlocutors, who had no mandate to even engage on Jerusalem, thereby "wasting" whatever idea he wanted to explore. This near-meltdown scene was unfolding in the street because we assumed that our residences were wiretapped and because the smokers needed to puff on their cigarettes. Hasson said he would resign from the delegation, and he withdrew from any further formal engagement with the Palestinians or the Americans. Of course, he continued to hang out with some of the Palestinians in their smoking huddles, using the opportunity to retrack Ben-Ami's ideas. Meidan-Shani did the same with the Americans.

Obviously, Hasson, and anyone except Sher, could not have known whether Ben-Ami was acting in sync with Barak. Sher wrote in his book that he had an honest and difficult conversation with Ben-Ami about staying within their mandate. But Ben-Ami claims that Barak's directive was broad and effectively allowed for such "explorations." Years later, Barak said that Sher and Ben-Ami went "beyond their mandate," but he never condemned them for doing so.

We don't know why the Palestinians responded the way they did. They were certainly surprised by Ben-Ami's ideas and must have understood how unprecedented they were. Hasson is probably right that they had no mandate to discuss Jerusalem beyond reiterating the formal mandate they received from Arafat. Perhaps they feared that Ben-Ami's "theoretical exercise" was a trick to expose their flexibilities, or perhaps it was sheer ignorance. But it is also true that they were forever suspicious of each other and did not want to be seen as weak on Jerusalem, a judgment that could terminate their political careers and place them and their families at risk. Furthermore, Ben-Ami's ideas required a nuanced acquaintance with the compound of Temple Mount, while we knew that the Palestinians were superficially prepared, at best.

Status Quo at the Holy Basin and the Old City

Printable maps at https://printable-maps.blogspot.com/2011/04/map-of-old-city-of-jerusalem.html

---

FAPS Article 4A: Holy Sites [Provisions 39–42]

39. The Parties are committed to the <u>freedo</u>m of worship in and access
    to holy sites subject to the requirement of public order …
40. The <u>Al-Haram Al-Sharif / Har HaBait / Temple Mou</u>nt and the
    <u>Haram Al-Ibrahimi / Me'arat HaMachpela / Tomb of the Patriarchs</u>
    are subject to <u>divine providence</u> and holy to Jews and Muslims alike.
41. The right of access to and worship in them will be guaranteed by the
    two states … There shall be freedom of worship in the Holy Sites …
42. There shall be freedom of access to holy sites in Jerusalem.

An elusive status quo is the ultimate reference point when it comes to discussing the future of Jerusalem. The challenge is that the status quo is not static and continuously evolves. It takes years of learning to fully understand its complexity, primarily at the Holy Basin. At three square kilometers, the Holy Basin encompasses the Old City and the Temple Mount within it; the City of David (*Silwan* to the Palestinians) to the south of the Old City, where the ancient capital of Israel built by King David has been excavated beneath a Palestinian-Jewish neighborhood; the Kidron Valley to the east, where Jesus

last prayed before his crucifixion; and the western slope of the Mount of
Olives, which overlooks the Old City and is covered by a huge Jewish cemetery and gorgeous church compounds that belong to the Russian Orthodox,
the Greek Orthodox and the Coptic Orthodox Church. Some of these structures are centuries old, dating to the Muslim and Crusader eras.

The Old City itself covers 0.9 square kilometers and houses more than
30,000 people, making it one of the most densely populated areas in the
world. It was walled by the Ottoman Empire in the 17th century and is
divided into four quarters: the Muslim Quarter in the northeast is the largest; the Christian Quarter in the northwest includes the Church of the Holy
Sepulcher; the Armenian Quarter in the southwest is the smallest; and Temple
Mount—al-Haram al-Sharif to Muslims and Har Ha'Bayit to Jews—occu-
pies the southeast corner. The Jewish Quarter is located among the Armenian
Quarter to the west, the Muslim Quarter to the north, and Temple Mount
to the east.

Temple Mount itself is roughly as large as the entire Christian Quarter.
Its monumental platform, built by Herod in the beginning of the first century, covers 37 acers and was built to support the awesome Second Temple,
which was one of the most magnificent buildings in the Roman Empire.
That platform now upholds two large mosques: the Dome of the Rock with
its golden cover that is the symbol of Jerusalem, and the Al-Aqsa Mosque.
The entire structure is the third holiest site in Islam, and its underground
space, known as Solomon's Stables, serves as another mosque, which can also
accommodate thousands.

The sacredness of Temple Mount to Judaism and Islam emanates from
the belief that God began the creation of the world from the Foundation
Stone, which is located under the Dome of the Rock. This is also where
Abraham bound Isaac before withholding the sacrifice. That legacy led King
Solomon, son of King David, to build the First Temple in that location circa
1000 BCE; it was destroyed by the Assyrians in 586 BCE. Seventy years later,
the Second Temple was built by the returning Jewish exiles on top of the
ruins of the First Temple. At the beginning of the first century, Herod rebuilt
the Second Temple. Its environs were the scene of Jesus's preaching and his

walk down Via Dolorosa to the nearby place of his crucifixion, where the Church of the Holy Sepulcher now stands.

Herod's structure was destroyed shortly thereafter by the Romans in 70 CE, and Jerusalem remained in ruins and poverty for centuries. In 632, it became a holy place for Islam with the legendary ascendence of the Prophet Mohammed to heaven from that same Foundation Stone. In the 11th century, Jerusalem's Muslim rulers built the two giant and magnificent mosques on the Herodian platform; they are still there. Altogether, some 1.9 billion Muslims, 2.6 billion Christians, and 16 million Jews, hold Jerusalem to be a sacred spiritual place.

The Herodian Platform is supported by four imposing walls, built of massive carved limestone blocks that were shipped from a nearby quarry and perfectly fit together. The blocks at the base of the wall are estimated to weigh as much as 20 tons and have withstood powerful earthquakes. The Western Wall of the compound is 457 meters long. One of its sections, 70 meters in length, is known as the Kotel, which means "the side wall." It is Judaism's holiest site since it was accessible to worshippers, who could pray close to the inaccessible ruins of the Second Temple and the Holy of Holies. The Kotel is bounded by Robinson's Arch to the south and by the Muslim Quarter to the north, but in recent years the spaces under the built-up Muslim Quarter were excavated, cleared, and opened to the public. They now serve as additional prayer halls.

Life in the Old City and on Temple Mount is shaped by ancient and longstanding traditions, as well as by a dynamic power struggle between Israel and the Palestinians. Most significantly, the government of Israel and the Jerusalem municipality have undertaken massive construction projects within and around the Holy Basin, and particularly in the Jewish Quarter. Areas of prayer for Jews have been expanded, and Jewish nonprofits and individuals are acquiring real estate in the non-Jewish quarters of the Old City and in key locations in Arab neighborhoods. Even Sharon owned a home in the Muslim Quarter, and small Jewish enclaves exist in Silwan above the City of David, Sheikh Jarrah and on the Mount of Olives. Furthermore, a popular Israeli movement is successfully increasing Jewish and Israeli visits to and prayers on Temple Mount itself—an area that used to be off-limits for religious Jews and most Israelis.

In addition, there has been a monumental effort to expose and prove the Jewish connection to Jerusalem. Extensive archeological excavations unfold, most notably, in the Kotel Tunnels, underneath the Western Wall and the Muslim Quarter; in the Davidson Park along the southern Wall; and underneath Silwan, where the City of David is being uncovered after lying in ruins for more than 1,900 years. Millions of tourists have now visited these sites and have the proof that Jews have a deeply rooted affiliation to Jerusalem and to Temple Mount, which makes Arafat's denial of that relationship laughable. At the same time, the Waqf—the religious Muslim trusteeship that manages al-Harem al-Sharif—has cleared the spaces underneath the Herodian platform known as Solomon's Stables, violating all best practices of archeology. Their goal was to eliminate any archeological trace of Jewish connection to that space and establish ownership of it by using the space as a large mosque. Their political objective was to preempt Ben-Ami's upstairs-downstairs idea for the Permanent Status of Jerusalem, which was described at the start of this chapter.

Names in Jerusalem keep changing too. Until the early twentieth century, the Arab population called Temple Mount by the name *Beit Al-Makdas*, which is an Arabic translation of the Hebrew term *Beit HaMikdash* and means House of Worship. That name references the First and Second Temples and fully acknowledges the Jewish history of that place. When the Palestinian national movement gained momentum in the 1920s, the name was changed to *al-Haram al-Sharif* (the noble sanctuary). In more recent decades, Palestinians have referred to the site as the *al-Aqsa Mosque*, inferring that the entire compound is a holy site and a huge mosque.

This background is essential for understanding what was at stake during the Camp David negotiations and why the status of Jerusalem was, and remains, one of the most complex diplomatic issues in the world. Reaching peace in Jerusalem requires surgical arrangements to address demographic, political, religious, security, and economic needs. Indeed, Jerusalem remains at the heart of the Israeli-Palestinian conflict, and the issues seem more intractable today than they were in 2000.

Yerushalayim and Al-Quds

FAPS Article 4: Jerusalem, Hebron and Holy Sites [Provisions 31–37]

31. <u>The Zone of Jerusalem (ZOJ) shall consist of</u> the territories within the <u>Municipal boundaries</u> of Jerusalem <u>and the adjacent Palestinian- and Israeli-populated areas</u> such as Abu Dis, Eyzariya, Ar-Ram, Az-aZaim, and Ma'ale Edumin, Givat Ze'ev, Anata, Michmash, and Givon.

32. <u>The ZOJ shall consist of</u> territories <u>under recognized Israeli sovereignty</u>, territories under <u>recognized Palestinian sovereignty</u>, and certain areas of East Jerusalem whose permanent sovereign state … shall be negotiated for an agreed period.

33. … present arrangements shall be revised to provide Palestinian neighborhoods in East Jerusalem with functional responsibilities in agreed municipal speres including agreed partition of powers and responsibilities in planning, municipal services and zoning, public order and law enforcement … and dispute settlement.

34. The ZOJ shall contain the respectively <u>recognized capitals of Israel and Palestine</u>: The Israeli municipality of <u>Yerushalayim</u>, which within its <u>recognized Israeli sovereign territories</u>, shall serve as the <u>united undivided capital of Israel</u> and the <u>seat of the Palestinian Embassy to Israel</u>. The Palestinian municipality of <u>Al-Quds</u>, within its recognized <u>Palestinian sovereign territories</u>, shall serve as the <u>capital of Palestine</u> and the <u>seat of the Israeli Embassy to Palestine</u>.

35. The ZOJ shall be managed as <u>a functional, environmental, and economic whole</u>, whose <u>unity shall be preserved</u>. Its urban needs and other issues of common concern shall be managed through agreed institutions and mechanisms to be provided for in the CAPS.

36. Israel and Palestine will aim to guarantee the free and <u>unimpeded movement of persons, vehicles, and goods</u> in the ZOJ subject to agreed arrangements and procedures.

37. Israel and Palestine shall reach an agreement on <u>special security arrangements for the ZOJ</u> including entrance and exit control in light of the city's status and particularly security arrangements necessary for the protection of religious sites …

Clinton Ideas: Jerusalem

The general principle is that <u>Arab areas are Palestinian</u> and <u>Jewish ones are Israeli</u>. This would apply to the Old City as well. I urge the two sides to work on maps to create maximum contiguity for both sides.

Regarding <u>the Haram / Temple Mount</u>, I believe that the gaps are not related to practical administration but to the symbolic issues of sovereignty and to finding a way to accord respect to the religious beliefs of both sides.

I know you have been discussing a number of formulations, and you can agree to one of these. I add to these two additional formulations guaranteeing <u>Palestinian effective control over the Haram</u> while <u>respecting the conviction of the Jewish people</u>. Regarding either one of these two formulations there will be <u>international monitoring</u> to provide mutual confidence.

(1) <u>Palestinian sovereignty over the Haram</u>, and <u>Israeli sovereignty over</u> (a) the <u>Western Wall</u> and the space sacred to Judaism of which it is a part; (b) the <u>Western Wall and the Holy of Holies</u> of which it is a part. There will be a fine commitment by both <u>not to excavate beneath the Haram</u> or <u>behind the Wall</u>.

(2) <u>Palestinian sovereignty over the Haram</u> and <u>Israeli sovereignty over the Western Wall</u> and <u>shared functional sovereignty over the issue of excavation</u> under the Haram and behind the Wall such that mutual consent would be requested before any excavation can take place.

My favorite subject in high school was history, and as a teenager I loved to hike in the Judean desert and around Jerusalem, where every stroll was a venture into the past. By the time I joined the ECF, I was confident of my knowledge about the history and geography of Israel and its capital, believing, like most Israelis, in a "unified Jerusalem" that is the "eternal capital of Israel."

But a few weeks into my tenure at the ECF, Hirschfeld and Pundak invited me to join them for a meeting at the American Colony in Jerusalem, which is a legendary Relais & Chateaux five-star hotel with a history dating back to the late 19th century. Like the King David Hotel in West Jerusalem, the American Colony is one of the most cosmopolitan places in the Middle

East and a meeting point for top-tier diplomacy, international business, and high-end tourism. On that day, as we drove from Jewish West Jerusalem to the Arab east side, Pundak marked the moment when we crossed the 1967 Lines. He described the American Colony as a "neutral meeting point" because of its location on the Arab side, proximity to the Jewish side, and international ambiance. Having a great Middle Eastern menu and outstanding service made the experience all the better.

That first trip was the beginning of a journey to explore the full geography, demography, and anthropology of Israel's capital through dozens of field visits. Tagging along with Pundak for these ventures was a privilege. He had the deepest love for the city and a nuanced acquaintance with it. The trunk of his car always held maps and aerial photos, which we studied diligently. Whenever possible, he would pull off at an observation point overlooking Jerusalem from different directions. We often travelled along seamlines between Jewish and Arab sections and between Jerusalem's municipal area and the West Bank, meeting the Palestinians and Israelis, Arabs and Jews, who lived there. Many times, we drove Pundik's Renault deep into a Palestinian neighborhood to meet a host, who was often a local Fatah leader. Although we were Israelis, and Israel was the formal sovereign in those areas, we stood out as foreigners, and we were out of reach of Israel's security forces. We knew there was risk, but we trusted our hosts, who eagerly engaged us in conversations or showed us around, often inviting us for tea and pastries.

Our goal was to gain a more nuanced and systemic understanding of Jerusalem to inform the economic, political, legal, and border arrangements that we would propose. Jerusalem's *municipal* area then housed 130,000 Palestinians in an urban sprawl of communities that stretched from Kafar Aqeb and Beit Hanina in the north, through an "eastern rim" that included Shuafat, Jabel Mukaber, Isawiya, Sur Baher, and Umm Tuba. The Palestinian residents of these areas are considered Jerusalemites and permanent residents of Israel who are entitled to Israeli citizenship and voting rights. In fact, if East Jerusalem were its own municipal government, it would be the largest Arab city in Israel.

During these trips, I discovered a Jerusalem that I didn't know existed. I realized that my friends and I were living behind "virtual walls" that hide the Palestinian areas and gently guide Jewish and Israeli locals and visitors to stay within the comforts of "Israeli Jerusalem." These virtual walls also guide many government agencies, as is evinced by the inferior quality of public infrastructure and services in the Palestinian neighborhoods compared to the Jewish ones: roads are narrow and bumpy, sidewalks are uneven or nonexistent, police as a public-facing law-enforcement agency is hardly present, and garbage cans are often full and uncovered. Arab Jabel Moukaber, for example, is separated from Jewish Talpiyot by a wide street. While many Palestinians from Jabel Moukaber commute daily into the Jewish areas for work, most residents of Talpiyot do not travel in the opposite direction. Even in the Old City, which has eight gates, Jews primarily use the western and southern entrances, close to the Jewish side, while Arabs use northern and eastern gates, leading to the Christian and Muslim quarters. It is unlikely to find an Arab East Jerusalemite sitting in an Israeli-Jewish café in West Jerusalem or vice versa, and most neighborhoods remain either "Jewish" or "Arab."

One day, Pundak and I visited the valley that separates Neve Yakov, the northernmost Jewish neighborhood in municipal Jerusalem, and Ar-Ram, an adjacent Palestinian community that is part of the West Bank. At the time, the two communities were divided by an open area about 200 wide. So close, yet so far: the gaps in the quality of life were astounding, beginning with the quality of the roads, street lighting, public parks, and garbage collection. The Israeli community, while poor, clearly belonged to a developed First World nation, while the other side was underdeveloped, and poverty-stricken. In 2003, the security fence would create a permanent physical barrier between the two neighborhoods along that narrow valley.

On another outing, we ventured into Beit Tzafafa, a Palestinian neighborhood in the southern part of municipal Jerusalem, just beyond today's Malcha soccer stadium, mall, and technology park. Between 1949 and 1967, Beit Tzafafa was divided by the ceasefire line, with its northern part in Israel and southern part in the West Bank. After the 1967 War, the entire village and its surroundings were annexed to Jerusalem and Israel. I had driven past that neighborhood dozens of times without ever getting off the highway to explore it, sit in one of its restaurants, or talk to its people. When I finally did all of that with Pundak, I was surprised to discover that many of its Arab residents spoke Hebrew and worked in middle-class jobs in Israel in the healthcare system, as teachers, or in the municipality. Although they saw themselves as Palestinians and hoped to see a Palestinian state, they also wanted to remain part of Israel. In Beit Tzafafa, too, Pundak and I were generously welcomed.

The mood was much different when we drove east into the Palestinian neighborhoods of Jabel Moukaber, Arab al Sawahrah, Umm Lison, Tzur Baher, and the more remote area of Kafar Akeb at the northern tip of Jerusalem. Each of these communities housed many thousands of Palestinians, although within municipal Jerusalem, they are part of an urban continuum that stretches into the West Bank. Their population includes those who hold a blue Israeli ID that allows them to receive Israel's government services, drive cars with yellow Israeli license plates, and work freely in Israel, as well as those who are residents of the West Bank, rely on services of the PA, and cannot enter Israel without special permits. The municipal border in these areas cuts through streets and backyards and separates clans into Israelis and West Bankers. When the Sharon government built the security fence in 2002–2003, a massive physical barrier split these communities.

Certainly, the Jerusalem that I experienced between 1995 and 2001 had been unified by law for about 30 years but was divided in its reality. All the Jewish neighborhoods of Jerusalem were integral to Israel, just like Tel Aviv, but the Palestinians who lived in the annexed Arab neighborhoods clearly had no affinity to Israel. Furthermore, the PLO instructed them to boycott the municipal elections and not to seek Israeli citizenship, the lack of which denied them decisive political influence. Their representatives could have made up one-third of the city council and added 15 percent to the representation of Arab parties, potentially tilting the entire balance of power in Israeli politics against the right wing.

During those years, as we were forming our outlook of Permanent Status in Jerusalem, I felt like I was being let in on a secret that only a handful of Israelis knew, even though it stared all of us in the face. Over time, the ECF team molded its vision of Jerusalem based on our hundreds of excursions and field meetings with Palestinians and Israelis from all sectors of the city; countless books and articles about the history, geography, culture, architecture, and sociology of Jerusalem; brainstorming sessions with academics and researchers; and, most important, intense deliberations among our team, in which we made sense of our experiences.

Envisioning Jerusalem in Permanent Status was an exercise in designing functional solutions to municipal problems, and in dealing with national and religious legacies that had lasted for millennia. For Israelis, the word "Yerushalayim" represents a Jewish concept that repeatedly appears in prayer books. *Yerushalayim shel Ma'ala* ("heavenly Jerusalem") embodies national yearnings and ideals of wholeness, heavenliness, peace, and purity, and could be "located" at Temple Mount and its environs. At the same time, *Yerushalayim shel Mata* ("mundane Jerusalem") is an earthly space of hustling and bustling, whose boundaries are ever changing based on political, security, and administrative considerations.

In Biblical times, "Yerushalayim" referred to the area of the City of David on a small, unimpressive mountain—Temple Mount, *Har HaBayit* in Hebrew—whose name derives from the Hebrew temple, *Beit HaMikdash*, that stood on its summit. The uniqueness of that mountain was in having its own water source, which made it defensible in times of siege. Over the centuries, Jerusalem was built and destroyed, rose and declined according to the strategic and political conditions in the region. In the 16th century, the Ottomans built walls, which now surround the Old City. Henceforth, the term "Yerushalayim" came to refer to the walled city and its immediate surroundings. But the location of Jerusalem, in a peripheral area of the vast Ottoman Empire, led to its decline into poverty and political insignificance.

In the early 20th century, following the British conquest of Ottoman Palestine in 1917, Jerusalem became central again, and served as the seat of the Mandatory government. Its development was boosted, and it expanded to include newly built Jewish neighborhoods primarily to the west of the Old City and Arab areas to its north. At the same time, the struggle between Jews and Arabs in Jerusalem intensified, with each national movement aspiring for the city to become the future capital of its state.

The division between West Jerusalem and East Jerusalem was created by the 1948 War and existed until the reunification of the city in 1967. During that period, West Jerusalem, or Yerushalayim, was the area controlled by Israel, while East Jerusalem, or Al-Quds, was the area controlled by Jordan, which included the entire Old City. The borderline between the two parts of the city ran through populated areas. It was originally drawn with a marker, a historic quirk that resulted in a 50-meter-wide no-man's lands. Close to the

Old City, Jordanian and Israeli positions were less than 100 meters apart, subjecting Israeli civilians to the whims of Jordanian soldiers. Indeed, houses in that area remain scarred with bullet holes until today. One major passage, the Mandelbaum Gate, allowed for limited movement between the two sides by diplomats, religious leaders, humanitarian cases and even tourists.

West Jerusalem of 1949-1967 was a small border city of roughly 38 square kilometers, serving as the capital of Israel and connected to Tel Aviv and to the coastal plain by a narrow road. It housed the Knesset and other government buildings, as well as two hospitals and two campuses of the Hebrew University, one of which was in an enclave surrounded by Jordanian territory. Its modest population included many politicians, diplomats, civil servants, and academics. The Old City was out of reach for Israelis and Jews, who could not pray at the Kotel, which could only be viewed from Israel by leaning out of a narrow window at the top of a church tower on Mount Zion.

Al-Quds—Arab East Jerusalem of 1948–1967—was even smaller than Israeli West Jerusalem, covering just 6.4 square kilometers. It included the entire Holy Basin—namely the Old City, the Valley of Kidron (Wadi al-Joz) and the Mount of Olives—as well as the Augusta Victoria Hospital and the Seven Arches Intercontinental Hotel, where the King of Jordan used to stay on his visits to al-Haram al-Sharif. The primary modern neighborhood was Sheikh Jarrah, bordering on the northern wall of the Old City, which served as a business center and included mansions of prominent Palestinian families such as Husseini and Nashashibi and a few European diplomatic missions. Outside its municipal area, East Jerusalem was surrounded by Palestinian villages, including Qalandiya, Beit Hanina, and Shuafat in the north; Anata and Az-Za'yim, Abu Dis, Al Sawahreh, Al Eizariya, Tzur Baher, and Jabel Mukaber, located from its northeast to its southeast; and Beit Tzafafa in the south, which separated Jerusalem from Bethlehem. In addition, following the 1948 War, two refugee camps emerged in the outskirts of Al-Quds, in Shuafat and Qalandiya.

During its Jordanian era, Al-Quds was an underdeveloped border town, notwithstanding its status as a holy city to Muslims. The 1948 War transformed it from a teeming commercial center of Mandatory Palestine to a backwater of Jordan. Nonetheless, for Palestinians, it remained the heart of

the West Bank, on a major transportation route (now called Road 60), which
connected Bethlehem, Hebron, and the southern West Bank with Ramallah,
Nablus and Jenin, and an international airport at Atarot to Jerusalem's north.
Meanwhile, another major road stretched from Jerusalem eastward, descend-
ing the Judean Mountains to Jericho in the Jordan Valley, where it connected
to the Allenby Bridge over the Jordan River, which then led to Amman. In
other words, nearly all traffic across the West Bank from north to south and
from east to west went through Jerusalem.

These legacies created four "historical traumas" that the Israeli side had
to address during the Camp David negotiations. The first was the siege of
1948, which was laid by Jordan on West Jerusalem and by Palestinian militia
on the road to Tel Aviv. In May 1948, the Jewish Quarter of the Old City
was decimated by the Jordanians, as were the Jewish communities of Gush
Etzion, south of Jerusalem. That wartime experience affected Israel's national
security strategy for decades, because Yerushalayim had to be protected from
any future attack at all costs. Hence, after the 1967 War, Israel made a gener-
ational effort to expand and bolster Yerushalayim. Its municipal boundaries
were enlarged to include a "circle" of mountains to its north, east, and south.
In that space, Israel built a belt of 11 neighborhoods, including Ramot Alon
and Ramot Shlomo in the north; French Hill, Neve Yaakov, and Pisgat Zeev
in the northeast; Talpiyot and Har Homa in the southeast; and Gilo in the
south. By 2000, some 130,000 Israelis lived in those neighborhoods. All of
that area became part of a "unified Jerusalem" that "will never be divided
again."

In addition, an outer circle of satellite communities was built around the
municipal borders: Gush Etzion was resettled to the south and the neighborhood of Gilo now separates Yerushalayim from Bethlehem; Ma'ale Adumim
and a cluster of nearby communities was built in the east and numbered
40,000 residents by 2000; and Givat Zeev, Psagot, Beit El, and other smaller
communities were built to the north of Yerushalayim to separate it from
Ramallah. The "Yerushalayim corridor"—referring to the narrow land strip
and road that connected West Jerusalem to the coastal plain—had been
expanded by many small communities to its north and south. Road 1 is now
an eight-lane highway parallel to a high-speed rail line. In addition, Highway
443 enters Jerusalem from the northwest, and an expanded Road 60 enters

the city from the south. Altogether, this massive development makes today's Jerusalem the largest that the city has ever been.

The second trauma was the political division of Jerusalem and the physical barrier that represented it. Immediately after the 1967 War, Israel demolished that wall and erased any other signs of partition, which were never to be recreated. Later, the areas of the no-man's zones became a major transportation route between north Jerusalem and the Old City, connecting Jewish and Arab neighborhoods and symbolizing for many the unification of the city. In any case, the "eternal unity of an undivided Jerusalem" became a slogan that all politicians swore by.

The third trauma involved a lack of access to the Kotel and other Jewish holy sites in the Old City and on the West Bank. Pictures of the liberation of the Kotel in 1967—after 1897 years of foreign rule and 19 years of denied access—captured a moment of national exhilaration. Hitherto, the space for Jewish worshippers at the Kotel was four meters wide, narrowly separating it from the Arab neighborhood of the Mughrabi. Immediately after the war, that neighborhood was evacuated to clear a large plaza that could accommodate tens of thousands of people. Since June 1967, at any moment of every day, Jews are praying at the Kotel. This legacy has made free access to the Kotel and to other holy sites in the West Bank an absolute requirement for a Permanent Status agreement. Whenever the Palestinians contested such demands, we reminded them that while Jews had no access to those sites under Jordanian rule, Muslims have access to their holy sites under Israeli rule.

The final trauma stemmed from the absence of international recognition of Yerushalayim, even in its Western part, as Israel's capital. UNGAR 181 declared Jerusalem a "corpus separatum," and even Israel's closest allies put their embassies in Tel Aviv. Therefore, receiving Palestinian and international recognition of Yerushalayim as Israel's capital was another critical issue during the Camp David negotiations. That is why Israelis were so appreciative of President Trump when he recognized Jerusalem as Israel's capital and moved the U.S. Embassy from Tel Aviv.

Heading into the Permanent Status negotiations in 2000, Israel and the Palestinians had conflicting expectations. Barak pledged that "Yerushalayim is the unified and undivided capital of Israel forever." Meanwhile, the Palestinians wanted the capital of Palestine to be Al-Quds. As Arafat eloquently put it in a famous speech: "Al-Quds! Al-Quds! Al-Quds!" By that time, the term *Yerushalayim* came to describe all Jewish areas of municipal Jerusalem, including the 11 new neighborhoods, as well as the Arab areas in the Old City and around the Holy Basin such as Sheikh Jarrah, Silwan, and Wadi al-Joz. However, for most Israelis, Yerushalayim did *not* include the Palestinian neighborhoods in the outer rim of municipal Jerusalem, which they could not name and never visited. Meanwhile, for the Palestinians, the term "Al-Quds" was expanded to include all the Arab neighborhoods of municipal Jerusalem, many of which were formerly part of the West Bank. Hence, conceptually, "Yerushalayim" and "Al-Quds" had a contested overlap, particularly in the Holy Basin and around the Old City. The challenge in the negotiations was to square those conflicting claims.

One answer was to expand the geographic scope of the city. UNGAR 181, which Israel accepted, and UNGAR 194, which the Palestinians uphold— both refer to the "area of Jerusalem."[33] UNGAR 181 even included a map of that area, designated to be a *corpus separatum* and remain under UN sovereignty. But the changes to the municipal boundaries made the notion of the "area of Jerusalem" elastic. In 1995, the Beilin–Abu Mazen Understandings proposed that the "area of Jerusalem" would house two capitals—*Yerushalayim* and Al-Quds—in one open metropolis. Such an arrangement would allow Palestinians to claim that Permanent Status was consistent with UNGAR 194 and for Israel to claim that Yerushalayim remained "undivided" with all its *Jewish areas* "united."

Barak's starting position affirmed Rabin's pledge to keep Jerusalem united and undivided. At face value, it meant that Israel's borders in Permanent Status must subsume the entire area of municipal Jerusalem, including its Arab neighborhoods with their Palestinian residents. The PLO would never agree to this demand, but it didn't make sense from the perspective of Israel's interests either. Barak wanted to secure a "peace for generations" by keeping Palestinians in Palestine and Jews in Israel. He fiercely argued against

---

33   UNGAR 194, Ibid, Article 8 referring to UNGAR 181 Part III Section B

any return of Palestinian refugees into Israel. So his demand to annex some 130,000 Palestinian Jerusalemites into Israel made no sense.

Ultimately, and after much hesitation, Barak embraced this demographic logic, turning Jerusalem's virtual walls into political borders. Namely, in Permanent Status, Jewish neighborhoods would be Israeli, while Arab neighborhoods would be Palestinian. The question remained regarding what to do with the Arab neighborhoods in the Holy Basin: the Muslim and Christian Quarters of the Old City, Silwan (atop the City of David), Sheikh Jarrah Wadi al-Joz, and the Mount of Olives? These areas were going to require a special regime, which divides sovereignty and powers. For example, the Muslim and Christian Quarters could fall under Palestinian sovereignty but be treated based on the model of Area B: under Israeli security and Palestinian civic law. In addition, there was Beit Tzafafa, which is encircled by Jewish communities.

The principle of Arab to Palestine and Jewish to Israel had challenging practical implications. Though some open areas allowed for a clear separation between Jewish and Arab neighborhoods, elsewhere, particularly in the Holy Basin, Jewish life and Arab life were closely entwined and could not be distinguished by a clear physical boundary. This principle also meant that the political border in the area of Jerusalem would be convoluted. Indeed, the security fence built by the Sharon government along the municipal boundaries of Jerusalem is some 200 kilometers long.

Also, keeping the city open for movement of goods and services and providing safety and security would be extremely difficult. In the Beilin–Abu Mazen Understandings, Jerusalem would remain open without a physical barrier, but Barak's team emphasized security considerations and leaned toward tighter separation, as did Dahlan. Finally, there was the question of sovereign contiguity: at the French Hill juncture, would Israel have contiguous a north-south sovereign corridor from Neve Yaakov to French Hill, while the Palestinians would have an overpass or underpass, or would the Palestinians have an east-west contiguous sovereign corridor from Beit Hanina to Shoafat, while Israel uses an overpass or underpass? These questions were raised and discussed in detail but were not resolved.

Hebron and Other Holy Sites

Source: Wikipedia

The Tomb of the Patriarchs (and Matriarchs) in Hebron—known as *Me'arat Ha'Machpela* to Jews and *al-Haram al-Ibrahimi* to Muslims—is an impressive 800-year-old structure erected atop a cave where Abraham, Isaac, Jacob, and Sarah are believed to be buried. Like Temple Mount, it is a holy site for both Jews and Muslims, and as such includes a mosque and a synagogue. The fact that the Bible clearly chronicles the purchase of the spot by Abraham lends Jewish claims to the burial site and the surrounding area extra power. Furthermore, a Jewish community existed in Hebron for centuries until a 1929 massacre by local Arabs, which drove Jews from their homes. But after 1967, Jews returned as Israelis and with the backing of the government, settled in Hebron, and built nearby Kiryat Arba, with a current population of 8,000.

In Hebron, approximately 80,000 Palestinians live alongside a few hundred Jews, most of whom are situated close to the Tomb of the Patriarchs. Friction between the two communities has turned Hebron into a microcosm of the Israeli-Palestinian conflict. Over the years, Palestinian terrorists have targeted soldiers and settlers, along with Israeli and Jewish tourists, while local Jewish settlers have assaulted Palestinians and vandalized their properties. The most devastating terror attack was carried out by Baruch Goldstein, a physician from Kiryat Arba, who gunned down 29 Palestinian worshipers in the mosque of the Tomb of the Patriarchs in February 1994. That terror attack ignited a response from Hamas in the form of deadly suicide bombings, which led to Israeli retaliations and ultimately to an escalation that derailed the Oslo Process. These events made the withdrawal of Israel from Hebron according to the Interim Agreement particularly challenging. Eventually, in January 1997, Netanyahu signed a special agreement toward the implementation of Oslo B in Hebron that divided its area into two sections, controlled by the PA and Israel.

To enhance security in Hebron, the IDF deploys significant forces and heavy-handed measures to separate the two populations and protect settlers and visitors. Consequently, many Palestinian businesses were driven out of the area, which was then sealed off to them. What remains is a security enclave around the Tomb of the Patriarchs, where there is free access to Jews and tourists, as well as monitored access for Muslims, and a small Jewish community is protected by a large military force in an area that is off-limits to thousands of Palestinians. For the Palestinians of Hebron, the reality of occupation is more vividly present than anywhere else in the West Bank.

Given that context, the proposed security arrangements in Hebron toward Permanent Status were as complicated as those in the Old City. Barak's position was that Israel should maintain sovereignty over the Tomb of the Patriarchs and Hebron's Jewish sections, as well as over a land corridor that connects it to the southern Israel-Palestine border, close to Arad. Meanwhile, the Palestinians seemed amenable to the principle that Hebron would require special arrangements for access and worship in Permanent Status, but they would not agree to Israeli sovereignty there, and we never negotiated that issue further. On that point, the 1995 Beilin–Abu Mazen Understandings and the 2003 Geneva Accord both placed Hebron and the Tomb of the Patriarchs under Palestinian sovereignty, while the Trump Plan followed Barak's approach in placing the Tomb of the Patriarchs, its Jewish surroundings, and the land corridor under Israeli sovereignty.

The sites of Rachel's Tomb, in Bethlehem, and Joseph's Tomb, in Nablus, both holy only to Jews, represented a second tier of importance to Israeli negotiators. Rachel's Tomb was simpler to manage because of its proximity to the southern border of Jerusalem. In Permanent Status it could be easily accessed by a narrow strip from Jerusalem, which could even fall under Israeli sovereignty or control. Joseph's Tomb, though, is in the heart of Palestinian

Nablus, which means that Israel needs Palestinian security forces to protect the site and guarantee access to it. Indeed, in the 20 years since the Camp David negotiations, Rachel's Tomb has been accessed quite smoothly, but worship at Joseph's Tomb has been a source of recurring and sometimes bloody friction. And while the Palestinians agreed with us that freedom to worship at holy sites was important to the Israeli-Palestinian relationship, we never got to discuss how that principle would apply at these locations. In any event, it seemed that if we ever did reach agreement on the more substantive issues, particularly that of Jerusalem, figuring out a plan for access to the Tomb of the Patriarchs, Rachel's Tomb, and Joseph's Tomb would not be an obstacle for an agreement.

There was a third group of holy sites as well: dozens of locations of biblical, religious, or historical significance for Jews across Judea and Samaria. In principle, we wanted to secure their preservation, as well as allow freedom of access to them and prayer at those of religious significance. Our initial reference point was the arrangements in the peace treaty with Egypt that secured the honorable preservation of four memorials—two of each country in the other's territory. Alas, when the Peace Administration compiled a list of such sites across the West Bank, we wound up with more than 40 locations, including Biblical sites, tombs of important rabbis, and archeological digs.

Initially, we wanted to make the list long to give us leverage in the negotiations. But once we saw our own creation, we realized that the Palestinians would not agree to such demands. Had we prioritized our list, we might have been able to negotiate particular arrangements for specific sites of particular importance to us. But with an extended list, the most we could hope for were broad principles that would be hard to enforce. Furthermore, when we raised the topic in preliminary discussions with the Palestinians, they demanded reciprocity, claiming that dozens of sites within Israel had similar historical, religious, or sentimental significance for them and needed to be preserved and accessible. Since some 450 Palestinian communities were deserted and destroyed in 1948, they had many options to choose from. Hence, our demands triggered their demands, which we could not accommodate. So, paradoxically, it was this category of "less important" sites that could have represented an unexpected and serious obstacle to reaching an agreement on Permanent Status.

Showdown at Camp David

Jerusalem was clearly going to be the hot-button issue of the Camp David summit, but Barak would not allow even referring to it ahead of the summit or in any preparatory work. He made an electoral pledge that a "united and undivided Jerusalem shall remain the capital of Israel forever," and any rumor to the contrary might have destabilized his coalition. Neither were the Palestinians interested in any in-depth discussion of Jerusalem; they simply held on to their demands without crisis or compromise.

But despite Barak's sensitivity, much preparatory work regarding Jerusalem did take place. It happened indirectly when we worked on other issues. Clearly, designing Permanent Status in Jerusalem would have shaped our approach to economics, security, borders, and civic affairs—in fact, to the entire FAPS. But the opposite was true as well: when we worked on security, economics, or borders, we discussed Jerusalem. In addition, as soon as Sher and I began to work on the backchannel in Sweden, we could formulate a draft agreement on Jerusalem, trusting that it would never be leaked. Yet again, the vast work that was done in various non-governmental settings, particularly the ECF, turned out to be extremely useful.

On the seventh day of the summit, with negotiations going nowhere, Barak convened our full delegation on the porch of his cabin for a long-overdue conversation about the future of Jerusalem in Permanent Status. Each of us was invited to share his thoughts and recommendations. Unlike most government meetings in which time is budgeted, Barak let us speak for as long as we wished, and some really took their time. This was an occasion when political platitudes would not suffice. Despite the range of the political outlooks among our delegation, which included some right-wing people, a surprising consensus soon emerged: the area of Jerusalem could accommodate two capitals, most of the densely populated Arab areas should be controlled by Palestine, and the Holy Basin should be subject to a special regime that respects its significance to Islam and Christianity. The general tenor was best captured by Minister Amnon Lipkin-Shahak, a lieutenant general in the reserves, who said: "When I sing *Jerusalem of Gold* [a famous Hebrew love song to Jerusalem], I don't think of Kafar Aqeb or Shuafat." It seemed as if we agreed that although Jerusalem should be unified and open, its borders could be adjusted to allow some areas currently within "municipal Jerusalem" to be included in Al-Quds.

There was no official summary to the meeting, although some of us, who appreciated the historicity of the moment, took copious notes. But the delegation gave Barak the mandate to negotiate the future of Jerusalem on these terms, although it was divided on the *approach* to such negotiations. Most of us—including Sher, Ben-Ami and me—recommended working our way from the easier issues to the harder ones. For example, let's first agree on the general principle that "the area of Jerusalem would house two capitals" or that "holy sites would be open to prayer and worship, subject to necessary security arrangements" before discussing the details of borders, sovereignty, and security. Such an approach would allow us to make progress, even if we didn't reach a FAPS at Camp David. That approach also made sense because we viewed the Palestinian side as disorganized, unprepared, and incapable of reaching decisions of historic magnitude.

But the dissenting side had one important member: Barak. After months of stalling (until April-May), and attempts to advance via backchannels, he was now designing a "moment of truth." He understood Arafat to be elusive, always preferring to delay a tough choice with the hope for a better offer. Therefore, only extreme pressure on Arafat, leaving him "nowhere to go," could yield an agreement. With everyone secluded in Camp David; without a majority in the Knesset or a government; with just 36 hours left before Clinton's departure to Japan; and with a standoff and a standstill between Israeli and Palestinian positions, this was the time to hit the nail on the head, tackling the toughest issue first, namely Temple Mount. Barak's logic was simple: if we cannot reach an agreement on Temple Mount, there would be no deal on Jerusalem and no FAPS. But if we agreed on a vision for the Old City, we would be able to finalize all the other issues. Barak argued that Arafat knew what he was willing to do to achieve peace, and only a bold Israeli proposal in front of Clinton in the pressure-cooker of Camp David could "smoke Arafat out of his cave" of non-engagement. It was a risky move that made sense in Barak's head and on whiteboards, but less so given the lack of trust among the leaders and the dynamic of the negotiations. Of course, Barak's approach was also shaped by his political reality: he had just lost his coalition and was heading to new elections. He needed a powerful narrative for his imminent campaign.

By that point, Ben-Ami had already raised with the Palestinians four possible approaches to sovereignty over Temple Mount, all of which were close to our redlines: that no one would be sovereign on Temple Mount, leaving the space subject to "divine providence"; that Israel and Palestine would share sovereignty over Temple Mount; that sovereignty would be divided, with Palestine controlling the upper platform and mosques, while Israel would control the space beneath the platform, known as Solomon's Stables; or that sovereignty would remain in the hands of the United Nations or some international consortium of nations that could include the U.S., the EU, Jordan, Saudi Arabia, or Morocco. Though not fleshed out, these ideas offered direction, focusing the parties on designing security and administrative arrangements that would allow the Old City to function.

At Camp David and in front of Clinton, Barak crystallized and focused Ben-Ami's ideas into one concrete offer: neither party would be the sovereign on the Temple Mount. However, Israel's sovereignty in the Old City would include the Kotel and its plaza, Robinson's Arch, the Southern Wall, and the archeological site of Davidson Garden; the Kotel Tunnel that runs along the Western Wall under the Muslim Quarter; Silwan and the City of David, including the excavations; and the Jewish and Armenian Quarter to the right of the Jafa Gate. Meanwhile, Palestine would hold sovereignty over the Christian and Muslim Quarters, which cover more than two-thirds of the Old City, as well as the Arab neighborhoods of Sheikh Jarrah and Wadi al-Joz. While Israel would remain responsible for security in these areas, the Holy Basin would be subject to special arrangements monitored by the international community to ensure freedom of movement and religious practice, particularly by Muslims and Palestinians on al-Haram al-Sharif.

Barak also suggested that the shared sanctity and international significance of the Holy Basin meant that neither party would be allowed to establish its seat of government there. Israel was not about to do that in any case, but we wanted to be sure that the Palestinians wouldn't either. Instead, because the government compound of Israel and the parliament of the PA were located roughly one kilometer from Temple Mount, we suggested designating a radius within which neither party could build its iconic government institutions.

Once those principles were established, our delegations could focus on the political borders that would separate Al-Quds from Yerushalayim.

As complicated as that all sounded in theory, the reality was sure to be even messier. But we weren't worried about that yet, and when Arafat refused to discuss Barak's proposals, we never had to. That said, the principles presented by Barak provided the foundations for the Clinton Ideas, which then served as the reference point for future negotiations, including between Olmert and Abu Mazen in 2008. Even the Trump Plan accepts some of these principles by suggesting that the Area of Jerusalem would house two capitals, with Al-Quds located adjacent to the current municipal border in the northeast area of Kafr Aqab and Shuafat or in Abu Dis; by acknowledging that Arab residents of Yerushalayim would be associated with Palestine; and by dividing sovereignty and administrative powers on Temple Mount, although it places the entire platform under Israeli sovereignty and *Jordanian* custodianship.

In the 23 years that have passed since the Camp David negotiations, Jerusalem has grown larger, more open, and more prosperous than ever before. The Jewish areas of the city have expanded further, and a network of roads and light rail interconnects its different neighborhoods. As significantly, a few Arab countries have signed peace accords with Israel despite the continued conflict with the Palestinians, and the U.S. has moved its embassy to Jerusalem. However, Palestinian attachment to Jerusalem has not waned and the city remains a sensitive flashpoint for conflict. Barak assumed that an agreement about the future of Jerusalem would be essential for Israeli-Palestinian peace, and his assumption holds today, as the struggle between Jews and Arabs over Jerusalem continues.

CHAPTER 8

FAPS Article 6:
Refugees

Clinton Ideas: Refugees

I sense that the differences are more relating to formulations and less to what will happen on a practical level. I believe that Israel is prepared to acknowledge the moral and material suffering caused to the Palestinian people as a result of the 1948 war and the need to assist the international community in addressing the problem.

The fundamental gap is on how to handle the concept of the right of return. I know the history of the issue and how hard it will be for the Palestinian leadership to appear to be abandoning this principle. The Israeli side could not accept any reference to a right of return that would imply a right to immigrate to Israel in defiance of Israel's sovereign policies and admission or that would threaten the Jewish character of the state. Any solution must address both needs.

The solution will have to be consistent with the two-state approach that both sides have accepted as a way to end the Palestinian-Israeli conflict: the state of Palestine as the homeland of the Palestinian people and the state of Israel as the homeland of the Jewish people.

Under the two-state solution, the guiding principle should be that the Palestinian state would be the focal point for Palestinians who choose to return to the area without ruling out that Israel will accept some of these refugees. I believe that we need to adopt a formulation on the right of return that will make clear that there is no specific right of return to

---

Israel itself but that does not negate the aspiration of the Palestinian people to return to the area.

In light of the above, I propose two alternatives: (1) <u>Both sides</u> recognize the <u>right of Palestinian refugees to return</u> to <u>historic Palestine</u>, or (2) Both sides recognize the <u>right of Palestinian refugees</u> to <u>return to their homeland</u>. The agreement will define the implementation of this general right in a way that is <u>consistent with the two-state solution</u>.

The agreement would list the <u>five possible homes</u> for the refugees: (1) The state of <u>Palestine</u>; (2) Areas in Israel being transferred to Palestine in <u>the land swaps</u>; (3) Rehabilitation in <u>host countries</u>; (4) Resettlement in a <u>third country</u>; (5) Admission to <u>Israel</u>. In listing these options, the agreement will make clear that the return to the West Bank, Gaza Strip, and areas acquired in the land swap would be the right of all Palestinian refugees.

… rehabilitation in host countries, resettlement in third countries and absorption into Israel will depend upon the policies of those countries. Israel could indicate in the agreement that it intends to establish a policy so that some of the refugees would be absorbed into Israel <u>consistent with Israel's sovereign decision</u>. I believe that priority should be given to the refugee population in Lebanon.

The parties would agree that <u>this implements UNGAR 194</u>.

Arab Peace Initiative

… calling for full Israeli withdrawal from all the <u>Arab territories occupied since June 1967</u>, in <u>implementation of UNSCRs 242 and 338</u>, reaffirmed by the Madrid Conference of 1991 and the land-for-peace principle, and …

Israel's acceptance of an <u>independent Palestinian state</u> with <u>East Jerusalem as its capital</u> … in return for the establishment of normal relations in the context of a <u>comprehensive peace with Israel</u> … the council … further calls upon Israel to affirm … achievement of a <u>just solution to the Palestinian refugee problem</u> to be agreed upon in accordance with UNGAR 194.

A Just Solution?

In the spring of 1997, Pundak and I visited the Dheisheh refugee camp in Bethlehem. We came to meet the leadership of the young guard of the local Popular Committee, a group that exists in, and represents, residents of every refugee camp. We were guests of the local branch of *Tanzim*, the paramilitary arm of Fatah, and were under their protection. As we made our way through the camp, we saw one- or two-story buildings with small street-front shops. The main streets were asphalted, but many of the side alleys were not, and there was no trace of any planning or zoning. The overall appearance was that of an extremely poor neighborhood. And the community center, where our meeting took place, was in a shabby building with a small central hall and four side rooms, furnished with simple plastic tables and chairs. The whole scene reminded me of the shantytowns of Africa, where I grew up.

When we sat in a circle, everyone introduced themselves. The personal stories of the Palestinians were different variations of the "party line" of their national struggle. Briefly, although they were born in Dheisheh some three decades after 1948, refugeeism and displacement were central to their identities. They detailed where their families came from in Israel (most came from the same area) and what they did before their uprooting. They then proceeded to describe a life of poverty and dislocation at the camp, and reiterated how sacred the Right of Return was to them and how they yearned for the return of their families to their ancestral homes to resume their lives as they were prior to their *naqba*. All of them spoke about deeds to property that their families kept, symbolized by the keys to the homes which they left behind.

After we heard their stories, Pundak posited a scenario in which a Palestinian state invites them to become its passport-holding citizens and stay in Dheisheh, which is developed into a modern neighborhood of Bethlehem. In such a scenario, he asked, would they still prefer to be a minority in Israel, hitherto their enemy, over living as citizens of their own independent country? Pundak's question generated a lively debate among them, and a good two hours later, a consensus seemed to appear: in such a scenario, their right of return to Israel might not be realized because it no longer made sense.

Pundak and I headed home encouraged. What we had heard from this authentic grassroots refugee leadership led us to believe that an agreement on ending Palestinian refugeeism was possible if a Palestinian state was established. But we failed to pay proper attention to the other tacit message of the day: arriving at such an outcome would require a lengthy engagement. There was a lot of letting go to do on their side.

An estimated 750,000 Palestinians left their homes during the 1948 War and were not allowed to return after it ended. Although many of those people have passed away in the intervening years, by 2000, "Palestinian refugees"—namely those who left in 1948 and their descendants—numbered 4.2 million people.[34] Currently, in 2023, the United Nations Relief and Work Agency (UNRWA) supports 5.3 million Palestinians who are still living in 57 refugee camps in Gaza, the West Bank, Jordan, Syria, and Lebanon. This is the longest-standing refugee problem in the world, a seemingly intractable matter for Israel and the Palestinians.

Surprisingly, Israelis and Palestinians agree on the most fundamental principle for the resolution of the refugee issue, which is that any solution must be a "just" one. That is the language used in multiple UN resolutions and in the 2002 Arab Peace Initiative. In fact, during the Camp David negotiations, Israel also demanded that any agreed resolution of Palestinian refugeeism in Permanent Status would constitute a "just solution." After decades of struggle, the Palestinian leadership had a similar interest, so the ideal of a "just solution" turned out to be as significant to the resolution of Palestinian refugeeism as the idea of 1967 Lines to the territorial dispute.

But we had radically different perceptions on what constitutes "justice" in this case. The Palestinian version is quite rigid, with roots in UNGAR 194 of December 1948—also simply known as "194"—which suggests principles for a final settlement of the Israeli-Arab conflict. Its Article 11 states that "refugees wishing to return to their homes and live at peace with their neighbors should be permitted to do so at the earliest practicable date…" This article is the foundation for the Palestinian claim for the so-called Right of Return and the source of whatever international legitimacy that claim may carry. 194 also resolved to compensate Palestinians—whether returning or not—for lost or damaged property. A fun fact is that six Arab League countries

---

34   In 2000, the population of 4,200,000 Palestinian refugees was divided between Jordan (~42%; 1,800,000), the West Bank and the Gaza Strip (~38%, 1,500,000), Lebanon (~10%; 400,000) and Syria (~10%, 420,000). Today UNRWA claims that number is 5.9 Million. (UNRWA, *Where We Work*, n.d. https://www.unrwa.org/where-we-work.)

voted *against* 194 and the Palestinian leadership rejected it as well because it accepted the legality of Israel. Notwithstanding their initial rejection, Arabs and Palestinians came to embrace 194 as the foundation of their claims against Israel.

Israel's view of "a just solution" rejects the Palestinian position and has been clear and consistent since 1948. In a nutshell: the 1947 1949 conflict was waged by the Palestinian leadership and five other Arab countries with the declared intention to destroy nascent Israel. Indeed, without exception, all Israeli communities conquered during the war were decimated and their populations were brutalized. The 1948 war began in November 1947 with six months of clashes between the Jews and Arabs of Mandatory Palestine. Upon the departure of the British on May 15, 1948, five Arab armies invaded Israel and had some initial successes in besieging Jerusalem and advancing toward Tel Aviv and Haifa. During that period, the Palestinian population—especially in communities that existed in proximity to Jews, such as in Jaffa, which is located between Tel Aviv and Bat-Yam—were called upon over Arab radio to temporarily leave their homes to "clear the way" for Arab armies to eliminate the Jewish state.

Later, as the IDF captured territory, it also ordered the evacuation and departure of many communities and their citizens that came under its control. In the end, an estimated 85 percent of the Arab population in Israeli-controlled areas left, and the rest stayed and became Arab-Israelis.[35] Those who left were not allowed to return, because they were part of an enemy population who could still be incited by the hateful leadership of Haj Amin Al-Husseini and his ilk. Furthermore, during and after the war, a roughly similar number of Jews that had been forced to leave Arab countries had immigrated to Israel. Technically, many of them were also refugees, yet they were readily absorbed by Israel as citizens, with many settling in "abandoned Palestinian homes." Other Palestinian infrastructure was damaged, and much property was destroyed or confiscated by Israeli authorities, making a return of refugees implausible.

---

35 Encyclopedia Britannica, *Resurgence of Palestinian Identity* (Encyclopedia Britannica, https://www.britannica.com/place/Palestine/Resurgence-of-Palestinian-identity).

There were also powerful principled reasons to deny their return. The Palestinians initiated the war and lost. There is a price for that. As David Ben-Gurion explained: "They lost and fled. Their return must now be prevented." Furthermore, following the two world wars, tens of millions of people—Greeks, Turks, Bulgarians, Germans, Poles, Ukrainians, and others—relocated from their places of residence to within the boundaries of their nation-states to establish long-lasting peace and stability. To the Israelis, that approach made sense. Just as Israel absorbed hundreds of thousands of Arab Jews, Arab countries should absorb a roughly similar number of now-displaced Palestinians.

The only reason that this logical outcome of mass exchange of populations did not come to pass were the powerful forces that united to prevent it. The Soviet-led communist bloc, the so called "non-aligned countries," and Arab countries shared an interest in preserving the conflict with Israel and in delegitimizing the Jewish state. The Soviet bloc labeled Israel as a Western outpost in the Middle East and sought to minimize its influence, while Arab leaders, near and distant, benefited from having an external enemy. Perpetuating Palestinian refugeeism was crucial for their goals, so much so that they introduced and passed a special resolution by the United Nations that would enshrine the status of Palestinian refugees for generations.[36] That resolution gave a permanent refugee status to those displaced by the 1948 War and to their descendants for generations to come.[37] Indeed, one could be a second-generation Canadian citizen and a third-generation Palestinian refugee at the same time! Moreover, a special agency, UNRWA, was created to serve Palestinian refugees while in exile and to maintain their status until they could "return to their homes." All refugees were then given documents that enshrine their status, and 58 temporary encampments of refugees were declared "refugee camps" in the West Bank, Gaza, Jordan, Syria, and Lebanon, all of which have been served by UNRWA since that time.

---

36 United Nations General Assembly Resolution 302.

37 A "Palestinian Refugee" is a the political-legal status of a person "whose normal place of residence was Palestine between June 1946 and May 1948, who lost their homes and means of livelihood as a result of the 1948 Arab-Israeli conflict." This definition also includes their descendants. Source: UNRWA, *Palestine Refugees* (https://www.unrwa.org/palestine-refugees)

Against this backdrop, it is easy to understand the perspective of ordinary Israelis, who dismiss Palestinian refugeeism as an issue that is artificially preserved to sustain the conflict. Most Israelis hold the demand for a Right of Return to be ludicrous and the claim that Israel is singularly responsible for creating and preserving Palestinian refugeeism, and therefore also for its resolution, to be an absurdity. This is partly why most Israelis have only a remote awareness of the existence of Palestinian refugees, and fewer still understand the issue's origins and complexity. Even for Israelis who support the Two-State Solution, it's clear that Palestinian refugeeism should be resolved in the Palestinian state and by Arab countries. This was also my mindset when I came into the world of Israeli-Palestinian peacemaking.

Meeting the Palestinian Narrative Firsthand

In September 1995, the ECF hosted the first-ever major trilateral meeting among Israelis, Jordanians, and Palestinians in collaboration with Data, our partner from Bethlehem, and Horizon, our partner from Amman. Three delegations of senior professionals met for three days at the Dan Hotel in Tel Aviv to discuss future economic relations among our countries.

As I had worked at the ECF for just two months, this was my first such gathering, and it required dressing up. For a tie, I chose a classic dark blue with a gentle pattern of doves, and Gary Sussman, my ECF colleague, taught me how to tie it. Henceforth, I would wear that "novelty tie" for important occasions related to the peace process—including in Sharm El-Sheikh, Camp David and to Clinton's White House—and it always became a conversation topic. I thought I looked sharp, and it was a good thing, because on the first evening of that event, Hirschfeld, ever susceptible to stage fright, gave me a five-minute notice to deliver the closing remarks in his name and then brief the press.

After a long day of deliberations, we took our guests to dinner at a restaurant in Jaffa. These were days of high hopes, and we felt the thrill of an exciting and new beginning of building a peaceful and prosperous future for our societies. After the 20-minute drive, we pulled up in an unpaved parking lot, close to where the Peres Center for Peace and Innovation stands today. Just as we disembarked the vans, one of the Jordanians began to wail loudly, as if he had just learned of a tragedy in his family. Falling to his knees, he kissed the dirt of the lot. The rest of us were speechless. I had never seen anything like it. His pants covered in chalky dust, he pointed to a nearby two-story Arab home. "This is it," he said in Arabic. "This is my home." The Palestinians and Jordanians walked over to hug and comfort him.

By the time we entered the restaurant a few minutes later, the mood had dramatically changed. It was now quite somber. The Israeli side was at a loss for words, and our Jordanian colleague became the center of attention. After he collected himself, he told us that his mother had left Jaffa in 1948 as a young girl with her family, moving to an area under Arab control in the West Bank. They thought they were leaving for a short while, but they eventually settled in Jordan and never returned to Jaffa. The girl, his mother, grew up and got married, but she never forgot about her family home in Jaffa. She showed them old pictures of the house and its surrounding area. And on his first visit to Israel, he had recognized the house, or at least so he thought.

It was a classic story of a Palestinian refugee-family of displacement and plight, but from an Israeli perspective that story also represented the most promising outcome that we could have hoped for. Our guest was an educated, senior professional in his field and a proud Jordanian, who represented his country in Tel Aviv, working with Israelis and Palestinians on peace-building. Upon coming to Israel, he had no personal plans of going to Jaffa, and it was we, his hosts, who coincidently took him there. Nor did he have plans to "return." But now, memories of his Palestinian heritage surfaced 50 years after his mother had left her home.

This experience and others—like the visit to Dheisheh—made me realize how formative the experience of refugeeism is to Palestinians, both as individuals and as a nation. I was intrigued to learn more, but there were only a handful of sources about the subject in Hebrew. So I wound up frequenting specialized bookstores in London and the Bookshop at the American Colony Hotel, where the owner, Munther Fahmi, became a friend and guided my journey of learning, as I pored over books, reports, photo albums, and primary sources. One book that had a lasting impact on me documented every Palestinian village and community destroyed or abandoned during the 1948 War—all 450 of them.

This journey helped me develop a deeper understanding of the Palestinian perspective. Intellectually, I began to understand why the 1948 War was their catastrophe, or *naqba*, as it affected all families and every fabric of their society. Visits to refugee camps enabled me to sympathize with the personal tragedy that came with becoming a refugee, often for life, and anyone could relate to the plight of losing a home or a livelihood.

Still, the more I dug in, the more it became clear to me that Israel's fundamental position on this matter was practical and just. A war of annihilation was waged against Israel's Jews. Luckily and skillfully, we emerged victorious. Considering the conditions of 1948, the plight of Palestinians as refugees was in many ways inevitable, but their status as refugees was preserved intentionally by Arab countries. Most important, I was convinced without doubt that the resolution of Palestinian refugeeism is essential for reaching Permanent Status and that it must take place in Palestine, not Israel. All my fellow Israeli negotiators agreed on these points.

Ending Palestinian Refugeeism

The official Palestinian position on their refugees was steadfast. In a nutshell, the PLO wanted Israel to accept exclusive responsibility for the creation, preservation, and resolution of the refugee issue. Once Israel accepted that responsibility, it would need to recognize the Right of Return of the refugees to their original homes, which were now in Israel. The refugees would then decide whether to return or not and would be entitled to compensation for their sufferings, with an added package given to those who chose *not* to return to Israel for the property they had left behind. For the Palestinians, that package would represent a just solution, and they stuck to that position before, during, and after our negotiations. To be fair, when presenting these demands, they always "assured" us that most refugees would *not* act on their Right of Return, preferring to stay in Jordan, Syria, and Lebanon or to repatriate to Palestine, where 40 percent of them were already living. In private, our Palestinian interlocutors dismissed these hardline positions as posturing, knowing that they were a non-starter for Israel and a turn-off even for some of their allies. In addition, they cited Arafat, who said that the PLO was ready to make "painful" compromises to accomplish peace, without explaining what those compromises might be.

Why did the PLO assume such an anachronistic and unrealistic position, antagonizing us and distracting themselves from building their future state with the people and money they could have? One reason was posturing in attempt to increase the financial compensation package for refugees. A stronger reason was intimidation by the powerful "refugee lobby," which was known to be aggressive and even violent. It was a lesson demonstrated in the aftermath of the Beilin–Abu Mazen Understandings in 1995. Abu Mazen, a refugee from Tzfat, allegedly agreed that the Right of Return would be implemented primarily in Palestine, with only a symbolic few going to Israel. In response, his house in Gaza was attacked by a mob, which was incited by rival politicians. Some even stipulated that Arafat himself had blessed the attack on Abu Mazen's house to teach his deputy a lesson about PLO hierarchy. In any case, that event was a warning to all future Palestinian negotiators.

We believed—and our Palestinian interlocutors confirmed in private— that Arafat could be flexible on *the framing* of the Right of Return and on its implementation primarily in Palestine. But that would only happen as part of an agreement on Permanent Status that provided for a Palestinian state that could absorb all refugees with the help of a generous economic package, thereby giving political and economic hope to *all Palestinians*. This point only enhanced the all-or-nothing dynamics of the Camp David negotiations, in which both sides foresaw either a finalized agreement or a total collapse of the political process. So while we assumed that an agreement could be reached on the resolution of Palestinian refugeeism, there was no prospect for showing any intermediate progress.

A central tenet of Oslo A was its "constructive ambiguity" regarding Permanent Status, which left the key outstanding issues unresolved. The hope was that the Interim Period of 1995–1999 would serve Palestinians for building their self-governing capacities, while improving bilateral relations and deepening trust with Israel ahead of Permanent Status negotiations. But when it came to the refugee issue, the Interim Period had the opposite effect, allowing radical Palestinian voices to mobilize and organize, and to shoot down any idea for compromise. Palestinian leaders who signaled flexibility on the issue of refugees were condemned, and the pragmatic approach to the resolution of Palestinian refugeeism lost ground.

The Interim Period also exposed the naïveté of well-meaning Western governments like those of the United States, Canada, and Britain. The preservation of Palestinian refugeeism was made possible by UNRWA, which was funded primarily by the U.S. and European governments. These governments may have had a faint logic to support UNRWA prior to the creation of the PA in July 1994 or to the Interim Agreement in September 1995. But once the PA was created, it made no sense that UNRWA continued to provide basic municipal services in refugee camps *in the West Bank and Gaza* on America's dime, instead of funneling those same hundreds of millions of dollars through the PA as part of its capacity-building and state-building efforts. Had that happened in the Interim Period, by 2000, during the Camp David talks, we would have faced a simplified refugee issue, and today, in 2023, we could have been edging toward three decades without UNRWA in the Palestinian areas and with many fewer refugee camps. And even if there was a logic to justify funding UNRWA until Permanent Status negotiations in 2000, why continue to do so after their collapse, in Gaza after Hamas took over, and in the West Bank when there are no negotiations now or moving forward?

Furthermore, the radicalization of the Palestinian positions on this issue was also paid for by the well-meaning governments of Canada and the UK. In 1997, I was invited to join the so-called Ottawa Process along with other Israeli, Palestinian, and international experts.[38] Our goal was to brainstorm ideas about the resolution of the refugee issue, and the highlight of that process was a conference about compensation schemes for Palestinian refugees. The entire effort was paid for by the government of Canada, which was the gavel holder of the Multilateral Refugee Working Group that was established following the Madrid Conference of 1991. Toronto's McGill University was engaged to lead this process, and it deploying a well-intentioned, highly informed, and friendly team. I had a nice personal connection with them.

In general, Canada has been supportive of the Two-State Solution, so it was most likely interested in deploying its precious foreign-policy budget on a pragmatic engagement among Israelis and Palestinians. Indeed, all the Israeli participants in the Ottawa Process were senior professionals and veterans of the Israeli peace camp, such as Prof. Eyal Benvenisti and Major

---

38 For a summary of the Ottawa Process from the Palestinian perspective, see Rempel, Terry: "The Ottawa Process: Workshop on Compensation and Palestinian Refugees." *Journal of Palestine Studies* 29, no. 1 (1999): 36–49. https://doi.org/10.2307/2676429.

General Shlomo Gazit. The conference was also very timely, taking place late in Netanyahu's tenure, when a change of power in Israel seemed imminent, opening the door to a resumption of Permanent Status negotiations. In other words, this was a time to be constructive.

Unfortunately, the conference went in the opposite direction when it was hijacked by radical Palestinian voices, many from the Palestinian Diaspora, as well as by their European and Canadian supporters. All of them colluded to present extreme positions that were synonymous with the moral, economic, and practical termination of Israel. The well-meaning organizers, helplessly bound by their role as even-handed facilitators, effectively lost control of their own conference, which turned into a hostile clash between the Israelis and that radical group. The Palestinians were so extremist that they even turned against the PLO, challenging its stature as a representative of the refugees and its power to make decisions regarding their claims. Specifically, they were suggesting that all refugees could "return" and that every single refugee could adjudicate a claim against Israel as part of a "just solution"—millions of claims by millions of individuals instead of one collective claim put forth by the PLO. This was not only ludicrous but ironic, because the PLO was founded to represent the refugees. The Israeli contingency was, of course, furious. I told our Canadian hosts that if the Israelis who came to Ottawa—leaders in the Israeli peace movement like Gazit and Benvenisti—were so outraged, then the Ottawa Process was useless and counterproductive. I felt for its organizers, whose party was rained on.

It didn't have to be that way. By the late 1990s, the work of peacemaking had become professionalized to a level at which we rarely experienced the kind of head-butting that happened in Ottawa. Meetings were substantive and practical, and participants were often very friendly between sessions. We had come to understand that political and historical debates were a waste of time compared with the potential of working together. Arguments about who created what problem or who was responsible for which injustice were checked at the door. Occasionally a heated debate erupted, but we learned to quickly get back to the work of designing peace and coexistence.

When Europeans joined our discussions, that constructive environment was at risk, because both sides became prone to posturing, knowing that our European colleagues were reporting to their governments. This happened

even when they confined their roles to those of convenors, facilitators, and
providers of professional expertise, and refrained from taking positions on
the substantive bilateral work of conflict resolution. But some European
NGOs simply stood with the Palestinian side and became mere detractors.
Their rationale was that the Palestinians were weak compared to the Israelis,
so the European intervention was required to counteract the asymmetry. In
our track-two work, this approach was nonsensical and often patronizing to
both sides, because the Israeli delegation was deeply committed to supporting Palestinian capacity-building. This happened in a range of areas, such as
health care, environment, water management, economics, and security, and
with funding from the government of Israel, including during Netanyahu's
first government in 1996–1999. Moreover, many of the Israeli experts volun-
teered for that work because they believed that sharing expertise was essential
for stable relations in Permanent Status.

Chief among such antagonistic European organizations was the Adam
Smith Institute, a group funded by the British government to help build the
Palestinian Negotiation Support Unit—known as NSU—that was created to
staff Palestinian negotiators. I first met members of the Adam Smith Institute
at the ECF office in Tel Aviv in the early summer of 1998, when they came to
meet Hirschfeld and our team. They arrived wearing thick British wool jack-
ets and drenched in sweat, which turned out to be symbolic of what was to
unfold. Mistaking the ECF for a potential ally and perhaps a confidant, they
tried to sell us on the view that international law, and specifically 194, should
be the starting point for negotiations and the foundation for the resolution of
Palestinian refugeeism. Hirschfeld tried to convince them that a creative and
pragmatic approach that balanced both sides' concerns, needs, and interests
would be far more constructive, that whatever would be agreed upon could
represent the "just solution" that the Palestinians sought, and that therefore
194 shouldn't be the starting point for negotiations but rather their endpoint.

The two sides were talking past each other, and Hirschfeld began to
lose his temper. He told the Adam Smith folks that lawyering up was a bad
idea for the Palestinians because Israel had a much larger pool of legal talent
to throw into a futile legal dogfight. He was trying to impress upon them
that the Israeli-Palestinian conflict would be resolved by politicians and not
between lawyers in courts, and that therefore it was better to focus on what is

feasible. Alas, the Adam Smith folks would not budge from their conviction. Hirschfeld had little patience with, and some contempt, for such purist idealistic interventions, and the meeting quickly deteriorated, with our guests receiving a piece of Hirschfeld's mind.

Nonetheless, the Adam Smith Institute would go on to spend millions of British pounds helping the NSU sharpen their legal arguments, which were rarely used during the Camp David negotiations or later. In 2011, thousands of NSU documents were leaked to the press, exposing a string of hawkish legalistic positions on all outstanding issues. These documents remain available online as a long-lasting proof for critics who claim that the entire effort to negotiate a peace treaty was doomed. I am sure that the British government, like the Canadian government, was convinced that their money was supporting peace. Sadly, in some cases, their work produced the opposite effect.

These events indicated that the Palestinian side was not ripe for resolving the refugee issue. We knew it ahead of the Permanent Status negotiations, because their political system was deadlocked and riddled with conflicts, which prevented any constructive discussion of that topic; they simply stuck to their default positions regarding responsibility, return, compensation, and 194. Astonishingly, after decades of struggle, they did not have a single concrete and feasible idea about how to address the plight of their own people. As strange as it may sound, it often felt like the Palestinian leadership didn't have a real interest or a sense of urgency in resolving the plight of its refugee constituency.

Why then did our delegation sink its teeth into the detailed resolution of Palestinian refugeeism? We could have played along with the Palestinians, ignoring the topic altogether or kicking the can down the road, since on this topic time was on Israel's side. With every passing year, decade, and generation, the refugees of 1948 grow older and fewer, the next generation intermarries with non-refugees and relocates out of the refugee camps, and the passion around this issue wanes. Well, Barak wanted End of Conflict and Finality of Claims, so we needed to identify every potential claim by any group of Palestinians and offer a way to address it. And the primary cluster of claims was related to the refugees and their descendants.

These circumstances left the Israeli side—primarily Sher and me—to formulate the article of the FAPS on Palestinian refugeeism, *without* Palestinian input. The benchmarks of End of Conflict and Finality of Claims meant that UNRWA had to be dissolved; refugee camps had to be formally integrated into the adjacent local municipalities; all Palestinians had to become citizens of Palestine or some other country; financial and property claims had to be addressed; and UNGAR 194, the Right of Return and a "just solution" had to be declared as "implemented." In Permanent Status, there could be no "Palestinian refugees," "refugee camps," UNRWA, or any further Palestinian claim from Israel emanating from the plight of the refugees. In this light, we articulated a coherent and comprehensive framework for resolving Palestinian refugeeism, walking on the razor's edge of balancing Palestinian and Israeli narratives, needs, interests, and concerns. Eventually, that draft agreement became the first and perhaps only comprehensive offer for the resolution of Palestinian refugeeism ever presented by Israel.

But the resolution of Palestinian refugeeism had much broader implications for Palestinian citizenry: in Permanent Status, Palestinians in the West Bank and Gaza—roughly 45 percent of all Palestinians, not including Arab-Israelis[39]—would become passport-carrying citizens of Palestine; Palestinians who end up on the *Israeli side* of the border, such as in Yerushalayim, would become passport-carrying Israeli citizens and residents; Palestinian refugees in Jordan, Syria, and Lebanon could choose between staying in place, repatriating to Palestine, or emigrating to other countries; and a tiny minority of humanitarian cases would be allowed to settle inside Israel. At that point, the plight of all so-called "displaced persons" who became refugees because of the 1967 war would be resolved as well, along with the plight of all Palestinian refugees.[40]

---

39   For example, see Media Line, *Report: 13.8 Million Palestinians Live Around the World* (July 12, 2021, https://themedialine.org/headlines/report-13-8-million-palestinians-live-around-the-world/#:~:text=There%20are%20some%2013.8%20million,West%20Bank%20ang%20Gaza%20Strip): 5.2 million live in the West Bank and Gaza, 6.2 million in Arab countries, and 0.7 million in other countries.

40   The number of displaced persons is estimated by Palestinian sources to be 300,000 based on Gussing Nils-Goran. *Report by the Secretary-General under General Assembly Resolution 2252 and Security Council Resolution 257* (United Nations, 1967, https://www.un.org/unispal/document/auto-insert-181277/).

The Perfect Directive for Responsibility and Return

FAPS Article 4: Refugees [Provisions 71–75, 92, 94–95]

71. The Parties are <u>cognizant of the suffering</u> caused to individuals and communities on <u>both sides</u> during <u>and following</u> the 1948 War. Israel further recognizes the urgent need for a humane, <u>just</u> and <u>realistic</u> settlement to the plight of Palestinian refugees within the context of <u>terminating the Israeli-Palestinian conflict</u>.

72. A resolution of the Palestinian refugee problem <u>in all its aspects</u> will be achieved through an <u>international effort</u> … Israel, in accordance with this article, will take part in this effort.

73. The termination of the Palestinian refugee problem shall incorporate possible <u>return to Palestine</u>, integration within <u>host countries</u> and immigration to <u>third countries</u>.

74. In light of the era of peace, the Palestinian party recognizes that the <u>right of Return</u> of Palestinian refugees shall apply <u>solely to Palestine</u>. Israel recognizes the <u>right of Palestinian refugees to return</u> to the Palestine.

75. Israel shall, as a matter of its <u>sovereign discretion</u>, facilitate a <u>phased entry of [XX] Palestinian refugees to its territories</u> on <u>humanitarian grounds</u>. These refugees shall be <u>reunited with their families</u> in <u>their present place of residence</u> in Israel, <u>accept Israeli citizenship</u> and <u>waive their legal status as refugees</u>.

---

92. The wishes and claims of the Palestinian refugees shall be taken into account to the extent and manner agreed between the Parties in the FAPS and CAPS.

94. Israel shall have <u>no further commitment or obligation</u> emanating from the Refugee issue beyond those specified in this Agreement [i.e the FAPS —GG].

95 The implementation of this Article and the completion of the Commission's work … shall <u>resolve the Palestinian refugee problem in a permanent way</u> that amounts to the <u>implementation of all relevant international resolutions</u> [i.e. 194 —GG].

Negotiations on the Palestinian refugee issue were deadlocked from the get-go and remained so until the last minute. Until April, neither side was in a hurry to progress, but as of May, the Israeli side was eager to move forward, as Barak began to eye the Camp David summit. Our team had to prepare for such a scenario, and Barak gave us the mandate to do so. Regarding Palestinian refugees, he may have not known the exact details of our proposal, but he saw its principles clearly: there could be no exclusive Israeli responsibility for the creation, preservation, or resolution of Palestinian refugeeism; no compromise of Israeli sovereignty; no recognition of the Right of Return to Israel; and no entry of refugees into Israel in any significant numbers.

From Sher's perspective as chief negotiator, this was an ideal mandate, because it established clear redlines but also allowed for significant flexibility. For example, within Barak's directive we could ignore the issue of responsibility altogether or just focus on a shared effort to resolve Palestinian refugeeism, as long as Israel's responsibility was not exclusive. On the Right of Return, Barak's directive meant that Israel could recognize the Right of Return to Palestine, to "their homeland," to the evacuated settlements, or even to the swapped territories, as long as they did could not "return" to Israel. We could also agree to entry of some refugees into Israel, as long as such entry was at Israel's discretion. In this regard, Israel's starting position indicated that 10,000 of the *original* 1948 refugees would be allowed to settle in Israel, with their families, on the grounds of "family reunification" or "humanitarian cases." Indeed, that principle was adopted in the Clinton Ideas, and it has been part of all negotiations ever since.

Beyond the challenge of Palestinian passivity and reluctance to put forward any concrete proposal, which I've discussed, there was also a gap in the approach to the negotiations. The Palestinian side wanted to first discuss the principles of the agreement and then deduct the detailed arrangements, while Israel wanted to first agree on the details of Permanent Status and then extract the principles of the FAPS. For example, the Palestinians demanded that Israel first acknowledge the Right of Return and "assured" us that the ensuing arrangements would ensure that most refugees would settle outside Israel. They wanted us to accept full and exclusive responsibility for the plight of the refugees and promised that Israel would not incur the economic costs of its resolution. Clearly, neither Barak nor any other Israeli prime minister could agree to such demands for one simple reason: we held those claims to be untrue and knew that even some Palestinian delegates held these demands to be an overreach.

One such moment tells the entire story. By Israeli law, every citizen who writes a letter to a government agency is entitled to an official response. In compliance, the Office of the Prime Minister, like other ministries, has a special team that responds to such letters, in most cases laconically. But some letters stand out. One day, the head of this team, a gentle woman who spoke Hebrew with a heavy British accent, approached me in the Aquarium and said: "We received this letter about Abu Mazen. I think it may be of interest to you." It came from a former academic who had researched the early days of the PLO. At the time, the rivals of the PLO were Arab governments who would not recognize it as the legitimate representative of the Palestinian people. Against this backdrop, in the early 1970s, Abu Mazen published a series of articles that blamed Arab countries for the creation and preservation of the refugee problem. These articles were golden for us and were immediately added to our stack of documents.

A couple of months later, in June 2000 at Andrews Air Force Base, one of the sessions was dedicated to the refugee issue. Expectedly, the Palestinian side began with their hardline claims on this issue, and the meeting quickly became tense, aggressive, and even hostile. This was a perfect moment to share these articles with them, and we did. The Palestinians did not even know that they existed. The meeting basically exploded.

Reverse Agrarian Revolution with $40 Billion

FAPS, Article 6: Refugees [Provisions 76–81, 83–86, 88–91]

76. An International <u>Commission</u> shall be established. Canada, the EU, Host Countries, ... Palestine [PLO] ... UN, the U.S., and <u>Israel shall be invited to participate</u>. Special attention ... to the <u>special role of ... Jordan</u> ...

77. An international <u>Fund</u> shall be established and supervised by the Commission and the World Bank ... It will <u>collect, manage and disburse the resources</u> pertaining to the rehabilitation of and compensation to Palestinian refugees.

78. The objective of the Commission and the Fund is to provide for <u>a comprehensive and conclusive settlement</u> of the Palestinian Refugee Problem <u>in all its aspects</u>.

79. The Fund shall establish and manage a <u>Registration Committee</u> in order to <u>compile a definite and complete register of property claims</u> of the refugees due to the 1948 War. The modalities ... of the registration of claims, their verification and pro-rata evaluation ... shall be determined by agreement upon the establishment of the Fund....

80. ... the <u>register of the claims</u> verified by the Registration Committee shall constitute <u>the definitive statement of all Palestinian refugees property claims</u>.

81. <u>Every Palestinian refugee-household</u> that became a refugee in 1948 or its direct decedents may, <u>within agreed period</u>, submit <u>one sole claim</u> due to the 1948 War ... <u>No further individual claims</u> may be filed <u>beyond the agreed date</u>.

83. The <u>rehabilitation of refugees</u> in their <u>current places of residence</u> or their <u>relocation</u> to their new places of residence shall be carried out on the basis of a comprehensive Programs for Development and Rehabilitation (PDRs). The PDRs will be concluded between the Commission, the Fund and <u>the relevant country</u> with the aim of enabling the refugee to rebuild his life and the life of his family.

84. The PDR shall provide for <u>gradual elimination of the formal and practical aspects of the refugee problem</u> including the <u>phased withdrawal of UNRWA</u> within 10 years and the transfer of its responsibilities to the Host Country, the provision of <u>full personal-legal status</u> to all refugees that wish to live in such Host Country and the settlement of its <u>national refugee-related claim</u>.

85. The Parties shall call upon the international community to support the permanent settlement of the Palestine refugee problem by <u>defining a Lump Sum [of XX]</u> and to develop <u>immigration options</u> for those refugees wishing to immigrate to third countries. The Lump Sum shall provide for <u>all the financial requirements for the comprehensive and final settlement</u> of the Palestinian refugee problem including those of <u>rehabilitation and all individual or collective claims</u>.

86. Eligibility of a claimant to property compensation shall be propor-
tionate, limited by and subject to the resources accumulated by the
Fund, as well as by allocations to rehabilitation programs. Transfer of
compensation to a claimant shall be conditioned by such claimant's
waiver of further proprietary claims.

88. ... Israel will address the issue of a financial annual contribution of
$[XX] for [XX] years.

89. The mandate of the Fund and the Commission shall be concluded
between the Parties in the CAPS based on this Article.

90. The Commission, the Fund and Palestine shall design and implement a PDR for the permanent resolution of the Palestinian refugee
problem in Palestine within 10 years of the conclusion of the CAPS.
Palestine shall view the implementation of this program as a final
settlement of its national claim in this respect.

91. UNRWA records shall be the main basis of the implementation of
this Article. Records from other relevant sources shall be subject to
the Commission's scrutiny and approval.

FAPS Appendix: Transitional Arrangements

1. Settlements, the majority of the inhabitants of which will express
their wish for relocation to Israeli Territories, shall be transferred to
Palestine in the context of the Israeli contribution to the settlements
of the Palestinian refugee problem.

As I educated myself about Palestinian refugeeism, I discovered an important
fact: during the period of the British Mandate, Palestinian society was highly
stratified, and a few families controlled the economy and owned most of the
land. An urban legend says that one family owned contiguous properties
from the Jordan River to the Mediterranean Sea. The practical implication
of this reality is that most Palestinians refugees who ended up in refugee
camps were dwellers on lands that were not their property. This fact posed a
significant challenge when we came to envision the resolution for Palestinian
refugeeism.

The Palestinians initially demanded an open-ended compensation scheme to refugees for their plight and for lost property. Meanwhile, in the spirit of Finality of Claims, Israel demanded a lump-sum agreement with a finite financial framework, which would also provide for a comprehensive economic package. The goal was to set the Palestinian economy on a path of long-term development that would benefit all Palestinians and particularly those still living in the refugee camps. Based on conversations with the U.S. government and the World Bank in Washington, we had the impression that as much as $40 billion could be allocated over 20 years for that purpose if an agreement on Permanent Status was reached. We had lots of money to play around with—in our dreams, of course.

The logic of having a lump-sum agreement went beyond achieving Finality of Claims. We wanted to allocate resources to infrastructure, housing, healthcare, and education, which favored public interest over individual rights. We also sought to reverse the Palestinian tendency to expand the definition of who was a refugee by incentivizing "real refugees" to disqualify "wannabe refugees" from the lists of UNRWA. Finally, a lump-sum would encourage refugees to settle their claims early when funds were available as opposed to withholding settlement until an indefinite future.

Alas, these goals were incompatible with Palestinian goals. If we made good on property rights, as the Palestinians demanded, a few wealthy families would get most of the money, notwithstanding the fact that many of them had never lived in a refugee camp and had significant business interests outside Palestine. Meanwhile those who needed the money most would get little or nothing. Such an outcome would be unjust, and could result in popular opposition to the agreement and lead to social unrest and political instability.

Israel had additional goals. We wanted the refugees to become citizens and permanent residents of the places where they were *currently* living. We assumed the Palestinian leadership would want that outcome as well to avoid a mass migration of poor refugees to nascent Palestine, which could crush its economy and create massive social and political ripple effects. Hence, we needed to figure out a way to phase the process, and to receive the consent of individual refugees and the willing participation of all Host Countries involved, primarily Jordan. We found a hook for our approach in a Palestinian book, which said that about half of the land of every Palestinian community was designated for public use: schools, roads, wells, waterways, and other community resources. It was an unverifiable piece of data, but it seemed plausible, and it was useful.

So we proposed that 50 percent of the monies allocated for the resolution of the refugee problem would go toward public works in Palestine and the Host Countries, based on the number of refugees they invited to stay. This meant that $20 billion of the aforementioned $40 billion would effectively be an economic assistance package for roads, water and sewage systems, schools, power plants, and other infrastructure projects. We expected that such a package would lure additional funds from international financial institutions, making an altogether hard-to-resist proposition. Based on our estimations, Palestine and Jordan would *each* get at least $8 billion for incorporating roughly 80 percent of the refugees between them, while Lebanon and Syria would each receive $2 billion if they invited the Palestinian refugees who live in their land to become their citizens. In addition, each Host Country would need to sign away any *national* claim against Israel, the international community, or the Palestinian state due to hosting the refugees hitherto and to assume the responsibilities of UNRWA, which would have to withdraw from their areas.

The other 50 percent of the funds—an estimated $20 billion—would go directly to refugee households: $16 billion to refugees in Jordan and Palestine, and $4 billion to refugees in Lebanon and Syria. This meant that Jordan and Palestine would each receive $800 million per year for 20 years through their economic development packages and the transfers to households. As a reference point, the entire U.S. aid package to Jordan in 2021 was roughly $1.7 billion, with about a third designated to military assistance.[41] Indeed, these would have been huge sums of money that could have upgraded economic development across the entire region. And we had no objection to prioritizing the treatment of refugees in Lebanon, as the Palestinians requested, because of their distressed conditions. For Israel, that package came with three conditions: that the household monies be linked to relinquishing refugee status; that those who renounced their property claims would be fast-tracked; and

---

41   U.S. Department of State, *U.S. Relations with Jordan – United States Department of State*, (U.S. Department of State, https://www.state.gov/u-s-relations-with-jordan/, September 16, 2022.)

that the monies be allocated to long-term personal investments and savings such as home ownership, small business loans, scholarships, and pensions.

A $20 billion budget of individual allocations for 4,000,000 refugees equates to $5,000 per person, including children of all ages. As Palestinian households are traditionally large, these payments would add up to $30,000 for a family of six. In Jordan, for example, the average annual income in 2000 was $1,700;[42] thus each refugee family could receive a life-changing sum equivalent to multiple annual salaries! Furthermore, this money would "travel" with the family, turning these former refugees into sought-after citizens who came with resources for development. We envisioned a competition among Jordan, Syria, Lebanon, and Palestine, each trying to attract the refugees to take the package and settle in their midst.

Fundamentally, this approach was inspired by the Marshall Plan, which allowed for the rebuilding of Europe following World War II. With equal import, we hoped to declare our economic package at the signing of the FAPS, heralding a period of long-term economic development. A similar understanding of the link between economic growth and peace-building informed the Trump Plan, but with a major difference: for us, economic development would be the consequence of peacemaking. For Trump, economic development was going to be the driver.

Was ours a fair proposal? I think it was. At the ECF, we estimated the value of the property that Palestinians had left behind in 1948. With Prof. Ezra Sadan, a world-renowned Israeli macroeconomist, we ran different extrapolations based on pre-war data from the British mandatory government. Using average annual interest rates over the 50 years since 1948, we landed on a valuation of 7 to 8 billion dollars in 1999 terms. Admittedly, the calculation may be seen as skewed downward in Israel's favor, but the Palestinian suggestion of using present-day valuation of the land made no sense, because it used Israeli growth rates to appreciate Arab properties, when no neighboring Arab country had grown at the pace of Israel. The Palestinian approach meant that in certain areas—like the Palestinian community of Sheikh Munis, which stood where Tel Aviv University is today—the value of

---

42   Macro Trends: Jordan GNI Per Capita 2000, *Jordan GNI per Capita 1978–2023,* (n.d. https://www.macrotrends.net/countries/JOR/jordan/gni-per-capita)

the property of a single community would be billions of dollars. In any case, our calculation gave us a sense of scale and confidence that $40 billion was a very generous sum to work with.

One way or another, we figured Israel would still end up dealing with two constituencies that would not finalize claims. Both were expected to be small: those who would insist on their personal Right of Return to Israel and those who would seek to pursue property claims through the courts. We believed that we created powerful incentives for refugees to settle in their places of residence, take the financial package, and move on with their lives. At the same time, we envisioned strong disincentives for individuals to continue the struggle, primarily by deferring the outstanding claims until after all other issues were settled, namely in 20 years.

Leaving such unresolved issues would have been a major compromise for Barak because it diminished his ability to point to Finality of Claims upon signing the FAPS and exposed him to criticism by the opposition. It also meant that we would accept that the PLO could not negotiate the private claims of refugees. Nonetheless, we believed that our approach represented a win-win-win for Israel, Palestine, and the Host Countries, as well as nearly terminating Palestinian refugeeism because UNRWA would be withdrawn, refugee camps would disappear from the maps and be integrated into nearby local towns, and most refugees would become citizens of Palestine or other states—as close to End of Conflict and Finality of Claims as politically possible.

Arab-Jews and Jewish Refugees

FAPS Article 4: Refugees [Provisions 71, 82, 96]

71. The Parties are <u>cognizant of the suffering</u> caused to individuals and communities on <u>both sides</u> during <u>and following</u> the 1948 War...

82. The parties agree that <u>a just settlement</u> of the Israeli-<u>Arab</u> conflict should <u>settle the claims of Jewish individuals and communities</u> that left <u>Arab Countries</u> or part of Mandatory Palestine due to the <u>1948 War and its aftermath</u>. An international mechanism affiliated with

> the above commission and Fund will be established to deal with such claims.
> 96. The Parties encourage the Refugee Multilateral Working Group to continue its work ... specifically focusing on those <u>individuals who personally became refugees during the 1948 War</u>.

Before our departure to Camp David, Barak asked Sher to meet with Prof. Shimon Shetreet, a distinguished scholar of law at the Hebrew University and a former minister and Member of Knesset for the Labor Party. Sher invited me to join him. Prof. Shetreet was born in Morocco and proudly represented the millennia-long heritage and legacy of that community. In 2000, he was the leader of the World Organization of Jews from Arab Countries (WOJAC), which represented Arab-Jews from across the Middle East, including Algeria, Morocco, Tunis, Libya, Egypt, Yemen, Syria, Lebanon, Bahrain, Iraq, and even non-Arab Iran. These Jews had lived among their Muslim and Arab neighbors for centuries, sometimes millennia, but when Israel was established and the Arab-Israeli conflict erupted, some 850,000[43] of them had fled their homes, often due to mob violence or state persecution.

WOJAC was monitoring the Camp David negotiations and saw a historic opportunity to achieve a few goals. Primarily, they wanted awareness and recognition of their plight and legacy. But they were also hoping to receive financial compensation for lost properties as part of the overall financial settlement of the Israeli-Palestinian conflict. Lastly, they wanted to counterbalance Palestinian claims against Israel with the story of the plight of Arab-Jews and their own financial and property claims, which totaled $30 billion.[44] Their claim was that a "just settlement" of the refugee problem, which is called for in 194, includes a resolution of their plight as well.

Undoubtedly, theirs was a story of mass displacement, deep trauma, and tremendous financial loss. And clearly the legacy of Arab-Jews was

---

43   World Jewish Congress, *The Expulsion of Jews from Arab Countries and Iran – an Untold History* (World Jewish Congress, n.d. https://www.worldjewishcongress.org/en/news/the-expulsion-of-jews-from-arab-countries-and-iran--an-untold-history)

44   Levin, Itamar. "Organization of Expatriates of Arab Countries: Value of Looted Jewish Property: 30 Billion USD" (Globes, 8/13/2001 https://www.globes.co.il/news/article.aspx?did=460965.)

overshadowed and sidelined by the Holocaust of European Jews and by the emergence of Israel. Nonetheless, I found it strange that WOJAC would want to associate the miraculous story of the in-gathering of the exiles into Israel with the story of Palestinian refugeeism. After all, a pillar of Zionism is that no Jew can ever again become a refugee if Israel exists.

Their demands took us by surprise, but we listened. Clearly, no Jew was demanding to "return" to an Arab state, so WOJAC's requests were primarily relevant to our negotiations regarding financial compensation for lost properties. And even in that narrower sense, the linkage with Palestinian claims created multiple practical and legal challenges. For example, Israel had an interest in conservative assessments of the value of Palestinian properties, while WOJAC had an interest in inflating the value of Jewish properties. Obviously, in a final agreement, there can only be one way of appreciating properties. Also, many Arab-Jews moved to other countries, such as the U.S., Brazil, Canada, or France. Therefore, while WOJAC claimed to speak on their behalf, Israel had no standing whatsoever in representing them.

A third concern was a country like Morocco, which had never expelled its Jews and was happy to welcome them back. What would be the implications of such a scenario for Israel's position that negated the Right of Return? Finally, while WOJAC engaged us as if we were negotiating a "broader" Israeli-*Arab* agreement, the FAPS was a "narrow" Israeli-*Palestinian* agreement. In sum, it made little sense to introduce the issue of Arab-Jews into the negotiations with the Palestinians.

The issue was also political. Members of Barak's coalition and lobby groups advocated on behalf of Arab-Jews and demanded that Barak include their issue in the FAPS, with the hope of currying favor with potential Sephardic supporters of the Labor Party. Therefore, Barak instructed Sher to take on WOJAC's demands and present them as Israel's. But when Sher raised the issue to Erekat, the Palestinian negotiator brushed him off, saying: "Why don't you go talk to the Arab countries?" In other words, the Palestinians were not a party to Israel's grievances on behalf of Arab-Jews. The exception to that principle were tiny Jewish communities that had been expelled from Gush Etzyon, the Jewish Quarter in Jerusalem, Hebron, Nablus, or Gaza before or during the 1948 War, most of whom could have already returned to their original communities if they so desired. We all acknowledged that Erekat had a point. Nonetheless, while we had a weak legal case, we had a strong historical case: the crisis of 1947–1949 created multiple cases of mass refugees, and the plight of Arab-Jews was as much a plight as that of the Palestinians.

Over the following years, the claims of Arab-Jews gained traction. Israel's government, under Likud prime ministers Sharon and Netanyahu in 2002, 2003, and 2010, recognized Arab-Jews and Iranian-Jews as "refugees" for whom Israel would seek compensation in future peace negotiations. In 2008, the U.S. Congress adopted a similar resolution.[45] The irony of these legislations is inescapable, and their political purpose is clear: to impede and, if possible, prevent future negotiations and agreements with the Palestinians. The fallacy and cynicism of that linkage between Israeli-Palestinian peacemaking and the plight of Arab-Jews was exposed by none other than Netanyahu and Trump. The Abraham Accords and normalization agreements with Morocco and Bahrain were signed without so much as a mention of the plight of their Jewish communities.

45   *House Resolution 185, 110th Congress (2007–2008): Expressing the Sense of the House of Representatives Regarding the Creation of Refugee Populations in the Middle East, North Africa, and the Persian Gulf Region as a Result of Human Rights Violations* (https://www.congress.gov/bill/110th-congress/house-resolution/185, April 1, 2008).

CHAPTER 9

Bilateral, Trilateral and Multilateral

Egypt: The Cornerstone

In January 2021, I arrived in Bahrain for the first time, with Betty. The Abraham Accords had been signed four months earlier, on September 15, but not much could happen among Israel, Morocco, the UAE, and Bahrain during the COVID19 pandemic. I came to Bahrain as guest of the Bahrain Centre for Strategic, International and Energy Studies, Derasat, which is Bahrain's leading think-tank but the visit was also an opportunity to meet Derasat's chairman, Shaikh Dr. Abdulla al Khalifa, who is the deputy secretary general of the supreme defense council and undersecretary for political affairs at the ministry of foreign affairs. In that capacity, Shaikh Abdulla played a leading role in forging Bahrain's normalization agreement with Israel as part of the Abraham Accords. My hosts were eager to learn about Israel's political system, and our first dinner lasted for three hours, creating a unique initial moment in the budding relationship between our two countries.

My talk at Derasat was titled *The Art of Strategic Surprises and Opportunities*. For that talk, I could have chosen many case studies of occasions on which Israel outsmarted its adversaries, but I decided to analyze the strategic surprise inflicted on Israel by Anwar Sadat, the president of Egypt from 1970 to 1981. During his tenure, and particularly by the 1973 War, Sadat masterfully transformed Egypt from a beaten country within the Soviet sphere, recently humiliated by Israel in the 1967 War, to a proudly victorious nation and an ally of the U.S. In that process, Egypt regained the entire Sinai Peninsula, which had been taken by Israel in 1967, and reopened the Suez Canal that had been blocked due to the conflict with Israel. The strategic cost for Egypt was also significant: peace with Israel led to its break with the Arab World, a military conflict with Libya and expulsion from the Arab League, which Egypt had led.

In focusing on Sadat, little did I know that he was admired by my Bahraini hosts. One of them told me that Bahrain's ability to establish normalized peaceful relations with Israel emanates from Sadat's legacy, and that the Abraham Accords are an outgrowth of the Framework for Peace in the Middle Peace, signed between Israel and Egypt in Camp David in 1978.

From 1948 to 1970, Egypt made the struggle against Israel its primary national-security priority. In the 1948 War, after initial successes, the Egyptian army was defeated, and the nascent IDF even invaded Sinai. At the end of the war, Egypt remained in control of Gaza, which it then used as a base for terror operations against Israel. It also sponsored the Fatah movement and the PLO as platforms for the continued Palestinian struggle against Israel. Arafat, who lived in Egypt at the time, was even rumored to be an agent of Egyptian intelligence. That approach subjected Egypt—under King Farouk, and then, following a coup in 1956, under Gamal Abdel Nasser, who was Sadat's ally and patron—to multiple military defeats and tremendous economic drain. It also cornered Egypt with the Soviet Bloc, which treated its Arab allies with a healthy dose of condescension.

Against that backdrop, after Sadat became president following Nasser's death in September 1970, he quickly moved to reframe Egypt's national security goals. His new approach could be framed as "Egypt first," and he quickly moved to effectuate it: in 1971 he alluded to a possibility of peace with Israel and then offered an interim separation of military forces as a launching pad for peace negotiations. Both overtures were rejected by Israel because "it is better to have Sharm El-Sheikh [the southern tip of Sinai] without peace than peace without Sharm El-Sheikh." As Israel ignored his outstretched hand, Sadat launched a total war against Israel in order to force Israel into a diplomatic process. In addition, shortly before the war, Sadat expelled all Russian military advisors and then accepted the diplomatic patronage of the U.S., led by President Richard Nixon and Henry Kissinger.

In 1974, Sadat signed with Israel an Agreement on Disengagement of Forces, similar agreement that he offered Israel in 1972, and in 1977, he stunned the world by traveling to Jerusalem and calling for peace. He then accepted the invitation to join President Carter for a summit at Camp David with Israeli Prime Minister Menachem Begin. Thirteen days later, on September 17, 1978, they emerged with the Framework for Peace in the Middle East, which included the outline of the Oslo Process and of the Israel-Egypt peace treaty. By 1982, all his goals were achieved: Sinai was in the hands of Egypt, the Suez Canal was reopened, and Egypt became an ally of the U.S. Sadly, Sadat did not see the full realization of his vision. He was assassinated by radical Islamists on October 6, 1981 at the commemoration for the 1973 War.

In its negotiations with Israel, Egypt insisted on reclaiming the entire Sinai Peninsula to the last square inch. But Gaza, which Egypt controlled from 1949 to 1967, was not part of its territorial aspirations. Historically, Gaza is beyond Egypt's eastern border, drawn in 1907, so it was always ruled through a military administration. Furthermore, Sadat understood that Gazans have more in common with fellow Palestinians than with millions of Egyptians. So he left the headache of Gaza to Israel.

But Sadat did not desert the Palestinian cause but rather reframed Egypt's leadership on the issue. The 1978 Camp David Accord inspired and guided the Oslo Accords with a five-year Interim Period of Palestinian self-government that was going to allow for resolving the outstanding issues toward Permanent Status. Furthermore, Egypt continued to play a central diplomatic role in Israeli-Palestinian relations through its close ties with Palestinian security forces in Gaza—first with the PA and then with Hamas—and through its influential diplomacy that reported directly to presidents Mubarak and As-Sisi. In the 1990s, that entire operation was led by Omar Sulieman, an intelligence officer turned diplomat and politician, who was also one of Mubarak's closest aides.

Egypt's key man in Tel-Aviv during the years of the Oslo Process was ambassador Mohammed Bassiouni. He and his wife, Nagua, were socialites, beloved by Israel's elite. They hosted many events and countless diplomatic and track-two meetings and were known for their generosity and hospitality. Whenever we would meet at Bassioni's residence, he would welcome us with tea and pastries in the spacious living room, and then show us to the dining room, where all sides would be seated at the large table. He would then "politely" leave the room to "let us do our work." Of course, we assumed that everything that we said was recorded by the Egyptian intelligence and by the Israeli intelligence, so even when we came out to the beautiful garden for a private conversation we would still whisper, covering our mouths with our hands.

The favorite part of every meeting at Bassiouni's house was when, after a couple of hours of deliberations, he would enter the room and say: "You have worked so hard. It's time to get a bite. The chef prepared *a little something* for you." We would then proceed to the next room where a full feast would be on display, enough to feed a platoon of hungry soldiers, with the best delicacies of Egyptian and Arab cuisine. Indeed, those legendary meals may have been the best investment of Egypt's intelligence's because they lured everyone to favor Bassiouni's hospitality.

Egypt's influence on the Oslo Process was very significant until 2001, but it grew even larger after Israel's Disengagement in 2005 and when Israel laid siege to Gaza following Hamas coup in 2007. Henceforth, Egypt controlled Gaza's access to the world and shuttled messages between entities that were officially at war with each other, namely Israel and Hamas, as well as Hamas and the PA. When military conflicts erupted in and around Gaza, Egypt would always play a crucial role in brokering ceasefires and would also mediate multiple other deals such as the exchange of 1,027 Palestinian prisoners for Gilad Shalit. These negotiations would often happen in Cairo, where Egyptian intelligence officers would shuttle between the two delegations. In fact, it is hard to imagine the progress that Israel and Hamas have made in stabilizing the situation around Gaza without Egypt.

Egypt's influence extends beyond Gaza to the PA and to Jerusalem. When Sadat came to Jerusalem in 1977, he insisted on praying at Al-Aqsa Mosque and visited the Church of the Holy Sepulcher not only to emphasize the centrality of Al-Quds to the Arab and Moslem world but also to embody his vision of peace in the Middle East. In 2000, after the Camp David summit, we asked Mubarak to convince Arafat to engage with and accept Barak's overtures on Jerusalem. But Mubarak refused to exert such pressure on Arafat, suggesting that we should explore a long-term interim agreement because the Palestinians were not ready for a comprehensive agreement. Their advice would prove to be wise. Sadly, Israel could not and would not act on it. Indeed, throughout the years, Egypt has been a force of stability and moderation.

This book begins and ends with quotes from Sadat because no other individual has done more for peace in the Middle East than him. In his remarkable account of Sadat's leadership, Henry Kissinger observed: "It was [and still is] too early to judge whether Sadat had started an irreversible movement of history…" Israel's agreements with the PLO, Jordan, the UAE, Morocco and Bahrain "stand as Sadat's vindication" but his bigger and more inspiring vision of peace was stopped short by his assassination. Kissinger testifies that in 1981 Sadat envisioned building a synagogue, a mosque and a church at mount Sinai.[46] Forty years later, that vision was fulfilled by the UAE, when it built the Abrahamic House in Abu Dhabi. Indeed, a direct line connects the 1978 Camp David Accords, the Oslo Process, the 1994 Peace Treaty with Jordan and the 2020 Abraham Accords, as well as Sadat's vision for Mount Sinai and the reality in Abu Dhabi.

Jordan: Missing in Negotiations

In the late 1990s—corresponding with my late twenties—I was a "young professional" in Tel Aviv whose profession was peacemaking, the focal point of global attention. My social circle included Israelis from NGOs and key government units, young diplomats and journalists from around the world, representatives of international organizations, and businesspeople who operated across the Middle East, when Tel Aviv was just becoming a global business hub. We shared the excitement of a thrilling moment in the history of Israel and the region, hanging out in Tel Aviv's cafes, at parties, and on local beaches, and then bumping into one another at conferences in Jerusalem, Cairo, Amman, and throughout Europe.

The star of that circle was a young Jordanian diplomat by the name of Imad Fakhoury. Charismatic, outgoing, genuinely nice, educated, polished, and smart, he was an immediate sensation in the salons of Tel Aviv and the first of many such remarkable Jordanians I met. Imad and the other Jordanians I worked with, in government and nonprofits, were always Britishly polite, pragmatic, professional, and gracious hosts. Food in Jordan was always

---

46   Kissinger, Ibid, pp. 261-276.

delicious, and there was fun to be had in Amman. These encounters built the "brand" of Jordan in my mind. And Fakhoury? Well, not surprisingly, he rose to become a minister and senior executive at the World Bank.

My first visit to Jordan with the ECF was in late 1995. When we drove through Amman, I noticed signs that displayed the slogan "One God, One Country, One King." Because Hirschfeld was a professor for Middle East history, an explanation quickly followed: After decimating the PLO strongholds in 1970, King Hussein embarked upon a national effort to coalesce Jordanian society by opening all circles of business, civil society, and government to Palestinians except for the air force, security services, and a few other key sectors, which remained reserved to Hashemites.

Indeed, some of the most senior Jordanian professionals and civil servants who we met were of Palestinian origin, including our partner and host, Rateb Amro, whose family originated in Hebron. I was impressed by the visionary leadership of Hussein, who, over three decades, led his country from the brink of a civil war into stability as a resilient society, which later withstood influxes of millions of refugees from Iraq and Syria. To symbolize that integration, King Abdullah II married Queen Rania, who comes from a Palestinian family in the West Bank, and their son and heir-apparent, Crown Prince Hussein II, will blend Hashemite and Palestinian origins on the future throne of Jordan.

That coherent national identity and distinct political culture contradicted a slogan often heard slogan from right-wing parties in Israel: "Jordan is Palestine." They claim that Jordan is an Arab state in the area that was "promised" to the Zionist movement in the Balfour Declaration in 1917. By acknowledging the Emirate of Transjordan in 1921, the Jews had already made their historical compromise with the Arabs. Since the 1948 War, Jordan's population has mostly been of Palestinian origin, so Israel does not need to compromise further by accepting a Palestinian state in the West Bank and Gaza. (We elaborated on these events in Chapter 2A, which is available on this book's website.)

While seemingly anachronistic, these ideas continue to inspire and inform some of Israel's far-right thinkers regarding the resolution of the Israeli-Palestinian conflict. As late as 2023, Betzalel Smotritch, the leader of Israel's National Religious Party and Minister of Finance in Netanyahu's Sixth Government, stood over a map of a "Great Israel" that incorporates the entire area of Jordan and the PA under Israeli sovereignty, denying that a Palestinian people ever existed.

At ECF, the first project I led focused on trilateral collaboration among Israel, the Palestinians, and Jordan. Whereas that project focused on *economic* relations, it also highlighted how critical Jordan would be to many other key areas of Israeli-Palestinian relations in Permanent Status—so critical, in fact, that the ECF leadership understood that a separate bilateral track of negotiations between Israel and *Jordan* would be required to envision the *trilateral* relationship among the three countries and ensure peace and prosperity in Permanent Status.

Because Crown Prince Hasan, Hussein's brother and then the heir-apparent, was responsible for the "Israeli file," a meeting was arranged for Hirschfeld with Hasan's senior advisor at a palace that was also a beach villa in Aqaba, clearly visible from Eilat, on the Israeli side of the border. Our goal was to explore the best way for Israel and Jordan to coordinate on Permanent Status negotiations.

That palace is one of the most elegant houses I have ever visited, exquisitely designed in a gorgeous mix of whites, blues, and yellows from floor coverings to furniture, table settings, and drapes. The food was delicious and the hospitality impeccable. As expected, the message we received was that Israel should negotiate its peace with the PLO while keeping in mind Jordan's interests. Our Jordanian interlocutor refused to detail what those interests were.

These experiences and lessons continued to guide me when I joined the peace administration and then the office of the prime minister. At the highest echelons of Israel's government, Jordan's stability and well-being were seen as crucial national interests. At the same time, there was no concrete understanding of Jordan's *particular* interests, which were affected by our negotiations with the PLO. We realized that some agreements with the PLO might be good for Jordan, while others might compromise its interests. Therefore, we anticipated that Jordan might side with Israel on some issues and with the PLO on others.

Meanwhile, neither our embassy nor the Mossad had the capacity to discuss these issues with the Jordanians, and none of our preparatory work at the peace administration analyzed the impact on Jordan of the negotiations with the PLO. In any case, through April 2000, there was little to report to the Jordanians, and as of May, negotiations were unfolding too quickly to keep Jordan in the loop. So, once again, the work, which was done by the ECF in 1998, became useful for our delegation.

We realized that Jordan's interest in Israeli-Palestinian Permanent Status had seven facets. On the issue of Palestinian statehood, we assumed that containing the constitutional and diplomatic reach of Palestine to its own residents and citizens, while preventing Palestine from representing *Palestinians in Israel or Jordan*, was as important to Jordan as it was to Israel. The two countries shared a concern over possible Palestinian irredentism and overreach into our societies, which would be inspired by a vision of a "Greater Palestine" that inherits the entire original territory of the British Mandate from the Mediterranean to the Iraqi border. Hence, we held Jordan's goals to be similar to ours: to establish that Palestine realizes the right of self-determination of *all Palestinians*, including those living in Israel and Jordan, but to limit the representative power of Palestine to its own residents and citizens.

Then there was the issue of borders. Israel's peace treaty with Jordan demarcated two sections of our bilateral border: a southern section from Eilat/Aqaba to the Dead Sea and a northern section from the Beit She'an Valley northward. Meanwhile, an entire stretch of Jordan's Western border—from the middle of the Dead Sea along the Jordan River to the Beit Shean Valley—was left in limbo until Israel and the Palestinians settled their territorial dispute. As I alluded to earlier, according to the Jordanians, until 1988, there was no need for a border there because both sides of the river in that area—the West Bank and the East Bank—were Jordanian territory. And even after Jordan no longer claimed the West Bank, they nonetheless rejected Israel's claim to it. In any case, we believed that Jordan would accept any agreement we reached with the Palestinians.

Jerusalem, and particularly al-Harem al-Sharif, was a much more complicated political challenge because of conflicting claims made by all three parties. The Hashemite Dynasty, which traces its lineage to the Prophet Muhammad, holds itself to be the custodians of al-Harem al-Sharif through the Jordanian Waqf and expects their status to be acknowledged and respected in any agreement between Israel and the PLO. Meanwhile, the Palestinians hold al-Harem al-Sharif to be the symbol of their national identity and seek to control it as well. These competing claims lead to constant competition between the Palestinian and Jordanian Waqfs, in which Israel has favored the Jordanians, and we knew that any FAPS would have to account for Jordan's role in Jerusalem. Indeed, the Trump Plan gave the Jordanian Waqf custody of al-Haram al-Sharif.

A fourth issue was security. In a scenario of peace and stability, Israel, Jordan, and Palestine would have multiple common interests against terrorism and radical Islam. But our concerns focused on scenarios in which Israel would fall into conflict with Palestine or Jordan. To Israel, Jordan was seen as an essential physical buffer against an eastern front, in which Syrian or Iraqi forces would use its territory or airspace to attack Israel. In this respect, Israeli and Jordanian interests were fully aligned, and we anticipated tacit Jordanian support of any credible need we would present to the Palestinians in this regard.

But the more contentious issue was the security arrangements along the Jordan-Palestine border. We never heard it explicitly from the Jordanians, but we believed that they would prefer to have American or Israeli forces stationed along the Jordan River in Barak's "sliver of sovereignty," thereby separating Jordan from Palestine. This made sense because Jordan did not harbor territorial ambitions toward Palestine, but Palestinian ambitions toward Jordan could not be ruled out. Hence, as Israel wanted protection against a threat from the east, we assumed that Jordan would want protection against threats from their west. Furthermore, tight Israeli control of all future crossing points would offer protection against terrorism to all three parties, and we assumed that Jordan would prefer to deal with Israel on such matters.

Another issue, of course, was the refugees. An estimated 40 percent of Palestinian refugees live in Jordan, numbering close to 1.6 million in 2000,[47] a number that ballooned to 2.3 million people in 2022.[48] That is roughly 20 percent of Jordan's population of 11 million. Though many of the sec-

---

47 UNRWA, *Total Palestinian Refugees (1950-Present)*, (at Jewish Virtual Library, 2020).

48 Dabash, Dina Dahood, *From Burden to Economic Asset: Palestine Refugee Camps in Jordan* (Urbanet, October 20, 2022).

ond- and third-generation refugees had married non-Palestinian spouses and moved out of the refugee camps, 10 sites in Jordan were still designated as "refugee camps" and operated by UNRWA. Therefore, any resolution of Palestinian refugeeism would have to be multilateral, consider Jordan's interests, and ensure Jordan's share of economic resources.

Economics and water were two additional areas that brought the three countries together. The water system of the Jordan River and the Dead Sea was shared not just as a source of water but also as a unique tourist destination that could attract millions of visitors, particularly Christians who would want to visit Jesus' baptism site in the Jordan River, Qasr al-Yahud (also known as Al-Maghtas or Bethany Beyond the Jordan), Jerusalem, the Sea of Galilee, Nazareth, and Bethlehem. Furthermore, the Jordanian economy was inseparable from the Palestinian economy in the West Bank, which was closely connected to Israel's, so we had to envision the three economies as one system.

As central as Jordan was to designing Permanent Status, it was never an official participant in the negotiations. Until after Camp David, we had not even discussed engaging its representatives. In fact, only when Permanent Status negotiation got serious did we think about bringing Jordan into the fold to secure its support for the FAPS. Sher and I began to design a secret memorandum of understanding between *Israel and Jordan* to ensure that Jordan's interests were protected and to guarantee its support. But in September the war broke out, and that dialogue never took place.

The signing of the Jordan-Israel Peace Treaty in October 1994 by Hussein and Rabin happened in two steps: first in the Arava desert on the border itself and then at the White House. Personal affection between the leaders was evident, and the peace treaty was framed as being long in the making, given the intimate relationship between the two countries for 25 years in the areas of security, water, and agriculture. But then and now, there has been strong vocal opposition in Jordan's media, civil society, and Parliament to normalizing relations with Israel. The Israeli-Palestinian conflict affects Jordanians on many levels, as I described above, and while the border is open for Jordanians and Israelis to cross, relations are not warm. Unfortunately, that is unlikely to change as long as the conflict with the Palestinians, particularly in Jerusalem, remains unresolved.

Economic Peace

FAPS, Article 7: Economic Relations [Provisions 98–101]

98. Israel and Palestine shall establish a <u>Free Trade Area</u> (PIFTA), which shall govern their trade relations. Thereafter, each party shall <u>independently determine and regulate its own tax policy</u>.

99. The PIFTA Agreement will address inter alia, the <u>border economic regime</u> (including ... customs stations...) ... rules of origin, transit arrangements, intellectual property, ...

100. The PIFTA shall come into being following the establishment of an <u>effective economic border</u>. Until such time ... the Interim Agreement .... shall remain in effect.

101. Each State shall <u>grant workers</u> of the other <u>access to its labor market</u>, without discrimination in comparison to third parties. Each State shall have the sole discretion to determine the policy and number of individuals of the other side eligible to work in its territory.

My first responsibility in the ECF regarding the peace process was staging 11 (yes, eleven!) task forces of Israeli, Palestinian, and Jordanian experts in areas that are important for future regional economic development such as trade, banking, customs, and taxation. The gaps in development between the Israeli economy and those of Jordan and the Palestinians were vast, and much of our work involved transferring knowledge and experience from senior Israeli professionals to their Palestinian and Jordanian counterparts. The effort, funded by the German Friedrich Neumann Foundation, was motivated by the mutual understanding that shared prosperity is crucial for stability in Permanent Status. We envisioned a Middle Eastern version of Benelux, the economic union forged by Belgium, the Netherlands, and Luxembourg, which seeded the European Union.

We knew that the pillar of such a trilateral framework would be the relationship between Israel and Palestine. So, in parallel to the trilateral task forces, in early 1998 we created yet another working group, funded by the Norwegian government. Our goal was to design and formulate a draft agreement on economic and trade relations in Permanent Status, which could replace the Paris Protocol that governs Israel's economic relations with *the PA* during the Interim Period, and, absent an agreement on Permanent Status, remains in effect today.

The effort—named "Economic Permanent Status" or EPS—was led by David Brodet and Dr. Maher al-Kurd. Brodet was then the recently retired director general of Israel's ministry of finance and former chief negotiator on the Paris Protocol. He was supported by other top professionals, such as Yoram Gabbay, former accountant general; Prof. Avi Ben-Bassat from the Hebrew University, who later became director general of Israel's ministry of finance; Arie Zeif, former director of the Israeli tax and customs authority; and Meir Linzen, an expert on international taxation who is now a managing partner of Israel's leading law firm. On the Palestinian side, al-Kurd was a veteran leader of the PLO and a negotiator in Oslo, and his team included senior economic and business leaders as well. I staffed and coordinated the Israeli team, which meant that I coordinated the entire effort. The full forum of the two delegations, numbering nearly 25 people, met every two or three months for three-day conferences in Jerusalem, Tel Aviv, or Oslo. In between the bigger gatherings, smaller task forces worked on specific issues.

We initially explored two models: one was a free trade area, FTA, whereby each country would keep its own economic regime of customs and other regulations, based on an economic border that separated the two economies. The other model called for establishing a customs union, which was based on a shared single structure of customs and other regulations to allow for free flow of goods and services *without* an economic border.

The challenge was that neither model was optimal. A customs union would allow for more economic movement, which would accelerate everyone's growth, but it would also subject all economies to instability due to overriding security concerns that might disrupt free movement. Furthermore, a customs union could not accommodate a special relationship between Palestine and Jordan, as the Palestinians envisioned, given the historic and social ties between the two societies. Meanwhile, an FTA would limit the access of Palestinian businesses to their main market in Israel but might be more appropriate to their development needs in terms of taxes, customs, standards, and other regulations. So, with a customs union being too "open," and a FTA being too "closed," we came up with a hybrid third option that would allow for plenty of free movement but also for distinct economic policies. That model was named after our project—the EPS Model—and our team formulated a full-fledged draft agreement around it.

Working on the EPS Model was my first experience in negotiating and formulating a draft agreement with the Palestinians. Though the exercise was technically non-governmental among nonprofits, and thus could be dismissed as a mock venture, both Brodet and al-Kurd gave it their full attention, knowing that every word and each concession would be carefully reviewed by peers and critics alike. Furthermore, economic relations were considered the easiest issue of Permanent Status, so failure to reach agreement would deliver a negative signal to other peacemaking efforts, just we were anticipating a renewed effort toward a Permanent Status agreement in the aftermath of the Netanyahu government.

When I reflect on that formative effort with hindsight of nearly 25 years, I spot patterns that would be repeated in later years, some even in government. First, the Israeli side put together the entire venture and looked out for all of the parties. In the EPS project, the ECF brought together the Norwegian funders and facilitators and engaged the Palestinian side. There was also equity in funding, even though salaries and cost of living were much higher in Israel. This was important to our Palestinian partners, but it wasn't merely generosity on the part of the ECF. First, we always had additional funding from Jewish philanthropists, while the Palestinians had no equivalent source. Furthermore, such projects were vehicles for the funding of Palestinian and Jordanian pro-peace civil organizations and the rewarding of their senior experts, who were early joiners of the peace movement. Indeed, for many, this was their first professional engagement with Israelis, and they later became avid advocates of peaceful coexistence. And when we saw nepotism—some of our salaried counterparts were family members—we ignored it.

Another precursor of future patterns was the Israeli side doing the bulk of the work, taking care of logistics, conducting the research, and formulating the drafts of what were to be joint documents. We didn't feel taken advantage of because that extra work, particularly formulating the drafts, had

many benefits. While we had to be loyal to proceedings and respect the interests of the Palestinian side, this pattern allowed us to frame the conversation
and advance the deliberations in leaps and bounds. Arguably, this may be a
byproduct of our different cultures, since Israelis tend to be more proactive.
But truth be told, we also had a substantial professional and administrative
edge, with a long bench of experts that had extensive experience in government work, academia ,and international negotiations. The Palestinians, and
to a lesser degree the Jordanians, had little of that. Some were businesspeople
or academics, but precious few, if any, had played at a high level in government or international affairs.

In this context, many of the sessions during the EPS Project were dedicated to knowledge-sharing. For instance, one of our tasks was to prevent
double taxation among Israel, Jordan, and the future Palestinian state—a
necessity for cross-border business, investment, and trade. During the process, funded by the Dutch government, Linzen and Dutch experts tutored
our Palestinian partners on international taxation. When we discussed trade,
Arie Zeif, former head of the Israeli customs and VAT authority, had to do
the same about tax systems. It did seem that the Palestinians and Jordanians
genuinely welcomed the opportunity to learn from us and then work on
future relations as equals.

That generosity extended to using the vast network of the ECF team
and our experts for introducing the Palestinian side to international organizations and experts. A highlight was a visit to Washington, D.C., which
Brodet organized with the help of Prof. Stanley Fisher, who was then deputy
director of the International Monetary Fund and later rose to become gov-
ernor of the Bank of Israel and vice chair of the Federal Reserve. The goal
of the visit was for Brodet and al-Kurd to receive feedback and endorsement
for the emerging EPS Model from the highest echelons of world economics.
The visit included meetings with the most senior professionals in the World
Bank, the IMF, and the U.S. Treasury, as well as with Washington think tanks
and elected officials. At the end of that visit, Brodet joked with me that most
financial leaders of most countries could only dream of the itinerary that I
experienced, but I could only dream of their travel accommodations... :)
And as a side note, during that visit I first met Salam Fayyad, who was then a
senior member of the IMF and later became prime minister of the PA.

The ECF never used our professional advantages to disadvantage the Palestinian side. We believed that Israel's interest would be best served by a thriving Palestinian state, and that getting the better of the Palestinians would break trust and eventually destabilize whatever arrangements are agreed upon. Therefore Israel's starting positions, as conceived and presented by the ECF, incorporated Palestinian interests and concerns, and always had a win-win outcome in view. When an evident clash of interests prevented us from doing that, we would be transparent about it and try to come up with creative solutions.

However, without fail, our first offer would be rejected by the Palestinians, often without specific or substantive feedback. We'd then come up with a second draft that was closer to the Palestinian positions, and inevitably that draft too would get pushed back, which led to a third proposal. Amid this dynamic, every concession that our team made became a stepping stone for the Palestinian side in the next round of discussions. There were obvious reasons for this routine: first, the ECF was more eager to close the deal within the time frame that was promised to funders, and our team of busy professionals were volunteering their time, so we had to keep things moving forward. Meanwhile, the Palestinians, who had little direct interaction with the funders and whose experts were often paid per meeting, had no similar sense of urgency. It sometimes felt as if we wanted to feed more than they wanted to be fed.

But there was another, more profound reason for their deliberateness: neither the Palestinians nor the Jordanians really knew what they wanted. Worse, they did not have the professional capacities that would allow them to figure it out ahead of engaging with us. They shaped their strategy and positions and clarified their interests through their responses to our proposals. In the few times we received an opening paper from them, the thinking represented within was basic.

In any event, by November 1998, we were ready to conclude the mock-agreement about the EPS Model at the residence of the Norwegian ambassador to Israel in Herzliya. It was the culmination of months of work on a mock agreement that we hoped would become the reference point and maybe even the actual draft of the economic chapter of the Permanent Status agreement.

The ECF side was again represented by Brodet, Linzen, Hirschfeld, Pundak, Karni, and me. Al-Kurd came with one other senior member of his delegation.

A lot was at stake for all parties. The ambassador and his team were under pressure from Oslo to deliver an outcome that would continue their legacy of bold diplomacy that had led to the Oslo Accords; compete with Stockholm's Beilin–Abu Mazen Understandings; and justify the massive financial investment that they had made. Within the ECF, we were hoping to demonstrate the full potential of our model of track-two negotiations that produce full-fledged mock agreements. Success would inspire all other working groups on Permanent Status that we were orchestrating and make fundraising easier. Indeed, a lot of money and credibility were at stake.

For al-Kurd, the stakes were higher still. He was struggling to preserve his position as a senior negotiator for the PLO. Being a chief signatory of a breakthrough mock agreement with a highly respected partner like Brodet would boost his stature, whereas failing to conclude such an agreement after lengthy deliberations could jeopardize his standing. Though he claimed to have Arafat's general endorsement for the exercise, figuring out the details was up to him, and he needed to avoid concessions that would be used by his political rivals against him. He too knew that he could not trust Arafat to back him up.

So, before signing the EPS Model, al-Kurd needed to put up a fight in the presence of his colleague to demonstrate that he was pushing the Israeli side to our limits. Anticipating this, ahead of the final meeting, Brodet asked our delegation to identify some outstanding issues within which he could make concessions to al-Kurd without compromising Israel's interests. We then met with the Palestinian side in the early afternoon to discuss a nearly finalized draft, which our team had prepared. Close to midnight, after having negotiated multiple bridging ideas, we still could not find a way to the finish line. Al-Kurd wouldn't budge. He wanted to discuss each topic on its own and expected Brodet to produce additional offers on the sticking points. But Brodet would only agree to a final package that concluded all outstanding points of the negotiations. It was as much a standoff on process as on substance. Neither Brodet nor al-Kurd would compromise.

Finally, Brodet made one last offer that encompassed all remaining points of disagreement. Al-Kurd said that it was not good enough. Signaling his colleague, he got up to leave. After gracefully thanking the Norwegian ambassador and his team for their support, and sincerely acknowledging Brodet and the rest of us for our efforts, he walked out of the residence. We were exhausted, and the Norwegians were clearly disappointed. So was I. Eight intense months seemed to have led nowhere.

But when I said as much to Brodet, he responded, "Maher is not going far. He left his keys on the counter." Indeed, a few minutes later, al-Kurd was back, to fetch his keys but also to issue his own take-it-or-leave-it idea. While outside the residence, he must have gotten a green light from Arafat, and now, around 2:00 AM, he was back in the game. Brodet tweaked al-Kurd's overture, and shortly thereafter they signed the document as the Norwegians brought out the champaign for the toasts. In the years to come, al-Kurd and Brodet remained strong advocates for their EPS Model. Staying friendly, they protected and defended each other's compromises. And when Ben-Bassat, a member of our team, became director general of the ministry of finance and led economic negotiations with the Palestinians, the EPS Model was his point of reference.

Water: Conflict to Peace-building

FAPS, Article 8: Water and Wastewater [Provisions 103–104, 106, 108–110, 113]

103. The Parties acknowledge the importance of water in meeting their vital needs. Accordingly, and with a view to continued cooperation in the spirit of goodwill, they have agreed on the following principles for the comprehensive and <u>final settlement of all the water and wastewater issues</u> between them.

104. The Parties further acknowledge their mutual need of <u>additional quantity of water</u> while recognizing their <u>existing natural resources are insufficient</u> … both parties accord special importance to the <u>development of new water resources</u> with emphasis on the desalination of sea water and brackish water and the reuse of treated wastewater.

106. Both parties <u>recognize their respective sovereign rights</u> over the water resources within their territory that are <u>not shared</u> between them.

> They further recognize the necessity to agree on the [*equitable and reasonable*] allocation for their shared water…
>
> 108. Both Parties attach great importance to protecting and preserving their water resources … they recognize that effective treatment of wastewater will contribute significantly to the protection of their water resources and may serve as an important source for additional water.
>
> 109. The parties will jointly approach the international community for securing the funds necessary for the implementation of all agreed water and wastewater projects.
>
> 110. … the parties undertake … to collect, treat, and reuse or dispose of wastewater originating in their territory … to preserve the quality of the shared water sources … preserve the quantity and ensure the quality of the current surface flows into Israel …
>
> 113. … the CAPS shall address additional issues including … a Joint Coordination and Cooperation Mechanism … Joint monitoring and supervision mechanisms … ownership of infrastructure … infrastructure crossing the territory of the other Party … dispute resolution … financial aspects …

In the 1990s, a popular topic among Middle East experts and geo-strategists was how future wars would be triggered over water. Key flash points were identified to be among Turkey, Syria, and Iraq over the Euphrates River; Egypt, Sudan, and Ethiopia over the Nile River; and between Syria, Lebanon, Israel, and Jordan over the Jordan River. Indeed, struggle over water has been a cause of conflict around the world and throughout history since the time of the Book of Genesis. But the Middle East seemed to be boiling over due to diminishing resources, exploding demographics and "desert expansion," which is how we used to refer to climate change 25 years ago. The precursor was the so-called War on the Water between Israel and Syria in 1966, when Israel fought to pre-empt Syria's attempt to divert the flow of the Jordan River from the Kinneret.

Looking ahead, experts observed that Israel, Jordan, and the Palestinians share a single water system, with sources in Syria and Lebanon that feed the northern Jordan River in Israel, which flows into the Sea of Galilee, which in turn empties into the southern Jordan River, which ends in the Dead Sea. Five countries having a direct interest in the same water system is a recipe for trouble. In addition, Israel and the Palestinians share underground aquifers and therefore sewage treatment concerns and related environmental issues. In total, most of Israel's water relates to areas that would be Palestinian in Permanent Status, while all of the Palestinians' water relates to Israel. But in hindsight, while the experts were correct in their forecasts about the wider Middle East, they were dead wrong about Israel.

On my first day at the ECF, I found a booklet with a glossy cover featuring a satellite image of the Middle East. Published a year earlier, it was authored by Dr. Yossi Vardi, who became director general of Israel's ministry of infrastructure at the young age of 28. In that booklet, Vardi shared a fantastic vision of the Middle East as a prosperous region fully open to the movement of goods and services. He outlined a network of transportation routes that would connect the Arabian Gulf with the Mediterranean Sea and Europe, Asia, and Africa. In his vision, goods from Europe that arrived in Israeli ports would be shipped by train to Jordan and then to Saudi, or oil from Saudi could travel through Israel, bypassing the bottlenecked Suez Canal. His work was aligned with, and supported by, Shimon Peres' vision of a new Middle East. In the hopeful early days of Oslo, it was legitimate to dream big.

An abundance of water was a pillar of Vardi's vision. He envisioned Israel's massive desalination sites fulfilling its own needs and providing for those of Jordan and the Palestinians, thereby making Israel an exporter of water. He foresaw water being pumped back into the Sea of Galilee to reverse its depletion, which in turn would allow for the reviving of the Jordan River, which would once again be an international tourist attraction and would reinvigorate the Dead Sea. As incredible as it all sounds even today, what Vardi dreamed is coming true: Israel has become a world leader in water desalination, and an exporter of water to Jordan and to the Palestinians. The depletion of the Sea of Galilee has been reversed, making possible the revival of the Jordan River and then the Dead Sea. Vardi's visionary thinking allowed for superseding the zero-sum paradigm that prevailed hitherto—namely, if the Palestinians have more water, Israel has less, and vice versa—with an exercise in expanding the pie; that is, more for everyone.

That vision inspired the article on water in the FAPS, which was negotiated by Dr. Noah Kinarti for Israel, and by his Palestinian counterpart, Dr. Samih al-Abid. Noah, who passed away in 2010. Kinarti was a member of Kibbutz Kinneret, which is on the shore of the Sea of Galilee. In Israel, such roots imply being hardworking, modest, down-to-earth, and practical. As an agrarian with a PhD in water, he understood his issue to the most minute nuance. Kinarti was a favorite of the ECF team—particularly Boaz—and had a special relationship of friendship and trust with Rabin and Barak. He also had excellent connections in the Arab communities and knew their language and customs. He respected them, and they reciprocated.

Kinarti met his professional match in al-Abid, a pleasant and professional civil servant in the PA, then serving as director general of its ministry of infrastructure, who rose to become deputy minister and then minister of planning. I believe that they met during the negotiations on the Interim Agreement in 1995, but I was introduced to them when the ECF formed the working group on water in early 1997 to prepare for Permanent Status negotiations. Initially, Kinarti was eager to share knowledge and al-Abed was eager to learn, which eventually allowed them to engage as professionals of equal standing and as friends. Incredibly, both wound up chairing the official delegations for the negotiations on water. They could have had endless, pointless arguments about international law and water rights, but they quickly focused their working group on pragmatic solutions toward mutual prosperity. Indeed, they were able to finalize the draft article on water in the FAPS, which was the *only* article that was ever fully agreed upon.

Who's Leaking the $100 Billion?

In 1998, an ECF team led by Boaz and me started toying with estimating the cost of implementing a comprehensive resolution to the Israeli-Palestinian conflict. The price tag quickly reached $100 billion over 20 years. On top of the $40 billion for Palestinian refugees, an additional $20 billion was earmarked for resettling about 80,000 settlers from dozens of communities in Judea and Samaria, and another $20 billion for the redeployment of the IDF from the West Bank and for constructing nearly 2,000 kilometers of border fences. A final $20 billion would go to the IDF to upgrade its capabilities, given its relocation from the West Bank and most of the mountaintops overlooking the Jordan Valley. This money would come from the U.S. and the so-called donor countries, which included the EU and other European nations, Canada, Japan, and even some Arab nations that supported the Oslo Accords.

The most sensitive piece of the package was the money attached to the relocation of settlers. Barak and others on our team were in communication with leaders of the settler movement, who were opposed to any territorial compromise. But those who were talking to us were also pragmatic and wanted to ensure that the FAPS addressed their concerns. For example, they wanted communities of settlers to have the option of communally relocating within Israel's borders to preserve their social makeup. They promised Barak that such relocation would go a long way to sweeten the bitter pill, which meant that the estimated cost of moving each family of settlers reached $1 million. However, that number would be offset by the fact that Israel was supposed to leave intact their communities with their infrastructure in the worth of billions to become upscale neighborhoods sold to Palestinian middle class. When Israel withdrew from Sinai in 1982, and from Gaza in 2005, every single building had been demolished. We were trying to avoid such wasteful devastation.

The ECF continued to work on the economic package until 1999. As our understanding of Permanent Status evolved, Boaz and I updated our assessments, and our presentation became more convincing. When we finally began to test our estimates on European and American diplomats and economists, their feedback was reassuring. They thought both the package and its allocations made sense.

Until May 2000, during the period of stalled negotiations, no one paid much attention to the size of the financial package. But in December 2000, negotiations became serious, and our delegation prepared for a possible clinching of a comprehensive agreement. In that context, the economic package would be integral to this final leg, not just among Clinton, Barak, and Arafat, but also as a means to mobilize the support of the Israeli and Palestinian publics, as well as of Jordan, Syria, and Lebanon.

We discussed the package with the Americans and its primary funders, and outlined it for the Europeans, particularly their special envoy, Ambassador

Miguel Moratinos. I still had access to the materials that Karni and I had prepared for the ECF two years earlier, and I shared them with Sher, who began to refer to them as part of his briefings. Though I don't remember any official decision being made, an economic package of $100 billion became a reference point for our work.

In June, at Andrews Air Force Base, ahead of the Camp David summit, we discussed it with the American Peace Team as part of our efforts to convince them that we were serious and ready. During that trip, the Israeli embassy organized a day of off-the-record meetings. We briefed the minority and majority leaders in the Senate and House of Representatives and key members of relevant committees that would have to bless the economic and security packages associated with a FAPS.

It was the first visit to Capitol Hill for most of us, and we got the dignitary tour of the building. I was awestruck; I think most of us were, One highlight for me was our time with Senator John McCain. I had known of his legendary courage in battle and captivity, but in the meeting, he projected as a serious politician and statesman. Well-briefed and up to date, he understood the issues at stake and asked smart questions. Clearly, he was extremely supportive of Israel. I felt I was in the presence of an exceptional person.

The most important meeting of the day, though, was with the pro-Israel lobby, AIPAC, which was going to be crucial for mobilizing the support of Congress for the economic package of the Permanent Status deal. AIPAC's delegation included about 10 top lobbyists, professionals, and lay leaders, and we were represented by Sher, Meidan-Shani, and me, accompanied by a representative of the Embassy. We didn't know much about AIPAC, so we relied on our briefing, which had AIPAC leadership leaning hawkish and many of them staunch supporters of Netanyahu, skeptical of the Oslo Process, and suspicious of Barak's recent overtures. So we walked into the meeting warily. We were going to ask for their discretion, understanding that in Washington that was a naïve expectation.

Still, we needed to find a way to earn their full and unequivocal support. In the first part of the meeting, Sher laid out the status of the negotiations and described the gaps on each of the major issues, avoiding disclosure of our true redlines and highlights of the discussions with Clinton's team. The AIPAC delegation seemed disappointed to hear a repetition of Barak's well-known positions and wanted some undisclosed briefings from the "room where it happens." But we didn't trust the confidentiality of the meeting, nor did we trust our own embassy diplomat, whose reports would reach Minister Levy, who opposed the negotiations.

After listening politely and asking some clarifying questions, the AIPAC group asked what we wanted from them. Sher began to describe a "theoretical scenario" of a conclusion of a FAPS, and then listed our security and diplomatic needs should a deal be signed. When we got to the economic package, he explained its logic and then dropped the number: 100 billion dollars. He said we believed Clinton would back it, but we would need their support to shepherd it through Congress. The number shocked them, in part because they misunderstood us to be requesting the entire package from the U.S., and not "just" $40–60 billion. One of them said with typical American understatement: "That is a lot to ask for these days." They didn't assure us that they would get Congressional approval for such a package, but we were confident that Congress would support the legislation necessary for implementing such a historic agreement. All in all, we left Washington thinking we'd had a great visit. Barak received our full report before boarding the plane back to Israel.

When we landed at Ben-Gurion Airport on Friday morning and were shocked by a front-page headline that screamed: $100 Billion: The Cost of Implementing the Permanent Status Agreement." The story laid out all the specifics of our proposal as discussed in Washington the day before. Sher was furious. We thought it was a devastating leak, designed to sabotage the negotiations and prevent a quick approval in Congress. We pointed a finger at AIPAC. Such a leak served both the opposition in Israel and the Republican Party in Washington, who did not want to allow Clinton a major foreign policy achievement. We shared our frustrations with AIPAC's representative in Israel, who denied everything. We did not believe them.

As Permanent Status negotiations got serious, leaks of our internal discussions were becoming a growing problem. We'd see ideas in the press that had been raised only in small fora and discussed in classified documents. With Barak's coalition disintegrating, and in light of his push for a summit at Camp David, each of these leaks frustrated Sher and our team. We accused

Barak's political team, who sat outside the Aquarium, of being the culprits and willing to sacrifice historic negotiations for short-term political interests.

The leaks were relentless, and Sher grew increasingly infuriated. When he became chief of staff, he wanted to stifle them by putting everyone at the Aquarium through a polygraph test to uncover the source. One day we raised the issue with Hasson, asking that he bring in the Shin Bet to carry out the tests. We were sitting in Sher's office, which is separated by a small hall from where Barak was sitting at that moment. Hasson responded by pointing nonchalantly in the direction of Barak's office and saying, "I will do it only if the first person tested is the Prime Minister himself." This was a stunning statement, effectively associating the leaks with Barak. Well, here was a new twist. Barak is, of course, entitled to say what he wants to whomever, even at the cost of making everyone suspicious of one another, of our diplomats, and of AIPAC. And when he does so, "leaks" become "briefings."

Years later, I befriended some senior AIPAC leaders. They remembered the incident and the insult. At least I had an opportunity to apologize. As for the economic package, $100 billion continued to be the number until the negotiations petered out and the Clinton presidency ended, in January 2001.

SECTION III

System Effects

CHAPTER 10

The Dream Peace Team

Making a Make-or-Break Moment

June 26, 2000, was my thirtieth birthday, marking the fifth anniversary of the meeting in Bethlehem that had launched my work on Israeli-Palestinian peacemaking. By that day it was clear that we were heading to a summit at Camp David, and our workload was tremendous, particularly with the American Peace Team in Jerusalem. There was no time for any personal matters. Nevertheless, late in the evening at the lobby of the David Citadel hotel, our delegations celebrated my personal milestone with a cake and toasts. It was spontaneous and modest, but also momentous because we knew that a historic event, which we were all going to be part of, was about to unfold, One toast followed another as my birthday became the pretext for thoughtful comments about the imminent historicity. Regretfully, I was too embarrassed to take notes on the brink of the most dramatic episode of my professional life.

The so-called Peace Team, led by the special Middle East coordinator, Ambassador Dennis Ross, was made up of outstanding individuals who represented different branches of the U.S. government. The highlight of their service, as a team, was during the Clinton Administration, through one of the most remarkable periods of American diplomacy in the Middle East or anywhere. Martin Indyk served as Ambassador to Israel; Rob Malley represented the National Security Council at the White House; Aharon Miller was Ross' deputy; Gamal Hellal was the team's diplomatic interpreter; and Jon Scwartz was their lawyer. In our eyes, it also included Dan Kurtzer, then Ambassador in Cairo. All of them had PhD-level educations and extensive experience in Middle East diplomacy. They knew Israel and the Palestinians. They were hardworking, passionate *mensches*, most of them Jewish, some with deep connections to Israel.

Their primary working assumption was good for Israel. It held that Israel's "security concerns" must be addressed for a peace deal to emerge. Israel's trauma was its pre-1967 "narrow waist," which placed its population centers under threat from the hilltops of the West Bank, and that trauma had to be alleviated in Permanent Status. But the challenge they faced was "containing" Israel's "security concerns" which expanded to incorporate a variety of other interests. For example, does Israel's security mandate sovereignty over the entire Jordan Valley, or perhaps only over a sliver of land along the Jordan River? Who should be stationed along that border: the IDF, American peace-keeping forces, or some international contingency force? And what kind of police and security forces would Palestine be allowed to have? In any case, this American approach gave tremendous leverage to the Israeli side. When we declared that a certain position emanated from a "security concern," the Peace Team would almost automatically support us.

The American team had its weaknesses too. The first was that they focused on reaching a declaration of principles and kept busy formulating and reformulating big-picture statements aimed at resolving the outstanding issues. The Clinton Ideas epitomize that approach. But when we needed more granular understandings that generated greater certainty about Permanent Status, it turned out that they had not sufficiently mastered the details, and this compromised their effectiveness as mediators.

The second weakness was the absence of a strong organizing framework on how to run the Permanent Status negotiations, as would be expected from a superpower that established Israeli-Arab peacemaking as a top foreign policy priority. Therefore, Barak was able to shape the diplomatic process and bring Clinton along to the radical idea of an all-or-nothing, moment-of-truth summit in Camp David. This happened through a series of steps that began with the Sharm Memorandum and the goal of reaching a FAPS with End of Conflict and Finality of Claims. It continued with dismissing any form of interim or partial agreement. In May 1999, Kurtzer warned that an attempt to reach a Permanent Status agreement would lead to a bloody war. This was the last time that I heard of such American concerns. Sadly, only after the collapse of the Camp David negotiations and the outbreak of the war in September-October did the U.S. re-seize the leadership of the peace process to generate the Clinton Ideas.

The collapse of the Swedish backchannel on May 23, 2000, was a major milestone for the Camp David negotiations. At that point, Barak began to push for the summit in Camp David, where either a historic breakthrough would be achieved or Palestinian rejectionism exposed. The "meltdown moment" that Barak had anticipated since the inception of his tenure was coming to fruition: his coalition was crumbling, soon relying on 47 Members of Knesset and on the support of Arab parties; negotiations with Syria collapsed and Israel was already out of Lebanon; the Palestinians were preparing for a possible violent clash that could subject Israel to harsh criticism from the international community for its reluctance to negotiate peace; and pressure on Israel to negotiate with the Palestinians was mounting from the EU, Egypt, and Jordan. Most important, Clinton was eager to make history, and Barak felt that he was the best friend that Israel could ever hope for in the White House.

In late May, Barak was alone in his view that we should go for an all-or-nothing summit. Sher, Ben-Ami, and our team advised him to try to further narrow the substantive gaps through additional negotiations. We agreed that the Palestinian leadership was too divided to negotiate an agreement—at that point Abu Mazen and Abu Alaa were not even speaking to each other—but we hoped that the Americans could still be effective mediators. But Barak concluded that there was no time left for additional maneuvering. He listened to the stern warnings from his intelligence officers and experts that the Palestinians were unprepared for a historic deal and that failure could lead to an eruption of violence. But he reframed the warnings as additional reasons for seeking a summit. His logic was that violence could erupt anytime and anyhow, and that Palestinian incompetence was not a bug, but a feature of their strategic approach designed to push Israel into gradual concessions.

Clearly, in Israel, Barak could decide to go for a summit, but Clinton, Secretary of State Madeleine Albright, National Security Advisor Samuel Berger, and Ross needed to be persuaded to call for it. By early June, Barak was pressuring the Americans to invite Arafat to Camp David, assuming that he would have to accept an invitation from Clinton. But the Peace Team was apprehensive about such a summit in fear that failure would compromise Clinton's legacy and cause a major setback to Israeli-Palestinian relations.

Their next move was to invite both delegations to Andrews Air Force Base for another round of negotiations with the goal of narrowing the gaps ahead of a summit. But the Palestinian team was clearly preoccupied with its internal rivalries, following the backchannel in Sweden and the now-overt clash between Abu Alaa and Asfour in one corner and the group surrounding Abu Mazen in the other corner. In addition, Dahlan and Rashid were consolidating their power to challenge both elder leaders. Expectedly, negotiations in Andrews were futile, and everybody knew it.

That meant that we had some time for shopping and for a night out in D.C. So, after an afternoon stroll among the base's stores, all of the Israelis were wearing bargain Old Navy khakis, which were not available in Israel then. In the evening, the Americans and Israelis frequented a famous steakhouse, while the Palestinians preferred a stronger experience of Washington's night life. In any case, the negotiation round in Andrews convinced Ben-Ami and Sher to support Barak in his conclusion that negotiations among our delegations had exhausted themselves. It was now time for the leaders to convene, since further progress would require Arafat's involvement.

Still the American team remained conflicted. We overheard them when both delegations stayed at the David Citadel hotel. Our team was assigned rooms above theirs, and through the open balcony door we could hear their fierce debates, which once even escalated to a screaming match. They converged on demanding assurances that Israel—namely Barak—would make significant overtures in Camp David, which would force Arafat to engage in serious negotiations and justify Clinton's decision to convene a summit. In other words, they wanted to negotiate with Israel about the contours of the FAPS! These dynamics were probably like the negotiations that took place ahead of the 2003 Roadmap between Bush and Sharon or in the lead-up to the Trump Plan in 2020.

But Barak refused to engage with Ross on the substance of the FAPS and continued to pressure the Americans to call for a summit. The Peace Team had a hard time refuting Barak's "brilliantly persuasive" arguments that emphasized the X factor of Clinton's extraordinary powers of persuasion and charisma, which could break the stalemate if everyone was huddled in secluded Camp David. Appealing to their desire for history-making, he insisted that now was the time to act, and that the risk was worth taking.

To further boost the American willingness to convene a summit, we designed another intervention. Sher and I divided the draft of the FAPS, which included as many as 180 provisions, into three groups of topics and formulated three *separate* documents. The first captured dozens of points that seemed to be "in agreement" based on previous rounds of negotiations, side conversations with the Palestinian delegation, and reports of our intelligence or public statements. To demonstrate Israel's seriousness, that list went far beyond niceties such as a "mutual desire for peace." For instance, it made clear that in Permanent Status there would be a Palestinian state in Gaza and the West Bank connected by a Safe Passage, that Palestine would be demilitarized but have its own security forces, and that all refugees would be allowed to return to Palestine. Furthermore, since this document outlined the *reality* of Permanent Status, each point reflected *mutual and interlocking* concessions. For example, the provision stating that "the Area of Jerusalem will house both Yerushalayim and Al-Quds…" embodied an Israeli concession of recognizing Palestine and its capital, Al Quds, as well as a Palestinian concession of recognizing Yerushalayim as the capital of Israel. These points may sound trivial, but it was the first time that an Israeli government had shared with the U.S. government in writing an outline of an agreement on Permanent Status. And even without any further additions, that document, if signed, could have constituted the most far-reaching articulation of Permanent Status to date.

The second document had about 20 "bridgeable points," at which we believed that strong and effective American mediation could bring the parties to additional understandings *before* a summit, or at least narrow the substantive gaps between them. We wanted the Peace Team to engage the Palestinians, and Israel, in identifying potential bridging formulas. For example, we believed that most disagreements regarding Palestinian statehood could be resolved ahead of Camp David. Just imagine Israel and the Palestinians coming out of the summit declaring that an agreement had been reached on establishing a Palestinian state, even if the details remain to be finalized.

The third document identified and isolated the "summit issues," which only the leaders could resolve as part of a comprehensive deal and a historic quid pro quo. We knew that Arafat could only make concessions regarding the Right of Return or the Old City of Jerusalem in the context of what he called a "peace of the brave" that provides for a Palestinian state and secures other core Palestinian interests. It was useless to negotiate these issues any earlier.

In a meeting at the residence of Ambassador Indyk, Sher gave the three documents to the Peace Team. Together, they balanced Barak's instruction that any Israeli concession must be reciprocated with the American expectation for assurances that Israel will make far-reaching offers in Camp David. In that meeting, Sher was acting as Barak's special envoy, bypassing Eran and the official channels of the Peace Administration. Framed as "non-papers" (working documents without any official logo or signature), the documents were deniable by Barak in case they were leaked. At the time, I thought that Sher was taking a risk and stretching his mandate, but seen with hindsight, he probably acted with Barak's blessing.

We expected the Peace Team to leap into action, engage the Palestinians to verify the points of agreement and bridge those of disagreement, energetically shuttling between the parties to prepare the summit. Unfortunately, that didn't happen. Perhaps Ross was focused on ensuring that Barak would be flexible on the big questions, so the Peace Team had no bandwidth for discussing dozens of more minor points. Perhaps they did not master the details of the FAPS to be able to engage in such negotiations. Also, at that point, roughly three weeks after the collapse of the backchannel in Sweden, the Palestinian leadership was torn by political infighting, and any attempt by the Americans to pressure them would have been quickly and easily brushed off. In retrospect, this was a milestone on the way to the failure of the Camp David summit.

When the Americans finally agreed that a summit represented the logical next step and were going to issue invitations to come to Camp David, Arafat needed to be convinced to accept. He feared being pressured by Barak and Clinton to unwanted concessions or being blamed for failed negotiations. Erekat suggested further deliberations before a summit was convened, but the Americans rejected his suggestion because the Palestinian side had not put forward any concrete proposals beyond rehashing their core positions. Furthermore, they were concerned that Arafat would act on his threats to declare independence unilaterally, risking conflict with Israel and blocking any possibility to negotiate.

At some point, Arafat understood that he could not prevent Clinton from calling a summit and that if he was invited, he would have to go. (As one of his negotiators told us, he wanted to be "dragged to Camp David kicking and screaming.") Eventually, Arafat had his way when Clinton promised him that there would be "no finger pointing." Namely, Clinton pledged not to blame either party in case the summit failed to yield an agreement. Through this brilliant diplomatic move, Arafat turned the table on Barak, placing the onus of the summit on Israel and the Americans. With a guarantee that they could walk away unharmed, Arafat did not really *have to* negotiate in Camp David. The Palestinian side came to the summit skeptical, but willing to be positively surprised.

Once the date for the summit was set for July 11 and the invitations were issued, the pace of events accelerated. Each delegation would have nine "delegates," led by Barak and Arafat respectively, and two "administrative staff," who would room in the service quarters on the edge of the compound. Immediately, a fierce competition broke out among a few dozen Israelis who saw themselves as potential delegates: Barak had at least 10 senior political and national security advisors; the negotiation team, led by Ben-Ami and Sher, included six people; the Peace Administration, led by Eran, Arieli and Crystal, had various committees; we needed a legal team; and Barak's coalition partners on the left yearned to engage in some real peacemaking. History was going to be made and everybody wanted to be a part of it, or at least have a front row seat at it.

There were political considerations as well. The support of the left for any FAPS was all but guaranteed. Meanwhile, some right-wing leaders from Likud, like Ehud Olmert, then mayor of Jerusalem, and Dan Meridor, formerly one of Netanyahu's ministers, seemed open to supporting an agreement. Barak was hoping to bring them into the fold by participating in the summit and co-shaping the FAPS. Their support would be crucial to legitimizing the agreement with the Israeli center-right public and in the Knesset.

Danny Yatom, Barak's chief politico-military advisor, and Sher were tasked with preparing the list of delegates for Barak to approve. I wanted to be part of the delegation but understood that it would be unlikely. Then Novik, always fully informed about what was going on, called me with a golden tip:

"You must go, and you will play a significant role. Title doesn't' matter. Even if you carry bags, you must be there." With this advice, I approached Sher: "The Americans invited nine delegates and two administrative staff. I should be the admin of the delegation." Sher immediately agreed. No senior member of government was willing to walk around Camp David with a badge of "an admin."

Making the final selection of the delegation to Camp David from among those who felt worthy of going became a delicate task. The Palestinian side was dealing with similar dynamics. To alleviate these tensions, Barak suggested "expanding the summit" to an additional location in nearby Emmitsburg, so that large delegations could participate. In case of a breakthrough among the leaders, those delegations would be activated to detail the FAPS. But the negotiations never got that far, and these delegates spent their days visiting nearby historical sites of the American civil war and supporting the local economy in malls. That is why dozens of Israelis and Palestinians can credibly claim that they participated in the Camp David summit.

Eventually, the delegation, led by Barak, included Sher and Yatom, Yanai for the IDF, Hasson for the Shin Bet, and Elyakim Rubinstein as our legal counsel. Rubinstein had Barak's trust and remarkable experience as the legal counsel of the ministry of defense, the chief negotiator of the Israel-Jordan Peace Treaty in 1994, and a veteran of the 1978 Camp David summit! He later rose to become chief justice. The politicians were Ben-Ami as minister of public security and co-chief negotiator; minister Amnon Lipkin-Shahak, who was also a former IDF chief of staff, known for his pleasantness, wisdom, and excellent relations with the Palestinians; and Dan Meridor, as the right-wing member of the delegation. Barak also brought Yossi Ginossar to be his backchannel to Arafat via Mohammad Rashid, who was part of the Palestinian Delegation. The administrative team included me and Einat Glouska, who was a secretary in Barak's bureau and the only woman in the summit, beside Secretary Albright and First Lady Hillary Clinton.

On July 8, our delegation left for Washington, and on July 9, we met the Peace Team and then Albright, which was an opportunity to wear my novelty tie. On July 10, Sher, Yanai, and I entered Camp David as part of the advance team. As we were handed our badges, I was surprised to see that I had been upgraded to a delegate with full access. When I saw Malley, who led the American advance team, he pointed at my badge and said: "I hope you appreciate it. When we saw your name on the Israeli list, we thought that you should be a delegate." On that day, security checks were more relaxed, and no one went through my luggage or asked me to surrender my camera. That made me the only Israeli delegate taking photos of our delegation.

Camp David is a magical place, secluded in the mountains of Maryland and tightly protected by the Marines and the Secret Service. It includes a presidential cabin, called Aspen, which is a gorgeous and spacious wooden house whose balcony overlooks a small golf course and has a magnificent view. There are additional bunks, some larger than others, as well as central cabins with meeting rooms, a lounge, a gym, a library, and a cinema. Naturally, Barak and Arafat got the two biggest and nicest cabins, where Begin and Sadat had stayed 22 years earlier, and the rest of us were housed in the smaller ones.

All cabins and facilities are interconnected by paths, and we roamed around by walking or by driving golf carts. There were fewer carts than delegates, so the initial assumption was that they would be shared. Apparently, it was assumed that we would leave the keys in the carts at our destinations so others could use them. But it was a hot and humid July, and this honor system quickly collapsed when some members, particularly of the Israeli delegation, kept the keys in their pockets. Nobody wanted to walk. Metaphorically, the resource of the golf carts was accumulating at the top, concentrated within our delegation. The Palestinians had to walk. The first intervention of our American hosts, as mediators, was to redress that imbalance and assign carts to each delegation. On our side, things really escalated when Danny Yatom himself—a major general in the reserves and a former head of Mossad—was forced to walk! That night, during our team meeting, he collected all the keys and assigned the "Israeli carts" to our delegation according to hierarchy. Hence, Camp David's little experiment of managing a scarce resource in the best spirit of a sharing economy collapsed and was replaced by tight central management. The irony of the situation did not escape Erekat, who joked to the Americans that they had just witnessed a local form of "Israeli domination." Henceforth, I moved around by hitchhiking or walking.

Barak's cabin—Dogwood—was adjacent to Clinton's Aspen. It had a small entrance corridor, which opened to a living room on the right, with sofas and a TV, and a dining room on the left, with a round table. The living room had a beautiful back porch with a garden table and chairs, and the dining room had an adjacent modest kitchen. In the back was a master bedroom and a smaller guest room. As soon as we moved in, we rearranged the furniture, turning Dogwood into our center of operations, with the entire team crowding Barak's space during the days and into the small hours of the night.

Dan Meridor and I were assigned to a room that had two single beds and basic facilities. I had deeply respected Meridor for many years, so it was an honor to be rooming with him. We did not spend much time in our cabin, but we still had some meaningful conversations. He was genuinely interested in the journey that had brought me to Camp David, and in the rationale of the FAPS. Assigned to the working group on refugees, he needed to climb a steep learning curve, and, to my surprise, there was a lot that I could share with him to get him up to speed.

Camp David Summit

The day-by-day story of the Camp David summit—from July 11 to July 25—has been written up many times from many perspectives, particularly in Sher's seminal book, *Within Reach*.[49] With the hindsight of 23 years, it is no longer as interesting to discuss or debate who said what to whom when and where. The bigger moves of the Summit, however, remain relevant to any future attempt to resolve the Israeli-Palestinian conflict.

In broad brushstrokes, the summit can be divided into four phases. Tuesday, July 11, to Saturday, July 15, was the exploratory phase. In parallel to four working groups, Clinton, Albright, and Berger met with Barak and Arafat and senior members of both delegations to explore the contours of the FAPS. The second phase—from Sunday, July 16, until Clinton's departure for the G8 Summit in Japan on the morning of Wednesday, July 19—was the peak of the summit, when big ideas were presented by Barak and then rejected by Arafat. During the third phase—from Wednesday, July 19, until

---

49   Gilead Sher, *Within Reach: The Israeli-Palestinian Peace Negotiations, 1999–2001* (Routledge Publishing, 2006).

Saturday, July 22—Clinton was in Japan and Albright was chairing the summit, while Barak and Arafat avoided each other, and low-key work took place in the working groups. The last phase began when Clinton returned from Japan on Saturday, July 22, to make a final push toward an agreement. His failure brought the summit to a close on Tuesday, July 25.

The opening session of the summit on Tuesday, July 11, produced iconic images. Our delegations were huddled in Laurel, the central building that houses the largest boardroom. Meanwhile, Clinton, Barak, and Arafat were orchestrated to walk together down a path dressed in smart casual outfits (except Arafat, who stuck to his military fatigues) and smiling to a pool of media representatives shouting questions and taking photos. When they reached the door, Barak wanted to show respect to Arafat by allowing him to enter the building first, and he placed an arm behind Arafat's back to gently push him forward into the hall. Alas, Arafat wanted to extend a similar gesture to Barak, and a funny shoving match erupted, with each man trying to push the other. That moment was televised all over the world.

The first plenary began with passionate speeches by Clinton, Barak, and Arafat about the momentous gathering, all of them pledging to do their utmost to bring peace. There was nothing groundbreaking in their messages. As pre-agreed, we were then quickly divided into four working groups on security, borders, refugees, and Jerusalem. Every member of our delegation was assigned to one or two fora, but we also met with the Palestinians in various other formats. Sher was concerned that most of our delegation did not have a detailed understanding of the "map" of Israel's interests or positions, nor did they understand the overarching framework of End of Conflict and Finality of Claims. Some of our delegates, like Shahak, Ginossar, and Rubinstein, were experienced international negotiators and deeply acquainted with the PA, but they were not up to date about the specific complexities of the FAPS and the work that had been done. Therefore, Sher joined the security and territory working groups and asked me to sit in on the refugees and Jerusalem groups. He also asked me to brief everyone, which I did, sometimes through in-depth sit-down conversations, but also during hurried walks into meetings. The members of our team needed to authoritatively represent Israel, regardless of how well they understood the subject matter.

Meanwhile, Clinton and his senior advisors met Barak and Arafat and other senior delegates to explore the principles of the FAPS.

During the first week, Barak was concerned with Palestinian "pocketing." He was upset with their dogged insistence on their "core positions," their reluctance to put forward any proposal, and with their strategy of turning any Israeli concession into the starting point of the next round of negotiations. So he forbade any exchange of documents, and all conversations were held orally within the framework of "nothing is agreed until everything is agreed." Therefore, we could not explore path-breaking ideas that would leap the negotiations to another level. At the same time, Barak did not want the Americans to document any Israeli positions, in the fear that they would turn into unreciprocated concessions. Meanwhile, the Palestinians were adamantly opposed to the Peace Team putting forward its own bridging proposals. They were concerned that such proposals would embrace the Israeli logic as a starting point for negotiations, force them into unwanted discussions, and place them on the defensive as naysayers. After all, they did not come to Camp David to close a deal. Hence, in all working groups, we and the Palestinians were both effectively posturing, and the summit was heading to a quick deadlock.

So the Americans put forward a document of principles. Our team felt that it was half-baked, and the Palestinians were suspicious that it had been coordinated with us. It definitely exposed the Americans' inability to bridge between the Israeli and Palestinian approaches to the negotiations, as well as between our positions. We wanted to extract the overarching principles out of concrete understandings, while the Palestinian side wanted to agree on the principles before detailing particular arrangements. Expectedly, both parties protested the American document, which was quickly withdrawn, demonstrating a surprising lack of determination. In retrospect, that was a pivotal moment that portended the failure of the summit, and by its fourth day, on Friday, there was no documented progress at all.

At this point, Clinton invited the working groups to report directly to him and his team. I joined Rubinstein, Abu Alaa, and Abu Mazen in reporting on the progress of the working group on refugees. The two PLO elders were now talking to each other again after their falling out in the aftermath of the backchannel in Sweden. They were now reunited by the "threat" of the ascending "young Turks," Dahlan and Rashid, who established an axis with Ginosar and the Americans to push toward a FAPS at the summit. Nonetheless, in Clinton's presence, both sides put their best feet forward. Clinton then masterfully summarized, without notes, the areas of potential agreement and asked us to work on them. Similar dynamics happened in the other working groups, so Friday evening came with a high note, which was followed by an unforgettable festive Shabbat dinner hosted by the Clintons, when Israelis, Palestinians, and Americans mixed around tables to celebrate Shabbat together. On the following day, we held "open discussions" in "Shabbat mode" without official note taking, so by the end of day five, the Americans still had nothing to show.

What may seem to be time wasted in water-treading was actually aligned with Barak's master plan for the summit. He didn't believe that any serious progress would be made until that elusive moment of truth when Arafat was forced to make a decision before the summit ended when Clinton left for Japan. But Clinton and his team, who were not advised of that outline, were getting antsy. Among our delegation, Ben-Ami, Sher, and others were also concerned with the lack of progress. On Saturday afternoon Sher made a move. While standing outside Clinton's cabin, he and I reached out to three members of the American delegation to informally discuss the *methodology* of the summit. They knew that we were heading into a crisis, and my impression was that they were at a loss. Given Barak's instructions, we could not actually hand them the same documents that we had given them in June, which stated all the areas of potential agreement, although I had them in my briefcase. But we made sure that they remembered their existence. We thought that with that in mind, they could de-risk the entire summit for everyone's sake. But later that night, the stakes were increased again.

On Saturday night, Clinton and the Peace Team sought to solidify the progress that they thought had been made on Friday. Clinton invited the leaders of the working groups on borders and territory to a meeting in his cabin. On this issue, the Americans shared the basic approach of Israel, which held the West Bank and Gaza to be *disputed territory* that should be divided between the parties. Hence Israel's willingness to withdraw from nearly 90 percent of the West Bank and all of Gaza—in addition to establishing a Safe

Passage, a terminal for Palestinians in Ben-Gurion Airport, and a platform for Palestinian use in the Ashdod seaport—was framed by Clinton as a "very generous" and "historic" offer, aligned with UNSCR 242, namely with the *English* version of 242 that Israel and the U.S. favored.

The Palestinians, however, remained steadfast in their position that the West Bank and Gaza were *occupied territories*. They reiterated that their historic compromise had already been made when they accepted Oslo A in 1993 and recognized Israel on 78 percent of Mandatory Palestine. In keeping with that longstanding principled position, they insisted to Clinton that the FAPS must embrace the 1967 Lines as the basis for future borders. They expected him to acknowledge that principle and its implication: that the area of Palestine should be equivalent to the entire West Bank and Gaza, which was the rightful implementation of UNSCR 242 as they understood it. They repeated their willingness to be flexible in addressing Israeli needs and concerns through land swaps and other arrangements once that principle was enshrined. Clinton saw this position as rigid and unconstructive, and felt that it deadlocked the negotiations.

At that point, Clinton rocked the boat. I am not sure whether his rage was planned or spontaneous, but our team reported that it was a show of real fury. He lashed out at Abu Alaa, accusing the Palestinian side of failing to appreciate what was being offered to them and warning them of missing a historic opportunity. Our delegation was obviously happy that Clinton was siding with Israel on that issue and pressuring Arafat to work within the Israeli and American framework. But, as Barak reiterated, Arafat was unlikely to give up on a fundamental principle before the last moment of the negotiations and without any assurances regarding Israel's concessions. Certainly no Palestinian negotiator would ever take the risk of making such a compromise on their own, and Abu Alaa, the most constructive and brave Palestinian negotiator, was the wrong target for Clinton's attack. Henceforth, Abu Alaa was sidelined or took a step back, and his withdrawal further compromised the probability of reaching an agreement.

In retrospect, instead of leaning on the Palestinians to accept the Israeli framing of Gaza and the West Bank being *disputed* territories, the Peace Team should have "expanded the pie" to accommodate both sides. For example, if Israel withdrew from most of the West Bank and transferred some lands to

Palestine as a land swap, and also gave the Palestinians assets that did not exist prior to 1967, such as a Safe Passage, an air terminal, or a seaport platform, this could be understood to be in compliance with both Barak's pledge not to return to the 1967 Lines and with Arafat's demand to receive the equivalent of 100 percent of the West Bank and Gaza. Embracing such an approach in Camp David would have required Clinton to challenge Barak and Arafat so that both sides could claim success. Indeed, that was the approach that the Peace Team eventually took in the Clinton Ideas, six months later.

Similarly, on the issue of refugees, our positions seemed to be opposing. Israel rejected the notion of the Right of Return, while the Palestinians demanded that the agreement would be based on UNGAR 194, which called for return or compensation. Hence, an agreement that established a universal Right of Return of refugees *to Palestine* and provided for entry into Israel of a small and limited number of refugees based on Israel's sovereign discretion could have been consistent with both sides. That principle too was part of the Clinton Ideas.

Of course, Clinton and the Peace Team had to explore top-down big-picture understandings among the leaders on the principles of the FAPS, as they did. At the same time, they should have worked bottom-up based on everything that had happened in the negotiations to that point by formulating their own draft-FAPS. Ben-Ami, Sher, and other key members of our delegation doubted Barak's all-or-nothing approach and were hoping that demonstrable progress at Camp David, even without an agreement, could give the diplomatic process more time. While Barak did not want the Americans documenting *our* positions, they could have articulated *their* impressions of the emerging agreement and prepared *their* version of a FAPS. Some of us were hoping that the Americans would change their mode of operation during the summit, but it didn't happen. I have no doubt that the summit failed primarily because of the gaps between Israel and the Palestinians. But it could have turned into a partial success if the Americans had been willing to exercise more political leadership and diplomatic creativity, which is what they eventually did come December.

The days in Camp David were intense, often stretching for more than 18 hours, well past midnight and sometimes until dawn. As secretary of the delegation, I was overwhelmed with participating in negotiation sessions, with assignments of summarizing meetings, and preparing talking points. Every night, Barak would hold a team meeting with the entire delegation, at which everyone would give updates about their formal and informal discussions with the Americans or the Palestinians and share their assessments and recommendations. Each person had dozens of such interactions every day. The meeting would conclude with Barak's always-insightful analysis and guidelines for the following day, which were turned by Sher and Yatom into assignments that were often carried out immediately thereafter. All of us would stay in Dogwood for a few more hours during which Barak would meet Clinton, often at midnight and even at 2:00 AM. While some of us were working in small teams, others were hanging out, chatting and snacking. Around midnight, which would be morning in Israel, there would also be briefings to and from Jerusalem. Indeed, Barak's Cabin was a beehive, buzzing with activity at all hours of the day and night.

The all-or-nothing architecture of the Camp David summit led to the focus on Jerusalem and to its dramatic peak from Sunday, July 16 until Clinton's departure to Japan in the morning of Wednesday, July 19. As mentioned, Barak's logic rested on two pillars: first, a breakthrough on Jerusalem clears the way for a FAPS, while impasse on Jerusalem blocks the entire agreement. Hence, a moment of truth for the Oslo Process required a moment of truth on Jerusalem. Second, Arafat would only expose his flexibilities under pressure and at the last minute. This is why Barak engineered his dramatic offer on Jerusalem in the presence of Clinton roughly 36 hours before the original end-date of the summit, when Clinton was scheduled to depart to Japan. And while this logic of the "matrix" might have made sense rationally, it also created a counter-rationale: Why would Arafat make a historical concession on Jerusalem before he was assured that his other key interests were addressed?

Israel's *initial* positions regarding Jerusalem, which were presented by Ben-Ami and Sher to Dahlan and Erekat on Sunday, July 16, were already far-reaching: the Area of Jerusalem would house two capitals of two states, Yerushalayim and Al Quds; the Palestinian outer neighborhoods would be part of Palestine and Al Quds; the inner neighborhoods that were close to the Old City, which were small, geographically contained, and encircled by

Jewish areas, would be under *Palestinian sovereignty* and Israel's security control; the Old City and Holy Basin would remain under *Israeli sovereignty*, while their Arab areas—Silwan and the Christian and Muslim Quarters—would be subject to a special regime and administratively connected to Palestine; and Temple Mount would be under international custodianship. We felt that this proposal addressed all of the Palestinians' key concerns. As extensive as it was, it still fell within the confines of the traditional positions of the Israeli peace camp, stretching them to the limit without going overboard.

The Palestinians seemed unimpressed by the dramatic offers. They wanted more, particularly Palestinian sovereignty over al-Haram al-Sharif. On July 17, without referring to the specific ideas that Sher and Ben-Ami had presented the day before, Arafat demanded that Arab Jerusalem in its entirety—including the Muslim and Christian Quarters and Temple Mount—would be under Palestinian sovereignty. He then pledged to accommodate Israel's needs in the Jewish Quarter and the Kotel. Arafat felt bullied by "Barak and his big brother," Clinton, and refused to budge from his core positions under their pressure.

Barak now faced a dilemma: Does he improve Israel's offer or back down, pack up, and leave? Clinton was clearly turning against Arafat. Barak thought that if he raised his offer he could tip Clinton over to break his pledge to Arafat of "no finger pointing," to publicly condemn the Palestinians for the failure of the summit, to endorse Israel's efforts of peacemaking and thereby, perhaps, consolidate Israel's positions as the "final take-it-or-leave-it proposition." Against this backdrop, on Monday, July 17, in the afternoon, our delegation gathered on the porch of Barak's cabin to discuss Israel's positions on Jerusalem. As I described earlier in the chapter on Jerusalem, the meeting lasted for hours, and every member of the team spoke at length while Barak listened intently. Without a formal conclusion, it seemed that most of us felt that Israel could do more in its quest for peace.

That night, around 10 PM, Barak choked on a cashew nut and needed a Heimlich maneuver, which I performed, to help him regain his breath. Around midnight he met Clinton to present his upgraded offer regarding Jerusalem. This time Barak agreed that the Palestinians would have sovereignty in the Palestinian neighborhoods of Jerusalem, including in the Muslim and Christian Quarters, but insisted that the Old City would be subject to an international regime and Israeli security. As for Temple Mount, it was to remain under shared or international sovereignty. This was a daring offer, probably as far as any Israeli Prime Minister could ever go. Israel had nothing left to give away; some members of the Peace Team even thought that Barak had gone too far.

But for Arafat, it was still not enough. He wanted Palestinian sovereignty over al-Haram al-Sharif. Throughout Tuesday, July 18, Clinton met with Arafat and pressed for a deal, to no avail. In the middle of that drama, around midday, Abu Mazen left Camp David for his son's wedding. He had been passive and unengaged throughout the summit, as if dismissive of its significance, but his departure felt to us like another blow to the pro-deal faction among the Palestinians in one of the most consequential moments for his people. With Abu Mazen disengaged and now gone, and with Abu Alaa sidelined, the "young Turks"—led by Dahlan and Rashid—were left carrying the torch of deal-making.

Eventually, Arafat sent a letter to Clinton thanking him for his efforts but rejecting Barak's offer. It read, in part: "If we cannot liberate Jerusalem now, someone will come who will be able to do it … I led the Palestinian People from Diaspora to a peace among the brave based on the international legitimacy … I will not be the Palestinian leader that will legitimize Israel's sovereignty over al-Haram al-Sharif. May God help us."

Upon learning of that letter—as no FAPS was going to be concluded within the original timeframe of the summit and before Clinton's departure to Japan—Barak decided to fold and return to Israel. He too sent Clinton a letter thanking him for convening the summit and for his tremendous efforts. Soon thereafter, a pile of luggage formed in front of Dogwood.

The Americans, however, were not ready to declare failure. They asked both parties to stay in Camp David until Clinton returned from Japan and resume the efforts to hammer out a deal. They suggested that Albright preside over the summit in his absence. While Barak did not want to be issuing empty threats, he also didn't want to pull the plug on Clinton's summit, which was convened under his pressure. At the end of another long team meeting, we unanimously advised Barak to stay. After an eventful day, at 11:00 PM Yatom informed the Americans that we wouldn't be leaving just yet. A similar process unfolded on the Palestinian side, and at close to 1:00

AM, Clinton visited the cabins of Arafat and Barak to thank both delegations for our efforts and for giving peace another chance. He encouraged us to press on while he was away, leaving in the following morning of Wednesday, July 19. After a long and eventful day, everybody was invited for a late-night snack at Laurel. In a surreal scene, when the delegations met, we all hugged one another, happy to have another chance at making peace.

Alas, that second effort failed as well. While Clinton had been gone, Barak refused to see Arafat, believing that he would not budge until Clinton returned. He asked us to vacate his cabin and used the time for in-depth conversations with key members of our delegation. The book in his hand was *Five Days in London*,[50] about Churchill's decision to reject the Nazi offer for a truce despite remaining alone in the aftermath of recent defeats in Europe. Churchill famously promised Britons "blood, toil, tears, and sweat," and shortly thereafter the Battle of Britain would rage. Barak, who loves history and admires Churchill, drew inspiration from the ability to make such a decision in the face of tremendous uncertainty and adversity. Clearly, Camp David was one of the most momentous events in Israel diplomatic history.

At the same time, these days were a bit slower-paced, and everyone got much deserved rest and some exercise. Israelis and Palestinians, including Barak and Arafat, could be seen in the gym and power-walking around the compound. In the evening, Albright invited both delegations to a night out at the presidential cinema, with popcorn, pizza and soda, which I missed because of some administrative assignment. Sher and I went for a run along the outer perimeter of Camp David and also found an hour to do some karate training. He was a level-five black belt, I was a level two black-belt, and Camp David is the most unique place I have performed *katas* in.

When Clinton returned on July 23, negotiations resumed. He immediately met with Barak but focused on Arafat, pleading with him to work with Barak's offer. On the following day, when it became clear that Arafat was reluctant to engage, the two leaders clashed, with no holds barred. In the heat of the discussion, Arafat tapped his childhood memories from Jerusalem

---

50   Lukacs, John. *Five Days in London, May 1940*. Yale University Press, 1999. http://www. jstor.org/stable/j.ctt1npwm3.

to reiterate the fallacy that Jewish affiliation with Temple Mount had been exaggerated to expropriate the Palestinians. Clinton then accused Arafat of not negotiating in good faith by refusing to present any constructive ideas. He threatened Arafat with being responsible for the failure of the summit, for the end of the peace process, and for a setback to the relations between the U.S. and the Palestinians. Arafat remained steadfast. Late in the evening, he delivered to Clinton his final answer that he would not betray his people and would rather die than forego Palestinian sovereignty at al-Haram al-Sharif.

At that point, Barak fully disengaged. Ben-Ami spoke passionately to Clinton and his team and to Erekat and Abu Alaa, anticipating the collapse of the Barak government, the demise of the entire Israeli peace camp, the discrediting of future peace efforts, and extended conflict and bloodshed. He also understood the inevitable impact on the Labor party and on his own political aspirations. His prophesies were all realized.

Erekat still tried to get something out of the summit by offering to prepare a joint statement that highlighted the progress that was made and pledged to continue negotiations. His offer reflected the Palestinian expectation that the summit would be a phase in larger negotiations. But Clinton and Ben-Ami dismissed his suggestions out of skepticism, exhaustion, or both. In truth, Erekat's idea could have been constructive if the Peace Team had prepared the ground for it. Indeed, the failure of the summit was bitter for all sides, and Israelis and Palestinians carry most of the responsibility, but its outcome could have been better if the Americans had managed the summit differently. Yes, this is hindsight, but it was also said in real time.

In the evening, Barak gave a second and final order to prepare for departure the next morning. Some members of our delegation withdrew to their cabins to sleep, others hung out in Dogwood, and Ginossar spent the final hours of the summit with Dahlan and Rashid, assessing the implications of the failed summit. Sher, Yatom, and I were working on the follow-up to Camp David, while Barak was on the phone briefing the media in Israel. We had just gone through 48 hours of non-stop top-stakes diplomacy, which left us simultaneously adrenaline-hyped and exhausted. After midnight, Sher and I and others went on a final walk around the compound. I knew that my prospects of ever returning to Camp David were slim.

As we walked past Aspen, Chelsey Clinton came out for her night walk. We knew she was there, studying for some exam, but hadn't seen her. She joined us, immediately changing the serious conversation into a cheerful one. After a while, she and I found ourselves alone, the two "young" people present at Camp David, although I was 10 years her senior. We walked around the perimeter and wound up sitting in the church. As the daughter of the most powerful couple in America at the time, she was polished, knowledgeable, educated, and interested in history and diplomacy. She knew how to ask questions, realized that a historic event had just taken place while she was cramming for an exam, and tried to understand what had happened. Our conversation helped me frame for myself the unfolding of the summit. "What's going to happen next?" she asked, and I answered: "Nobody knows. Next could even be war." There was heavy silence. The whole scene was surreal. By the time we got back, it was dawn.

On Tuesday, July 25, after 14 days of nonstop action, we left Camp David. Our delegation briefly posed for a photo in Dogwood, with me wearing my novelty tie. After a short ceremony with a small honor guard of Marines, we boarded Marine 1, the presidential helicopter, and flew to Andrews Air Force Base to return to Israel. The view of Washington was gorgeous, but we were solemn and our hearts were heavy. Before boarding the plane to Israel, Barak gave a short briefing to the media, framing the summit as his courageous attempt to make peace that the Palestinians had rejected. We were physically and emotionally exhausted, having just emerged from a major historical event whose consequences would take years to unfold. When we landed at Ben-Gurion, Nava, Barak's then-wife, hugged and thanked me for saving his life, but it felt like that incident had happened ages ago. An hour later, I climbed the stairs to my third-floor Tel-Aviv apartment. A giant bouquet of flowers from a close friend awaited. I then went out to my neighborhood café. The juxtaposition of what had just happened in Camp David and the life-is-going-on in Tel Aviv was mind-boggling.

Battle Over the Narrative

In the latter days of the summit, some of the Palestinian delegates were antsy to embark on their summer plans, mostly passing time in and around Arafat's cabin. They came to Camp David with low expectations, fed by the downplaying of the summit by the Americans, who wanted to get Arafat to accept Clinton's invitation. In their mind, Camp David was supposed to be a top-level brainstorming session about Permanent Status and a milestone in the continued process of negotiations. They certainly didn't expect a make-or-break summit, like Barak planned for them. Our intelligence warned us that about that mindset, but Barak believed that Arafat and the Palestinian delegation would rise to the occasion. So, we were confounded by their attitude of continued low-stakes engagement, even when faced with a high-stakes opportunity to make history for their people.

For Barak, Camp David was pivotal and consequential. While Clinton was in Japan, Barak began to prepare for a possible negative response from Arafat and a failure of the summit. He ordered Arieli to prepare a strategic alternative of a unilateral realignment of Israel in Gaza and the West Bank, which could lead to a *reality* of two states for two people. But Barak's immediate next move was a massive stealth campaign of public diplomacy, perhaps singular in its ambition and scope. Barak understood that the eyes of the world were set on Camp David, and now everyone will want to know what happened. He foresaw a "battle of narratives" about the summit among Israel, the U.S. and the Palestinians. He wanted Israel to frame the narrative of Camp David and Clinton to validate Israel's framing despite his pledge to Arafat of no finger pointing.

So Barak directed Yatom and Sher to launch a globe-trotting public-diplomacy operation that would establish the story of the summit as: "Israel offered. Palestinians walked away. Israel has no partner for peace *at this time*." He emphasized to us the importance of being first to provide an in-depth report on the summit, and not just a caption, and wanted to cover the world within a few days. He also stressed the significance of first-hand testimonials, which is why he wanted our delegates to deliver his message as opposed to our embassies' diplomats. Sher and I crystallized talking points for everyone to use, and Yatom divided us into teams of one or two delegates. Travel plans were prepared for each team, covering a total of nearly 100 countries, and meetings with top local officials were secured in each stop. In some cases, our representatives were to hold their briefings in the airport and spend less than a day before flying to their next destination. I was originally scheduled to fly on a route that included Moscow, Singapore, and other Far East destinations and even Jakarta! But in the last minute, Sher decided that he needed me in Jerusalem.

Barak's public-diplomacy operation was remarkably successful and framed for the world the story of Camp David. That narrative—"Israel offered a most generous peace. Arafat rejected. There is no Palestinian partner for peace at this time"—had a lot of evidence to build upon, including the mounting number of personal testimonies that began to come out of the summit. By the time the Palestinians regrouped in late August, they faced a diplomatic avalanche, which put them on a global defensive. Their narrative—to the extent that they were even able to crystallize one—was sidelined.

And Barak continued. He now needed Clinton to validate Israel's story through his personal testimony for the sake of history, for pressuring the Palestinians to curb their demands and for his imminent political campaign. Barak wanted to stand for reelection as the person that would turn every stone in his quest for peace, without compromising Israel's security. His request from Clinton was just to describe what happened at Camp David. Ironically, such factual description meant finger-pointing at Arafat, which Clinton promised not to do. By that time, secret negotiations had already resumed in Jerusalem, and I believe that both leaders were contemplating a second summit in the fall. So Clinton too had an interest in setting the stage for further diplomatic progress, by revealing the potential progress that could have been made if Arafat would have been more engaging. Eventually, Clinton laid out his perspective on the Camp David summit, which reinforced and validated Israel's narrative.

Barak's narrative was evidently effective in allowing Israel to frame the global mindset regarding the summit. Its power emanated from its truth. But I contested it on one crucial point. My truth was that Israel "did not have a partner for *an agreement on End of Conflict and Finality of Claims* at that time." As I mentioned earlier, as of April, I have concluded that we should have allowed a Palestinian state to come into being in *provisional* borders, which would have then allowed us to negotiate a long-term *interim* agreement that narrows the scope of the conflict, without dramatic society-tearing historical compromises. That approach, building on the Interim Agreement of 1995, would have been doable for the Palestinians and, so I believed, better for Israel. Alas, polls repeatedly indicated that the Israeli public did not support another interim agreement with the Palestinians, and Barak would not even consider that option. So our acting as if a FAPS was the only path forward was true from the political perspective, but from the strategic perspective we had another option.

Within the otherwise frustrating context of a failed peace process and then a bloody war, Barak achieved all his diplomatic goals, placing Israel as the "good guy" in the Camp David negotiations, despite months of stalling until May 2000. Alas, Barak's diplomatic success only accelerated the effectuation of Ben-Ami's prophesy from the last day of Camp David about the imminent downfall of Barak, the Labor Party, Israel's Peace Camp and of the prospects for peace.

After a short while, the Israeli and Jewish peace camp, who believe in the Two-State Solution, began to reject Barak's narrative that Israel had "no partner for peace." They sought to show that Barak made critical mistakes and therefore shares responsibility for the failure in Camp David. They highlighted his inability to connect with Arafat and argued that Israel's take-it-or-leave-it propositions were pre-mature, half-baked, and fell short of what was essential for the Palestinians to accept. Therefore, the peace process is still alive and should be pursued.

Throughout that period, when Barak said that Israel had "no partner for peace" he would then qualify with the reservation "at this time," thereby keeping the door open for a change of circumstances that would allow for further negotiations and potentially another summit. But that nuance was immediately ignored by the Israeli and Jewish rightwing who celebrated his testimony that there is "no partner," casting aside the nuance of "…at this time."

For the Palestinians, Camp David became a diplomatic fiasco, which was at scale with their setback in 1991 after supporting Saddam Hussein and Iraq's invasion of Kuwait. The onus of the failed summit was placed on them by Israel and Clinton, and they faced an uphill battle of public diplomacy against a coherent Israeli narrative. And the final blow to the international standing of Arafat and the PLO came with the outbreak of the war in late September and then when he failed to accept the Clinton Ideas. Arafat was blamed for supporting the violence despite progress in the negotiations, for avoiding American and European attempts to cease fire, for having lied to Barak,

Clinton and the Europeans and for failing to seize on the historic opportunity that he was granted. Indeed, the period of May 2000 to January 2001—including Sweden, Camp David, the outbreak of the war and the Clinton Ideas—created an unmitigated diplomatic disaster for the Palestinians.

Clearly, they too had a case to be made and a narrative to be told. They could have pointed to the distrust that was built during the Interim Period and continued during Barak's tenure, which the summit could not dispel. They could have blamed the lack of personal chemistry between Barak and Arafat or called for continuing the negotiations based on what had been achieved. Who could have rejected such a Palestinian presentation?

It took the Palestinians a year to present their own perspective, defending their conduct in Camp David. In August 2001, 10 months into the Israeli-Palestinian War, Agha and Malley published an essay in the New York Review of Books titled *Camp David: A tragedy of Errors*, where they presented an alternative description of the summit. While they placed some of the responsibility on Barak and Clinton, they too concluded that Arafat and the Palestinian leadership "...never really understood what was offered." Ross and I wrote rebuttals, which led to Agha and Malley writing a fourth article that led to a response from Barak himself, which triggered another article by Agha and Malley. That entire back-and-forth, between August 2001 and June 2002—framed as *Camp David: An Exchange*—became one of the most authoritative sources about the unfolding of the summit.

In 2003, I got a call from Clayton Swisher, who was a member of the security detail of Albright. He stood out among the often blank-faced bodyguards by being curious and energetic. While expected to be a fly on the wall in Albright's presence, Swisher was intrigued by the history that was unfolding in front of his eyes and taking mental notes. We were of roughly similar age, and he reached out to me a few times during the Camp David negotiations to strike a substantive conversation about what was going on. Three years later, he told me that he left the State Department, joined a thinktank and wrote a book about titled *The Truth About Camp David*.

In his book, Swisher assigned the failure of the summit to Israel and the US, who allegedly colluded against the Palestinians. While I had many factual comments to his work and did not agree with his analysis or conclusions, my biggest reservation was with the title of his book. I suggested one small change:

to call the book <u>A</u> *Truth About Camp David*, namely capturing Swisher's perspective, which would then allow me to respectfully offer some comments ... but he refused, saying that the title was controlled by the publisher.

Once published, Swisher's well-resourced book became a hit among Palestinians and their supporters as the authoritative narrative about Camp David. Its credibility emanated from the messenger: an unbiased American who testified about his personal experiences, conducted massive research and formed his own opinion. Meanwhile, Swisher moved on to become an award-winning journalist for Al Jazeera, who continued to work on the topic of Israeli-Palestinian relations for years to come.

In conclusion, Barak's diplomatic triumph turned out to be a pyric victory. When he returned to negotiations, he was seen as detached from reality: why negotiate with Arafat or the Palestinians, who are "not a partner?" And later: why should Israelis vote for Barak to wage peace when there is "no partner"? For waging war, Israelis preferred Sharon, who went on to achieve a huge electoral victory over Barak in the elections of February 2001.

Clinton Ideas

Clinton Ideas Concluding Remarks

I believe that this is the outline of a fair and lasting agreement.

It gives the Palestinian people the ability to determine their future on their own land, a sovereign and viable state recognized by the international community, Al-Quds as its capital, sovereignty over the Haram, and new lives for the refugees.

It gives the people of Israel a genuine end to the conflict, real security, the preservation of sacred religious ties, the incorporation of 80 percent of the settlers into Israel, and the largest Jewish Jerusalem in history recognized by all as its capital.

This is the best that I can do. Brief your leaders and tell me if they are prepared to come for discussions based on these ideas. If so, I would meet them next week separately. If not, I have taken this as far as I can.

These are my ideas. If they are not accepted, they are not just off the table, they also go with me when I leave office.

The paradoxes of Barak's positions following the Camp David summit were perplexing. Above board, he was bashing the Palestinians and claiming to have "unmasked Arafat" to discover that he was not a partner for peace. At the same time, Barak authorized near immediate return to negotiations ahead of a possible second summit that was supposed to be much better prepared, with an American document of principles as a basis for negotiations.

We met with the Palestinian delegation dozens of times in August and September in stealth mode, being snuck into hotel suites from back doors. Everyone's favorite was the gorgeous presidential suite at the King David hotel that has a magnificent view of the Old City. The raging war made it regularly available for our use. We made steady progress, which prepared the ground for a crucial meeting between Barak and Arafat on September 25, that opened the door for the most successful round of negotiations in Washington on September 26-28. By that time, we were discussing specific formulations regarding Permanent Status, without giving the Palestinians the draft FAPS we had. A second summit seemed imminent.

But on September 28, Sharon's visit to Temple Mount triggered a chain of events that led to an all-out war. Three major attempts to stop the violence by Albright in Paris on October 4, by Tenet on October 12, and by Clinton and Mubarak in Sharm El-Sheikh on October 16-17 failed and the second summit was put on hold. At that point, all parties understood that the peace process may be tabled for years, denying Clinton and Barak the agreement they desired.

In mid-November circumstances changed again. Throughout that period, Ben-Ami, Sher and our delegation continued to meet with Palestinian negotiators, primarily Erekat and Dahlan, while Shahak and Ginossar maintained their backchannel with Arafat via Rashid. Strangely, despite the bloodshed, suddenly all parties converged toward another swing at an agreement. An undecided presidential election between Gore and Bush gave Clinton additional time to cement his legacy as a statesman. On December 9, Barak declared a special election for the premiership to be held in February 2001, and wanted to sign a FAPS so that the vote would become a de-facto referendum. And Arafat was under pressure—coming from Egypt and other Arab countries, as well as Dahlan and Rashid—to consolidate the incredible gains he made in the negotiations and launch a Palestinian state in all of Gaza and nearly all the West Bank with Al-Quds as its capital in control of al-Haram al-Sharif, and with a minimum of $20 billion seed funding.

Against this backdrop, Clinton was willing to make his final attempt to bring about Israeli-Palestinian peace. In late December, our delegations were invited to Bolling Air Force Base to "renew negotiations." The goal was to help the Peace Team crystallize a document of principles about Permanent Status that would serve as a basis for the second summit led by Clinton. It was surprisingly nice to spend time with our Palestinian interlocutors. Strangely, we felt like brothers-in-arms, belonging to a tiny group that was fighting for peace when everyone else was at war. We discussed measures for stopping violence in parallel to working with the Peace Team. Highlights included a work meeting at the White House and a late-night cannot-be-seen-together meeting with Malley in a Dunkin Doughnuts restaurant, where Sher and I ironed out key points about the refugees.

Finally, on Saturday, December 23, on Christmas Eve, both delegations were invited to the White House and were brought into the cabinet room in the West Wing. Everyone dressed up to the occasion, with me wearing my novelty tie, ahead of a historical moment. Upon entering the room, Clinton warmly shook our hands and thanked each of us for our work. The juxta-position of the war at home and the friendliness among the delegations in Washington could not be starker. The Americans sat on one side of the cab-inet table with Clinton in the middle, and Sher and Erekat split the other middle side of the table with both delegations seated to their respective sides. I was sitting at the far end of the Israeli delegation.

Clinton then read a carefully crafted statement, which was a condensed version of a FAPS with big-picture guidelines for the resolution of all out-standing issues. It was the synthesis of the American approach to peacemaking, often offering two or more options for the parties to work with. In a nutshell, Clinton's ideas called for a demilitarized Palestinian state to be established in 95-99 percent of the West Bank and in Gaza, including land swaps in an area equivalent to 1-3 percent of the West Bank, a safe passage and other territorial perks. Arab Jerusalem would become Al-Quds and serve as capital of Palestine while Jewish Jerusalem becomes Yerushalayim and the recognized capital of Israel. Additional surgical arrangements would divide sovereignty in the Holy Basin and on Temple Mount. Palestine would accommodate

Israel's key security concerns and the refugees would be allowed to return to Palestine, while Israel takes a small number of them at its discretion. Clinton further suggested that an agreement based on his ideas would constitute End of Conflict and its implementation will lead to Finality of Claims.

My role was to capture Clinton's every word, but at some point my computer ran out of battery and began to beep loudly, interrupting the President's speech and sending everyone to a burst of laughter. After the President was done and left the room, Ross re-read the president's ideas to ensure that both sides have an absolutely accurate record.

In conclusion, Clinton said: "I believe that this is the outline of a fair and lasting agreement…" and proceeded to summarize their highlights, as quoted at the top of this section. He then asked us to "…brief our leaders and tell me if they are prepared to come for discussions based on these ideas." Namely, his ideas were a package to be considered as a whole, not to be picked and chosen from. Clinton continued: "If so, I would meet them next week separately … [and] if my ideas are not accepted, they are not just off the table, they also go with me when I leave office." His final words were deeply personal and so true: "This is the best that I can do … I have taken this as far as I can."

On December 31, after extensive deliberations, the Government of Israel accepted the Clinton Ideas as a basis for negotiations provided that the Palestinians do the same. Since we anticipated that Arafat would come back with a "yes, but…," trying to pocket achievements and clinch further concessions, we added a detailed annex of our own reservations to be used when negotiations resume.

Joining Sher to deliver the response to Clinton and his team on January 5 would be my last official visit to the White House. We walked through corridors of the West Wing to Clinton's Oval Office. Brown boxes for packing were everywhere, and pictures were off the walls in anticipation of Clinton's imminent departure. The scene was surreal. He graciously received us in his office for Sher to brief him on Barak's decisions. Meanwhile, Arafat took a few more days and on January 7, Erekat delivered a response that included reservations to key principles in the Clinton Ideas, as well as requests for clarifications that would have required extensive additional negotiations. Clinton and the Peace Team, as well as Barak and our team, concluded that this was

Arafat's way to pass on the Clinton Ideas. Perhaps he thought Bush would give him more than Clinton, despite a direct message from Bush's team that "Bush would not touch the Israeli-Palestinian peace process with a ten-foot pole" (yes, it's a quote), if Arafat declines on Clinton's proposals.

A final round of negotiations in Taba in late January was a political show. Three weeks before election, Barak wanted to demonstrate to the Israeli public that hopes for peace were still alive with him, and the Palestinians wanted to demonstrate to the world their commitment to peacemaking. In the absence of agreement on the Clinton Ideas as a basis for further negotiations, both sides retracted to their past positions. Nonetheless, this was the first time that we shared with the Palestinians a detailed map of our offer regarding permanent borders, and it was also the first time that the Palestinian side presented its own territorial proposal on a map. The big difference between the maps was the settlement blocs: Israel wanted wide "corridors" connecting the blocs to Israel totaling 7.5 percent of the West Bank, while the Palestinians offered "balloons," namely connecting the blocs to Israel via roads, that amount to 4.5 percent of the land. It was also the first time that we officially negotiated the refugee issue.

Two weeks later, Sharon won the elections decisively. As Ben-Ami predicted on the final night at Camp David and after seven months of violence, the Israeli Peace Camp was now decimated. A nine-months effort—from May 2000 to January 2001—to reach a historic peace agreement between Israel and the Palestinians ended.

With the hindsight of two decades, the Clinton Ideas are the biggest missed opportunity of the Camp David negotiations. As Sher wrote:[51] "... one can only imagine what could have happened in Camp David if Clinton would have presented these ideas to Barak and Arafat in July at the summit, with six months remaining in office to iron out the FAPS." Sadly, an initial version of the Clinton Ideas was presented at Camp David on July 13, but was then retracted by the Americans under the protests of both delegations. It pains me to think about that lost opportunity. At the same time, the Clinton Ideas remain the most long-lasting legacy of that period. If negotiations on Permanent Status ever resume with American participation, the primary reference point would be the Clinton Ideas.

---

51   Sher, *Ibid*, p. 201

Quartet Roadmap

The Camp David negotiations and the Clinton Ideas were shaped by the Oslo Process, which envisioned a Palestinian state established as *an outcome* of an agreement on Permanent Status between Israel and *the PLO*. Such agreement is a massive political undertaking requiring resolution of all outstanding issues emanating from the historic conflict; bringing into being a Palestinian state in *permanent* borders; and shaping state-to-state relations between Israel and Palestine. Given the enormity of the task, understandably, all attempts to achieve a FAPS failed. For sure, by 2003, when the war between Israel and the Palestinians had been raging for two and a half years, the notion of such a FAPS was no longer relevant.

That reality led to the reimagining of the peace process by Israel, Bush and the so-called Quartet of countries, including the US, the EU, Russia, and the UN. Their idea was to reverse the diplomatic process by first establishing a Palestinian state in *provisional* borders and then reaching Permanent Status. For Israel, that sequence represented a significant shift: Now, a Palestinian state would emerge *before* peace and without End of Conflict, so statehood was no longer the tradeoff for peace. Nonetheless, Israel accepted the Quartet Roadmap, but the Palestinians eventually did not, so the Roadmap's original concept did not leave a lasting impression.

In parallel to the diplomatic efforts to end the war and resume the peace process, Sharon led massive unilateral moves. In 2002 he initiated the construction of the security fence along a potential future border between the two states roughly following the 1967 Lines, with deviations to include the settlement blocs and most of the municipal areas of Jerusalem. This was a monumental project designed to stop terrorists from freely moving into Israel, but it also signaled that the vast majority of the West Bank, on the Palestinian side of the fence, would eventually become Palestine. Sharon then led the Gaza Disengagement in the summer of 2005, whereby Israel fully withdrew from Gaza, including from three settlements in the northern West Bank. Had Sharon continued for another term—he suffered a terminal stroke in 2006—we may have seen additional unilateral moves in the West Bank of dismantling isolated settlements and perhaps even recognizing the PA as a state. Clearly, in 2001-2005, Bush and Sharon were able to turn the lemons they were handed into lemonade.

If Bush's first tenure was marked by progress toward separating Israel and the Palestinians, the second tenure was a setback. In the aftermath of Israel's Gaza Disengagement, the Olmert Government was willing to seek a FAPS, but the U.S. naïvely insisted on holding the long-promised elections to the Palestinian National Council, which is the parliament of the PA. Polls of Palestinian public opinion indicated majority support for Abu Mazen's pro-Oslo Fatah party, and everyone hoped for a vote of confidence in the peace process. But analysts failed to appreciate that the voting system was based on districts. While Hamas was disciplined in running one candidate per district, supporters of Fatah were split between a few contenders. Thus, despite Fatah winning the "popular majority," Hamas won most of the seats in the PLC and was set to lead a government that rejected the Oslo Accords in violation of the agreements with Israel.

This would have been an unacceptable outcome, so Israel and the U.S. demanded that the incoming Hamas Government ratifies and abides by the agreements. Hamas rejected this demand, and the ensuing standoff sent the PA into a constitutional deadlock that lasted 18 months. In Gaza, violent clashes erupted between Dahlan's forces and Hamas. In June 2007, Hamas mounted a coup that ousted Fatah and the PA from Gaza. Henceforth, the PA has been divided between Hamas-controlled Gaza and a PA-controlled West Bank.

At that point, in November 2007, the Bush Administration convened Olmert and Abu Mazen in Annapolis for a conference that re-launched negotiations on a FAPS, based on the Roadmap. That would be the second major attempt to reach a FAPS. Alas, the Annapolis embraced two conflicting approaches: one, based on the Oslo Process, preceded a Permanent Status agreement to statehood, while the other, based on the Roadmap, favored statehood first. Furthermore, they seemed to ignore the breakup between Gaza and the West Bank, perhaps with the hope that it would be temporary, while negotiating an agreement with a demilitarized Palestinian state in *permanent* borders. Strangely, Bush did not insist on his own novelty—the Roadmap—which would have been a better framework for negotiations between Israel and *the PA* toward a Palestinian state in *provisional* borders, initially in the West Bank. That misjudgment led to the inevitable failure of the Annapolis Process by January 2009.

While the Camp David negotiations and the Annapolis Process ended in failure and while both discussed similar issues, the underlying reasons for that outcome were utterly different: the unified PA of 1999-2000 was different from the bifurcated PA of 2006-2008; the Clinton Ideas were the outcome of the Camp David negotiations, and could have been the starting point of the Annapolis Process; and the Roadmap did not exist for the Camp David negotiations, but was available to Bush, Olmert and Abu Mazen.

What If You Fail? We'll Try Harder!

In 2013 I was invited to meet one of the top advisors to secretary of state, John Kerry, who was leading another attempt to broker a peace deal between Israel and the Palestinians on behalf of President Obama. The Israeli side was led by Netanyahu, through his chief negotiator, Yitzhak Molcho, and Foreign Minister Livni, while the Palestinians were once again represented by Erekat. We met at the David Citadel hotel in Jerusalem. We had known each other since the formative experience of Camp David and have been friendly ever since. He told me that as a veteran of the Barak peace team and a leader of "an influential think tank" I was part of a group of Israelis that the U.S. was eliciting feedback from.

I think that both of us expected a calm meeting. He began by laying out Kerry's vision for the negotiations. Their underlying assumption seemed to be that in 2000 Israel and the PLO were close to an agreement, but the diplomatic *process* was mismanaged by the Americans, who were dominated by Barak. Clinton was too emotionally and closely involved in a hands-on manner, and therefore lost his leverage on both parties. Now, Obama and Kerry, with the support of some veterans of the Clinton Peace Team, wanted to "pick up where we left off" and "finish the job." The x-factor would be a different American approach to mediations. This time the U.S. was going to be forceful with *both* parties and optimize the timing and nature of the Presidential intervention by Obama. The goal was to reach a FAPS that would establish a Palestinian state alongside Israel and resolve all the outstanding issues. They felt they had a much better chance now, 13 years after the Camp David negotiations and with Abu Mazen leading the Palestinians.

I was stunned. As I mentioned earlier, I agreed that the U.S. could have better managed the Camp David negotiations. But what if Barak was correct to observe that a comprehensive peace agreement was not feasible? What was the impact of the split between Gaza and the West Bank, which rendered the demilitarization of Palestine impossible? Furthermore, the capacity of the PLO to ratify an agreement was compromised by the rise of Hamas, and the ability to implement a FAPS was partial at best. The effect of these realities was ignored or dismissed by the Kerry team.

There was a high alternative cost as well for those who believe that Israel's existential interest is to secure a *reality* of two-states-for-two-people. Pursuing a FAPS that seeks a Palestinian state in *permanent* borders based on the Oslo Process prevents pursuing a long-term *interim* agreement that establishes a Palestinian state in *provisional* borders based on the Roadmap. Indeed, a political process based on the Roadmap would have been a lower-hanging fruit; could have also served Palestinian interests; and may have secured Obama a historic achievement. Meanwhile, a third presidential failure to reach a FAPS—by Clinton, Bush and now Obama—could have terminated prospects of ever achieving peace.

"Last time [in 2000] we overheated the system, it exploded into a war with thousands of casualties" I said. "Well, this time is different … Abu Mazen is in power, and not Arafat," he said "and you [Israel] have full security control of the West Bank to prevent terrorism." That was true, but Hamas controlled Gaza with the ability to rattle the political process through acts of strategic terrorism and even a full-on military confrontation. Indeed, in July 2014 Hamas kidnapped and murdered three Israeli boys, which led to Operation Cast Led in Gaza. Furthermore, twice in the past—in 1987 and in 2000—we had the illusion of tight control of the Palestinian areas but ended up with large-scale confrontation.

"Did you conduct a thorough debrief of the 2000 negotiations? Have you articulated the lessons?" I asked. He obviously thought they did. I thought they did not. "How will you know that your approach is succeeding or failing?" I pressed. "We won't fail this time. The President is very committed to succeeding," he answered. "What if you fail to reach an agreement?" I pressed. "We'll try harder." He responded. "Do you have a plan b?" I asked. "Our plan b is to try harder on plan a." "Did you consider the approach of the Quartet Roadmap of seeking a Palestinian state in *provisional* borders instead of pursuing a FAPS?" He didn't answer. We kept going back and forth. We were friends. We knew our stuff. Both of us were passionate about this topic. He was confident that Obama and Kerry could make history. I walked away from the meeting distraught, confident that they were going to miss a historic opportunity. I felt he was upset and disappointed with me. I was upset and disappointed with them. Indeed, the third attempt to reach a Permanent Status deal under Obama failed without a legacy.

Trump Plan: A New Baseline

On January 28, 2020, in a White House press conference, President Trump unveiled *Peace to Prosperity: A Vision to Improve the Lives of the Palestinian and Israeli People*. The so-called Trump Plan was framed as "a proposal to resolve the Israeli-Palestinian conflict, outlining the terms of an agreement to be eventually signed by both parties and clear all claims between them." Shortly thereafter, Netanyahu called the Trump Plan "the Deal of the Century" and said that Israel had never had a better friend in the White House.[52]

In its quest to achieve peace, the Trump Administration, pledged to break with the worn paradigms of past approaches to the resolution of the Israeli-Palestinian conflict. Their primary novelty was their process: They worked closely with the Israeli side to present the Palestinians with a take-it-or-leave-it proposition. In parallel, Trump "reshaped the playing field" with dramatic diplomatic moves in favor of Israel in order to pressure the Palestinians to negotiate on his terms and accept his proposals: He moved the American embassy to Jerusalem, defunded UNRWA, began to refer to the West Bank as Judea and Samaria instead of "Occupied Palestinian Territories," recognized Israel's sovereignty in the Golan, blocked and sanctioned the International Court of Justice and recognized the legality of the settlements.

Israel's rightwing initially celebrated the Trump Plan because it represented an acceptance of many rightwing claims. Netanyahu went as far as describing its presentation as "a historical moment for Israel and Zionism on par with 1948 and 1967." Indeed, the Trump Plan recognized Israel's claim for sovereignty over a unified Jerusalem and all settlements in Judea and Samaria and the Jordan Valley; accepted Israel's position that the West Bank

---

52   BBC News, *Netanyahu: Trump Middle East Peace Plan "Deal of the Century"*, (January 28, 2020. https://www.bbc.com/news/av/world-middle-east-51289277).

is a "disputed territory" over the Palestinian position that it is an "occupied territory;" and allowed Israel to annex 30 percent of the West Bank without equitable land swaps. It also established that Israel's security must shape any future arrangements and recognized that the establishment of Palestine is subject to Israeli and American discretion and not a pre-ordained outcome of an inalienable right of the Palestinian People. Some critics denounced these conditions as "impossible" or "fantastic."[53]

The Palestinian leadership immediately rejected the Trump Plan in its entirety without even engaging with its specific language. The mirror image of Israeli gains were Palestinian losses. The Trump Plan breached many of the PLO's long-held positions such as its demand for an equivalent of 100 percent of the West Bank and Gaza, territorial contiguity, dismantling all settlements outside the settlement blocs and a capital in east Jerusalem. Most importantly, the establishment of Palestine was deferred for years and subjected to Israel's whims.

Alas, the absence of a Palestinian interlocutor, which is often seen as the biggest flaw of the Trump Plan, may turn out to be the key for its lasting impact. Abandoning any pretense of "fairness" or "evenhandedness," the Trump Plan is skewed in favor of Israel in its underlying principles and specific provisions, which is evidenced by Netanyahu's wholeheartedly embracing it. Toward its formulation, Trump and Netanyahu, and their teams, worked on all outstanding issues, and as Trump wanted his plan to receive support from America's Arab allies such as Saudi Arabia or the Gulf States, he extracted a-priori concessions from Netanyahu.

The result is an unexpected validation by Netanyahu of the Two-State Solution, of key aspects of the Oslo Process and of pillars of Permanent

---

53   Re Impossible: Federman Josef and Riechmann Deb, *Trump Peace Plan Delights Israelis, Enrages Palestinians* (AP News, May 1, 2021. https://apnews.com/article/donald-trump-ap-top-news-international-news-jerusalem-politics-f7d36b9023309ce4b1e423 b02abf52c6).
Re Fantastic: Boot Max, *What Trump and Netanyahu Just Unveiled Was a PR Campaign, Not a Peace Plan* (Washington Post, January 28, 2020. https://www.washingtonpost.com/opinions/2020/01/28/what-trump-netanyahu-just-unveiled-was-pr-campaign-not-peace-plan/).

Status, which were negotiated by Barak and Olmert[54]—all without *any Palestinian reciprocity*. For example, the Trump Plan is based on the principle of two-states-for-two-people;[55] the Area of Jerusalem is envisioned to house the Palestinian capital;[56] the 1967 Lines are the reference point for future territorial arrangements and there will be land swaps;[57] a safe passage will connect Gaza and the West Bank, which are a "single territorial unit;"[58] there will be special arrangements for Israeli military presence in the Jordan Valley; Palestinian refugeeism exists and should be resolved by a return to the newly established Palestinian state and by dismantling UNRWA; and an economic package, inspired by the Marshall Plan,[59] will provide for Palestinian economic development.[60] In fact, the Trump Plan is remarkably similar to the positions of Barak ahead of the Camp David summit and before substantive engagement with the Palestinians, and includes most of the components required for a Two-State Solution.

The Trump Plan was declared in January 2020 at the White House in a festive event, celebrating its many achievements for Israel. But it quickly hit a wall when the Jewish and Israeli rightwing realized that it was premised on the Two-State Solution and included Israeli acceptance of a Palestinian state, albeit conditional. To address that frustration, Netanyahu pledged to annex unilaterally the Jordan Valley and West Bank settlements, which were assigned to Israel according to the plan. The upcoming Israeli elections provided a powerful incentive to act swiftly. However, the Trump White House poured cold water on these intentions by forcing a joint Israeli-American committee to delineate the border of the annexation.

---

54   Arieli Shaul, *Understanding the Trump Plan*, (Israel Policy Forum, July 2020, israelpolicyforum.org/wp-content/uploads/2020/07/Understanding-the-Trump-Plan.pdf).

55   Trump Plan, *Ibid*, p. 3

56   Trump Plan, *Ibid*, p. 17

57   Trump Plan, *Ibid*, p. 11-12

58   Trump Plan, *Ibid*, p. 12

59   Spetalnick Matt, and Holland Steve, *White House's Kushner Unveils Economic Portion of Middle East Peace Plan*, (Reuters, June 22, 2019 https://www.reuters.com/article/us-israel-palestinians-plan-exclusive/exclusive-trumps-economy-first-approach-to-mideast-peace-built-on-big-money-projects-idUSKCN1TN0ES).

60   Trump Plan, *Ibid*, p. 32

The Netanyahu government, which was formed in May 2020, called for such annexation by July 1. When Netanyahu came to implement that decision, he quickly encountered the complex dilemmas, which would emanate from securing hundreds of kilometers of convoluted borders, protecting isolated settlements and the roads that lead to them, dealing with an enclave in Jericho; or turning 60,000 Palestinians in the Jordan Valley into Israeli citizens—just as we did in Barak's Peace Administration. Furthermore, military intelligence warned against the destabilizing effects of annexation on Jordan and the PA, that could lead to synchronized protests and armed resistance from Gaza and in the West Bank and distract Israel from its campaign against Iran and Hezbollah.

Another source of resistance came from the international community, particularly Europe, Jordan and Egypt, as well as Gulf states. Jordan threatened to freeze the Peace Treaty with Israel and the EU warned Israel with sanctions.[61] Most importantly, the Trump administration itself expected Netanyahu to accept the entire Trump Plan and not to pick and choose a few provisions that worked in Israel's favor, while Democrats, led by Joe Biden, categorically rejected any unilateral annexation altogether. Eventually, in a stunning turn of events, annexation was abandoned when the leaders of the UAE offered Israel a historic normalization agreement in its stead, and the Abraham Accords with the UAE, Bahrain and Morocco came into being in September 2020.

But the unintended historic effect of the Trump Plan may still be ahead of it. It embodies the gradual acceptance by Israel's moderate rightwing of the Two-State Solution and of key ideas of the Oslo Accords, which have been a part of Permanent Status negotiations since 1995. Indeed, the Trump Administration nudged Netanyahu, his inner circle, Likud and others in the Israeli rightwing in a way that no Democratic American President, Israeli leftwing party or Palestinian or Arab interlocutor could have. It created a 'ceiling' for the demands and expectations of any future Israeli government from the Palestinians and a new *baseline* for any future negotiations.

---

61   Landau Noa, *Eu Discusses Sanctions against Israeli Annexation That Will Not Require Consensus*, (Haaretz, May 15, 2020. https://www.haaretz.com/israel-news/. premium-the-eu-discusses-sanctions-against-israeli-annexation-that-will-not-require-consensu-1.8849054).

Wedge Issue

Why would the U.S. even care about Israeli-Arab and Israeli-Palestinian relations? During the Cold War and into the 1990s, there was a clear geopolitical logic for doing so. The Israeli-Palestinian conflict was perceived to be the heart of the Israeli-Arab conflict and a source of regional and global instability, so stable relations between Israel and the Palestinians was important for keeping world peace and energy prices low. Furthermore, the great-power competition with the Soviet Union and the influence of American Jewry focused American diplomacy on our region, turning the Israeli-Palestinian conflict into the one to solve for leaders who aspired to make history and have a shot at the Noble Prize for peace. Indeed, Nixon, Carter, Bush 41, Clinton, Bush 43, Obama and Trump gave it their best attention and effort.

Many of these conditions are no longer in place: The plight of the Palestinians is not a top priority for the Arab world, as Israel, the PA and even Hamas-controlled Gaza are co-existing with mild flareups, little bloodshed and few human rights violations compared to other conflicts. Key Arab countries are developing relations with Israel, as they pivot their economies away from dependency on oil and toward innovation and entrepreneurship. Meanwhile, the west no longer depends on Arab oil and gas, and the U.S. is effectively energy independent. In addition, America's competition with Russia and with rising China is played out in other regions, so the interest in solving the Israeli-Palestinian conflict declined.

Furthermore, American politics is also changing. For about 20 years— from the Oslo Accords in the early 1990s until the mid-2010s—support for Israel and for the Two-State Solution were mainstream bipartisan positions endorsed by Republicans and Democrats and by most Jewish organizations. A president that advanced them was guaranteed to receive widespread support. But in recent years, that consensus has dissipated. Republicans support Israel's policies in Judea and Samaria and have effectively detached from the Palestinians to the point where many reject the Two-State Solution altogether. Among Democrats, while some maintain the traditional support for Israel, others, on the progressive side, are critical of its policies particularly regarding the Palestinians. For the former, the Clinton Ideas would be "anti-Israel" and for the latter they would be "anti-Palestinian."

For sure, the U.S. has many interests in the Middle East such as strengthening its relations with its allies, blocking Chinese and Russian influence, or
preventing Iran from becoming a nuclear power. This means that keeping
the Oslo Process and the PA alive or preserving the stability of Jordan are
clearly important. But, in the absence of a clear American national security
interest or a clear political interest to do so, why would any American president even prioritize peacemaking between Israel and the Palestinians? There
is no good answer to that question. So attention and budgets have shifted to
other theatres and the remarkable Peace Team disbanded and retired with no
equivalent to continue its legacy.

CHAPTER 11

The Butterfly Effect that Changed the Middle East

Barak and Arafat Engaged

With the hindsight of more than two decades, the 10 days from September 25 to October 4, 2000, were the turning point for the Oslo Process, Israeli-Palestinian relations, the Palestinian national struggle, Israel, and even the broader Middle East. In those days, and in the weeks that followed, I had a front-row seat at a live demonstration of system effects, in which Israel and the Palestinians transitioned from near-breakthrough in the peace negotiations to all-out war. In the years that passed, Israelis and Palestinians kept blaming each other for what transpired. But from my vantage point, neither party planned this explosion, wanted a war, or was exclusively responsible for its tragic outcome. A combination of small things making big impacts and of big moves having no impact fueled the fire of conflict until it was out of control.

This was also the moment when I saw the Prime Minister of Israel at his weakest, reminding me of the famous scene in The Little Prince when the king gives orders that no one executes. Barak wanted matters to go one way, but they went in the opposite direction: he wanted to calm things down, but events were conflagrating; he wanted de-escalation but he got an escalating war; he wanted a peace process, but it was irrevocably derailed. Meanwhile, Arafat, at the peak of his stature and within reach of incredible historic achievements for his people, wanted an even better deal, but his actions derailed the Palestinian national movement, dismembered the PA, and prolonged the plight of Palestinians by decades.

On an early fall evening of Monday, September 25, 2000, exactly two months after the Camp David summit ended, Arafat's helicopter made its way through Israel's skies. It landed at the helipad of Kochav Yair, a community east of Tel Aviv, where Barak lived. This would be Arafat's second and last visit to Israel as leader of the Palestinians. In his first visit, he came to Leah Rabin's home to console her after the assassination of her husband, Yitzhak. Now he came to have dinner at Barak's home to rebuild their relationship.

That dinner was the culmination of two months of intensive diplomacy. Shortly after Camp David, in August, negotiations discreetly resumed with strong American and Egyptian backing. We met our Palestinian interlocutors and the American Peace Team in suites of luxury hotels in Jerusalem and at the residences of the Egyptian and American ambassadors in Herzliya. In parallel, Shahak and Ginossar regularly met with Dahlan and Rashid to ensure effective communication between the two leaders, and Dani Abraham, a Jewish American billionaire who dedicated himself to bringing Israeli-Arab peace, also shuttled between them. All of these efforts had a similar goal: to resume Permanent Status negotiations toward a second summit that would lead to a FAPS.

In Kochav Yair, Barak and Arafat, accompanied by their senior advisors, including Ben-Ami and Sher, broke bread together. Then the two leaders spent an hour on Barak's balcony in a private conversation. When they reemerged into the living room, Arafat was grasping Barak's forearm in friendship. Together, they instructed their delegations to go to Washington, D.C. to hammer out a FAPS. The rest of our negotiation team was at Ben-Gurion Airport, waiting for the final confirmation to board the flight. A new phase in the Permanent Status negotiations was about to begin.

That night, Barak and Arafat had another sensitive issue to address. It was the forthcoming visit of MK Ariel Sharon to Temple Mount. Sharon felt challenged by Netanyahu, who had retired from politics after his loss to Barak in 1999 and was now contemplating a comeback bid for the leadership of Likud. He wanted to reassert his leadership of his party and the right wing. A morning stroll, accompanied by bodyguards, police, fellow parliamentarians, and many journalists to the most contested spot in the Middle East, seemed to make perfect political sense. The timing—right before the Jewish holidays—and the rumors that Barak was negotiating over Jerusalem made that visit even more attractive.

Barak did not want Sharon to visit Temple Mount, but Attorney General Rubinstein advised that he could not lawfully prevent a sitting MK from doing so. Many Israelis, including the chief of the Jerusalem police, and Palestinians, asked Barak to overrule Rubinstein, to no avail. Some even speculated that Barak saw political and electoral benefits to Sharon's provocation because it would offer a glimpse into what his premiership would entail. In any case, Barak needed Arafat's understanding and collaboration for the visit to unfold without turmoil, and Arafat grudgingly went along.[62]

From the Peak of Peacemaking…

The next morning, we landed in Washington and were driven in a motorcade to the Ritz Carlton hotel. Under heavy security, in the presidential suite, the Israeli and Palestinian delegations engaged in parallel discussions. The security teams negotiated Sharon's upcoming visit to Temple Mount, while the rest of our delegations discussed key issues of the FAPS. The atmosphere was good: serious and constructive.

We made progress on both fronts. The security teams coordinated Sharon's visit down to the last detail. Hasson and Dahlan spent hours on the phone with Jibril Rajoub, head of Palestinian security in the West Bank, and with his colleagues. Everybody understood Sharon's political need for a photo on the Temple Mount, and therefore his visit could be short in time and limited in scope. Sharon's team was aware of these arrangements and on board with that plan as well.

We also made headway with the political negotiations. In Camp David we never got to discuss the FAPS in detail and review with the Palestinians provisions of the draft agreement, which the Israeli team had been formulating. In Washington, we took that next step, crystallizing areas of agreement and better understanding the sticking points. The concluding meeting with Albright on Thursday, September 28, in her office on the top floor of the State Department building, was upbeat, and the view of Washington that day was stunningly beautiful.

---

62 Lahoud, *Rajoub warns of riots if Sharon visits Temple Mount today*, ND, p. 1. See also Rubinstein, *Kindling a Religious War*, ND. p. 3.

Immediately thereafter, Sher and I went to our embassy and sent a detailed report to Barak, which we concluded with the words, "We may have passed the point of no return," referring to the status of the negotiations ahead of a second summit. From there, we flew to New York to return to Israel. An El Al flight was held back so that we could make the connection. We landed in Tel Aviv the following morning, on Friday, and drove straight to the prime minister's office in Jerusalem.

By that time, Ben-Ami had already been appointed as Israel's minister of foreign affairs, taking over the position from David Levy, who boycotted the Camp David summit and resigned afterward. Ben-Ami was also our co–chief negotiator and minister of public security, responsible for the operations of the police during one of the most sensitive and explosive periods in Israel's history. Altogether, that was a handful, and he had to prioritize his attention, managing the portfolio of public security with a more hands-off approach.

On that Thursday, at 11:00 AM Israel time, while we were still in Washington, Sharon and other MKs from Likud visited Temple Mount. They followed the agreed plan, but a group of Palestinians began to protest the visit. The Jerusalem police dispersed the rioters to protect Sharon, and both sides had minor casualties with no deaths—all within what could have been expected. Nonetheless, Sharon's visit was framed by many Palestinians as a provocation, despite its being short and fully coordinated. When we landed in Israel on Friday and were briefed about recent developments, we got the impression that everything was under control and still within what had been anticipated. Nobody imagined that a chain reaction had been ignited which would unravel the peace process and instigate a major war that would claim the lives of thousands.

... To an Israeli-Palestinian War

During the flight to Tel Aviv, Ben-Ami, as minister of public security, needed to choose Israel's next police commissioner. The leading candidate was the chief of the Jerusalem police, deputy commissioner Yair Itzhaki, who was an experienced, outspoken, and charismatic officer, known to be moderate in his deployment of police force. The other was deputy commissioner Shlomo Aharonishki. When we landed, Ben-Ami told Aharonishki that he was getting the top job, and informed Itzhaki that he was being passed on. A press release followed in short order.

From his meeting with Ben-Ami, Itzhaki went to his command post overlooking the Kotel plaza, roughly one kilometer in aerial distance from the office of the prime minister, where Barak was situated, and half a kilometer from the ministry of public security, where Ben-Ami was working. Itzhaki's mission was simple: to preserve public order and to protect the safety and security of the tens of thousands of Jews who were praying at the Kotel. But the architecture of Temple Mount made that goal hard to achieve. As I described earlier, the mosques are located on top of a huge stone platform with the capacity of 400,000 worshipers, making Temple Mount one of the largest places of worship in the world. The plaza of the Kotel is about 30 meters beneath that higher platform that supports the mosques. On that Friday, on the eve of the Jewish new year, Rosh HaShana, the Kotel Plaza was at capacity and some 150,000 Palestinians were attending Friday prayers at the mosques.

During the weeks prior to Sharon's visit, the flames of conflict had been fanned. Rumors about an imminent historic deal on Jerusalem, which would include bitter compromises for both sides, were spreading. Each public focused on its own concessions. On the Israeli side, many politicians including Sharon pledged unrelenting opposition to any compromise on Temple Mount. On the Palestinian side, Hamas fomented protests and violence to derail the peace process and to challenge Arafat and his Fatah party. In the aftermath of Sharon's visit on Thursday, mosques across the West Bank and among Arab-Israelis incited the public to come to Al-Aqsa to protect it from the Jews. So on Friday, thousands came to Jerusalem to protest Sharon's visit, seeking a fight and revenge.

Meanwhile, Barak wanted to prevent escalation. His delegation was coming off a week of significant progress in the Permanent Status negotiations toward a FAPS, which could become his platform in the imminent elections. His directive was clear: to contain protests and minimize violence and casualties so that negotiations could continue uninterrupted. Our Palestinian interlocutors also wanted as little violence as possible. They too wanted to advance toward a historic agreement with Israel.

Serving these goals by police requires authority, wisdom, experience, professionalism, decisiveness, and moderation. But Itzhaki and the entire Jerusalem police were distracted and frustrated by being stepped over by Ben-Ami. After the prayers, around midday, Muslim rioters began to throw stones from the upper platform of the mosques onto the Kotel Plaza. They also assaulted the small police contingency that was stationed on the edge of Temple Mount. The Jerusalem riot police now needed to curtail stone-throwing from the top platform, to evacuate the lower Kotel plaza, and to defend their own force, which was being attacked. A bit later, Itzhaki decided to leave the safety of his command post to lead his forces on the front line. In the field, he was soon hit on the head by a stone, lost consciousness, and was evacuated to the hospital. This was a turning point. Itzhaki's less experienced deputy assumed command, and shortly thereafter he ordered the riot police to storm and evacuate the platform of the mosques. The inevitable outcome was escalation of violence and Arab casualties.

On that Friday morning, Barak convened with Yatom, Sher, and other advisors at the Aquarium to monitor events in the Old City. We counted on the coordination with the Palestinian security forces to keep things "under control." Although intelligence officers, journalists, and Palestinians warned us of an angered mob of young men who were flocking to Temple Mount, I don't remember being alarmed by their reports. And even if we had been alerted, I doubt that we could have contained the tremendous force that was being unleashed.

As violence was escalating on Temple Mount, Rajoub and his forces tried to calm things down on the Palestinian side. They demanded that the Imams and the Waqf call upon the protestors to withdraw and disengage from the police. They were also frantically calling their Israeli counterparts—Ben-Ami on the political level, Sher and the negotiation team and their contact people in the Israeli security forces—to restrain the Jerusalem police. But Ben-Ami was sidelined by the events, although, to be fair, he could not have done much either.

In the battle fog, those at the Aquarium could not form a clear picture of what was happening on Temple Mount. Updates were coming in through the standard communication channels via Barak's military secretary, through our cell phones, and live on the radio. I remember that day as complete chaos. For a few hours, the government of Israel effectively lost control of its Jerusalem police, which lost control of events in the heart of the Old City.

Palestinian aggression on the platform and even in the mosques was fierce. Our police forces were attacked by large groups of rioters armed with stones, batons, and other cold weapons, turning the platform into a war zone. Police responded harshly, including with live fire, to contain the violence, stop the riots, and push the rioters out of Temple Mount. Violence then spilled over to nearby areas inside the Old City and in Arab East Jerusalem. Dozens of Israeli police were wounded, while the Palestinian side counted seven dead and dozens of wounded from East Jerusalem, the West Bank, and Arab-Israeli communities. This mix of casualties turned out to add even more fuel to the fire, merely 36 hours after leaving Washington and in direct opposition to Barak's directive.

That night, as every Jewish family gathered around the holiday table, Israel was supposed to quiet down. In the late afternoon, when events seemed to subside, we joined our families. The contradiction between the peaceful holiday environment in my hometown of Holon and the violence in Jerusalem was surreal. The following day was going to be explosive. On our side, soldiers were called up from their holiday vacations and forces were deployed across the West Bank, East Jerusalem, and Gaza. Meanwhile, the Arab streets were boiling with humiliation and rage.

One of the most important practices instituted by the Oslo Accords was the Joint Patrols of Israeli and Palestinian police, who would together oversee the implementation of the agreements and resolve local problems. In practical terms, these were convoys of two vehicles, one Israeli and one Palestinian, which were manned by Israeli and Palestinian teams of police. As they spent many hours together and broke bread, some became friendly and then friends. But on that Saturday morning, a Palestinian policeman shot his Israeli counterpart dead in revenge for the events in Al-Aqsa. Immediately the Joint Patrols were halted, and a symbol of the Oslo Accords was gone, shattering the trust between Palestinian police and Israeli security forces.

Later that day, tens of thousands of Palestinians joined widespread violence and raging protests in dozens of locations across the West Bank, in Gaza, and in Arab East Jerusalem. Worse yet, Palestinian policemen—armed with weapons given to them with Israel's blessing as part of the Oslo

Accords—fired at Israeli forces, who returned fire. Despite Barak's interest in calming the violence, a few Palestinians died and many others suffered severe injuries. Demonstrations on the following day were even more violent.

On Saturday, September 30, television screens around the world were dominated by one of the most tragic and iconic pieces of footage of the Israeli-Palestinian war. It came from Netzarim Junction, in the middle of the Gaza Strip. Netzarim was a tiny Israeli community in the middle of a Palestinian urban continuum that was home to more than 1,000,000 Palestinians and stretched from Gaza City in the north to Khan Yunis in the south. Netzarim, like few other settlements, symbolized Israel's imposing presence in the heart of the Palestinian areas because its protection required significant Israeli military forces and impeded the daily lives of Palestinians.

On that day, following the violence in Jerusalem, Palestinian policemen on one side of the junction were exchanging fire with Israeli soldiers on its other side. The crossfire was caught on camera, which also filmed a father holding his six-year-old son and crouching for cover against a wall behind a concrete cylinder. The boy, Mohammed, was hysterical, and the father, Jamal al-Durrah, is seen waving desperately to stop the shooting. Eventually, some bullets hit them, and Mohammad is seen slumping. The child died soon after.

The gut-wrenching images were broadcast in France and became viral around the world, with a voiceover telling viewers that Mohammed and Jamal were shot by Israeli soldiers. Millions of people were enraged, particularly in the Arab world, and Mohammed al-Durrah became an instant martyr. Huge demonstrations took to the streets, and Egyptian and Jordanian leaderships became concerned for their own stability. The IDF quickly accepted responsibility for the shooting, issued an apology, and pledged to investigate the incident. In addition, a call was arranged between Barak and Arafat to calm the violence down. They promised each other to act accordingly, but our intelligence indicated that Arafat did not fulfill his promise, fueling speculation that he had planned the violence and wanted its continuation.

Soon after Mohammed al-Durrah's death, Sher was approached with serious claims that Mohammed was killed by Palestinian bullets and that the footage was mixed by the Gaza-based Palestinian crew of France 2 in order to implicate Israel. But we did not want to deal with these claims and wanted them buried. First, Sher knew Charles Enderlin, the station's bureau chief in Israel, and I had also gotten to know him during my year at the prime minister's office. He was an Israeli whose son served in the IDF. We could not believe that he would be involved in editing footage to defame Israel. Second, Barak's overall directive was to calm things down, which is why the IDF quickly accepted responsibility and apologized. We were hoping that the story would die, and contesting the footage would only keep it alive. Nonetheless, a few Israelis and French Jews persisted in challenging the credibility of that report in court. Eventually, three legal actions in France ruled for France 2 and Enderlin in 2006, against them in 2007, and ultimately for them in 2013. In any case, the photos of Muhammed al-Durrah and his story became iconic for the Palestinian struggle, and they remain so.

On Sunday, October 1, Arab-Israelis took to the streets incited by claims that Israel was taking over Al-Aqsa and infuriated by the casualties in Jerusalem, including in their own communities. Protests simultaneously erupted in many towns and villages, where rioters blocked major transportation routes and clashed with police. In the mixed cities of Jaffa, Akko, and Haifa, where Arabs and Jews live side by side, protestors advanced toward the tourist and Jewish areas. The result was huge traffic jams all over central and northern Israel at the end of a national holiday, just as hundreds of thousands were returning from vacations. Specifically, hundreds of families who were driving on highways close to Arab communities were suddenly and traumatically caught in the middle of violent protests, in fear for their lives.

Police were stretched thin by rioting events all over the country. They were instructed to contain the demonstrations and push the protestors off the main roads. Undertrained and ill-equipped, they resorted to firing their weapons, killing 11 Arab-Israeli citizens and wounding dozens, with some shot in the back by snipers from a distance. This was a shocking outcome. In the West Bank we were in a political conflict, a war waged between the IDF and armed Palestinians. But in Israel, this was a clash between police and citizens. After decades of efforts to integrate the Arab minority into Israeli society, a deep rupture was revealed. Police came under tremendous criticism, and these events would eventually cost Ben-Ami his political career.

How could violence escalate so fast and get so far out of control? Part of the answer dates to May 1996, during Netanyahu's first term, when Israel and the Palestinians went through another round of violence, known as the Kotel Tunnel Riots. The trigger was the opening of a 250-meter-long tunnel, which had been excavated for years, along the basement of the Western Wall under the Muslim Quarter. It had a southern entrance from the Kotel plaza and a northern exit in the heart of the Muslim part of the Old City. Its purpose was to allow visits to the magnificent archeological findings from 2,000 years of Jerusalem's history, and included a pavement area built by King Herodes in the first century of the current era. A section of that tunnel was the closest point to the Holy of Holies of the Solomon Temple, which was built nearly 3,000 years ago. The tunnel was a narrow one-person-wide passage, and its opening was at the same time a safety requirement, a crowd-management necessity, and a political statement.

The Palestinians saw the opening of the Kotel Tunnel as an Israeli attempt to unilaterally change the status quo in the Old City during the Interim Period and ahead of Permanent Status negotiations by placing a symbolic stake under the Muslim Quarter and in its heart. For Hamas, it was an opportunity to challenge Arafat and the PA for their failure to "protect Al-Quds and Al-Aqsa." An immediate eruption of violence followed, quickly spreading across the West Bank and to Gaza. It was during these clashes, that Palestinian police fired at Israeli forces for the first time with the weapons that they had received as part of the implementation of the Oslo Accords. On the Israeli side, the conduct of the Palestinian police was seen as an utter betrayal. Seventeen Israeli soldiers and nearly 100 Palestinians died before calm was restored, and the violence demonstrated the fragility of Israeli-Palestinian relations a few years into the Interim Period.

The death of 17 soldiers, many of whom were shot by Palestinian police, shocked the Israeli public. It also triggered extensive debriefing in the Central Command of the IDF, which was responsible for the West Bank under the command of Major General Moshe "Bougi" Ya'alon, who later rose to become a lieutenant general, IDF chief of staff, and minister of defense. Ya'alon assembled a team of military strategists to design a better response in the event that violence erupted again. The multitude of Israeli casualties and the rapid escalation of violence almost beyond control were unacceptable.

Ya'alon's team observed that Israeli soldiers were ill-trained: hundreds of thousands of bullets had been fired, but only a few hit their targets, and many of the casualties were not considered "legitimate" or "quality." Namely, the soldiers failed to nip violence in the bud by hitting the chief rioters and instigators. At the same time, they unintentionally injured and killed nonviolent protesters and even bystanders, unnecessarily causing further escalation.

In the bigger picture, Ya'alon's team was concerned that an indecisive outcome of such clashes would be perceived by Palestinians as weakness, erode Israel's deterrence, and encourage the PA to use even more violence. Such an unending "virtuous" cycle of violence and counter-violence would lead to loss of lives and could have political implications. The primary worry was mounting international pressure on Israel to take unwanted action and accept unreliable and hostile international peacekeeping forces in the West Bank and Gaza.

Ya'alon's team came up with a new approach to create a lasting deterrent effect on the Palestinian side. Their objective was to effectively neutralize the *main perpetrators* of violence *before* it escalated, whenever possible non-lethally; to avoid Palestinian casualties among the uninvolved; and to prevent Israeli civilian or military losses. They envisioned the outcome of the next conflict as decisive, deterring the Palestinians from using violence against Israel for years to follow. In effectuating this "operational idea," every Israeli infantry soldier was trained to be a better shooter, and many were trained as sharpshooters and even snipers. An emergency plan called Field of Thrones was designed, designated weapons and ammunition were purchased, and all relevant units were trained.

By October 2000, the IDF was prepared for conflict. Since April, prior to Camp David, our intelligence indicated that Arafat was gearing up for a possible violent clash with Israel if he failed to achieve his political goals through negotiations. This would be a limited confrontation with the objective of garnering international support and coercing Israel into additional concessions. In response, the IDF stood on high alert, and battle plans, like Field of Thrones, were ready for activation. After Camp David, Barak even signaled to the Palestinians that Israel was aware of their hostile considerations by explicitly referring to the possibility of violent clashes and pledging that the IDF would prevent it. My impression was that by the fall, some IDF commanders even sought conflict and its escalation. For them, the mere fact that

Arafat contemplated a violent conflict to advance his political goals proved that Israel's deterrence capability needed to be reestablished.

The combined effect of all these loosely related events and dynamics was shocking: When violence erupted, Barak would give daily directives to restore calm and lower the flames of conflict. Alas, every day would end with multiple Palestinian casualties, both dead and wounded, and even further escalation. As planned and rehearsed, soldiers were firing fewer bullets from the safety of a greater distance, but, contrary to plans, they were more lethal. The rioters sought confrontation and got it, at a high cost in blood.

The raging violence created an immediate rift between the Palestinian and Israeli delegations. We knew of the progress that just been made in Washington and suspected Arafat of cynically using violence to push Israel toward more concessions, signaling that he would not compromise any further. Meanwhile, the Palestinians thought that Israel's "excessive use of force" was a ruthless attempt by Barak to coerce them into an agreement that entailed unacceptable compromises. Even our most moderate Palestinian counterparts were infuriated by the harshness of Israel's response, pointing out that some 50 Palestinians had been killed, and hundreds severely wounded, while the number of Israeli fatalities was two. They spoke passionately about their casualties and were clearly distraught by the situation.

The Palestinian population, incited by Hamas and other radical groups, was boiling with resentment, demanding revenge. There was tremendous popular pressure on the security forces of the PA and on all political leaders—including those who embraced the Oslo Process and abandoned the armed struggle—to "protect their people." One of them was Marwan Barghouti, the leader of Tanzim, a paramilitary militia of Fatah. I met Barghouti together with Hirschfeld and Pundak a few times in Jerusalem. He used to wear a black leather jacket, chain-smoke cigarettes, and project street smarts, energy, and charisma, spiced with a sense of humor. Following Oslo A, he embraced the Two-State Solution, withdrew from the armed struggle, and had his people cooperate with Israeli security forces. Multiple times they protected Israeli civilians who lost their way in Palestinian cities and refugee camps by bringing them back safely to an Israeli checkpoint.

Eventually, Barghouti caved under that pressure too and allowed his people to join the fighting by forming the Al-Aqsa Martyrs' Brigade. His subsequent arrest and conviction for multiple terror acts and murders was a symbolic moment in the collapse of the peace process. He has been in jail ever since, for more than two decades, but he remains a two-stater. Some hold him to be a leader of the Palestinian people in the aftermath of Abu Mazen's reign and speak about him as a potential local version of Nelson Mandela in his capacity as a peacemaker.

Negotiating Under Fire

Within three days of Sharon's visit to Temple Mount, violence escalated until the PA seemed to have lost control of the crowds in the streets and of its own police. Nonetheless, Barak and others on the Israeli side still thought that Arafat had the power to end the violence, and therefore pressured him to do so. Not everyone agreed, and some on our side, primarily Ben-Ami, questioned whether Arafat was still in control of the tiger that he had been trying to ride. In any case, all of us agreed that the Palestinian negotiations team had no influence over Arafat and could not stop the cascading events. Therefore, when we pushed them to negotiate an agreement on ending violence and resumption of Permanent Status talks, we exacerbated their conundrum. As Dahlan told us, in a very calm voice: "We will not be able to sign an agreement with you unless a few Israelis die. Palestinians would not accept an agreement when they think that you bullied us into submission." Of course, we harshly objected to the notion that more Israelis would have to die to warrant a ceasefire and for peace to be reached. But from their perspective, his words made sense.

At that point, Arafat became the focus of Israeli, American, European, Egyptian, and Jordanian diplomacy, all appealing to him to end the conflict. Being the center of such attention, he had no interest in quickly stifling violence. Indeed, we knew from our intelligence that he spoke from both sides of his mouth: saying to diplomats who came to see him that he wanted to bring violence to a halt, but then also ignoring, blessing, and even encouraging the Al Aqsa Martyrs' Brigades and Tanzim to continue their clashes with and even terrorism against Israel. Arafat's actions led to even more focus on him, which he seemed to relish.

These dynamics did not escape Israeli media, which began to harshly criticize Barak for "negotiating under fire." So Barak instructed us to stop the negotiations on the FAPS and focus exclusively on reaching an agreement on the cessation of violence. He did not want to be seen as bending under pressure. The diplomatic process seemed to be deadlocked yet again.

Within less than a week of Sharon's visit, Israel entered a state of siege: the political process collapsed; hundreds of local violent clashes took place every day across the West Bank and in Gaza; there were multiple terror attacks; and violence spilled over into Israel, with mass riots by Arab-Israelis disrupting major highways and daily life in Tel Aviv, Jerusalem, Haifa, and elsewhere. In the following weeks, nearly all tourists would flee the country; Israel's economic boom would come to a sudden halt; mass demonstrations against Israel would take place around the world; and all international media platforms like CNN and the BBC would turn against Israel.

When the war escalated, Sher finally succumbed to Barak's pressures to officially assume the role of chief of staff, which had been vacant for months, in addition to serving as chief negotiator. So he and I officially transitioned to the bureau of the prime minister. Henceforth, we would be working out of the Aquarium in Jerusalem and the ministry of defense in Tel Aviv.

During these early days of fighting, our negotiation team, led by Sher, was tagging along with Barak. We were sidelined by the violence, as Barak's calendar was filled with briefings with the IDF, the Shin Bet, police, and his other security advisors. But there was a lot of diplomacy taking place as well, particularly with the Americans, Egyptians, and Jordanians on stopping violence and returning to negotiations. The Americans were gasping to understand how the progress that was just made in Washington turned into such a fierce conflict. They could not afford time-consuming detours at the end of Clinton's presidency. The Jordanians—as custodians of the al-Harem al-Sharif—had to get involved in a conflict that the Palestinians dubbed "the Al-Aqsa War." They were also concerned about mass protests that could destabilize the kingdom. The Egyptians saw themselves as patrons of the Israeli-Palestinian political process, treated Gaza as their backyard, and held Arafat to be subject to their influence. They wanted stability and political progress, so if the West Bank and Gaza spiraled out of control, their stature and interests would be compromised as well.

Throughout those days, we were also in constant communications with our Palestinian counterparts and with the heads of their security forces. On October 2, our team, led by Ben-Ami and Sher, met with Erekat, Dahlan, and others. Driving the roads of the West Bank and Gaza at night had become dangerous, so the Shin Bet transported the Palestinian delegation from set meeting points into Israel, then snuck them into the meeting rooms through back corridors of hotels that were being abandoned by their patrons. Some Palestinians, like Erekat, were opposed to violence on principle and believed in a "nonviolent struggle." Others thought that a conflict with Israel was against Palestinian interests because they were within reach of their dreamed-of Palestinian state, with Al-Quds as its capital and a $20 billion seed funding to kick it off. They feared the loss of these achievements and wanted to seize the opportunities that they presented. In addition, the heads of their security services were concerned about the integrity and cohesion of their organizations, whose members were under pressure to break rank and join the fighting.

That specific meeting, on Day Five of the conflict, was very emotional. Both sides were angry and frustrated. And then, in a deeply human moment, Erekat told us of his son, Ali, then 16 years old. In the past, Erekat had proudly boasted that Ali was part of Seeds of Peace, a youth movement of Israelis, Americans, and Palestinians. Now, Ali was bullied by his classmates for his father's role in the peace negotiations and was challenged to prove his patriotism by confronting Israeli soldiers. Erekat was obviously concerned for Ali's safety, and worried that his son's entire upbringing would collapse. He choked up when he spoke.

Ours was just one of a few channels of communication between Barak and Arafat that continued to operate throughout the conflict, seeking to end violence and resume negotiations. A week into the crisis, everyone involved concluded that changing course required bringing the leaders together. That is how we got to Paris.

On October 4, a week into the war, Albright, Barak, and Arafat, together with the Israeli and Palestinian delegations and the Peace Team, convened in Paris at the residence of the American ambassador. While Albright shuttled between the leaders, the negotiation teams worked out a draft agreement to end violence and renew the political process. It was printed, corrected, and reprinted. Finally, close to midnight, it seemed that an agreement was reached, formulated on a draft with many strikeouts, additions, and corrections. It was messy but looked done.

This was the moment to sign whatever was agreed upon, or at least initial the draft. But President Jacques Chirac got word of the imminent agreement being forged in his backyard in Paris and wanted to be updated. He too had a stake in the negotiations: considering France to be a world power, he wanted his country to play a leading role in an EU-led international inquiry committee that would investigate the eruption of violence—a truth committee of sorts. He "offered" to deploy French military forces on the ground in Gaza and the West Bank as part of a peacekeeping contingency, which really meant that he expected the Palestinians to insist on that demand.

Israel did not want to have French forces deployed in the West Bank or Gaza because of France's legacy of pro-Arab policies and politics. The Americans did not want France there either. And while the Palestinians were happy to have French forces on the ground that were more sympathetic to them, this was not high on their agenda. So, in the closing of the agreement, this point was dropped. But nobody informed the French.

Over a midnight dinner in the Elysée Palace, Chirac was hostile to the Israelis, accusing Israel of excessive use of force that led to numerous Palestinian casualties. He then asked for an update on the emerging agreement, only to learn that there would not be French forces on the ground. He quickly turned to Arafat and said, "How could you have compromised on this very important point?" Arafat, without hesitation, looked at his chief negotiators, Erekat and Abu Alaa, and muttered something, which either meant that no such compromise was ever made or that he was not aware of it. His senior negotiators were surprised, and the agreement was upended.

The Israeli side was frustrated to the point of rage. When the parties returned to the residence of the American ambassador it was nearly 2:00 AM. Arafat then decided to withdraw to his hotel, leaving Erekat and Abu Alaa to deal with the exhausted Israeli team. Albright was fuming, demanding that Arafat stay in place. She rushed out of the residence, waving and yelling at the guards not to open the gates, so as to prevent Arafat from leaving. But the negotiations collapsed without an agreement to stop the bloodshed, which would claim thousands more lives.

After the failure to achieve a ceasefire in Paris, violence spread further. Mass Palestinian protests morphed into targeted terrorist attacks when the Tanzim (the military wing of Fatah) and the Al-Aqsa Brigades escalated their actions. Some hit cars along the roads of the West Bank, while others attacked targets within Israel proper. They fired on and terrorized Gilo, a southern neighborhood of Jerusalem, which was in the line of fire from nearby PA-controlled Beit Jala. Israel was now pushed to transition from a defensive containment of violence to offensive seizure of areas of the PA to prevent such attacks on its civilians.

Thursday, October 12, marked another tragic milestone in the escalation. Two uniformed Israeli reservist military drivers were on an administrative assignment north of Jerusalem and south of Ramallah. They took a wrong turn and were stopped by a checkpoint by Palestinian police. Instead of being sent back in the right direction, they were taken into custody at the Ramallah police station. Shortly thereafter, news of the two detained Israeli soldiers spread, and a mob besieged the station demanding to lynch them. The policemen eventually allowed the crowd to storm the building and capture the two Israelis. Meanwhile, word of the unfolding story got to the international media in Ramallah, who flocked to the scene. Minutes later, the soldiers were beaten to death in the station and their mutilated bodies were thrown headdown out of the windows of an upper floor to be further brutalized. Iconic footage caught the murderers waving their bloodied hands in celebration and was broadcast all over the world, including to millions of Israelis.

That morning, at the ministry of defense in Tel Aviv, all of us—the negotiation team and Barak's advisors, secretaries, administrative staff and security detail—were huddled watching the savagery in Ramallah on a large TV screen. We had gone through two weeks of violence, but everybody understood that this event represented a turning point because of the infuriating brutality on prime-time TV inside a police station, whose policeman had been armed by Israel to protect peace.

While we were all in the hallway, Barak was conferring with his military and security advisors in his office down the hall. Minutes later, we watched

on TV as the Palestinian mob suddenly escaped from the building and its surroundings. An Israeli warning had preceded a missile attack from helicopters,
which demolished the station. It was a response made in rage, again broadcast
to a global viewership. Over the following years, Israel would apprehend and
jail all the people who participated in the murders. But on that day, for those
soldiers, we could do nothing.

After Albright's failure to achieve a ceasefire in Paris, Clinton decided to
throw another log onto the Israeli-Palestinian fire. George Tenet, the director
of the CIA, was close with the Israelis, but also with the Palestinian security
forces, who the CIA trained and funded. Tenet may have had the best chance
to de-escalate the conflict and bring about a resumption of negotiations.

Alas, October 12 was an unfortunate day for Tenet to land in Israel.
After the atrocity in Ramallah and Israel's retaliation, his mission collapsed
before it even started. He had his meetings, but nothing came from them,
especially since Israel knew that Arafat was playing a double game: while he
sent Dahlan to talk with Tenet about stopping violence, he also encouraged
the Al-Aqsa Brigades, Dahlan's rivals, to continue their attacks against settlers
and soldiers. It was a typical Arafat maneuver: supporting Dahlan with one
hand and undermining him with the other. Our intelligence incriminated
Arafat, who may even have wanted Barak to know what he was doing. The
breakdown of trust between Barak and Arafat was absolute, and Tenet could
not salvage it. He left empty-handed on the following day.

Five days later, Clinton decided to make a dramatic personal intervention
by calling for an emergency summit in Sharm el-Sheikh, Egypt, on October
17–18. It was a desperately improvised attempt to save the peace process.
There was no time to prepare, and our channels of communications with the
Palestinians were barely intact.

The general idea was that Barak and Arafat would issue an unequivocal
call for ending violence that would be witnessed and sponsored by Clinton
and the Americans, as well as by Mubarak and the Egyptians, who would also
monitor its implementation. The joint statement in English was supposed
to be followed by coordinated translations into Hebrew and Arabic. Arafat's
statement in Arabic was very important to us because of his double game. For

example, in English, he used to speak about reaching "peace" but in Arabic he would refer to a *hudnah*—a long-term ceasefire that also meant a continued long-term struggle.

We flew to Sharm and gathered in the local convention center, where every delegation was assigned a room. Naturally, the Egyptian section was the largest; it covered half of the floor. The second-largest section was given to Arafat and the Palestinians, and then came the American quarters. The Israeli delegation was given a tiny room at the end of a corridor. Our hosts were signaling to us in every possible way that they didn't appreciate how Israel had handled the conflict.

The Egyptian intelligence was always aggressive with us, but this time they outdid themselves. Arab streets had been burning with newly intensified anger about Israel since the Al-Durrah incident two weeks earlier, and these sentiments were now directed at us. As soon as we got out of the motorcade that brought us from the airplane to the convention center, Barak's bodyguards formed a tight circle around him and an immediate second circle around his close advisors, including Sher and Yatom. (I was within that second circle.) We then walked to the convention hall. But as we passed through the doors, Egyptian security men elbowed their way through our group, violating all diplomatic protocols, and dividing our delegation into two sections, Our bodyguards started shoving the Egyptian security people, and the situation soon bordered on a brawl. Those in the front with Barak entered the building. Those in the back were held outside. One of them was pushing a trolley that carried our portable printer. Another was carrying Barak's personal luggage.

We were upset, but we also had a big meeting to run. Barak threatened to abort the conference and return to Israel immediately unless our team was allowed to reunite and he got his luggage. Those things happened gradually. Barak's luggage was brought in by Egyptian security first. Then the rest of our team joined. The printer was returned an hour later. Our security people immediately confiscated it, and later told us that it was bugged and had to be destroyed.

When we entered the small side room assigned to us, the head of our security team declared that the room was only for snacking and napping. No substantive conversations or work could take place there, because it too was bugged.

Where would we work? We took a short tour of the building and randomly chose a section of a corridor's wall near an electric socket. "You'll work from here," the security man said to me. And that's what happened: we pulled over a table and a few chairs, isolated our space, and established our "office" in the corridor.

The entire conference was the most hostile that I've ever participated in. There was no trust among any of the groups in attendance. Nevertheless, under pressure from Clinton and Mubarak, Barak and Arafat formulated a joint declaration that called for an immediate cessation of violence. These words, however, were empty. Violence continued.

Barak and Arafat Disengaged

The collapse of the Camp David negotiations into a violent confrontation, along with the disintegration of Barak's coalition, inspired Shimon Peres to make a bid to replace Barak as the Labor Party candidate for the premiership. Peres—former premier in 1985–1986 and again in 1995–1996, following Rabin's assassination—argued that he stood a better chance to beat Sharon in the coming general elections. He also claimed to be better suited to negotiate with Arafat the final act of the Oslo Process, which he had co-created with Rabin. So while Israel was locking horns with the Palestinians, its own leadership was torn by infighting.

The clash between Peres and Barak/Ben-Ami was long in the making. Barak's relationship with Peres had lasted decades but had been strained since 1995, when Barak joined the Labor Party and associated himself with Rabin, Peres' intra-party rival. Both Rabin and Peres were then disappointed when Barak described the 1993–1995 Oslo A and Oslo B Agreements as "Swiss cheese" that was full of holes. And after the loss to Netanyahu in 1996, Peres' people accused Barak of undermining their campaign so that he could assume the leadership of the Labor Party. There was no love lost, and no trust, between the two men or between their teams.

Nonetheless, when Barak became chair of the Labor Party and then prime minister, Peres expected to be given a senior leadership position, as Barak's second-among-equals and "big brother." But Barak would not be dominated or outshone by Israel's elder statesman, who also had the legacy of surprising his premier with successful back-door negotiations, most notably in London in 1988 and Oslo in 1993. Barak was suspicious that Peres would pull another backchannel on him, so he gave him a humiliating junior portfolio, as minister for regional cooperation, which Peres then ceaselessly used as a platform for diplomatic initiatives.

The relationship between Peres and Ben-Ami was tenuous on different grounds. Ben-Ami's personal story—coming from an immigrant family from Morocco and rising to become an Oxford professor and a star ambassador—made him a political silver bullet for the Labor Party. Peres sponsored Ben-Ami's political rise, but somewhere along this journey, they had a falling-out. Throughout the peace negotiations, Peres gave Barak and Ben-Ami the feeling that he could do a much better job himself, criticizing their approach and actions off-record, and after Camp David also on-record.

So Barak and Ben-Ami saw Peres as operating like a prime-minister-in-waiting. He met with heads of states, and on his travels he was willingly treated with the highest diplomatic protocols. He continually angled to take over the Palestinian file from Ben-Ami. Naturally, Peres' criticism of the negotiations' management implicated Sher and our entire team. Logically, we knew that his critique was a challenge to Barak, but emotionally, members of our team took his criticism personally and developed a grudge.

These dynamics were exacerbated after Camp David, when Peres openly criticized Barak for his management of the summit and for his inability to bond with Arafat, as he and Rabin had done. Against this backdrop, as Barak maneuvered to block Peres' bid for the leadership of the party, he was forced to establish a ministerial Peace Cabinet that included Peres and other senior politicians. Negotiations with the Palestinians were going to be managed by committee, which made Sher's work even more complicated.

This background is necessary for an understanding of the meeting with Arafat on November 2. All previous attempts—by Albright in Paris; by Tenet; and Sharm by Clinton—had failed to end the violence, but Barak insisted on prioritizing a ceasefire agreement. Meanwhile Barak's left-wing coalition partners in the Peace Cabinet pressured him to make another bold move toward a FAPS. Peres wanted to lead that last effort by establishing a direct channel with Arafat, and Barak was willing to let him fail. Eventually, a meeting between Peres and Arafat was scheduled for November 2 in Gaza, with the participation of Peres' chief of staff, Avi Gil, and Sher. The formal goal was to finalize the agreement, which had been negotiated in Paris a month earlier. Sher had Meidan-Shani, Hasso, and me join as well, and we took a draft of the desired agreement with us.

Before we left Jerusalem, Barak met with Peres, Gil, and Sher and made one additional concrete request: to secure from Arafat the jailing of Hussein Abayat, commander of the Tanzim in the Bethlehem area and an active terrorist perpetrating attacks against Israelis and the firing on Gilo. Barak saw this as a litmus test for Arafat's seriousness in ending violence and a chance to test Peres' clout as well. In private, Barak asked Sher to keep a watchful eye on Peres, not to leave him alone with Arafat, and to make sure that Peres was not taking some wild initiative that Barak would not approve of. He warned Sher of "Peres' fantasies."

Off we went from Jerusalem in an armored and armed motorcade full of bodyguards from the famed 730 Unit of the Shin Bet. After all, a former prime minister of Israel was traveling to Gaza for an entire evening in the middle of a war. The GMCs were packed with people and equipment. I was squeezed in a middle seat, my briefcase on my knees and my legs on a metal box—probably some communication equipment or ammunition. As we entered Gaza, we met Palestinian security personnel who led us through the pitch-dark streets. We were driving very fast, and I remember thinking that we were more likely to get hurt in an accident than by terrorists. Everyone was hanging onto their seats. No one spoke. From where I sat, I had a limited view of Gaza, and it was dark and quiet.

After what seemed like a long drive with many turns, we arrived at Arafat's compound around 10:00 PM, anticipating a meeting with Arafat and a session of negotiations with the Palestinian delegation. But Arafat had other plans for that evening. Wearing his military fatigues, with Erekat and Dahlan and other members of his inner circle around him, he warmly greeted us and was clearly happy to see Peres.

Arafat then invited us to have dinner and led us to a large dining hall with an oval table. He sat in the middle with his top advisors at his sides. Peres sat across from Arafat, with Sher and Gil beside him and the rest of our delegation on the farther flanks of the table's "Israeli side." A healthy and delicious dinner was served: grilled fish cooked in olive oil and lemon, thinly cut and mildly spiced vegetable salad, and other Palestinian dishes. Arafat graciously hosted us in the best spirit of Arab tradition. Each of us handed him our plate and he filled it himself, making comments about how olive oil was good for our veins and heart and how the fish were fresh out of the sea of Gaza. He then made sure that the servers gave us seconds, encouraging us to eat well. It was as if he was making the point that the conflict was not personal. Arafat and Peres, both known to be night owls, were alert and in good spirits. Arafat kept mentioning his "brother Rabin," probably to distinguish him from Barak, and the overall atmosphere was very friendly.

Arafat's residence seemed modest. After years of hearing about his alleged corruption, it was not nearly as lavish as I had expected or as luxurious as I have seen in other Arab countries. But the rumors about Arafat's healthy eating habits were definitely confirmed that night.

After deserts—excellent Arab pastries and delicious mint tea—we moved to the hospitality room. Arafat and Peres sat close together in armchairs, and the two delegations were seated on long sofas on opposing sides of the room, facing each other. After a few minutes of general discussion about the political situation in the Middle East, Arafat asked to have a one-on-one discussion with Peres, who immediately agreed. I would not be surprised if that moment had been pre-orchestrated by Peres' team. At any rate, Sher, who was under direct instruction from Barak *not* to leave Peres alone with Arafat, had to respectfully step out with Gil and the rest of us. We were escorted to another big room with a long boardroom table. More tea and pastries were served.

On the wall of that cabinet room, a huge mural sculpture was hanging, some 18 feet long and nearly six feet wide. I asked our host from Arafat's bureau about it. He proceeded to explain in detail every section and image in the mural, which was a depiction of the history and struggles of the Palestinian People, beginning with the Muslim era in the seventh century, on the right side. Moving leftward, each section described a different era: the Christian Crusades, the Byzantine period, and so on. The far left was dedicated to the *naqba* and to Israel's "oppression." I was stunned: in Israel we were taught that there was no Palestinian People at all, at least until the later 20th century, and that the concept was "made up" and "fictitious." Yet here I heard a detailed narrative that extended back for centuries. I made an alarming realization: the underlying story of that mural was about a Palestinian People who had repeatedly been able to overcome their rulers and conquerors. The implication was that like the crusaders, Ottomans, and British, who had all come and gone, so had the Jews come, and at some point, so would they be gone. In the long term, Palestinian resistance would prevail. Why would such people agree to an End of Conflict and Finality of Claims?

After some 45 minutes, Arafat and Peres came into the room. They seemed content with their discussion. Peres announced that the meeting was over and that we'd be leaving. Sher was sidelined. Nothing would be negotiated that night. On our way out, our Palestinian hosts bid us warm farewells, and Arafat insisted on kissing each of us on the cheeks, as he often did.

It was after midnight when we left Arafat's residence, and the drive out of Gaza was as speedy as the one coming in. Meanwhile, Peres updated Barak and Sher that, per Barak's request, Arafat had promised to arrest Abayat, keep him in jail, and order him to stop his terror activities. By the time we got back to Jerusalem, it was the middle of the night.

On the following day, the European envoy, Ambassador Moratinos, arrived in Israel. He met Barak, who told him about the Peres-Arafat meeting and asked him to verify with Arafat that Abayat would be jailed. Moratinos then traveled to Gaza, met Arafat, and reported back to Barak that Abayat was indeed destined to remain jailed, off the streets and away from his terrorist activities. A few days later, on November 9, an Israeli Apache helicopter fired a Hellfire missile at a car in the Bethlehem area, killing Abayat. He was evidently not in jail. Abayat's elimination was the first of many "targeted preventive actions" by the IDF against Palestinian military operatives. For Barak, this was yet another proof that Arafat could not be trusted.

What Really Happened? Depends on Who You Ask!

From May 2000 to January 2001, on many Thursday afternoons, I was invited to the headquarters of the research-and-analysis division of the military intelligence in Tel Aviv, aka the research division *(Hativat HaMechkar)*. That recurring meeting was born out of frustration that despite the billions of dollars that Israel invested in its intelligence, our delegation, working on the primary agenda of the Prime Minister, was *not* getting the decision-support that we needed. Lieutenant Colonel Ephrain Lavie, the head of the research division's "Palestinian Theater" and a member of our delegation, brought me together with two young and brilliant officers. One of them, Major Dror Shalom, would rise to become a brigadier general and commander of the entire research division, and then would move on to lead the politico-military unit in the ministry of defense.

The research division has played a legendary and crucial role in Israel's national security and strategic diplomacy. With access to Israel's most brilliant analysts, its role is to make sense of all the information gathered by the different agencies, form an assessment of Israel's military and diplomatic condition, present that assessment to the prime minister and the security cabinet, and then support the most important military and diplomatic operations. Most vitally, the research division is responsible for providing a warning about imminent wars or security threats. Hence its assessments and recommendations, accurate or misguided, could direct billions of dollars of spending, ignite a preemptive war, or allow an imminent threat to be disregarded. In a world of disinformation and conflicting political interests, the ethos and stature of the research division emanates from the supreme talent of its soldiers, the analytical rigor of its work, and its legacy of speaking truth to power.

A primary method of the research division is called "highlighted important information" *(Tziyun Yediot Chashuvot* or TZIACH), which prioritizes efforts to gather and analyze information. Specifically, the TZIACH determines which elements of the information that is gathered by listening devices and from spies makes its way to decision-makers. Against this backdrop, Sher's and my frustration during the Camp David negotiations was that the research division was not fine-tuned to support our diplomatic efforts. Lavie repeatedly briefed us that Arafat was interested in signing an agreement that conformed with the "core positions" of the PLO, namely, borders based on the 1967 Lines; Arab Jerusalem, with Al-Quds, as capital; and a just resolution to the refugee problem. He also warned that if negotiations failed to achieve these goals, Arafat might unilaterally declare a Palestinian state, even at the risk of a limited conflict with Israel.

That analysis had two major weaknesses. First, it could not anticipate the effect of Barak's actions, particularly his stalling of the negotiations until May and then his quest for a moment-of-truth summit in Camp David by July. Second, it had remained static for many years, perhaps since 1988 or

1993, while the dynamics among the Palestinian negotiators were changing weekly and even daily. The information that Arafat would need to get
the equivalent of 100 percent of the West Bank and Gaza in order to sign
an End-of-Conflict and Finality-of-Claims agreement was obviously very
important, but as negotiators we were interested in other questions: What
were the relations within the Palestinian delegation? What was the quality
of their preparations? What would their positions be? Who's more inclined
to compromise? Who has Arafat's ear? What's going on among Abu Mazen,
Abu Alaa, Abed Rabbo, Dahlan, Rashid, and Erekat? What did they think
of us? Did they understand our message? Furthermore, beyond the issues of
Jerusalem, borders, and refugees, which repeatedly appeared in the assessments, several secondary issues were also important for the FAPS but never
made it to the reports we saw. It turned out that much of this information
was plentifully available. And if it was not, we wanted our needs to affect the
TZIACH. That's why Lavie invited me to speak directly to Shalom and the
other analysts. And expectedly, I learned a great deal from those meetings.

The analysis of the Palestinian positions, which was presented by the
research division dozens of times ahead of Camp David, created a "conception": an overarching framework that guided all policy and decisions. Barak,
who was a former commander of the intelligence branch, diligently read the
entire analysis and not just its highlights. He concluded that Arafat would
not budge from his core positions and finalize a FAPS unless very specific
conditions were created: a compelling offer by Israel that was credibly close
to Israel's redlines, presented to Arafat by Barak himself; massive pressure on
Arafat, namely by Clinton and the Egyptians; and a clear deadline that forced
Arafat to make a historic decision. Hence the architecture of the Camp David
summit.

When we returned from Camp David, the Palestinian perspective on
the negotiations was framed by the research division as "more of the same."
Namely, Camp David was just an episode in an extended political process,
so a return to negotiations in August and September was expected and welcomed. Arafat remained loyal to his core positions and was still considering a
unilateral declaration of independence.

But now their assessment included another conspicuously dangerous ele-
ment: the Palestinians felt that Israel was repeatedly improving its offers. They

compared Barak's positions in April, before Sweden; during the backchannel in Sweden; ahead of Camp David; and then in September and concluded that there was no reason to compromise just yet. That was a slippery slope on which Israel's statements about "reaching our rock-bottom positions" lost their credibility. In retrospect, this was another cause of the ferocity of the conflict that erupted following Sharon's visit. In any case, the research division also insisted that Arafat was willing to risk a limited conflict to advance his political goals. I don't remember a single clear warning that we were sliding into an explosive situation that could lead to an all-out war. Certainly there was no warning that the war would last three years and claim thousands of lives.

After Sharon's visit to Temple Mount and the ensuing eruption of violence, there was one commonality between us and the Palestinians: each side seemed to attribute to the other side some masterminded Machiavellian intention. The Palestinian side believed that Barak had deliberately inflicted casualties and devastation on them to deter additional demands from Israel and coerce Arafat into accepting his offers. But while some senior IDF officers certainly sought to escalate the conflict once it erupted to reestablish deterrence, I can testify that Barak wanted the opposite: to calm things down. Meanwhile, many Israelis came to believe that Arafat had initiated the war to squeeze more concessions out of Israel, and that he never intended to have real peace. In this context, I can testify that I never saw or heard any clear evidence for these accusations against Arafat prior to October 2000 or in the early phases of the conflict. To the contrary, our intelligence officers repeatedly said that Arafat was interested in reaching a deal with Israel, albeit on his terms, and that he was surprised by the violence and experienced a loss of control. Indeed, the notion that such a bloody war may have been *unintended* was unfathomable to both sides, but even more unfathomable to me is the notion that Arafat intended to launch a total war with Israel and we knew nothing about it.

Notwithstanding the debate regarding the beginning of the war, it is clear that once violence erupted, Arafat encouraged the riots and did not prevent their escalation to terrorism. At that initial phase, he saw value in the conflict for his strategic interests. While the Israeli and Palestinian publics were *not* aware of the dramatic progress in the negotiations since Camp David and particularly in Washington, Clinton, Mubarak, Abdullah, Barak, and European leaders were fully cognizant thereof. Therefore, they could appreciate the interplay between violence in the streets and diplomacy and negotiations ahead of a potential second summit. What seemed to most people like uncontrolled tit-for-tat escalation was in fact a power play between Israel and the PA, Barak and Arafat, that was part of a broader political process. In this contest, Arafat had the upper hand in his quest for his national goals, as evidenced by the Clinton Ideas, which represented clear progress for the Palestinians compared to Barak's offers in Camp David.

By early 2001, it seemed that Arafat lost control of the level of violence, which escalated into a "war of terror" led primarily by Hamas, Islamic Jihad, and Fatah's Al-Aqsa Martyrs' Brigades. It targeted Israel's civilian population with dozens of deadly suicide bombings that caused hundreds of casualties. In response, the Sharon government ordered the recapturing of the West Bank to weed out the terror network, and eventually, Israel laid siege to Arafat's headquarters in Ramallah until his departure to exile and death in November 2004.

In parallel to these events, the narrative in Israel regarding the Camp David negotiations crystallized. It now held that Arafat had never accepted Israel's existence and legitimacy and that he continued to seek its elimination by insisting on the Right of Return. Hence, the Camp David negotiations represented a continuation of the PLO's Phased Plan, albeit implemented with diplomatic tools. Once diplomacy exhausted itself, the war represented a logical next step and was pre-planned to force Israel to accept a Palestinian state *without* Finality of Claims, specifically regarding the return of the refugees.

The most vocal advocate of that view was Amos Gilead, a brilliant, outspoken, and charismatic veteran intelligence officer who rose to the rank of major general before heading the politico-military unit of the ministry of defense. As early as April 2000, he warned that Arafat had no intention of signing an agreement and was preparing for a conflict with Israel. The collapse of the Camp David negotiations and the eruption of violence following Sharon's visit were presented as proof of his forewarning. Hence, Israel's response to Palestinian aggression had to be harsh to "teach them a lesson."

The alternative view, consistently held by Lavie throughout that period,[63] argued that Arafat wanted to sign a historic agreement with Israel based on the PLO's "core positions" and that any conflict Arafat contemplated was in service of that objective. Meanwhile, the eruption of violence in September was "organic" and "bottom-up" fueled by widespread frustrations with Israel and *with the PA*, as well as by incitement by Hamas. Therefore, the violence *could not* serve as proof that Arafat doesn't want peace and masterminded the entire conflict.

Furthermore, Lavie argued that in Arafat's mind, negotiations never reached the final stage at which both leaders must forge a give-and-take package of historical decisions. Arafat felt that he was *promised by Clinton* not to be bullied to a decision in Camp David, as Barak planned; that his actions in Camp David were consistent with his promise to Clinton; and that his response to the Clinton Ideas in January was a "Yes, but…," leaving the door open for further negotiations. Hence, from Arafat's perspective, negotiations were halted after Taba in January, before being exhausted. In other words, the Palestinian side refused to accept Barak's framing of a moment of truth, which, in their minds, was artificial and never really happened.

The difference between Gilead and Lavie was formative: the former claimed that war and future conflict with the Palestinians were inevitable. The latter claimed that war was unintended and a political process is feasible. Furthermore, Gilead offered a narrative that had a clear, even simplistic line of progression. Meanwhile, Lavie described a complex reality dominated by the law of unintended consequences.

Initially, in late 2000 and early 2001, Lavie was sidelined and disadvantaged in their debate. Gilead was his senior, and therefore had access to the prime minister, the security cabinet, and the media. It was his responsibility to present the assessment of the research division, adding his interpretation, while many ministers do not have security clearance to read the full analysis, and even those who do often don't take the time to do so. But when both men retired from service, their debate became public and on equal footing.

---

63   Yoav Stern, Haaretz, *A Baseless Conception,* (קונצפציה חסרת בסיס - כללי - הארץ), June 13, 2004)

At that point, it was Lavie who received the backing of senior officers of the intelligence branch, including a couple of its former commanders.

"Walking back the cat," or sometimes simply "cat walk," is a technique that intelligence analysts use to learn from their mistakes of assessment. It is applied when a surprise occurs, highlighting a failure of analysis and a gap in the available intelligence information. Such "cat walk" works its way back from the "intelligence gap" examining every step of analysis and piece of information that contributed to the mis-assessment, often identifying disinformation, unreliable sources, double agents, or simply bad or wrong thinking.

Because the outbreak of the war with the Palestinians and its tragic consequences were unexpected, a cat walk was inevitable. It produced the two schools represented by Gilead and Lavie, whose dispute goes to the core ethos and operations of Israel's intelligence services: To what extent can decision-support to the prime minister deviate from raw information? Could a senior officer use his access to top decision-makers to offer an additional interpretation of the analysis and do so without a similar level of rigor? To what extent should intelligence analysis serve the political interests of politicians and needs of public diplomacy, such as defaming Arafat? And at what point did the conception about Arafat's actions become a dogma that blocked any information or analysis to the contrary?

Ironically, Israel would come to name the violent clash with the Palestinians as "the Second Intifada" or "the Second Palestinian Uprising." That name references the first Intifada of 1987–1991, when Israel was in full control of the West Bank and Gaza with no Palestinian statehood on the political horizon. Meanwhile, Palestinians call these events "the Al-Aqsa War," which means the War for Jerusalem. But given the progress in the negotiations in 2000 toward a Palestinian state with Al-Quds as its capital, the violence was neither an "uprising" nor was it a "war for Jerusalem." From my perspective, it was simply an Israeli-Palestinian war!

SECTION IV

The Path Forward

CHAPTER 12

One-State, Two-States, Three-States...

Oslo Process on Life Support?

This book was written and published over three and a half years—from October 2019 to July 2023—with one scenario in mind: somehow, sometime the elusive condition of "ripeness" will emerge that will allow for another attempt to resolve the Israeli-Palestinian conflict and even reach peace. At that point, so Ari and I hope, this book will be useful and available to the women and men who will be tasked with transforming one of the longest-standing conflicts of the modern era.

In December 2022, Tom Friedman of the *New York Times* observed that the Israeli-Palestinian peace process is neither dead nor alive; "it's in hospice."[64] In demonstrating how near death the Oslo Process is, Friedman describes the loss of commitment to the spirit and intentions of peacemaking. At the same time, the Oslo Process is still alive, because the key institutions that it created—primarily the PA in Areas A and B, and its security and economic relations with Israel—continue to function. Friedman also eloquently observed that the "the alternative to the Two-State Solution will not be a stable One-State Solution. It will be the 'One Big Mess Solution,'" namely a reality that is worse for most stakeholders, except perhaps Iran and Hamas.

Ari and I accept Friedman's premise as the point of departure for the final section of this book: at this point, in the summer of 2023, the Oslo Process and the Two-State Solution are in limbo, neither "alive" in the sense that

---

64 Thomas Friedman, What in the World Is Happening in Israel? (*New York Times*, December 15, 2022).

Israel and the Palestinians are on track toward peace, nor "dead" in that the PA has disintegrated. Our question is, Where are things heading?

Is This Book a Requiem?

Those who claim that "the Oslo Process is dead" refer not only to the condition and direction of Israeli-Palestinian relations, particularly in the West Bank, but also to the intentions of the parties. Indeed, prospects for resuming negotiations with the goal of reaching peace seem more unlikely now, perhaps than ever before, since 1993. On the Israeli side, it has been 10 to 15 years since the last efforts to reach a FAPS, by Olmert in 2008 and by Netanyahu in 2014. Thereafter, all Israeli governments, led by Netanyahu, Bennett and Lapid, have avoided negotiations on Permanent Status, while gradually expanding settlements in the West Bank.

Netanyahu's sixth government, established in November 2022, represented an aggressive departure from the Oslo Process. It made annexing the West Bank an official goal. It then cancelled the law that allowed for the Gaza Disengagement of 2005 and prevented Israelis from resettling areas in northern Samaria that were also evacuated by the Sharon government. Betzalel Smotrich, Netanyahu's coalition partner and head of the National Religious Party, calls for canceling the Oslo Accords and dismantling the PA. With those positions, he was appointed minister of finance and a minister in the ministry of defense, responsible for key areas in the West Bank. Netanyahu then approved significant expansion of settlements in strategic locations that will circumvent a contiguous Palestinian state. Indeed, most of Israel's right wing denies the idea of Palestinian statehood altogether, rejecting even Netanyahu's famous Bar Ilan speech in 2009, in which he endorsed the principle of two-states-for-two-people. They also would not even accept the Trump Plan, because it recognized the possibility of a Palestinian state, albeit subject to many conditions. In fact, most Israeli politicians, including some in centrist parties, reject the notion of ever having a Palestinian state or another withdrawal.

At the same time, reality on the ground is making separation between Israel and the Palestinians in the West Bank ever more difficult. The numbers of settlers and settlements in Judea and Samaria have doubled since 2000 to nearly 465,000 settlers in nearly 130 communities. These settlements range from large modern townships with tens of thousands of people, like Ariel or Ma'ale

Edomim, while others are much smaller communities. There are also 146 "out-posts"—caravans on hilltops and single-family farms—some of which are "illegal" because they were not properly established. An additional 234,000 Israelis live in the neighborhoods of expanded Jerusalem, beyond the 1967 Lines.[65]

Furthermore, the trauma of the Gaza Disengagement makes future withdrawals much less likely. The thousands of rockets that have rained on Israel from Gaza cancel Israel's ability to relinquish security control in the West Bank, like it did in Gaza. And the number of potential evacuees—as many as 100,000 in the West Bank, compared to just 7,000 in Gaza—make such mass relocation of population a political impossibility. In the years that have passed since Camp David, Shaul Arieli has continued to monitor the development of settlements in the West Bank and has repeatedly claimed that separation between Israel and the Palestinians allowing for a viable contiguous Palestinian state is still possible. He may be right. But the political ability to do so doesn't seem to be there.

On the Palestinian side, Gaza and the West Bank have been separated since 2007. As a result, they can no longer be referred to as a "single territorial unit," and the PLO can no longer credibly claim to be the "sole legitimate representative of the Palestinian People." With Gaza is armed to its teeth and weapons readily available across the West Bank, nor can anyone imagine a "demilitarized Palestinian state." These notions had been cornerstones of the Oslo Process and premises of all attempts to reach peace, from the Beilin–Abu Mazen Understandings to the Trump Plan.

Meanwhile, the PA in the West Bank is authoritarian, corrupt, and failing, losing the legitimacy of its authority and its effective control of some key areas that fall to the rule of armed groups and local clans. The number of Israelis killed and wounded in terror attacks is rising, as Hamas, local gangs, and individual operatives become bolder. In addition, the imminent battle for succession—Abu Mazen is 87 years old and has been in power for nearly 20 years—is already enhancing instability and disunity. Against this backdrop, Israeli forces expand operations in the heart of Palestinian cities, and the number of Palestinian casualties, both armed and civilian, is spiking

---

65   Source: The Jerusalem Center for Public Affairs,

to unprecedented levels. An accelerating cycle of violence seems to be leading toward an ethnic national struggle, which could force Israel to expand its hold even farther into Area B and even Area A.

And in the broadest possible scope, the terms of the Permanent Status deal are getting tougher for *both sides*: for Israel, the original logic of "land for peace" has been long abandoned with regards to the Palestinians. Past withdrawals did not bring peace, and many Palestinians continue to reject Israel with support from Iran and other radical forces. The Trump Plan may be seen to represent a "smaller tradeoff" of "land for security," but security will likely remain a challenge for years to come, even under Trump's terms. Similarly, the Palestinians cannot hope for a deal like the one offered to them in 2000. Settlements and Israeli presence in Jerusalem have expanded, and Israel's demands for security arrangements have escalated. Any Palestinian leadership will have a hard time accepting such terms.

In this context, this book could be read as a requiem for the Oslo Process by those who accept this analysis and hold these trends to be inevitable. Thirty years after the historic agreement in Oslo in 1993, its vision of peace and coexistence among two secure and prosperous states, which are national homes to two peoples, may be disintegrating into a morass of violence and hopelessness. The work of peacemaking may have turned into Mission: Impossible. In that case, Ari and I hope that we have conveyed the patriotism, thoughtfulness, courage, and passion, as well as the limitations, complexities, and even cynicism of the Israelis, Palestinians, Americans, and others who have attempted to reach Permanent Status. Yes, this book singles out and highlights my experiences during the era of Barak and Clinton, but this salute goes to all teams on all sides from 1993 up until today.

A Requiem? Not Just Yet

But just as you are about to close the chapter on Israeli-Palestinian peacemaking in our generation, please remember the hard facts: *most Palestinians and most Israelis do not want to share a society*, because we have distinct cultures, legacies, and destinies. We speak different languages, and most of us are either Jewish or Muslim. While we have been in conflict for more than a century, neither wants to rule the other. According to polls, a vast majority of Palestinians wish for the establishment of their state *alongside* Israel and not in its stead. And most Israelis—even within Israel's right wing—don't want to annex the Palestinians of the West Bank and integrate them into Israeli society.

Furthermore, there are powerful political forces that maintain the Oslo Process and the PA and keep the Two-State Solution alive, even if Hamas controls Gaza. Domestic- and foreign-policy interests of the U.S., Egypt, Jordan, the UAE, Morocco, Bahrain, the EU, and other countries require the Oslo Process to continue. And as long as there is a peace *process*, Israel's control of the Palestinian population can be seen as *temporary*, which is essential for Israel's stature among the international community. Such a peace process is also vital for the unity of American Jewry and world Jewry, including all of the leading American institutions. In the absence of a commitment to a peace process, they will be unable to sustain their support for Israel.

Hence, these forces converge to restore stability whenever violence erupts and threatens to terminate the Oslo Process. Every few months or years, Israel and Hamas go through a cycle of mutual aggravations that escalate into local violence, which may include launching of rockets at Israel and IDF attacks on Gaza. Such action creates international pressure on both sides to calm down, with the U.S., Egypt (in Gaza) and Jordan (in Jerusalem and the West Bank) as the primary stabilizers.

These dynamics are evidenced by the fact that Israel's right wing—counting the tenures of Netanyahu, Bennett, and Sharon—which rejected the Oslo Accords, has in fact kept the accords in force and the PA in existence. For nearly two decades, they have transferred billions of dollars to the Palestinians; withdrawn from and stayed out of Gaza; co-existed with Hamas; worked closely with Egypt and Jordan; and, in signing the Abraham Accords, relinquished any intentions of annexing the West Bank unilaterally.

Indeed, an entire theory, Shrinking the Conflict *(Tzimtzum HaSichsuch)* about reducing friction between Israel and the Palestinians, became popular in Israel and was embraced across the middle section of Israeli politics. It was led by Israel's leading political philosopher, Dr. Micha Goodman,[66] who lives in a settlement in the West Bank.

---

66   See Dr. Micha Goodman, *Catch-67: The Left, the Right, and the Legacy of the Six-Day War* (Cantor and Blackstone Publishing, 2018).

At first sight, it may seem that Goodman's theory has little new in it. After all, similar ideas—such as seeking long-term interim arrangements or agreements, proposing unilateral withdrawals, and implementing various initiatives for decreasing friction between Palestinians and the IDF—have been percolating since the failure of the Camp David negotiations in 2000. Strategies such as upgrading the PA into a state with limited powers were developed in detail by the Reut Institute under my leadership as far back as 2004. Key elements were even integrated into platforms of political parties or became standing orders of the IDF, particularly under the command of Gadi Eizenkot.

With a deeper look, Goodman's ideas become distinct owing to one key factor: their messenger. His identity legitimizes his ideas as a foundation for the political platform of the moderate right wing in Israel, which has a vested interest in preserving the Oslo Process. A friend of mine, a senior Israeli diplomat with strong right-wing views and credentials, believes that Israel's relations with the Palestinians are stable in their current format and can last for "even 50 years." As someone who vehemently protested the Oslo Accords, he would now discourage their cancelling and the dismantling of the PA. He is one of a few right-wing leaders who publicly acknowledged that the Palestinians are "indigenous to the land" alongside the Jews, and that their national story cannot be dismissed. Nevertheless, he believes that Israel's rightful sovereignty over unified Jerusalem, Judea, and Samaria represents a supreme national interest that is worth significant risks and sacrifices. Therefore, the Oslo Accords allow for Israel to control Judea and Samaria without directly governing the Palestinian population. From Goodman's perspective, Israel has no interest in cancelling the Oslo Accords or in resolving the conflict with the Palestinians in the West Bank.

When pushed to go beyond ideological arguments to make practical points, he highlights the unacceptable security risks for Israel as a result of withdrawing from the highlands of the West Bank, which would put Israel's coastal plain under threat. He argues that the prospects of reaching an agreement on Permanent Status are too slim because the outstanding issues are too complex and the gaps in positions too wide. Hence, any attempt to reach such an agreement could lead to another war. Therefore, better to be safe without negotiations than sorry with a failed agreement. Finally, he would argue that "the Palestinians are not ready for peace" because their leaders have not accepted the notion that "Israel is a Jewish state" or that "Israel is the nation state of the Jewish People" or some version of that idea.

This is not such bad news—so his argument goes—because "time is working on Israel's side" via the expansion of Jerusalem and settlements that strengthen Israel's hold on Judea and Samaria. Since nearly all Palestinians are self-governed by the PA or Hamas, they are not "occupied" by Israel. And the Abraham Accords are a powerful proof that Israeli-Arab peace can progress without Israeli-Palestinian peace. In fact, the Arab world seems to have moved on from the Palestinian issue.

As a final point, my friend notes that Abu Mazen is nearing the end of his reign without an heir-apparent, and the PA is heading toward extreme instability. Therefore, Israel must preserve its control of that territory to be able to stabilize it, and thus prevent its seizure by Hamas or radicalization in favor of Iran, or even a collapse into absolute civic disorder. Furthermore, he says that "the political situation in Jordan could change." Being a diplomat, he was saying-without-saying that the Hashemite dynasty could be replaced by a government that would revive the notion of "Jordan is Palestine," thereby alleviating the pressure on Israel to accommodate Palestinian self-determination in Judea and Samaria.

This elaborate thinking among Israel's moderate right wing creates a powerful coalition to preserve the Oslo Process. It converges with similar political interests of Israel's left-wing and centrist parties, which also support the continuation of the status quo around Gaza and in the West Bank. All left-wing Israelis and many who define themselves as centrists believe in the moral and strategic need to end the occupation of the Palestinian *population* and in the justified inevitability of Palestinian statehood. But with no sense of urgency to act on the Palestinian issue, and in the absence of popular support or parliamentary majority, other issues take precedence.

Highlighting the powerful political forces that *preserve* the status quo of the Interim Period clouds the fundamental changes that consolidate *a reality* of two-states-for-two-people ahead of any agreement on Permanent Status. First among them is Gaza, where Hamas has controlled two million Palestinians since 2007 with de-facto recognition by Israel, Egypt, and key players in the international community. A resilient equilibrium has emerged to pre-serve Gaza's quasi-independence. Notwithstanding the mutually harsh rhet-oric, the new status quo around Gaza seems to stand on three pillars: one is Israel's defensive capabilities by Iron Dome and the new border fence, offen-sive capabilities, which repeatedly stun Hamas military leadership, and deep intelligence. A second pillar is economic and social: tens of millions of dollars are transferred to Gaza monthly in cash by Qatar via Israel; thousands of Gazans are employed in Israel; goods are exported from Gaza through Israeli seaports and airport; Gazan businesspeople move back and forth regularly; many patients from Gaza enter Israel daily for treatment; and Gaza's long-term energy, water and sewage infrastructure is built with Israeli approval. On the Israeli side, such stability allows for unprecedented prosperity among the communities adjacent to the border, where fields are safely cultivated up to the last meter next to the border fence. It also allows Israel to focus on other more burning frontiers, such as within the West Bank, in Syria, and against Iran.

The third pillar is political. By withdrawing to the 1967 Lines, Sharon established a "permanent border" between Israel and Gaza. Thereafter, Israel declared Gaza to be a "foreign territory" and has avoided any territorial claims in Gaza. And while Hamas rejects Israel's right to exist *in principle*, it has not made any *specific* claim for control of any *particular* location along its border with Israel, as if saying, "We reject the idea of Israel, but we recognize the reality of Israel and accept the border between us." Even during the flareup between Gaza and Israel, both sides made sure to avoid significant casualties and uncontrolled escalation. Since 2005, Israel has never tried to recapture Gaza, and many Israeli politicians who campaigned to topple Hamas and reconquer Gaza have turned their attention and agendas elsewhere. Four Israeli prime ministers—Olmert, Netanyahu, Bennett, and Lapid—have pre-sided over that new reality.

A second important trend toward a two-state reality is the convergence of Israel's moderate right-wing parties around the notion that there will be two polities west of the Jordan River, in addition to Gaza. In endorsing the Trump Plan, Netanyahu accepted the outcome of a Palestinian state in 70 percent of the West Bank in addition to land swaps around Gaza; Bennett called for "annexing Area C" to Israel, namely, relinquishing Areas A and B to the Palestinians; MK and former minister of defense Avigdor Lieberman repeatedly agreed to relocating settlement communities in peace. His support of a "demographic swap" in Permanent Status implicitly holds the 1967 Lines to be a reference point for future border arrangements. Trump and Netanyahu too endorsed "demographic swaps," and all agree that a Palestinian state will include, at a minimum, 40 percent of the West Bank in Area A, in addition to Gaza. That is a whole lot of progress, especially in the absence of any negotiation with or reciprocity by the Palestinian side.

Compare, for instance, Barak's positions upon entering Camp David in July 2000 with the Trump Plan of January 2020, which Netanyahu accepted. Both were formulated without serious engagement with the Palestinians and are remarkably similar: the Palestinian state would cover 80–86 percent of the West Bank in addition to Gaza; refugees would be allowed to return to Palestine; there would be two capitals in the Area of Jerusalem: Yerushalayim and Al Quds; functional responsibilities on Temple Mount would be divided; and all settlements and the Jordan Valley would remain under Israeli sovereignty.

As mentioned, when Bennett thought in detail about Permanent Status, he landed on calling for annexing Area C. This means that he accepted the delineations of the Oslo Accords, particularly the Gaza-Jericho Agreement, and acknowledged that Palestinian territory would cover at least 50 percent of the West Bank in Permanent Status, in addition to Gaza. Bennett also said that the PA would have "augmented powers and responsibilities" compared to those granted to it by Oslo B, while Barak agreed to a Palestinian state "with limited powers" and the Trump Plan introduced the concept of "limited sovereignty." Namely, Bennett, Barak, Netanyahu, Olmert, and the Trump Plan are speaking about roughly similar outcomes using different captions. They agreed that the detailed powers of Palestine would emanate from its agreements with Israel, that Palestine will have most sovereign powers in civic and economic affairs and that Israel should control the perimeter of the Palestinian state and its airspace.

A third powerful trend toward a two-state reality comes straight out of the hawkish positions of Netanyahu's current all-right-wing sixth government.

The positions of its far-right parties—calling for cancelling the Oslo Accords; declaring sovereignty over Judea and Samara, thereby annexing the West Bank to Israel; dismantling the Civil Administration, for ruling Palestinians directly—highlight and crystallize their own paradoxes. In April 2023, the PLO advocated a resolution in the UN General Assembly to submit to the International Criminal Court that Israel has de-facto annexed the West Bank. Such a decision is seen by the PLO as an essential stepping stone toward establishing that Israel is an "apartheid state," which would lead to its isolation and sanctioning. Notwithstanding the fact that the goal of annexation is part of the platform of Netanyahu's current government, Israel protested the decision by the UN, citing opposition to any unilateral action. How ironic... This turn of events made it clear that Israel needs the Oslo Process to claim that the control of the Palestinian population is *temporary*, not permanent, so as to block accusations of being an "apartheid state."

Furthermore, Netanyahu's government actions dispel the ambiguity regarding the future of the West Bank, which forces the U.S. and other countries to reprioritize the Israeli-Palestinian conflict. Furthermore, a growing number of Israelis now understand that full annexation of Judea and Samaria without equal political and economic rights would be untenable domestically and would meet fierce civic opposition. It would also severely compromise Israel's international standing, even among friends and vital allies such as the United States.

Indeed, Netanyahu's government is exacerbating the great conundrum of Israel's national security: as it pushes to expand Israel's presence in the West Bank, it risks the entire settlement effort; as it seeks to consolidate control over Palestinians, it nurtures the counter-forces of separation; as it seeks a shared society with Palestinians in the West Bank, it distances itself from world Jewry; and as it seeks to perpetuate its presence in Judea and Samaria, it threatens the future of Israel. And the biggest paradox of all: What if the U.S. government suddenly accepts Netanyahu's position against a Palestinian state ever being established within a Two-State Solution? What would Netanyahu's position be then, regarding the permanent *rights* of Palestinians under Israel's control forever?

Palestine First, Last, or Nascent?

The confluence of these dynamics indicates another window of opportunity to separate Israel from the Palestinians and thereby resuscitate the Two-State Solution. Clearly, peace may not be achievable in the foreseeable future, but the current situation in the West Bank is sub-optimal as well. Ari and I wrote this book in anticipation of that moment, whenever it comes, so that politicians and negotiators will be able to best design the political process.

The starting point of any future negotiations will be better, compared to 1999, in a few critical ways. First, the *minimal* positions of any Israeli government, including right-wing ones, will be the Trump Plan, which Netanyahu endorsed. Second, the zone of possible agreement on Permanent Status was determined by the Clinton Ideas. Third, the Quartet Roadmap has outlined an alternative diplomatic path, in which a Palestinian state is established *before* Permanent Status emerges. Finally, the Saudi Peace Initiative, endorsed by the Arab League, gives Israel invaluable assurances about the benefits of a Permanent Status deal. None of these reference points existed for Barak and our team in 1999.

In particular, the Roadmap highlights key dilemmas regarding the logic and structure of the political process: Is the geographic scope of future negotiations the West Bank, or also Gaza? What type of agreement: a Permanent Status agreement or a long-term interim agreement? Should a Palestinian state be established before or after a Permanent Status agreement? And should Palestine emerge from an agreement or only following Israeli unilateral recognition? The answer to these questions will design the diplomatic initiative and determine its prospects of success. We write "initiative" in singular because the experience of the Oslo Process indicates that every Israeli coalition and government can have *only one* meaningful political overture with the Palestinians *per tenure*, because the huge resistance it will face will cause its inevitable downfall.

For many, especially on the left, the architecture of the Oslo Process, which calls for a Permanent Status deal through direct negotiations, remains the only legitimate and viable diplomatic path to achieving peace. The weakness of that approach is its all-or-nothing nature, whereby "nothing is agreed until everything is agreed," tying an agreement in one area to agreements in all other areas. As mentioned earlier, such a comprehensive agreement that resolves the historical issues, provides for establishing a Palestinian state within *permanent* borders, and regulates its future relations with Israel is a monumental political endeavor, and likely to fail. This approach has guided all attempts to reach Permanent Status except the Quartet Roadmap.

From Israel's perspective, the primary weakness of the Oslo Process is its subjecting Israel's vital interest of ending the control of the Palestinian population to Palestinian consent. This conditionality gives the Palestinian side significant leverage in the negotiations, because accepting their own statehood is existentially important for Israel. Furthermore, given the breakup between Gaza and the West Bank, settlement expansion, the firing of rockets into Israel, and multiple other realities, a FAPS that is based on the Oslo Process and seeks End of Conflict and Finality of Claims is not in the cards.

But not all is lost. As I've said, my doubts about the approach of Oslo were seeded already in April 2000, before the Camp David summit. That is why Ari and I believe in the Roadmap approach, which offers an alternative less-for-less logic, focusing on establishing a Palestinian state within *provisional* borders, creating a two-state reality, and eliminating the threat of the One-State Solution. With End of Conflict, Finality of Claims, and peace postponed, Israel *and Palestine* will be able to shape Permanent Status in a gradual manner.

The Trump Plan, which only the Israeli side agreed to, will be the inevitable starting point of such negotiations. While it was designed as a reference point for *Permanent Status*, it is more relevant as *a* benchmark for a *long-term Interim Agreement,* where Palestine has more powers than the PA yet not all its powers in Permanent Status, and Palestinians have more sovereign freedoms but not all freedoms. After its establishment, Palestine can work with Israel to shape state-to-state relations in areas such as economics, security, and water. The primary advantages of this Palestine-first approach lie in its accommodating the split between Gaza and the West Bank and in allowing for further de-occupation of Palestinians in the West Bank toward greater political separation from Israel *before* all outstanding issues are resolved. Another benefit is opening the door for resolving the refugee issue within Palestine, before Permanent Status—all without contradicting Hamas ideology, which can accept a *hudnah* with Israel in exchange for Palestinian statehood.

Should a new reality of two states—Palestine and Israel—be shaped through negotiations and agreement, or by unilateral action of Israel? Conventional wisdom holds negotiations and unilateralism to be mutually exclusive, with negotiations being the opening act and unilateralism being the fallback. Indeed, negotiations have been the foundation of the Israeli-Palestinian peace process since 1993, with the exceptions of the 2005 Gaza Disengagement and the 2020 Trump Plan.

But as we saw with Barak and Olmert, it is nearly impossible to declare failure of negotiations and switch to unilateralism, even in the outbreak of war, because there is always an additional idea to explore under domestic or international pressures. In August 2000, after the failed Camp David summit, Barak instructed Shaul Arieli to plan for unilateral separation from the Palestinians. But he then faced tremendous pressures from within his coalition and from the Americans to give negotiations another shot (in August and September), and another (after the outbreak of the war), and another (after Albright, Tenet, Clinton, and Peres failed to bring about a ceasefire), and another (after Arafat did not accept the Clinton Ideas). So, next time around, Israel will have to choose: to lead with negotiations or with unilateral actions.

It would be an illusion to assume that a long-term interim agreement whose centerpiece is establishing a Palestinian state within *provisional* borders is easier to reach than a Permanent Status agreement. There are substantive gaps, and long-term interim agreements are as complex to negotiate as a Permanent Status deal because they will require not only division of powers on land, air, sea, and all civil spheres but also understandings about how to manage the outstanding issues, which are deferred to future negotiations. In addition, as explained in chapter 4, in 2004, the Palestinian side shifted from seeking a state as soon as possible, even within provisional borders and with partial powers, to demanding full resolution of all outstanding issues as a precondition for any agreement with Israel that ends occupation. Hence, many Palestinians oppose interim arrangements without assurances that permanent borders will be based on the 1967 Lines. On the Israeli side, opposition to interim agreements extends beyond ideological hawks who oppose any withdrawals to those who oppose interim agreements because they transfer assets without the ultimate reciprocation of End of Conflict and Finality of Claims.

Thus, it may be that there is no ripeness for an interim agreement either. In this light, it is easy to understand the premise of the Bennett-Lapid government: nothing will happen because nothing can happen.

Against this backdrop, Sharon's unilateralism may represent the only viable approach if neither a Permanent Status deal nor an interim agreement are feasible. Kudos to him for rejecting all advice and offers to negotiate Israel's withdrawal from Gaza in 2005 to "get something in return." Sharon understood that any such negotiations would prevent Israel from leaving Gaza altogether because no agreement could be reached. How so? Imagine the Palestinians saying to Sharon: "What will be the borders of Gaza that you will be withdrawing to?" Well, the answer was that Sharon was pulling back to the 1967 Lines and dismantling all settlements in Gaza, but he could not declare a precedent that would affect Jerusalem and the West Bank. Therefore, his choice was simple: successful unilateral extraction from Gaza or failed negotiations and staying in Gaza. In our opinion, he chose right!

So long as Hamas is firmly in control of Gaza, any future version of Israel's unilateralism must assume three polities: Israel, a Palestinian entity in the West Bank, and Hamas' Gaza. It also must assume that the PA will become a state, albeit with limited powers, and that Gaza is *already* a liberated Palestinian territory with its own destiny. Since 2000, all Israeli premiers except Bennett—namely Sharon, Olmert, Lapid, and Netanyahu—*explicitly* acknowledged that there will be a Palestinian state in the West Bank. Even Bennett—by refusing to claim sovereignty over Area A and Area B and speaking about "a PA with augmented powers"—*tacitly* acknowledged that Permanent Status includes a Palestinian polity in the West Bank. Meanwhile, all American presidents since Clinton have endorsed the outcome of Palestinian statehood. The exception to this trend is Netanyahu's current sixth government. In other words, the PA's long-term stature as a state seems undisputed by the international community and by most Israeli governments.

Without getting too deep into the weeds of international law, this general agreement about the future of the PA *as a state* qualifies it as a "nascent state," which is a political entity whose *future* statehood is undisputed but does not *yet* have the full qualities of a state. Israel was a nascent state between November 1947 and May 1948, as was East Timor in 2000 and as other countries have been. The PA being recognized as a nascent state would represent a significant upgrade from the Oslo Accords, which subjected its permanent political status to the outcome of negotiations. Once the PA is declared a "nascent state," the outstanding question about its future shifts from the destination—whether it will be a state or not—to the way to get to statehood, and to its exact powers.

It also means that important processes of upgrading the PA's powers and responsibilities can take place even before another "big agreement" is signed. The Interim Agreement already grants the PA powers and responsibilities in many areas, including policing, planning and zoning, sewage, education, transportation, judiciary, and health. Once recognized as a nascent state, additional powers can include a Palestinian currency, an independent Palestinian customs envelope, foreign embassies in Ramallah and diplomatic representations abroad, and PA membership in international organizations. This approach requires no formal agreements and is entirely within the power of both sides.

And what about Gaza? It is understandable for Israelis to think of Gaza as a unitary demonic entity of people who hate Israel, want its destruction, and actively work toward that goal. But we must always remember that a relatively small group of Hamas politicians and militants controls most Gazans, who are struggling and poor. During conflicts with Israel, that civilian population—with its children, elderly, people with disabilities, and even uninvolved adults—is defenseless against the collateral damage of Israel's military action. For instance, Operation Protective Edge of 2014 is estimated to have damaged or destroyed 96,000 Gaza homes, sending tens of thousands into homelessness.[67]

Furthermore, the leadership of Hamas is not monolithic. Within the framework of the "struggle" against Israel that rejects its legitimacy, they have a diversity of views. Some believe in the armed struggle and oppose any notion of collaboration with or "normalization" of Israel. Others hold the long view that allows them to recognize the "reality" of Israel and seek to exist alongside it based on a *Hudnah* and a set of arrangements that are mutually

---

67   See Ynet, *UN Doubles Estimates of Destroyed Gaza Homes* (December 19, 2014 https://www.ynetnews.com/articles/0,7340,L-4605408,00.html).

beneficial. Needless to mention that in Gaza there are other political views to the "right" of Hamas, like Islamic Jihad, but also supporters of Fatah and the PA.

The Oslo Accords treat Gaza and the West Bank as a "single territorial unit" within the PA. That approach made sense until June 2007, when Hamas took over Gaza, and perhaps also for the following years when Hamas was challenged to bring Gaza back under the umbrella of the PA. These hopes are now bygones, and Israel is looking at a reality of two distinct Palestinian polities. What then should Israel's policy be? The second Netanyahu governments of the 2010s worked with the PA and with Hamas in Gaza as two separate entities. This was a necessity, because the two would not come together, and was an outcome of Israel's interest to bifurcate the PA.

The separation between Gaza and the West Bank was always presented as an anomality that needed to be corrected. Even the Trump Plan re-embraced the founding principle of the Oslo Process of "Gaza and the West Bank as a single territorial unit" and framed the resolution of the PA's constitutional crisis as an internal matter and as a precondition for Palestinian statehood. This approach subjects any progress toward ending Israel's control of the Palestinian population to the resolution of the PA's crisis, and therefore blocks any path to a new diplomatic initiative.

We suggest an alternative approach, which seeks separate peaceful coexistence with the PA in the West Bank and with Hamas' Gaza. Whereas a comprehensive agreement would not be feasible, new diplomatic avenues toward stable political separation between Israelis and Palestinians can emerge. Israel can recognize the PA as a nascent state and support a gradual process of capacity- and institution-building and of resolving the territorial disputes. In Gaza, with no territorial claims, Israel can continue to work with Hamas as an independent Palestinian polity that declared war against Israel and needs to be tamed, in keeping with the approach of the Netanyahu and Bennett-Lapid governments. Such a direction can open the door for bolder diplomatic initiatives in the future. Yes, it is a paradox that credible and viable *unilateral* options may enhance the prospects of a negotiated settlement, but this point goes beyond our book.

What's the Agenda?

DOP / Oslo A, Article V: Transitional Period and Permanent Status [Provisions 2–3]

2. …Permanent status negotiations will commence as soon as possible, but not later than the beginning of the third year of the interim period [i.e. May, 4, 1996 —GG] <u>between the Government of Israel and the Palestinian people's representatives</u>.

3. … these negotiations shall cover <u>remaining issues</u>, including: <u>Jerusalem</u>, <u>refugees</u>, <u>settlements</u>, <u>security</u> arrangements, <u>borders</u>, relations and cooperation with other neighbors, and <u>other issues of common interest</u>.

Sharm Memorandum, Article 1: Permanent Status Negotiations

1. In the context of the implementation of the <u>prior agreements</u>, the two Sides will resume the Permanent Status negotiations … based on <u>the agreed agenda,</u> i.e. the specific issues reserved for Permanent Status negotiators and other issues of common interest.

Every textbook about the art of negotiations highlights the importance of the agenda and of the sequence of discussions. Determining them often requires its own complex deliberations. Strangely, this was not the case for us. During the Camp David negotiations, the agenda was largely predetermined by prior agreements to include territory and borders, the future of settlements, refugees, security, Jerusalem, water, and economic relations. We were also going to negotiate the establishment of a Palestinian state, which is the keystone of all other understandings. Neither side raised questions about the agenda, nor did we ever debate its particulars.

Still, that agenda comes with baggage. In 1948–1949, UNGAR 194 and the Lausanne Conciliation Commission called for tackling the "other questions" of territories, refugees, and Jerusalem, and even statehood, toward reaching the "final status" of the conflict between the newly formed Israel and its Arab neighbors. That agenda was later referred to in the 1978 Camp David Accords between Israel and Egypt [68] and in the 1991 Madrid Peace Conference, before being endorsed by Oslo A and shaping what became the Beilin–Abu Mazen Understandings. By 1999, that agenda was accepted by all parties, and it continues to define Israeli-Palestinian negotiations today.

The challenge with that agenda derives from its being primarily backward-looking, seeking to solve past grievances, instead of focusing on establishing good relations in Permanent Status. Theoretically, we could have worked on a different agenda that orients deliberations toward designing a viable Two-State Solution. We could have clustered in one working group all issues related to borders, including Jerusalem, Hebron, land swaps, and, if necessary, isolated settlements. The final output of this group would have been a map. A second team could have focused on establishing the Palestinian state and on its constitutional attributes, namely on how Palestinian self-determination will be realized. Its deliberations should have addressed Palestine's diplomatic relations with Israel, the future of the PLO, the personal status of all refugees, and Israel's concerns regarding potential outreach of Palestine to Arab-Israelis.

A third team could have focused on managing the "special sovereign arrangements" in each other's territory. Its portfolio would have included the Safe Passage between Gaza and the West Bank through Israeli territory, as well as Palestinian platforms in Israeli seaports, terminals in Israeli airports, installations for desalination and sewage treatment in Israel, and any other such permanent Palestinian presence in Israel territory. Its agenda would also have included Israeli access to Jewish holy sites in Palestine, such as the Tomb of the Patriarchs, Rachel's Tomb, or Joseph's Tomb; Israel's use of Palestinian airspace; Israel's "sliver of sovereignty" along the Jordan River; early-warning stations on West Bank mountaintops; or areas for Israeli military deployment in the Jordan Valley. These issues are bound together because of the clear tradeoff they create in peace and conflict.

Most important, we should have designated one team to work on all matters related to the seamless, safe, and secure movement of goods, services,

---

68   The 1978 Camp David Accord, *Ibid*, Preamble, articles 1–3.

and people—Israelis, Palestinians, and internationals. Finally, another working group would have worked out all of the civic affairs that shape ordinary state-to-state relations. Although little is "ordinary" in Israeli-Palestinian relations, there are areas in which internationally accepted norms and procedures prevail, such as standards, postal relations, banking, telecom, and consular affairs. In fact, during the Interim Period many of these issues had already been covered, so we were not starting from scratch.

Dismantling Myths

My introduction to the politics of Jerusalem took place in 1995 in a meeting between Hirschfeld, Pundak, and Faisal Husseini. We met at the Orient House, a grand villa then considered to be the seat of the Palestinian government in East Jerusalem. It was built by the Husseini family in the late 19th century and remained family owned. Walking into that building was a bit surreal. Though we were in Israeli-controlled Jerusalem, members of the Palestinian security force stood guard in outfits and with mannerisms that they had clearly picked up from their Israeli counterparts. We were allowed into the compound only after Husseini's head of office came to greet us and walk us in.

I had known Faisal Husseini to be an enemy of Israel and a descendant of a family that included notorious anti-Semites. His father, Abdelkader Al-Husseini, led the Arab military forces against the Jews in 1948 and had a reputation for charisma and viciousness. His uncle, Haj Amin Al-Husseini, led the Palestinian struggle against the Zionist movement in the 1930s and 1940s, including during the Arab revolt of 1936–1939, which led him to become a supporter of Hitler and Nazi Germany. In 1948, he led the Palestinian rejection of the UN Partition Decision (UNGAR 181) and rallied the Arab population against nascent Israel.

Faisal Husseini was groomed for leadership since birth in Cairo, allegedly played with Arafat as a child, and as a young adult became a founding member of the PLO, joining its armed struggle. He was jailed multiple times by Israel in the 1980s and used his captivity to learn Hebrew. In later years he became more moderate in his views, and following the first Palestinian uprising and the Gulf War, he joined the Jordanian-Palestinian delegation to the Madrid peace conference in October 1991. In its aftermath, he became a leader of the Palestinian peace camp, holding the "Jerusalem file" in the PLO and the PA. He also led the Arab Studies Society, a non-governmental organization with the official mission of documenting Palestinian presence in Jerusalem, which also served as his political platform, allowing him to receive funds for his activities from international supporters, primarily European.

Faisal Husseini was the first Palestinian leader I met. We conversed in English, but when he wanted to emphasize a nuance, we would use a Hebrew word or idiom. He was calm and polite, even when we were discussing contentious issues, and generous with his time and hospitality. Because he trusted Hirschfeld and Pundak, their conversations were candid, and as their assistant, I sat in on intimate political conversations about the Oslo Process, Israeli-Palestinian relations, the PLO, the PA, and other Palestinian leaders, learning more as I took notes than any school could teach. Husseini died of a heart attack in 2001 at 60 and was buried in the Muslim cemetery on Temple Mount following a funeral attended by hundreds of thousands of Palestinians. Shortly thereafter, Sharon ordered the closing of the Orient House.

Israel has travelled a long way since its rejection of the idea that a Palestinian people even exists. In the 1970s, leaders like Uri Avnery, Matti Peled, Aryeh "Lova" Eliav and Abie Nathan spoke about the Palestinians as a people had a leader, Arafat, and deserved a state. They were all considered left-wing radicals and treated as outcasts. Nathan, a former Air Force pilot, flew his plane to Egypt in 1966 to demonstrate that peace was possible and was later jailed for meeting Arafat in 1989. But their views eventually became widely accepted in Israel, even within the right wing.

On the Palestinian side, there were equivalent voices. In the 1970s and 1980s, some PLO leaders dared to call for recognizing Israel and forge peace with it, against heavy criticism and threats to their lives. In 1978, Said Hammami was assassinated after publishing two articles in the *Times* of London calling for a two-state solution, and in 1983 Isam Sartawi was murdered for taking similar positions. The lesson is that the deconstruction of untrue myths often begins with dissident subversive voices, which are silenced by those invested in the current conflict. But their persistence can be transformative.

The takeaway of their stories is that reaching peace requires contending with our own founding myths, which often cancel the narrative of the other side. This is difficult because most myths are seeded in some truth, which is then wrapped in fallacies and disinformation.[69] Reaching peace requires deconstructing these myths, owning up to our shortcomings, accepting that the other side too has its truth, and thereby allowing an area of reconciliation and agreement to emerge. This is a national process that transforms the political leadership and the public, and it may require decades and even generations, but it begins with personal experiences.

I went through that process in many instances during my years at the ECF and while in government. (I've shared some of these experiences in this book.) I also saw my colleagues in the negotiation team go through their own reckonings, particularly during our *internal* deliberations. To begin with, in Israel, many uphold the myth that ours is a story of "a people without a land who came to a land without a people." In reality, to justify the partition of Mandatory Palestine in 1936, we had to acknowledge that hundreds of thousands of Arabs lived in Ottoman Palestine when the first Jews arrived in the 1880s. Another myth was that the Palestinians are not a people who deserve political rights. Today, most Israelis consider the political rights of Palestinians as a fact of life.

Both delegations—Israelis and Palestinians—went through an accelerated process of contending with their founding myths during the Camp David negotiations. When our delegation prepared its proposal for the resolution of Palestinian refugeeism, we had to acknowledge that Israel contributed to the mass displacement of Palestinians, even if that outcome is justified by the conditions of the 1948 War. At the same time, the Palestinian side had to acknowledge that the Arab side made a major contribution to Palestinian refugeeism as well. And with regards to Jerusalem, a senior Palestinian negotiator confided in me that he always believed that the Jewish connection to Temple Mount was exaggerated for political reasons to deny Palestinian association with the place. But his experiences during negotiations sent him on a journey of learning that enlightened him to the depth of Jewish affiliation with Temple Mount. And these are just a few examples out of many.

---

69   See Shaul Arieli, *Exactly How Did It Happen? 12 Israeli Myths about the Israeli-Palestinian Conflict* (Aliyat HaGag U'Miskal, May 2021 – In Hebrew).

In 2009, I led a team from the Reut Institute, which designed and pioneered the strategic response to the delegitimization of Israel and the BDS Movement, then emerging as a global challenge. We identified London as the hub of the global anti-Israel movement and traveled there for a field visit and research tour. We met with Ambassador Ron Prosor and the team at the Israeli embassy, as well as all major British Jewish organizations, journalists, and thought leaders. Inspired to "know the enemy," we also asked to meet with leading critics of Israel and even leaders of the anti-Israel movement.

An unforgettable highlight of that visit was my meeting with one of the most senior leaders of the Islamic Brotherhood in London, who had global influence, including with Hamas in Gaza. The introduction was made by a Palestinian friend, and we had a long and pleasant meeting over mint tea and Arab pastries at a local Muslim charity. Our candid conversation covered history, philosophy, and politics, including the Camp David negotiations, the Israeli-Palestinian war, the PA and Hamas, the Gaza disengagement, and even the prospects of a Hamas government surviving the blockade imposed on Gaza by the Olmert government. He was polite, soft-spoken, and very well educated, including about Zionism and Israel. After nearly three hours, we parted with a handshake. Of course, a detailed report to Israel followed.

That meeting stands out in my memory not just because of my host, a sworn enemy of Israel and, to a degree, of the Jewish People. It was also the first time that I heard from a Palestinian leader a detailed explanation of the concept of *hudnah*, which illuminated for me the diplomatic opportunity that may emerge for Israel from that ideological adversity. I learned that while Hamas will not accept the *legitimacy* of Israel, at least for the foreseeable future, it may be willing to recognize the *reality* of Israel's existence and coexist alongside it.

Meanwhile in Israel, the Olmert-Livni government was up in arms against Hamas, imposing a blockade on Gaza to force Hamas into submission. I realized that it was a futile effort and paradoxically only emboldened Hamas. Indeed, the blockade led to multiple rounds of violence, in which Israel fought Hamas without seeking its demolition. It would take another decade—and many casualties—before ripeness would be reached on both sides, and the Netanyahu and Bennett-Lapid governments effectively accepted the idea of a *hudnah*. Indeed in February 2021, Israel and Hamas agreed to lay a gas pipe from Israel to the Gaza power station. And by 2023, thousands of Gazans were entering Israel each week for work, business, and medical treatment. In 2009, who would have believed that such a reality could emerge?!

The Elusive Quest for Ripeness

Between 1993 and 1995, ripeness for an agreement emerged between Israel and the PLO. Arafat and the Tunis-based PLO's old guard were eager to engage with Israel, in fear of being sidelined by the young guard that had arisen in the West Bank and Gaza following the first Palestinian uprising of 1987–1991. They needed international recognition following the colossal mistake of supporting Saddam Hussein and his conquest of Kuwait. In Israel, a newly elected Rabin government—contending with the rising threat of Iran, absorbing one million immigrants from the Soviet bloc, deadlocked by the collapse of the Jordanian option, and needing to reignite the economy—was ready to explore new opportunities. Many other factors, some of which are entirely intangible, like the mix of personalities involved, created the conditions for the Oslo Process to come into being. Similarly, ripeness allowed for the peace treaties between Israel and Egypt to be signed in 1978–1979 and for the Abraham Accords in 2020. Without ripeness, no agreement is possible. When ripeness is the air, hitherto-decades-old insurmountable problems can be creatively resolved in days or hours.

Ripeness is the concept that political scientists and experts on negotiations use to describe the unique set of political, strategic, and personal circumstances that create the conditions for an agreement to be reached. Barak referred to ripeness as "synchronization of clocks." In July 2000, he failed to engineer ripeness by having Clinton convene all parties in secluded Camp David and by putting forward dramatic offers. Before and after the summit, Barak and Arafat only met a handful of times and communicated primarily through their representatives, via public messages, and by authorizing or preventing actions. Meanwhile, Olmert worked directly with Abu Mazen through a series of lengthy personal meetings. Alas, in the absence of ripeness, neither Barak nor Olmert reached a FAPS, and since 1995, the Israeli and Palestinian political clocks have never synchronized again.

The closer we get to an agreement, the harsher and more violent the opposition becomes on both sides. In 1994–1996, terror attacks and political assassinations by Israelis and Palestinians derailed the Oslo Process. In the fall of 2000, a confluence of forces led to a war that blocked the Camp David negotiations. Such opposition to a negotiated settlement stems from ideological reasons and strategic considerations. There are many Israelis and Palestinians who believe that "time is working on their side." Palestinians point to powerful trends in American and European politics against Israel, such as the rise of the progressive movement in the U.S.; to the growing power of international legal institutions; to successes in delegitimizing Israel; and even, recently, to the political divides among Israelis and between Israel and the U.S. They are encouraged by the speed at which the Soviet Union and white South Africa imploded and anticipate that Israel may go through a similar decline that will lead it to withdraw unilaterally from the West Bank.

Meanwhile, Israelis who believe that time is working on their side point to the expansion of settlements, the continued separation between Gaza and the West Bank, emigration of Palestinian youth, and the marginalization of the Palestinian plight in the Arab world, as demonstrated by the Abraham Accords. Some even hope for and anticipate a seismic event in Jordan or in the West Bank that will cause the emigration of hundreds of thousands of Palestinians and irreversibly shift the area's demographics in Israel's favor. Such Israelis and Palestinians are bitter enemies, but aligned in opposing any resolution of the conflict, building off each other to create a vicious cycle of violence and hostilities against mutual recognition and peace.

In Israel's relations with the Palestinians, we hold most of the *tangible* assets, primarily land and powers of government. Meanwhile, the Palestinians hold *intangibles* such as accepting Israel, helping with its security, and recognizing its legitimacy. That's why we speak about "land for peace" or "land for security," namely tangibles for intangibles.

This basic tradeoff also affects the approach to the negotiations: in Camp David, our delegation generally focused on practical arrangements, while the Palestinian side wanted to lead with declaratory statements. For example, they wanted Israel to recognize the Right of Return based on UNGAR 194, and then discuss how it would be implemented, with few if any refugees returning to Israel. We wanted clarity about where refugees would live in Permanent Status before acknowledging that such arrangements represented the implementation of 194.

Furthermore, it is rarely a good time to negotiate. Both sides prefer negotiating from "a position of power," but when they are strong, why compromise? In Israel, there is the added difficulty of short and unstable tenures that last two to three years, and peace negotiations with the Palestinians can severely shorten even that period. For example, Rabin was elected in 1992 and signed the Oslo Accords from 1993 to 1995. By 1995, his government faced bitter and violent opposition, and most political analysts forecast Rabin's electoral defeat. Netanyahu was elected in 1996 and signed the Wye River Memorandum in 1998, after which his coalition disintegrated. In other words, if an Israeli government decides to change the status quo with the Palestinians, it must do so rather quickly, at the beginning of its tenure.

Meanwhile, on the Palestinian side, powerful forces work in the "opposite" direction toward prolonging negotiations. The inherent instability of Israeli politics challenges their decision-making: Why sign with Barak in late 2000, if his government was likely to fall shortly thereafter? And why sign with Olmert in January 2009, if he's under mounting pressure to resign? Furthermore, since their decisions are equally painful, the Palestinian leadership comes under internal pressure to escalate demands from Israel and to expand the agenda of the negotiations. With longer tenures—Abu Mazen has been in power for 19 years and counting, and Arafat reigned for decades—the temptation to defer decisions and wait it out for a better opportunity grows. And with all these dynamics at play, ripeness is ever more elusive.

What's Patriotic about Peacemaking?

In the spring of 1995, I was accepted to the prestigious cadet course of the Foreign Service to become a diplomat. Pursuing that opportunity would have been a natural choice for an admirer of the great statesmen of Zionism. I hoped that being part of the foreign service would place me "in the room where it happens." Alas, the historical drama of the peace process with the Palestinians was unfolding right then, while being an aspiring diplomat meant deployment in some foreign land, away from the action.

Meanwhile, I knew that somewhere in Israel, groups of people were shaping the future of our country and, by implication, of the Jewish People. Everyone heard about Rabin, Peres, or Beilin, and their chief negotiators, Savir, Gil, Lipkin-Shahak, and Uzi Dayan. But I realized that behind them—advising, researching, and strategizing—were hundreds of others. And I wanted to be one of them. I also realized that only lucky ones get to do so, and that being a diplomat in the foreign service was not necessarily the best path for getting there. In simple terms, I did not want to be assigned to a distant embassy when history was being made in Jerusalem.

That dilemma—between service as a diplomat and wanting to be involved in statecraft now—led to my meeting with Hirschfeld, which I described in the opening chapter of this book. When he offered me the chance to work for the ECF on the Oslo Process, I found my backdoor entrance to history-making, at the price of foregoing a childhood dream and a diplomatic career. On July 11, 1995, I started working with the ECF. Five years later, and on July 11, 2000, the Camp David summit began.

Zionism—the outlook that calls for the Jewish People to have a state in the Land of Israel, where it realizes its right of self-determination—has been a Jewish prayer for nearly 1,900 years. Since the destruction of the Temple in 70 CE and the final demolition of Jewish life in the Land of Israel by the Romans in 132–135 CE during the Bar Kochva Rebellion, Jews around the world have yearned to return to Zion. But for centuries, devoted prayers for mass return to Zion in the "end of days" were not compounded by any practical vision for repatriation.

Enter Theodore Herzl in 1896 with his new concept of "political Zionism." He called for the Jewish People to ingather in Zion to build a sovereign state that would secure its future. Herzl published books, established institutions, and embarked on a relentless diplomatic campaign to spread his thrilling idea to a thirsty audience. Henceforth, the accumulated achievements of the Zionist movement, with the backing of world Jewry, have been mind-boggling: establishing sovereignty and achieving international legitimacy, mass immigration of millions of people, incredible economic growth, bewildering scientific and technological successes, one of the most remarkable military forces in the world—and this is just a partial list.

A backbone of these achievements has been the bold diplomacy of the Zionist movement and Israel, which was led by world-class diplomats including Herzl, Chaim Weitzman, David Ben-Gurion, Golda Meir, Abba Eben and Shimon Peres. Their entire effort had one primary goal: to secure the fundamental legitimacy, well-being and security of the State of Israel with Yerushalayim as its capital. Indeed, since the humble beginnings of Herzl's efforts, the Zionist movement has experienced remarkable diplomatic successes, including the 1917 Balfour Declaration and the ensuing 1920 San Remo Conference; the 1936 Partition Plan, which laid the ground for the 1947 UN Partition Decision that enshrined the idea of a Jewish State; diplomatic recognitions by U.S., the Soviet Union, and eventually by most countries; the alliance with France and then with the U.S.; the 1978–1979 peace treaties with Egypt; the 1994 peace treaty with Jordan; the 1993–1995 Oslo Accords; the 2020 Abraham Accords; and the relocation of the U.S. Embassy to Jerusalem. There were also monumental achievements in terms of determining the territorial space of Israel. In 1979 and 1994, Israel's borders with Egypt and Jordan were irrevocably established. In 2000, the Barak Government aligned itself along the internationally recognized borderline with Lebanon, which was further formalized in 2022 by the Bennett-Lapid government. In 2005, Sharon aligned Israel with Gaza along the 1967 Lines.

Consequently, finalizing Zionism's 140-years-long effort to secure its space among the family of nations now requires a permanent border with Syria in the Golan and with the Palestinians in the West Bank. It is a paradox that the ultimate achievement for Zionism in securing a territory for the Jewish People hinges on having a bilaterally agreed and internationally recognized border with the Palestinians, with no further claims. That final phase of establishing Israel's borders in Judea and Samaria is also the most difficult, because of their ancestral significance and security concerns. It is also difficult because Iran and other radical forces want Israel to remain embroiled with the Palestinians, thereby overstretched in conflicts that will lead to its ultimate implosion.

The Oslo Process and the Camp David negotiations forced Israelis and Jews to face the most difficult national decision of our generation. The excruciatingly painful price was going to be withdrawal from our ancestral lands and the relocation of tens of thousands of settlers. The benefit: a final "stamp of approval" for Zionism coming from its primary adversary, namely the Palestinian national movement. With permanent borders with Palestine, most of Israel's borders would have been determined, except for that with Syria. A journey of nearly 20 centuries of exile without sovereignty and of 120 years of a modern national movement would have come to an epic close when the Jewish People has a finite, undisputed space, recognized by the PLO, by Palestine, and by other Arab countries. The prospects of inevitable bloodshed, moral decline, and eventual political defeat would be replaced by a grand historical achievement.

EPILOGUE

Gidi's Lessons for Aspiring History Makers

Being involved in international negotiations is thrilling. It requires passion, discipline, diligence, professionalism, intellect, and an engaging personality. It is a team effort in which different members play distinct roles. It often ends in frustration, but when it succeeds, after months and years of work that culminate in a game-changing agreement, the sense of satisfaction is elating and sometimes lifelong.

Most international negotiations—such as those on trade, taxation or communications—are highly intricate and very technical. They are led by experts, and even highly informed people may not be able to follow their details or fully understand their implications. As important as these agreements may be, they are unlikely to create headline news or generate passionate public debate. Ratification and implementation are often led by career civil servants.

But negotiating peace treaties between warring parties like Israel and the Palestinians is impassioned. Millions of people have strong views about the outstanding issues, and any concession is often portrayed as unnecessary, defeatist, and even as a betrayal. Opposition to such negotiations may topple governments and lead to violence, making failure more likely than success. And when efforts reach fruition and an accord is forged, significant criticism, protests, anger, and rage are sure to follow. If you perform a momentary act of courage in battle, you may be rewarded with honors, but if you undertake equally patriotic work of peacemaking, you will be guaranteed resentment by parts of the community that you sought to serve.

In July 1995, at 25, I finished my military service. I then decided to dedicate the next chapter of my life to serving the long-term well-being of my society by helping to end control of the Palestinian population. I hold this to be one of the most acute challenges facing Israel and the Jewish People. I supported Rabin's political vision and hoped to play a role in effectuating it. For the following five and a half years I was part of excellent teams that worked to end the conflict with the Palestinians in one of the biggest historical dramas of that decade.

I was very lucky to be invited to join Israel's peace delegation, but it was also deliberate: I chose to be in that field, I prepared myself for a possible moment of high service, and I had the intuition and determination to transition into government when Barak was elected. It was the first chapter of my career, and it was formative and exciting.

In the years that followed, I took on other endeavors in the Israeli and Jewish public sphere, like founding and leading a think tank and initiating a global humanitarian venture. And while I remained involved in various efforts to help resolve the Israeli-Palestinian conflict, nothing compared to the personal and professional experience of my days in the Barak Government.

In later years, I was often asked to distill my personal lessons about being "in the room where it happens." Of course, there are many generic guidelines—such as the importance of hard work, mentors, humility, reliability, diligence, networking, and professionalism—that are universally applicable. But in closing this book, I want to share some personal insights about my journey, whose goal has been to help make a historical difference for my community and society. These insights boil down to the following:

One: Dedicate yourself to a big problem. If the urge to make history is burning in you, single out a big juicy intractable challenge, which is acutely significant for the future of a community that you passionately care about. You must "fall in love" with that problem because it will consume your professional and even personal life for years to come. My "juicy problem" was transforming Israeli-Palestinian relations from conflict to peaceful coexistence. For a young Israeli who cares about the Jewish People, it doesn't get much bigger or more complex than that.

Two: Pledge a decade. If you are committed to making a dent in your problem, you must assume that it will take you a decade to do so. Making such a long-term commitment will allow you to build foundations of knowledge, experiences, and relationships, which will be essential for your ascent to positions of influence and authority. In 1995, I gave myself five years to work on Israeli-Palestinian peacemaking, but the highlight of my journey came in the sixth year, when I joined the government of Israel, and it continued until the eighth year. Yes, I may have worked very hard to merit that opportunity, but truth be told: I also had a lot of luck.

Three: Become indispensable to the greats. Once you choose your problem and pledge a decade, you must work for a great team or person in that field. Initially, you should be ready to carry their bags, work around their schedules, be their driver, manage logistics, take their notes, do their research, draft their documents, and execute their projects. Your reward is simple: an opportunity to be in the room where significant things happen regarding the problem that you "fell in love with." Over time, as you earn the trust of your bosses, they will come to rely on you, see you as their partner, and even treat you as a colleague, which is when you become their person for special requests and delicate missions. In my case, I was a major in the Navy on a fast track for promotions. I then left my military service and cut my salary by half to work on the peace process with Novik, Hirschfeld, Pundak, and Karni. While they operated out of a "small" nonprofit, the ECF, they had a groundbreaking record, a huge vision, and boundless ambition. I could not have had a better introduction to the heart of peacemaking in the non-government world, and it later opened the door for me to join government. And yes, many times, I carried their bags!

Four: Become the expert on "your problem." Your problem creates its own unique field of knowledge, which integrates multiple academic disciplines. You must master it. Yes, there are many senior people who you can learn from, but within a few years, you should become one of a handful of experts on *your problem*. "My problem" involved Israeli-Palestinian peacemaking, Permanent Status, and reaching a FAPS. It required me to dive into issues as diverse as international law, development economics, international trade, taxation, sovereign water rights, management of airspace, the geography of Jerusalem, and the history of Palestinian refugeeism. You will also need to chart your own unique intellectual path. Don't look for an academic degree that is aligned with the frontiers of the issue that you spend your life on, because it doesn't exist. Nor should you expect to meet experts that can answer all your questions. Instead, you should seek the company and guidance of experienced people and prominent scholars, read many books and publications, bring your insights together to "make sense of things," and build your private library of publications that you can go back to for reference.

Five: Go to the edges of your system. "Your problem" has its own ecosystem of governmental and non-governmental organizations; entrepreneurs and corporations; leaders and influencers; important locations in and outside your city, in your country and abroad; journalists and artists; books and publications. Sure, it's convenient to stay in your comfort zone, namely, in my case, by roaming among conferences, universities, think tanks, and receptions in Tel Aviv, Jerusalem, or New York. But your most important learning happens when you go to the frontiers of that ecosystem on site visits and field trips. Such experiences sharpen your outlook and allow you to be authoritative on "your problem." I read many books about Palestinian refugeeism and Hamas, but my visits with Pundak to the Dheisheh refugee camp and to the Palestinian areas of Jerusalem, as well as spending time with a leader of the Islamic Brotherhood in London, were unforgettable and formative. I met many academics and credentialed experts, but learned the most from journalists, social activists, junior officers, and diplomats who dared to operate on the front lines.

Six: Understand your side. Leading on your problem will require adaptations that will be controversial within your community and society. You may be avant-garde, but others may require more time to adjust. You must strive to understand their concerns by applying the same kind of intellectual rigor, curiosity, and openness to your own people as you are applying to the other side. I deeply cherish the insights, knowledge, and experiences that I have gathered with Israelis and Jews who are considered "right-wing" or "hawkish," who oppose the Oslo Process and any compromise with the Palestinians. Some of them have become my close friends. In an era when many of us are confined to our political echo chambers, and when algorithms of social media feed us with information that reinforces our existing views, actively seeking a personal engagement with different outlooks among our community and society is vital for making your path more accurate and effective. I hope that you could see the influence of these relationships across this book.

Seven: Be ready to de-myth. Those on the "other side" of your problem— however you define "your side" and the "other side"—have an outlook, narrative, history and rationale that are enshrined in facts, books, movies, museums, and other places. You must seek to deeply understand your "other side." In my case, "my side" is Israel and the Jewish People in their full diversity, and the "other side" is Palestinian society. Hence, a credible effort to understand the Palestinian outlook was essential for my work, both for legitimacy with the Palestinian side and for my ability to work with Israelis and Jews. It is also invaluably important for your ability to identify possible areas of agreement and avenues for making progress on your problem. I am one of few Israelis who read the detailed Palestinian reports about their *naqba*. I learned that the myth that Jews were "a people without a land that came to a land without a people" is simply false, because a thriving Arab society existed in Ottoman and Mandatory Palestine when Jews repatriated. And while I developed sympathy for the tragedy of individual Palestinians and their communities and was strengthened in my conviction about Israel's approach regarding Palestinian refugeeism, I also came to see the zone of possible agreement on this issue.

Eight: Find partners on the "other side." One of the most important lessons I learned at the ECF is about the importance of finding partners among Palestinians and in Jordan who would work toward designing a shared future. Such partners on the other side will enrich you with invaluable insights about their side and empower you to say to your side that your ideas are feasible. The challenges that they face in their society resemble the challenges that you face in yours. You'll need to support them as they support you so that together you can drive the change you believe in.

Nine: Think about government service. Life in the non-governmental world may seem flashier and more free-spirited compared to a government career. But, over time, a properly placed mid-level civil servant can have a huge systemic impact. I had a taste of both—non-governmental and governmental work—and can testify that in my late twenties, it was much more exciting to work at a cutting-edge nonprofit. But by my late thirties, some of my friends in government were moving mountains.

Ten: Master the arts of systems and networks, leadership and strategy. Making a difference for your society requires you to understand systems and networks and master the arts of strategy and leadership. These fields are essential for any endeavor to drive a societal transformation. If I need to name one seminal book to master, it would be *Leadership Without Easy Answers* by Ron Heifetz, because it teaches about the dynamics of societal change and how to lead when you have "authority" and, equally important, when you don't.

Finally, Margaret Mead famously said, "Never doubt that a small group of thoughtful committed individuals can change the world. In fact, it's the only thing that ever has." That is true in my experience. It has been a highlight of my professional life to belong to a group that never doubted its ability to change the world.

Acknowledgments

The primary thank-you goes to my wife and the rock of our family, **Betty Grinstein**, and to my partner, best friend, and co-author **Prof. Ari Afilalo**. Without them, this book would not have been written. In October 2019, they colluded to get me to commit to write this book. Nearly four years later, it is published just in time to commemorate 30 years since the first Oslo Accord was signed.

Betty is the matriarch of our family and the love of my life, blessed with powerful intuition and outstanding courage and boldness. For years, she has been urging me to put pen to paper and bring together my experiences and lessons. But I always had a good enough reason to defer: "Too busy," "People have moved on," "The peace process is dead," etc. But she insisted for the sake of history, Israel, the Jewish world, and our children. Without her vision and drive, there would not be a book.

Prof. Ari Afilalo has been my brother-from-another-mother, and our friendship and partnership span multiple areas of our lives. His co-authorship, vision, wisdom, and support have been invaluable to this creation. Ari is a lawyer and professor of law at Rutgers University—this is his sixth book—and he also inspires with his social conscience, generosity, and service to our community. He and his wife, Brigitte Dayan, lead the West Side Sephardic Synagogue and are pillars of Jewish life in the Upper West Side of Manhattan. We are lucky to have them in our lives.

Ari and I are also grateful to all those who read the manuscript and shared their feedback. In alphabetical order: **Dr. Shaul Arieli, Dr. Yossi Beilin, Jason Greenblatt, Dr. Yair Hirschfeld, Jonathan Kessler, David Makovsky, Ambassador Dennis Ross,** and **Gilead Sher**. A special thank-you goes to **Sam Feldman** and **Ilay Kielmanowicz**. Sam is a recent graduate of Yale, and an outstandingly smart, hardworking, and diligent young man. He will go very far, and we are proud to be his first book credit. Ilay is a rising junior majoring in history and psychology at the University of Missouri – Columbia. Their diligence and insights have made this book distinctly better. **Yadin Eldar** worked with me in the earlier phases of writing the manuscript. Amazingly, he was in high school at the time.

This book would not have been published on time for the thirtieth anniversary of the Oslo Process without the dedication and commitment of **Ilan Greenfield of Gefen Publishing,** his son, **Binyanmin Greenfield** and their team. Six months ago, we met in Ilan's office, and incredibly now the book is out. Ilan went above and beyond to make it happen. Ari and I cannot thank him enough. In this context, a token of gratitude goes to **Avi Jorisch** for insisting on my meeting Ilan. We are also grateful to **Gershon Burstyn**, **Gary Belsky**, and **Neil Fein** for the diligent editing that made the book more readable and fun, without compromising our personal touch.

The closing of this book is also my once-in-a-lifetime opportunity to express deep gratitude and appreciation to the individuals who inspired, trusted, empowered, and taught me. **Dr. Yair Hirschfeld** introduced me to the world of peacemaking and track-two diplomacy as my first boss at ECF. From him I learned the art of diplomatic entrepreneurship, of turning thoughts into ideas and ideas into strategies and projects. For me, he embodies the brilliance and courage to pursue one's beliefs. In the presence of **Dr. Nimrod Novik**, ECF Chair, I witnessed the supreme art of backchannel diplomacy, and from him I learned that even when one pieces together global initiatives, it is always important to dot the i's and cross the t's. His elegance—including his outfits, hairstyle, cigars, and fountain pens—is singular. He is one of the most talented and capable diplomats I have met. From **Boaz Karni** I learned the significance of logistics, surgical financial management, and the potential of lifelong loyalties. Boaz has supported Yossi Beilin for 40 years and has been a powerful force behind many of his groundbreaking initiatives. Their partnership could be the subject of its own book.

I deeply miss **Dr. Ron Pundak Z"L**, who passed away in 2014. Trained as a historian, journalist, and intelligence officer, Ron dedicated his professional life to peace and coexistence among Jews and Arabs and between

Israelis and Palestinians. While he worked on top-level diplomatic initiatives such as the Beilin–Abu Mazen Understandings, he also pioneered bottom-up, people-to-people Israeli-Palestinian collaboration, particularly in the medical field, to help many thousands of people. He would always—literally 24/7—be ready to help a Palestinian doctor or patient, whom he may have never met, cross the border into Israel for training and treatment. Ron taught me the art of execution and to never take no for an answer when you believe in the cause. He would always find time for his passion for the arts and for his lay leadership at the Tel Aviv Museum, and his house with Tula, his wife, was a shrine for aesthetics. I will also remember him for introducing me to espresso.

In government, **Gilead Sher** stands out in my journey for giving me the opportunity to work at the Bureau of the Prime Minister and for being an inspiring role model. He was the best boss and mentor one could ask for, and he trusted, empowered, and protected me in the shark tank of the Aquarium. Gilead commanded authority and respect for his ethics, and professionalism. Secretaries, staff, leaders, experts, peers, and our Palestinian counterparts deeply appreciated him. While he was outstandingly hardworking and productive—we sometimes scheduled work meetings for 1:00 AM—he always found time for calls with his wife and kids, for his IDF reserve duties as a brigadier general, for training in karate as a level-5 black belt (including at Camp David), and to advise a struggling artist or poet. Before and after his government service, Gilead led his law firm and later became an expert in negotiations and the Chair of the Sapir College in Sderot, among many other contributions to society. His book *Within Reach* is the most trusted account of the Camp David negotiations.

Another token of gratitude goes to **Baruch Spiegel**, former Deputy Coordinator of Government Activities in the West Bank and Gaza, who was the commander of the famed Golani Brigade. Baruch—a brigadier general in the reserves, who still serves in active duty—is a man of peace. He has forged inspiring bonds with his Jordanian counterpart, **General Mansour Abu-Rashid**, who has also become my friend and partner in peacemaking. Baruch has always gone out of his way to preserve and nurture peace between Israel and the Palestinians and Jordan, even in the most challenging of times. He has been my go-to person in all things related to the work of peace.

Finally, a special word of appreciation and gratitude goes to **Danny Abraham**, founder of Slim-Fast and a visionary entrepreneur and philanthropist. Danny's lifelong passion was to have Israeli-Arab and Israeli-Palestinian peace, and he used his fortune to support the S. Daniel Abraham Center for Middle East Peace in Washington, D.C. For nearly two decades, Danny lived as a self-appointed special envoy, relentlessly shuttling among Washington, Jerusalem, Cairo, Amman, Damascus, and any other location to realize a Two-State Solution. I hope that Dani sees peace in his lifetime.

I have engaged with many politicians over the years, across the political spectrum, but I have only worked for **Ehud Barak** for two years and around **Yossi Beilin** for five years. I wrote extensively about Barak in this book, so I would like to add a few words about **Beilin**. Yossi Beilin is a legendarily outstanding, radical and, influential politician. The partial list of his political impact includes launching the Oslo Process and then leading the Beilin–Abu Mazen Understandings, the Beilin-Eitan Understandings with Likud MK Mickey Eitan, and the Geneva Accords. Beilin also founded Birthright Israel and envisioned and led Israel's unilateral withdrawal from Lebanon. He is the only minister to shut down his own ministry, twice(!), because it "wasn't necessary." Yossi is also an accomplished author and thought leader who has published a few books and hundreds of articles. He is an intellectual who believes that any political, diplomatic, and social activity must have solid foundations in research and strategy. His freezingly air-conditioned office with classical music playing in the background, thousands of books along the walls, and a clean desk with sharpened pencils was always a hub of diplomatic and policy entrepreneurship.

Along my journey of and quest for peacemaking—including in the ECF, in the Bureau of the Prime Minister, in backchannel negotiation—particularly in Madrid in 2006–2009 and in Reut—I worked with hundreds of uniquely talented individuals as bosses, peers, mentors, colleagues, and interlocutors. They were Israelis, Americans, Palestinians, Jordanians, and Europeans, and with some I have forged long-lasting friendships. Mentioning just a few risks disappointing others, but I would be remiss if I didn't name **Gary Sussman** and **Daniel Levy, Ron Shatzberg** and **Michal Schwartzman** from the ECF;

Prof. Shlomo Ben-Ami, as well as **Dr. Shaul Arieli, Dr. Tal Becker, Moty Cristal, Yisrael Hasson, Ephraim Lavie, Pini Meidan-Shani,** and **Daniel Reisner** of the negotiation team; **Yoram Raved** and **General (Res.) Giora Eiland** from the backchannel in Madrid; and members of the American Peace Team including **Amb. Martin Indyk, Amb. Dan Kurtzer, Dr. Aharon Miller, Amb. Rob Malley** and, especially **Amb. Dennis Ross**, who has been a friend and a mentor.

A special word of acknowledgement, friendship, respect, and gratitude goes to Palestinian and Jordanian friends, interlocutors, or partners in peace-making. **Dr. Hussein Agha** and **Dr. Ahmed Khalidi**, with whom I spent hundreds of hours, stand out because of their intellect, immense knowledge, passion, pragmatism, and commitment to peace. In 1969, Agha was accepted to Oxford University and was invited to a meeting with PLO leaders Arafat and Abu Jihad, who congratulated him and asked about his plans. Agha answered: "I plan to go to South Lebanon with a gun and fight the Israelis" to which Arafat and Abu Jihad replied: "No, you should go to Oxford, seek Israelis, and engage them in discussions." Indeed, Agha and Khalidi have been in conversations with Israelis ever since and with representatives of all Israeli organizations. Their knowledge of Israel is singular. They were my primary teachers about Palestinian history and society and are the most creative and talented negotiators with whom I have ever worked. Agha's surprising personal story was yet another nudge to question the myths about Palestinians that I grew up with. I am proud to call them friends.

During the Camp David negotiations, I struck up a special connection with **Dr. Saeb Erekat**, then Chief Negotiator, who passed away in 2020. Saeb was warm, smart, funny, and, at the same time, a passionate fighter for the Palestinian people and for the cause of peace. I also felt a personal connection to **Gaith Al-Omari**, my counterpart in the Palestinian delegation, from the moment we met. His professionalism, generosity of spirit, cool-headedness, and charm have nurtured our friendship. Earlier in my journey, it was **Dr. Samir Hazboun** and his team from Bethlehem, and **Dr. Rateb Amro**, his son **Mohammad Amro,** and their team from Amman who introduced me to the Arab world. All made a mark on my journey and on who I am. I thank them all.

Seek Peace and Pursue It...

In mid-February, 2023,10 Palestinians made their way from Ramallah, Hebron, and Nablus to Tel Aviv to participate in a workshop organized by Tikkun Olam Makers (TOM), a venture of the Reut Group, which I founded and serve as its President. In Tel Aviv, at the makerspace of the Kibbutzim College, they met with dozens of Jewish and Arab Israelis to build wheelchairs for toddlers. In the evening, after a beautiful and festive dinner, they drove back to their homes in the PA, taking the completed wheelchairs with them to be distributed within their communities. The entire event was sponsored by USAID as part of the Nita Lowey Middle East Peace and Prosperity Act (MEPPA).

That workshop took place during one of the most difficult periods for Israeli-Palestinian relations since the signing of the Oslo Accords in 1993. A new Israeli government was taking a hard-line approach, Israelis suffered terror attacks, and IDF military action against terrorists led to many Palestinian civilian casualties. Hopefully, by the time you read these lines, the situation will have improved, but I am afraid we are heading into a dark period.

By 2009, my diplomatic activities had subsided, but the urge to contribute to peacemaking remained. When we launched TOM as a national and global platform for innovation around needs of people living with disabilities, the elderly, and the poor, we also envisioned it as a platform for humanitarian collaboration across religious, political, and national lines. We were inspired by the teachings of Rabbi Lord Jonathan Sacks ZT"L, who famously said, "The best way to heal a broken society is to build things together."

Henceforth, TOM has operated in 35 countries and in 150 locations. Each of these places is important to us, and particularly those across the Middle East, our work in which was made possible by the Abraham Accords. But the work that brings together Jews and Arabs within Israel, and Israelis and Palestinians, is our highest passion.

Believing in peace is a deeply rooted outlook. It upholds an absolute moral and practical obligation to seek a reality of coexistence in mutual respect and tolerance. I may have been distant from the diplomatic work of peacemaking for more than a decade, but the desire to contribute to peace has not left me. For six and a half years, between 1995 and 2001, I worked in the realms of strategy, policy, and diplomacy. In the following decade, I did so through various track-two and backchannel fora. Today, I focus on creating, preserving, and strengthening human personal connections, doing my bit to keep the hope for peace in our lifetime.

Glossary of Terms

11/1917	**Balfour Declaration**	A letter from Lord Balfour to Chaim Weitzman, leader of the Zionist movement, recognizing the right of the Jewish People to a national home.
1937	**Peel Commission**	The Pill Commission, established by the British government following the eruption of the Big Arab Revolt (1936–39) was the first to suggest the Two-State Solution.
11/1947 to 7/1949	**1948 War**	A war between the Jewish and Arab communities in Mandatory Palestine (11/47–5/48), which then expanded to a war between Israel and Egypt, Jordan, Lebanon, Syria, and Iraq. Israel won the war, which secured the existence of Israel. It also resulted in the creation of Palestinian refugeeism, which Palestinians refer to as their *naqba* (catastrophe).
11/1947	**UNGAR 181 / Partition Decision**	181 called for a partition of Mandatory Palestine into a Jewish State, an Arab State, and an international area primarily in Jerusalem. The Jewish side accepted 181 and the Arab side rejected it. The 1948 War began on the following day.
12/1948	**UNGAR 194**	194 provided a general outline for the resolution of the Arab-Israeli conflict. Its primary lasting impact is on the Palestinian position regarding the resolution of Palestinian refugeeism.

6/1967	**1967 War**	A war between Israel and Egypt, Jordan, and Syria, which ended in an Israeli victory and the taking-over of Sinai, Gaza, Jerusalem, the West Bank, and the Golan Heights. The Palestinians refer to the 1967 War as their *naqsa* (defeat).
11/1967 and 10/1973	**UNSCRs 242 and 338**	242 and 338 call for Israeli withdrawal and peaceful resolution of the Israeli-Arab conflict. They serve as benchmarks for any political process.
9/1978 and 3/1979	Israel-Egypt Camp David Accord and Peace Treaty	The Camp David Accord of 1978 provided a framework agreement for the resolution of the Israeli-Arab and Egypt-Israel conflicts. Its annex outlined a future political process for the resolution of the Israeli-Palestinian conflict. The Peace Treaty of 1979 created peace between Israel and Egypt.
10/1991	**Madrid Conference**	A conference gathered in Madrid to begin the Israeli-Arab peace process. The Palestinian side was represented in a Jordanian-Palestinian delegation. The Madrid Process launched multilateral groups, such as on water or refugees, and bilateral negotiations.
9/1993	**Declaration of Principles (DOP) / Oslo A Exchange of Letters**	DOP / Oslo A is the first of the "Oslo Accords" and provided the framework for the "Oslo Process." It was signed in secrecy on August 20, 1993, and then in Washington, D.C. on September 13, 1993, by Rabin and Arafat, together with an exchange of letters of recognition between Israel and the PLO.
	Permanent Status	The status of Israeli-Palestinian relations when all "outstanding issues" had been resolved. It was assumed that in Permanent Status the Two-State Solution would be realized.

As of 9/1993	**Oslo Process**	A political process designed to lead to Permanent Status.
	Oslo Accords	A series of agreements between Israel and the PLO that were signed as part of the Oslo Process. The most important Oslo Accords are the DOP / Oslo A (9/93), the Gaza-Jericho Agreement / Cairo Agreement (9/94) and the Interim Agreement / Oslo B (9/95).
5/1994	**Gaza-Jericho Agreement** / Cairo Agreement	This agreement realized the opening phase of the Oslo Process by designating Gaza and Jericho as the first territories of the PA. Its implementation allowed for the return of Arafat to Gaza (7/94), for elections for the PA institutions, and for the Interim Agreement / Oslo B (9/95).
	Paris Protocol	The economic annex of the Cairo Agreement (5/94) that regulated economic and trade relations between Israel and the PA. It remains in effect.
	Interim Period	A five-year period (5/94–5/99) designated for Palestinian self-government and capacity-building toward Permanent Status.
9/1995	**Interim Agreement** / Oslo B	This agreement regulated relations between Israel and the PA during the five-year Interim Period and provided for three "further redeployments" (FRDs). At the end of FRD3, Israel should have stayed only in areas of the West Bank that would be negotiated toward Permanent Status.
	Area A, Area B, Area C	The West Bank and Gaza were divided into three areas: Area A had full security and civic control by the PA (today 18% of the West Bank); in Area B there was Israeli security and Palestinian civic powers (today 22% of the West Bank); Area C was under Israeli control (today 60% of the West Bank).

1/1997	**Hebron Agreement**	In FRD1, Israel was supposed to withdraw from six Palestinian cities to be turned into Area A. Under Rabin, Israel withdrew from five cities (Jenin, Nablus, Ramallah, Bethlehem, and Jericho). Netanyahu renegotiated the terms of the withdrawal from Hebron.
10/1998	**Wye River Memorandum**	An agreement signed by Netanyahu and Arafat about the implementation of FRD2 and other outstanding issues of the Interim Agreement.
9/1999	**Sharm el-Sheikh Memorandum**	An agreement between Barak and Arafat about the implementation of the remaining parts of FRD2 and about the structure of the negotiations on Permanent Status. It introduced the goals of reaching a FAPS and a CAPS.
12/2000	**Clinton Ideas** also known as Clinton Parameters	A set of principles for reaching Permanent Status presented by Clinton in December 2000. The government of Israel conditionally accepted the Clinton Ideas, while Arafat rejected a few parameters and is seen as rejecting the Clinton Ideas.
4/2003	**Quartet Roadmap for Peace**	A framework for the Israeli-Palestinian peace process, which is based on establishing a Palestinian state within *provisional* borders ahead of reaching Permanent Status. It was accepted by Israel's Sharon government and rejected by Abu Mazen.
8/2005	**Gaza Disengagement**	Israel's unilateral full withdrawal from Gaza to the 1967 Lines, including the extraction of all settlers.

| 1/2006 to 6/2007 | **Hamas take-over of Gaza** | A political process that includes the Hamas victory in elections to the Palestinian Legislative Council (PLC) (1/06); multiple failed attempts to reach a national unity government; violent clashes between Hamas and Fatah in Gaza; and finally a violent takeover by Hamas of PA institutions in Gaza (6/07). |
| 2007–08 | **Annapolis Process** | A negotiation between the Olmert-Livni government and Abu Mazen on Permanent Status, sponsored by President George W. Bush. It was launched following the takeover of Gaza by Hamas. |

Glossary of Names

The following glossary of names gives a brief background on the key characters featured in this book, highlighting their involvement with the events discussed herein (all dates are based on Wikipedia):

Israelis	**Role During Oslo Process and Camp David Negotiations**
PM **Itzhak Rabin** z"l 1922–1995 Assassinated	Rabin served as Prime Minister of Israel in 1974–77 and 1992–95 on behalf of the Labor Party. He **was assassinated** while in office (11/95). Rabin's former positions included Minister of Defense during the First Palestinian Uprising (1987–88) and Ambassador to Washington and IDF Chief of Staff during the 1967 War. He signed **the DOP / Oslo A (9/93)**, **the Gaza-Jericho Agreement / Cairo Agreement (5/94)**, **the Interim Agreement / Oslo B** (9/95), as well as the Peace Treaty with Jordan (10/94). Rabin won the 1994 Nobel Prize for Peace together with Peres and Arafat.
PM **Shimon Peres** z"l 1923–2016	Peres was Prime Minister of Israel in 1984–86 and replaced Rabin (after his assassination) from 11/95 to 5/96 on behalf of the Labor Party. He later served as President of Israel (2007–16). Peres held multiple other portfolios during a political career spanning 55 years. During the Oslo Process, Peres served as Minister of Foreign Affairs under Rabin (1992–95) including Oslo A, the Gaza-Jericho Agreement and Oslo B, as well as the peace treaty with Jordan. He won the 1994 Nobel Prize for Peace together with Rabin and Arafat. During the **Camp David negotiations** under Barak, Peres served as Minister for Regional Cooperation.

PM
Benjamin
Netanyahu
Born 1949

Netanyahu was Prime Minister of Israel in six different tenures. During his first tenure (1996–99), he signed the **Hebron Agreement** (1/97) and the **Wye River Memorandum** (10/98).

During his second tenure (2009–13), corresponding with President Obama, he delivered the **Bar-Ilan Speech** (6/09), in which he embraced the Two-State Solution, negotiated a Permanent Status deal with Abu Mazen, and allowed for working relations with Hamas in Gaza, including a swap of 1,027 prisoners in exchange for Gilad Shalit.

During his fourth tenure (2015–20), he endorsed the **Trump Plan** (1/20), which represented major concessions by a right-wing premier.

Throughout his premiership, he allowed for settlement expansion primarily within the settlement blocks. Alas, the platform of his sixth government (as of 2022), aligned with far-right parties, calls for annexing the West Bank and allows for massive expansion of settlements across the West Bank.

PM **Ehud**
Barak
Born 1942

Barak was Prime Minister of Israel in 1999–2001 and served as Minister of Foreign Affairs (1995–96) and IDF Chief of Staff (1991–95). He signed the **Sharm el-Sheikh Memorandum** (9/99); **negotiated with Syria** (10/1999–4/2000); **withdrew from Lebanon** (5/2000); led the **Camp David Negotiations** (5/2000–1/01), including during the **Camp David summit** (7/2000) and the **Clinton Ideas** (12/2000). The Israeli-Palestinian War (also referred to as the Second Palestinian Uprising) erupted during his tenure (9/2000). After his premiership, Barak served as Minister of Defense under Netanyahu (2007–13).

PM **Ariel**
Sharon z"l
1928–2014
Stroke in
2006

Sharon was Prime Minister of Israel in 2001–05, after Barak and before Olmert. During his premiership, in accord with U.S. President George H.W. Bush, Israel ended the war with the Palestinians (2000–03) and built the security fence; the Quartet introduced the **Roadmap for Peace** (4/2003); and Israel **Unilaterally Disengaged from Gaza** (8/2005). Sharon was the first Israeli PM to meet with Abu Mazen in Jerusalem under a protocol of head of state.

PM **Ehud**
Olmert
Born 1945

Olmert was Prime Minister of Israel in 2006–09, after Sharon and before Netanyahu. During his tenure, **Hamas won the elections** to the Palestinian parliament (1/2006) and then **took over Gaza** (6/2007). He led the **Annapolis Process** with Foreign Minister Tzipi Livni and negotiated a FAPS with Abu Mazen (11/2007–9/09). Olmert received Abu Mazen at his official residence in Jerusalem. During the **Camp David negotiations**, Olmert was Mayor of Jerusalem and kept an open channel with Sher.

Prof. **Shlomo**
Ben-Ami
Born 1943

Ben-Ami served as Minister of Public Security, Co-Chief Negotiator, and Minister of Foreign Affairs under Barak (1999–2001), and as a Member of Knesset and contender for leadership of the Labor Party. He assumed ministerial responsibility for the police killings of 11 Arab-Israelis.
Ben-Ami is an Oxford and Tel Aviv University professor of history and a former ambassador to Spain. After his government service, he led the Toledo institute out of Spain, which hosted a backchannel in Madrid from in 2006–09. He has written books about Israeli-Palestinian relations and published many articles.

Gilead Sher
Born 1953

Sher served as Barak's Chief Negotiator (8–9/1999 and 5/2000–3/01) and later Chief of Staff (8/2000–1/01). He led the negotiations on the **Sharm el-Sheikh Memorandum** (9/99), and then the **backchannel in Sweden** (4–5/2000), and the **Camp David negotiations**.

Sher's book, *Within Reach: The Israeli-Palestinian Peace Negotiations, 1999–01* is considered the seminal record of that period. He is a founder and managing partner of a law firm; an expert in international negotiations, a professor at Rice University; a brigadier general in reserves for the armored corps; a political activist; and a level-5 black belt in karate.

Amnon Lipkin-Shahak z"l
1944–2012

Lipkin-Shahak was chief of staff of the Israel Defense Forces (1995–98) before entering politics (1999–2001), serving as Minister of Transportation and Minister of Tourism. During his military service he led many operations against the PLO in Lebanon.

As Deputy Chief of Staff, he co-led the Israeli delegation for the negotiations on the **Gaza-Jericho Agreement / Cairo Agreement** (5/1994) and the **Interim Agreement / Oslo B** (9/1995). As chief of staff, he participated in ending the **Kotel Tunnel Riots** (9/1996) and in the **Hebron Agreement** (1/1997). As a minister in Barak's government, he participated in the **Camp David negotiations**, and together with Yossi Ginossar, he led a backchannel with Arafat and participated in the **Camp David summit**.

After his government service, he went into business, but endorsed the **Geneva Initiative** (10/2003). Lipkin-Shahak was deeply respected by Arafat and the Palestinian side.

Shlomo Yanai, Mike Herzog, Yisrael Hasson, Pini Meidan-Shani, Ephraim Lavie, and Daniel Reisner

Members of Barak's delegation to the **Camp David negotiations** under Eran and then Sher and Ben-Ami (8/1999–3/2001):

General Yanai was Head of the Strategic Branch of the IDF and led the negotiations on security. Brigadier General **Mike Herzog** (later Ambassador to Washington) was Head of Politico-Military Affairs in the IDF Strategic Branch. Herzog continued to serve in Israel's delegations under Olmert and Netanyahu until 2014.

Meidan-Shani represented the Mossad and **Hasson** the Shin Bet. Both were "Arabists." **Lavie** was the team's intelligence officer.

Reisner is an international lawyer and headed the international law department of the IDF. He is a veteran of many negotiations.

Yossi Ginossar z"l (1946–2004)

Ginossar was Deputy Head of the Shin Bet and specialized in Gaza and Lebanon before being forced to retire and then turning to business. He served as backchannel special envoy to Arafat for Rabin, Peres, Barak, and even Sharon and Netanyahu. In that capacity, Ginossar participated in the **Camp David summit** and arranged Arafat's first trip to Israel for a condolence visit to Leah Rabin.

Ginossar developed a very lucrative business partnership with Rashid, Arafat's economic advisor, that was based on Dahlan's power as head of Preventive Security.

On a personal level, Ginossar lost his son in combat in Gaza.

Amb. Dr. Oded Eran Born 1941

Eran was a senior diplomat and ambassador to the EU and Jordan. He was appointed by Barak to be chief negotiator and head of the **Peace Administration** in 10/1999 (after Sher stepped down) and served in that capacity until 6/2000. His counterpart was **Abed Rabbo**. He participated in the **Camp David summit**.

Dr. Shaul Arieli and Moty Cristal

Colonel (Res) **Arieli** was the director of the **Peace Administration** and a veteran of the negotiations on the **Interim Agreement**. He later led the negotiations on the **Geneva Accord** and became a leading expert on Israeli-Palestinian relations, with special focus on maps (https://www.shaularieli.com/en/homepage-2/). Arieli has pubѳlished many books and articles.

Cristal served as deputy head of the **Peace Administration** and is an expert in negotiations. He too has published many articles about Israeli-Palestinian negotiations.

Dr. Yossi Beilin
Born 1948

As Deputy Minister of Foreign Affairs under Peres in the Rabin Government (1992–96), Beilin led the initiation of the backchannel that led to the **DOP / Oslo A**. His other positions included Government Secretary, Member of Knesset, and minister in various portfolios.

Beilin co-founded **the ECF** in 1990 and served as its president. In 1994–95 he co-led the **Beilin–Abu Mazen Understandings**, as well as the movement for the **unilateral withdrawal from Lebanon** (1998–2000) and the **Geneva Accord** (2003) among many other initiatives. He is also the visionary behind Birthright Israel (1993–99).

Beilin has published many books and hundreds of articles.

Dr. Yair Hirschfeld
Born 1944

Hirschfeld co-led (with Pundak and **the ECF** team) the non-governmental phase of the **Oslo Process** (11/1992–4/93) and remained a member of the Israeli delegation until the signing of the DOP (8/93). As the director of ECF he co-led the negotiations on the **Beilin–Abu Mazen Understandings**.

Within the ECF, Hirschfeld led dozens of initiatives in **track-two diplomacy**. His initial work in that field among Palestinian leadership and leaders of the Labor Party began in the 1980s. He co-founded the ECF in 1990 and led it until 2020. He is also a professor of Middle-East History at the University of Haifa and has published several books about his work.

Dr. **Ron Pundak** z"l (also spelled Pundik) 1955-2014

Pundak co-led (with Hirschfeld and **the ECF** team) the non-governmental phase of the **Oslo Process** (11/1992–4/93) and remained part of the Israeli delegation until the signing of the DOP (8/1993). He also co-led with Hirschfeld the track-two diplomacy that led to the **Beilin–Abu Mazen Understandings** and the negotiations on the **Geneva Accord**. Pundak pioneered many people-to-people initiatives and then led the Peres Center for Peace (2001–12) and the **Geneva Initiative** (2003–14).

Dr. **Nimrod Novik** Born 1946

Dr. Novik has served as Chairman of **the ECF** since its founding, and as such co-guided the negotiations on the **Oslo Process** (11/1992–8/93), the **Beilin–Abu Mazen Understandings,** and the **Geneva Accord**. In 1997–98, he led the ECF's diplomatic work to get the Palestinian side to say yes to PM Netanyahu, which led to the **Wye River Memorandum** (10/1998).

Novik has been particularly close with the Egyptian leadership and has been involved in dozens of backchannel diplomatic initiatives. He now serves on the board of the **Israel Policy Forum**.

During the 1980s, Novik served in Israel's embassy in Washington and as Foreign Policy Advisor to Peres. He became a businessperson in the early 1990s and was one of the pioneers of international oil and gas projects in the Middle East.

Boaz Karni Born 1953

Karni is a co-founder of **the ECF** and has been a longstanding supporter and partner of **Dr. Beilin**. He led the back office of the ECF and provided essential operational support and substantive input to Beilin, Hirschfeld, Pundak, and others during negotiations of the **Oslo Process** (11/1992–8/93), the **Beilin–Abu Mazen Understandings** (1994–95) and on the **Geneva Accord** (3/2003). Karni has been involved in hundreds of initiatives related to Israeli-Palestinian peace since the late 1980s.

Palestinians

Yasser Arafat Arafat was the legendary chairman of the Fatah party, and
1929–2004 of the PLO since 1964 including in Jordan (until 1970),
Lebanon (until1982) and Tunis (until 1994). He also
became chairman of the PA in 1994. He led the armed
struggle of the PLO.

As chairman of the PLO, Arafat signed **Oslo A** and the **letters
of recognition** with Rabin (9/1993); the **Cairo Agreement
/ Gaza-Jericho Agreement** with Rabin (5/1994); **Oslo B
/ Interim Agreement** also with Rabin (9/1995); the **Wye
River Memorandum** with Netanyahu (10/1998); and the
Sharm el-Sheikh Memorandum with Barak (9/1999). He
did not accept the **Clinton Ideas** (1/2001).

Arafat died in exile in Paris in 11/2004, after being besieged
by Sharon in his Ramallah office (3/2002–10/04).

Abu Mazen Abu Mazen comes from a refugee family from Safed (Tzfat).
/ Mahmoud He is one of the founders of the PLO, and one of its first
Abbas leaders to moderate toward Israel in the 1980s and embrace
Born 1935 the Two-State Solution.

Abu Mazen was considered second in the PLO hierarchy
and played a leading role in the **entire Oslo Process** as head
of its Negotiation Department. Since Arafat's death (11/04),
he has served as Chairman of Fatah, the PA, and the PLO.

Abu Mazen's representatives negotiated the **Beilin–Abu
Mazen Understandings** (1994–95), and he participated
in the **Camp David summit** and negotiated a FAPS with
Olmert (2007–09). He is the only Palestinian leader to
have visited PM Sharon and PM Olmert in Jerusalem.

Abu Alaa Abu Alaa, originally from Abu-Dis, near Jerusalem, is one
/ Ahmed of the founders of the PLO, who served in multiple roles
Qurei with a primary focus on economics. His positions included
1937–2023 chairman of the PLO's Palestinian National Council (PNC)
and the PA's Palestinian Legislative Council (PLC). Abu
Alaa was of the first Palestinian leaders to moderate toward
Israel in the 1980s and embrace the Two-State Solution.

Abu Alaa's **meeting with Hirschfeld in London** (11/1992)
led to the launch of the back channel in Oslo, which he led
till the **DOP / Oslo A** (9/1993). He later served as Chief
Negotiator on the **economic agreement / Paris Protocol**
(5/1994), on the **Cairo Agreement / Gaza-Jericho
Agreement** (5/1994), and on **Oslo B / Interim Agreement**
(9/1995).

Abu Alaa was assigned to lead the **backchannel in Sweden**
(5/2000) and participated in the **Camp David summit**,
where he clashed with Clinton.

Abu Alaa was deeply respected by the Israeli side for his
courage and skills of negotiation.

Dr. **Saeb
Erekat**
1955–2020

Erekat came from a Jericho family, was a U.S.-educated
academic and then journalist, and then a political activist, spokesperson, negotiator, and politician for the PLO,
reaching the level of minister in the PA.

He was part of the **Jordanian-Palestinian delegation to
the Madrid Conference** (10/1991). Considered a loyalist
to Arafat, he became chief negotiator in the later phases of
the Oslo Process, including at **Wye River Memorandum**
(10/1998) and during the **Camp David negotiations**,
beginning with the **Sharm el-Sheikh Memorandum**
(9/1999), at the Camp David summit, and until the end
of Barak's tenure. During this period, he often served as a
personal interpreter for Arafat.

Erekat continued to lead Palestinian negotiations and
to head the Negotiation Support Unit (NSU) during
the **Annapolis Process** (2007–09) and the leak of the
Palestinian papers (1/2011), after which he resigned; he
was reinstated by Abu Mazen.

Dr. Nabil Shaath (born 1938)

Dr. Shaath comes from a refugee family from Safed (Tzfat) and became an academic with an MA and a PhD from the University of Pennsylvania. He was considered "foreign minister" of the PLO and served in various roles, such as chief negotiator and PA Minister for International Co-operation (PA's unofficial minister of foreign affairs). In 2003 he became acting prime minister of the PA.

Shaath was an influential figure throughout the **Oslo Process** and during the **Camp David negotiations**, including at the **Camp David summit**.

Yasser Abed Rabbo
Born 1945

Abed Rabbo comes from a refugee family from Jaffa and joined the Marxist-socialist factions of Popular Front and Democratic Front, later to become a staunch supporter of the Two-State Solution. He is a member of the executive committee of the PLO and a minister in the PA.

Abed Rabbo served as the head of the Palestinian delegation and chief negotiator during the first phase of the **Camp David Negotiations** (10/1999–5/2000) working with Oded Eran. He participated in the **Camp David summit** and later led the Palestinian team that formulated the **Geneva Accord**, which he signed with Dr. Beilin.

Hasan Asfour
Born 1950

Asfour is a Fatah and PLO leader from Gaza and a PA cabinet member. Together with **Abu Alaa** and **Al-Kurd**, he was part of the negotiations on **Oslo A / DOP** (1–9/1993) and continued to work closely with Abu Alaa as negotiator in various phases of the Oslo Process. He was assigned by Arafat to **the backchannel in Sweden** (5/00). Asfour was a bitter rival of Abu Mazen.

Dr. **Maher** **Al-Kurd** Born 1947	Al-Kurd earned a PhD in Economics from the University of Leipzig, Germany. He was one of the early members of Fatah and the PLO, focusing on economic roles, including advisor to Arafat. Al–Kurd was involved—together with Abu Alaa Asfour—in the negotiations leading to the **DOP / Oslo A** (1–9/1993). He later served as Deputy Minister of National Economy of the PA (1996–2006). In that capacity, he led the negotiations on the **EPS Model** with the ECF. He has remained involved in track-two and back-channel diplomacy ever since.
Faisal Husseini 1940–2001	Husseini was one of the founders and leaders of the PLO. He held the "Jerusalem File," operating out of the **Orient House**. His father and uncle were leaders of the Palestinian national movement and enemies of the Zionist movement. Husseini sat in Israeli jails and then became a leader of the Palestinian peace camp.
Mohammed Dahlan / Abu Fadi Born 1961	Dahlan was born in Gaza to a refugee family. He led the Fatah youth movement, Fatah Hawks, and was jailed by Israel, where he learned Hebrew. In 1994, Dahlan was appointed to lead Preventive Security in Gaza, which became his power base and put him in regular contact with Shin Bet and the CIA. In this capacity he controlled the border crossings and the collection of taxes. His alliance with **Mohammed Rashid** and **Yossi Ginossar** is believed to have generated significant income to all parties. Dahlan participated in the **Camp David negotiations** and in the **Camp David summit**. He was the chief point of contact with Israel and the U.S. during the early phases of the war (as of 9/28/2000).

Dahlan went on to become a senior politician and minister in the PA He worked with and challenged Arafat and Abu Mazen on issues of reform and anti-corruption within Fatah, the PA, and the PLO. He then became the main opposition to Hamas in Gaza until the **Hamas coup** (6/2007), after which he left Gaza.

In 2011 he was accused of murdering Arafat, was expelled from Fatah, and went into exile in Abu Dhabi. Some say that Dahlan contributed to shape the Israel-UAE normalization agreement within the **Abraham Accords**.

Jibril Rajoub / Abu Rami

Born 1953

Hussein Al–Sheikh

Born 1960

Rajoub and Al-Sheikh (along with others) led multiple local or specialized security forces within the PA.

Rajoub is currently a senior politician for Fatah, and he also leads the Palestinian Football Association and the Palestine Olympic Committee, among other positions. In the 1980s, he was a militant and was arrested multiple times, served 17 years in Israeli jails, and became a leader of Palestinian prisoners. In jail he became fluent in Hebrew and translated Begin's autobiography into Arabic. Rajoub eventually arrived in Tunis and returned with Arafat to the West Bank, where he became head of **Preventive Security** (1994–2002). In this capacity, Rajoub was the point person for coordinating the **visit of MK Sharon on Temple Mount**, which led to the eruption of the war.

Al-Sheikh, born in Ramallah, is a politician and secretary general of the PLO Executive Committee who now serves as head of the PLO **Negotiations Affairs Department**. He was held in Israeli jails multiple times in the 1980s, where he learned Hebrew. During the Interim Period he served in Preventive Security and as secretary general of Fatah in the West Bank.

Mohammed Rashid	Rashid, of Kurdish-Iraqi origin, became Arafat's "money man" responsible for designing the financial structure of the PLO and the PA.
Gaith al-Omari	Al-Omari is a Jordanian human rights lawyer, who became Secretary of the Palestinian delegation to the **Camp David negotiations** and participated in the **Camp David summit**. He later became advisor to the prime minister of the PA, Salam Fayyad (until 2006). Al-Omari is a Senior Fellow at the Washington Institute.

Americans

President **Bill Clinton** Born 1946	Clinton was president of the U.S. in 1993–2000 and supported the Oslo Process from 1993. His presidency covered **Oslo A / the DOP** (9/1993), the **Gaza-Jericho Interim Agreement / Cairo Agreement** (5/1994), and the **Interim Agreement / Oslo B** (9/1995) with PM Rabin; the **Hebron Agreement** (1/1997) and the **Wye River Memorandum** (10/1998) with PM Netanyahu; and the **Sharm el-Sheikh Memorandum** (9/1999), **negotiations with Syria** (10/1999–4/2000), the **Camp David summit** (7/2000) and the **Clinton Ideas** (12/2000) with PM Barak. Clinton's secretaries of state were **Warren Christopher** (1993–97) and **Madeleine Albright** (1997–2001). His national security advisors were Tony Lake (1993-97) and Samuel (Sandy) Berger (1997–2001).
President **George W. Bush** Born 1946	Bush served as president of the U.S. in 2001–08. His presidency covered the **Quartet Roadmap** (3/2000) and Israel's **Unilateral Disengagement from Gaza** (8/2005) with PM Sharon and the Annapolis Process with PM Olmert (2007–09). Bush's secretaries of state were **Colin Powell** (2001–05) and **Condoleezza Rice** (2005–09). His National Security Advisors were **Condoleezza Rice** (2001–05) and Stephen Hadley (2005–09).

| President **Barack Obama** Born 1961 | Obama served as president of the U.S. in 2009–16. His presidency covered the U.S. peace effort led by Secretary of State Hillary Clinton (2009–12) and Secretary of State John Kerry (2013–16), both working with Abu Mazen and with Netanyahu.

Obama's secretaries of state were **Hilary Clinton** (2009–13) and **John Kerry** (2013–17). His national security advisors were **James Jones** (2009–10), **Tom Donilon** (2010–13), and **Susan Rice** (2013–17). |
| President **Donald Trump** Born 1946 | Trump served as president of the U.S. in 2017–20. He recognized **Jerusalem as Israel's capital** (12/2017) and Israel's sovereignty of the **Golan Heights** (3/2019); defunded **UNRWA**; presented the **Trump Plan for Peace and Prosperity**, which was endorsed by Netanyahu (1/2020); refused to support Israel's unilateral annexation of the **Jordan Valley** (spring 2020), and led to the **Abraham Accords** (9/2020).

Trump's Secretaries of State were **Rex Tillerson** (2017–18) and **Mike Pompeo** (2018–21). Trump's son-in-law, **Jared Kushner**, serving as senior advisor, led the work on the Trump Plan with Ambassador to Israel **David Friedman** and Special Envoy, **Jason Greenblatt**. |
| Amb. Dr. **Dennis Ross** Born 1948 | Ross served in various capacities relating to the Israeli-Arab peace process, both in the State Department and the White House under presidents Bush (Sr.), Clinton, and Obama. Ross began his career focusing on U.S.-Soviet relations.

Ross led the U.S. **Peace Team** as the special middle-east coordinator and thereby served as chief negotiator for Clinton throughout the **Oslo Process** from the **Madrid Summit** (10/1991) until the **Clinton Ideas** (12/2000), and he worked on the **Israel-Jordan** and **Israel-Syria** negotiations. Ross also served the Obama Administration during the **Annapolis Process** (2007–08). |

Between and after his terms of government service, Ross served as a senior fellow at the Washington Institute and published many books and articles, including his account on the Israeli-Arab peace process, *The Missing Peace*.

Amb. Dr. **Martin Indyk** Born 1951

Indyk served as ambassador to Israel twice (1995–97 and 2000–01) during the **Camp David negotiations**. He was a senior member of the Peace Team under Clinton and served as special envoy for Obama and Kerry (2013–14). In these capacities he was involved in the **Oslo Accords**, negotiations with **Syria** and **Jordan**, and in the **Camp David negotiations**, including at the **Camp David summit**.

Prior to, between, and after his periods of government service, Indyk worked at and led AIPAC, the Washington Institute, the Saban Center at the Brookings Institute, and at the Council of Foreign Relations. He published multiple books and many articles, including his account of the Israeli-Arab peace process, *Innocent Abroad*.

Dr. **Rob Malley** Born 1963

Malley served in Clinton's National Security Council (1994–2000) including as executive assistant to the national security advisor, Sandy Berger, and as special assistant to Clinton. In these capacities, he was involved in the **Wye River Memorandum** (10/1998), the Israel-Syria negotiations (12/1999–4/2000), and the **Camp David negotiations**, including at the **Camp David summit** and toward the **Clinton Ideas** (12/2000). Malley coauthored with Hussein Agha three articles in the **New York Review of Books**, *Camp David: The Exchange*.

During the Obama Administration, Malley was the chief negotiator on the nuclear deal with Iran, and under Biden he served as special envoy to Iran. Between the Clinton, Obama, and Biden administrations, Malley led the International Crisis Group. In this capacity, he met with and called for diplomatic engagement with **Hamas** (as happened).

Amb. Dr. **Daniel Kurtzer** Born 1949	Kurtzer was a diplomat and served as U.S. ambassador to Egypt (1997–2001) under Clinton and to Israel under Bush (2001–05) during the **Quartet Roadmap** (4/2003) and the **Gaza Disengagement** (8/2005). Earlier in his career, he served in the U.S. embassies in Cairo and Tel Aviv, as well as in Washington. After his government service, Kurtzer became an academic at Princeton and a public intellectual publishing books, articles, and policy papers.

Dr. **Aaron David Miller, Gamal Helal, and Jonathan Shapiro**

Miller, Helal, and Shapiro were members of the U.S. Peace Team who participated in the Israeli-Jordan and Israel-Syria negotiations, as well as in the entire **Oslo Process** during the Clinton Administration:

Miller was a senior member of the Peace Team who served six presidents between 1988–2003, including as Deputy Special Middle East Coordinator. He later joined and led the Woodrow Wilson Center and the Carnegie Endowment and became a public intellectual.

Helal is an Egyptian-American diplomat and interpreter who served presidents Clinton, George W. Bush, and Obama. His wisdom as a diplomat was respected by all parties.

Shapiro served as the legal advisor of the Peace Team and was considered to hold its "organizational memory."

Europeans

Amb. **Miguel Angel Moratinos** Born 1951

Moratinos is a senior Spanish diplomat and politician who served as the European Union special representative for the Middle East (1996–2003) representing European interests following the **Barcelona Declaration**. His tenure covered the first Netanyahu Government (1996–99) and the **Camp David negotiations** up until the **Quartet Roadmap**.

After his role with the EU, Moratinos entered Spanish politics to become a parliamentarian and minister of foreign affairs. He currently serves as UN High-Representative for the Alliance of Civilizations.

Front and Back Cover Photos

Pictures are described top to bottom and left to right:

Picture 1   *Front:* Begin, Carter, and Sadat at the signing of the Egypt-Israel Peace Treaty on March 26, 1979, at the White House South Lawn. *(Credit: White House)*

Back: Begin and Sadat at the King David Hotel in Jerusalem during Sadat's historic visit on November 19, 1977. *(Credit: Sa'ar Ya'acov, LAAM)*

Picture 2   *Front:* Rabin, Clinton, and Arafat at the signing of the Declaration of Principles (Oslo A) on September 13, 1993, at the White House South Lawn. *(Credit: Vince Musi, the White House)*

Back: Rabin, Arafat, and Peres after receiving the Nobel Prize for Peace in Oslo, Norway, on December 10, 1994, Oslo, Norway. *(Credit: Sa'ar Ya'akov, LAAM)*

Picture 3   *Front:* Rabin, Clinton, and Jordan Prime Minister Abdelsalam Majali signing the Israel-Jordan Peace Treaty at the Arava border, October 26, 1994. Standing: Elyakim Rubinstein, Warren Christopher, unknown, President Ezer Weitzman, King Hussein, unknown, Crown Price Hasan. *(Credit: Sa'ar Ya'akov, LAAM)*

Back: Hussein and Rabin at the White House on July 25, 1994. *(Credit: Sa'ar Ya'akov, LAAM)*

Picture 4   *Front:* Barak, Clinton, and Arafat in Oslo, November 2, 1999. *(Credit: Amos Ben Gershon, LAAM)*

Back: Barak, Albright, and Arafat at Camp David on July 20, 2000. *(Credit: White House)*

Picture 5   Front: Arafat, Hussein, Clinton, and Netanyahu at the sign-
             ing of the Wye River Memorandum at the White House on
             October 23, 1998. *(Credit: Sa'ar Ya'akov, LAAM)*
             Back: sitting: Clinton, Arafat, Netanyahu. Standing: Nabil
             Abu Rudeineh (Arafat's chief of staff), Gamal Helal (U.S.
             Peace Team), Shlomo Yanai (head of IDF's Strategic Planning
             Branch), Dr. Nabil Shaath, Dani Naveh (government secretary)
             at the Wye Plantation summit on October 20, 1998. *(Credit:
             Avi Ohayon, LAAM)*

Picture 6   *Front:* Sharon, Bush, and Abu Mazen at the conference for the
             presentation of the Quartet Roadmap for Peace in Aqaba on
             June 4, 2003. *(Credit: Avi Ohayon, LAAM)*
             Back: Sharon, Bush, and Abu Mazen in Aqaba on June 4, 2003.
             (Credit: Avi Ohayon, LAAM)

Picture 7   *Front:* Olmert, Bush, and Abu Mazen at the Annapolis
             Conference on November 27, 2007. *(Credit: Avi Ohayon,
             LAAM)*
             Back: Abu Mazen, Bush, and Olmert at the Annapolis
             Conference on November 27, 2007. *(Credit: Avi Ohayon,
             LAAM)*

Picture 8   *Front:* Netanyahu, Obama, and Abu Mazen at the White House
             on September 2, 2010. *(Credit: Moshe Milner, LAAM)*
             Back: Netanyahu and Abu Mazen at the White House,
             September 2, 2010. *(Credit: Moshe Milner, LAAM)*

Picture 9   *Front:* Netanyahu and Trump at the White House on February
             15, 2017. *(Credit: Avi Ohayon, LAAM)*
             Back: Trump and Netanyahu at the Oval Office on February
             15, 2017. *(Credit: Avi Ohayon, LAAM)*

Picture 10   *Front:* Minister of Foreign Affairs of Bahrain Dr. Abdullatif bin Rashid Al-Zayani, Netanyahu, Trump, and Minister of Foreign Affairs for the United Arab Emirates Abdullah bin Zayed Al Nahyan at the White House on September 15, 2020. *(Credit: Joyce N. Boghosian, White House)*

Back: Al Nahyan, Al-Zayani, Netanyahu, and Trump—both pictures at the signing of the Abraham Accords at the White House on September 15, 2020. *(Credit: Joyce N. Boghosian, White House)*

"Peace is a dynamic construction
to which all should contribute, each adding a new brick."

President Anwar Sadat, December 10, 1978
acceptance speech upon receiving
the Nobel Prize for Peace[70]

---

70   As quoted from Henry Kissinger, *Leadership: Six Studies in World Strategy* (Penguin Press 2022, p. 267)